Lecture Notes in Computer Science 8193

Commenced Publication in 1973
Founding and Former Series Editors:
Gerhard Goos, Juris Hartmanis, and Jan van Leeuwe

Jörn Altmann   Kurt Vanmechelen
Omer F. Rana (Eds.)

Economics of Grids, Clouds, Systems, and Services

10th International Conference, GECON 2013
Zaragoza, Spain, September 18-20, 2013
Proceedings

 Springer

Volume Editors

Jörn Altmann
Seoul National University, College of Engineering
Department of Industrial Engineering, Technology Management,
Economics, and Policy Program (TEMEP)
1 Gwanak-Ro Gwanak-Gu, 151-744 Seoul, Korea
E-mail: jorn.altmann@acm.org

Kurt Vanmechelen
University of Antwerp
Department of Mathematics and Computer Science
Middelheimlaan 1, 2020 Antwerp, Belgium
E-mail: kurt.vanmechelen@ua.ac.be

Omer F. Rana
Cardiff University, School of Computer Science and Informatics
Queen's Buildings, Newport Road, Cardiff CF24 3AA, UK
E-mail: o.f.rana@cs.cardiff.ac.uk

ISSN 0302-9743   e-ISSN 1611-3349
ISBN 978-3-319-02413-4   e-ISBN 978-3-319-02414-1
DOI 10.1007/978-3-319-02414-1
Springer Cham Heidelberg New York Dordrecht London

Library of Congress Control Number: 2013948097

CR Subject Classification (1998): C.2, H.2, K.6, K.4, H.4, H.3, J.1

LNCS Sublibrary: SL 5 – Computer Communication Networks
and Telecommunications

Typesetting: Camera-ready by author, data conversion by Scientific Publishing Services, Chennai, India

Printed on acid-free paper

Springer is part of Springer Science+Business Media (www.springer.com)

Preface

This year marks the 10th anniversary of GECON, the International Conference on the Economics of Grids, Clouds, Systems, and Services. In 2003, three years before the launch of Amazon's EC2 Cloud computing offering, this event was jointly initiated by members from the research and industry communities, to explore the problems at the interface of economics and IT. Its main focus at that time was the need to develop business models and economically inspired forms of resource allocation for grid computing systems in order to increase their availability, sustainability, and efficiency. Many of the models proposed in this event over the years have now turned into reality, and its widened scope is more relevant than ever considering the recent developments in our service economy with respect to (automated) trading, pricing, and management of services.

For a decade, the conference has brought together the research and practitioner community that works in the area of economics and computer science to address this emerging interest in infrastructure, platform, and software services. This includes the operation and structure of the service market, the alignment of cost, revenue, and quality-related objectives, and the creation of innovative business models and value chains. GECON has been unique in bringing together both technical and micro/macro economic aspects associated with the management and operation of services over distributed infrastructures. This year's conference, GECON 2013, continues this work.

GECON 2013 took place in the beautiful city of Zaragoza (the capital city of the autonomous community of Aragon). The city is famous for its folklore, a renowned local gastronomy, and landmarks such as the Basílica del Pilar, La Seo Cathedral, and the Aljafería Palace. Holding GECON 2013 in Zaragoza allowed us to combine a beautiful environment with intensive discussions on interdisciplinary research on economics and computer science.

This year again, we received a number of high-quality paper submissions. Each submission received a minimum of three reviews by members of an international Program Committee. Our final program consisted of seven sessions (three of which were work-in-progress sessions). The schedule for the conference this year was structured to encourage discussions and debates, with discussion time included in each paper presentation session, led by the session chair. We believe such discussion sessions are essential in order to boost more open and informed dialogue between presenters and the audience, and to enable the presenters to better position their work for future events and to get a more informed understanding of the impact their work is likely to have on the research community. The presentation sessions were:

Session 1: Business Models
Session 2: Energy Consumption
Session 3: Resource Allocation
Session 4: Work in Progress on Resource Allocation
Session 5: Work in Progress on Pricing
Session 6: Quality of Service
Session 7: Work in Progress on Utility and ROI Modelling

Session 1 started with the paper by Eetu Luoma on "Examining Business Models of Software-as-a-Service Firms", which focuses on how business models, using two examples of companies offering Software-as-a-Service (SaaS), differ from other (more traditional) software vendors. The authors derive useful comparisons that may be of benefit to vendors intending to operate in the SaaS market. The next paper by Kaufmann and Ma on "Cost Efficiency Strategy in the Software-as-a-Service Market: Modeling Results and Related Implementation Issues" identifies various features that SaaS vendors can use to distinguish themselves, with a particular focus on costs for clients and vendors, leading to a discussion about mechanism design choices in a SaaS market. Dutta and Hasan's subsequent paper on "How Much Does Storage Really Cost? Towards a Full Cost Accounting Model for Data Storage" addresses the commonly held misconception that with increasing availability of providers, storage costs have decreased. They consider a variety of factors that influence such costs – and not just the cost of the storage media – thereby providing the basis for an "accounting model" for storage.

Session 2 focused on the emerging interest in energy management and cost in Cloud systems. The paper by Cambazard et al. entitled "Constraint Programming Based Large Neighborhood Search Approach for Energy Minimization in Data Centers" presents an approach for the allocation of virtual machines to servers with time-variable resource demands on data centers – in order to minimize energy costs. The authors discuss this approach in the context of the EnergeTIC project. The next contribution by Cauwer and O'Sullivan entitled "A Study of Electricity Price Features on Distributed Internet Data Centers" considers how the design of Internet Data Centers and energy cost prediction regimes impact overall energy usage (considering factors such as price variability and time lag between geographical locations). The last paper in this session by Katsaros and Stichler on "Quantifying Ecological Efficiency in Cloud Computing" provides a methodology for calculating the ecological efficiency of virtual machines within a Cloud infrastructure. Their work is motivated by the question whether the economic and ecological efficiency of Cloud computing can be measured in practice (in real time).

Session 3 focused on resource allocation – one of the most widely researched areas within Cloud computing (and in previous GECON conferences). The contribution by Hernández et al. entitled "Cost Evaluation of Migrating a Computation Intensive Problem from Clusters to Cloud" identifies how an Amazon EC2 instance could be used as an alternative to a heterogeneous computing system used previously for supporting semantic annotation of educational resources at a university. The outcome provides a useful comparison about issues that need to be considered for migrating an application to a public Cloud infrastructure. Leon and Navarro present their work on "Incentives for Dynamic and Energy-Aware Capacity Allocation for Multi-Tenant Clusters", identifying how incentives could be developed to enable users to report their actual resource requirements to an infrastructure provider. Such reporting could be used as a basis to improve resource sharing (in a multi-tenancy environment) and reduce energy costs. The contribution by Banares et al. entitled "Revenue Creation for Rate Adaptive Stream Management in Multi-tenancy Environments" describes how a multi-tenancy Cloud infrastructure could be used to support stream processing from multiple users (with different customer classes). They outline how rate adaptation of a stream and dynamic resource allocation could be used to ensure penalties are minimized by an infrastructure provider.

Session 4 consisted of work-in-progress papers that deal with resource allocation problems. In "Scheduling Divisible Loads to Optimize the Computing Time and Cost", Natalia Shakhlevich revisits the problem of finding Pareto optimal solutions to divisible load scheduling problems that require optimization of both time and cost. The paper addresses the issue that common conceptions on divisible load scheduling, such as the necessity to spread load evenly on all processors and to fix the sequence of the processors in a non-decreasing order of their cost/speed characteristic, do not hold in general, and proposes alternatives strategies. In "Preference-Based Resource Allocation: Using Heuristics to Solve Two-Sided Matching Problems with Indifferences", Haas et al. apply genetic algorithms to the problem of allocating resources through two-sided matching on the basis of preference rankings rather than monetary valuations. Their heuristics yield superior results compared to standard algorithms, given the choice of appropriate objective functions. They also demonstrate the use of a penalty in such functions for unstable pairs, in order to achieve stable matches that perform well with respect to both fairness and welfare. Finally, in "Advanced Promethee-Based Scheduler Enriched with User-Oriented Methods", Moca et al. analyze the performance of a scheduler that optimizes user satisfaction when scheduling bag-of-tasks applications on hybrid distributed computing infrastructures (DCIs). These consist of desktop resources, Cloud resources, and best effort Grid resources. The user satisfaction function is based on a combination of makespan and cost metrics.

In session 5, work-in-progress on pricing was presented. Philipp Berndt and Andreas Maier from Zimory, a company offering Cloud management software, propose an alternative to the current pay-as-you-go flat-rate pricing schemes that are combined with overbooking strategies as adopted by many Cloud providers. In "Characterizing Sustainable IaaS Pricing", they highlight the issues with the existing billing approach and conduct a game theoretical analysis based on an asymmetric non-cooperative game. The authors subsequently propose a hybrid billing approach wherein a flat part of the rate deals with a minimum guaranteed level of performance, while a flexible part of the rate deals with resource usage beyond the flat rate portion. In "Towards a PaaS Architecture for Resource Allocation in IaaS Providers Considering Different Charging Models", Vieira et al. discuss the consumer-side problem of selecting the optimal charging models when mapping PaaS workloads and associated QoS requirements to VM allocations. In addition, they also present an additional charging model in the form of time-slotted reservations and present an integer linear programming model for optimizing the scheduling of requests.

Session 6 on quality of service began with a contribution by Khan et al. entitled "Towards Incentive-Based Resource Assignment and Regulation in Clouds for Community Networks", which investigates how a Cloud infrastructure could be supported within community networks (which are primarily volunteer-driven networks using off-the-shelf communication equipment to address the Internet access and service needs of a particular community). They focus on how incentive mechanisms could be developed to enable users to participate and contribute applications within such networks. The contribution by Baker et al. entitled "Towards Autonomic Cloud Services Engineering via Intention Workflow Model" describes how user requirements, captured using situation calculus, could be mapped into a workflow model that can be enacted over a Cloud infrastructure. The particular contribution of this paper is a description of how high level user objectives can be mapped into concrete services, which can then be composed to carry out these requirements. The authors also briefly describe how non-functional requirements such as fault tolerance and resilience can be addressed using this approach. The final contribution in this session by Oberle et al. entitled "End-to-End Service Quality Considerations for Cloud-Based Applications" identifies current limitations with offering end-to-end QoS within a Cloud environment that is often composed of multiple, independently operating business entities (often with contrasting and competing requirements). They describe the limitations of establishing service level agreements in this context and how standardization could play an important role towards achieving such end-to-end QoS objectives.

The final work-in-progress session on "Utility and Return on Investment Modelling" began with the paper by Haile and Altmann entitled "Estimating the Value Obtained from Using a Software Service Platform", which focuses on understanding benefits provided to users as service platforms and, in particular, the applications they offer within the market place. This work considers service variety, perceived usefulness, and the number of users associated with services as key parameters in understanding how they provide value to users. The paper by Franke et al. entitled "An Experiment in SLA Decision-Making" uses an experimental-economics approach to solicit the views of 16 professionals working in IT management, to better understand their choices. The results indicate that IT management practitioners do not behave as expected utility maximizers – as often assumed by other researchers. The final paper in this session by Naldi et al. entitled "Information Security Investments: When Being Idle Equals Negligence" focuses on the relationship between investments made in infrastructure to reduce the expected loss due to a potential attack and subsequent revenue loss due to a malicious attack on a system. The authors determine the potential investment threshold that a company must consider compared to making no investment.

We would like to wholeheartedly thank the reviewers and Program Committee members for completing their reviews on time, and giving insightful and valuable feedback to the authors. We would also like to extend our thanks to the organizers at the University of Zaragoza and to Ivan Breskovic of the Vienna University of Technology for their assistance this year. Furthermore, we would like to thank Alfred Hofmann of Springer for his support in publishing the proceedings of GECON 2013.

August 2013

Kurt Vanmechelen
Jörn Altmann
José Ángel Bañares
Omer F. Rana

Organization

GECON 2013 was organized by the University of Zaragoza, the Technology Management, Economics, and Policy Program; Seoul National University, the School of Computer Science; Cardiff University; and the University of Antwerp.

Executive Committee Chairs

Jörn Altmann — Seoul National University, South Korea
José Ángel Bañares — University of Zaragoza, Spain
Kurt Vanmechelen — University of Antwerp, Belgium
Omer F. Rana — Cardiff University, UK

Program Committee

Rainer Alt — University of Leipzig, Germany
Marcos Dias de Assunção — IBM Research, Brazil
Hermant K. Bhargava — UC Davis, USA
Rajkumar Buyya — University of Melbourne, Australia
Ivona Brandic — Technical University of Vienna, Austria
Ivan Breskovic — Technical University of Vienna, Austria
Jeremy Cohen — Imperial College, London
Costas Courcoubetis — Athens University of Economics and Business, Greece
Karim Djemame — University of Leeds, UK
Torsten Eymann — University of Bayreuth, Germany
Thomas Fahringer — University of Innsbruck, Austria
Bogdan Franczyk — University of Leipzig, Germany
Saurabh Garg — IBM Research, Australia
Wolfgang Gentzsch — The UberCloud, Germany
Thomas Hess — Ludwig-Maximilians-Universität München, Germany
Matthias Hovestadt — Hanover University of Applied Sciences, Germany
Chun-Hsi Huang — University of Connecticut, USA
Bahman Javadi — University of Western Sydney, Australia
Odej Kao — Technical University of Berlin, Germany
Kibae Kim — Seoul National University, South Korea
Stefan Kirn — University of Hohenheim, Germany
Tobias A. Knoch — Erasmus University, The Netherlands

Bastian Koller   HLRS, Germany
Harald Kornmayer   Duale Hochschule Baden-Wuerttemberg
                                   Mannheim, Germany
Dimosthenis Kyriazis   National Technical University of Athens,
                                   Greece
Byungtae Lee   KAIST, South Korea
Hing-Yan Lee   National Cloud Computing Office, Singapore
Jysoo Lee   KISTI, South Korea
Leandro Navarro   Universitat Politècnica de Catalunya, Spain
Marco A.S. Netto   IBM Research, Brazil
Dirk Neumann   University of Freiburg, Germany
Dan Ma   Singapore Management University, Singapore
Richard T.B. Ma   National University of Singapore, Singapore
Steven Miller   Singapore Management University, Singapore
Ashraf Bany Mohammed   University of Ha'il, Saudi-Arabia
Karsten Oberle   Alcatel-Lucent Bell Labs, Germany
Manish Parashar   Rutgers University, USA
Dang Minh Quan   National Economics University, Vietnam
Rajiv Ranjan   University of Melbourne, Australia
Peter Reichl   Telecommunications Research Center Vienna,
                                   Austria
Rizos Sakellariou   University of Manchester, UK
Satoshi Sekiguchi   AIST, Japan
Arunabha Sen   Arizona State University, USA
Gheorghe Cosmin Silaghi   Babes-Bolyai University, Romania
Burkhard Stiller   University of Zurich, Switzerland
Bruno Tuffin   IRISA/INRIA, France
Dora Varvarigou   National Technical University of Athens,
                                   Greece
Gabriele von Voigt   University of Hanover, Germany
Stefan Wesner   HLRS, Germany
Phillip Wieder   GWDG, Germany
Ramin Yahyapour   GWDG, Germany
Rüdiger Zarnekow   TU Berlin, Germany
Wolfgang Ziegler   Fraunhofer Institute SCAI, Germany

Steering Committee

Jörn Altmann   Seoul National University, South Korea
Rajkumar Buyya   University of Melbourne, Australia
Thomas Fahringer   University of Innsbruck, Austria
Hing-Yan Lee   National Grid Office, Singapore
Jysoo Lee   KISTI, South Korea
Steven Miller   Singapore Management University, Singapore

Dirk Neumann   University of Freiburg, Germany
Omer F. Rana   Cardiff University, UK
Kurt Vanmechelen   University of Antwerp, Belgium

Sponsoring Institutions

Telefonica, Madrid, Spain
Nerion Networks, Zaragoza, Spain
Seoul National University, Seoul, South Korea
University of Cardiff, Cardiff, UK
University of Antwerp, Antwerp, Belgium
University of Zaragoza, Zaragoza, Spain

Table of Contents

Session 4: Work in Progress on Resource Allocation

Session 5: Work in Progress on Pricing

Session 6: Quality of Service

Session 7: Work in Progress on Utility
and ROI Modeling

Examining Business Models
of Software-as-a-Service Firms

Eetu Luoma

University of Jyväskylä,
P.O. Box 35 (Agora), 40014 University of Jyväskylä, Finland
eetu.luoma@jyu.fi

Abstract. The paper focuses the attention to different business models
and intended strategic aims of the firms providing Software-as-a-Service
(SaaS). SaaS vendors have been said to challenge the business practices of
the existing vendors providing proprietary or customer-specific solutions.
The current studies on the topic have shown that SaaS is different from
preceding software business models, but consider and emphasize SaaS
business model as an invariable configuration. This case study compares
two SaaS firms with different backgrounds and reveals characteristics of
two very different SaaS business models. The findings indicate that along
with SaaS vendors providing only standard software applications and focusing on cost efficiency, there are vendors who provide more specialized
software applications and complement the SaaS offering with services
required by larger customers.

Keywords: Software-as-a-Service, Business Models, Strategies.

1 Introduction

This paper contributes to the growing body of literature on Software-as-a-Service,
which is one of the Cloud Computing service models. Technically speaking, the
term Software-as-a-Service (SaaS) refers to an application running on top of
cloud infrastructure and to an application delivered and used over the Internet
and provisioned by the users themselves [1]. From the software systems outsourcing perspective, SaaS is different from preceding custom-tailored, product
software and application service provisioning models. By adopting a SaaS offering the end-user organization outsources all the software-related functions to
the service provider [2], from requirements specification, implementation, deployment to operating. SaaS model is therefore considered in this paper as both
technical and business innovation.

Scholars have called for more studies on the business aspects of Cloud Computing [3], [4]. Searching the contemporary literature, we found that the business
related studies on SaaS consider the benefits and issues of the SaaS model, client
side perceptions and adoption, characteristics and business models of the SaaS
providers and discrete aspects of the SaaS business model. Need for "rich understanding on the complex phenomenon" has been identified in the previous literature [2], [5] and we also found shortage of studies capturing the aims and outlooks

J. Altmann, K. Vanmechelen, and O.F. Rana (Eds.): GECON 2013, LNCS 8193, pp. 1–15, 2013.
© Springer International Publishing Switzerland 2013

of SaaS vendors, which would provide a view to the development of the whole transforming software industry. Further, Currie et al. [6] suggested more in-depth case-based investigation of the differences in vendors business models and offerings.

The aim of this paper is to respond to the calls referred to above, generating two contributions to the literature on SaaS from the business viewpoint. First, the paper examines the different characteristics of SaaS firms; in other words, we compare operations, revenue logics and structures of software firms. This is accomplished by taking business model as the unit of analysis for our empirical study. Second, we consider the scope and aims of the SaaS firms, and changes thereof, to suggest potential courses of future developments in the software markets. Finnish software firms were selected as a target group that addresses the concerns of this study. In the context of a software market affected by the global competition, two research questions are of particular interest in this study: 1) What are the characteristics of different SaaS business models? 2) How are the SaaS vendors changing their business model?

In essence, business model is a description of how company operates and how it makes money [7]. The term has also been used to classify operating firms [8], [9]. While the concept is causing controversy and discussion in the research community (see e.g. Porter [10] and George and Bock [11]), this paper relies on the conclusion by Zott et al. [9] that there is a widespread acknowledgement of business model as a new unit of analysis. The current paper also submits to the views that business model emphasizes holistic approach, seeks to explain for both value creation and capture and considers both a focal organization and its surroundings [8], [9].

The incentive to address the questions above emerges from recent claim by Andriole [12]. He suggests that software renting (i.e. software acquired as a service and paid per use) will radically change the software business setting, by breaking down the positions of big proprietary software vendors. In addition to major decrease in costs to acquire and deploy software, Andriole argues that SaaS entails increase in end-user involvement in software development. Active users are affecting the software requirements and design. Combined with component architectures, this enables improved flexibility and, above all, increase in the speed of deploying new software capabilities. In case SaaS offers both cost-efficiency, flexibility and speed, the software firms providing proprietary solution or custom-tailored projects are unlikely not to take action, but we can assume them to change their business to match the customers needs. For that reason, the practical motivation behind of this paper is to demonstrate possible transformations from business models based on solutions and projects to business model with Software-as-a-Service offering in its core.

This paper is outlined as follows: We begin by summarizing and discussing the business-related literature on Software-as-a-Service. After methodological considerations of our empirical study, the findings of the study will be presented, followed by discussion. To conclude, the contributions and limitations of the study are discussed.

2 Existing Literature on SaaS Firms

To start with an overview of the relevant literature, recent empirical studies have examined both demand and supply of Software-as-a-Service. Most common topics looking at the client side include consideration of pros and cons of SaaS [13],[14],[15],[16] discussion of service quality and related expectations by SaaS customers [17],[18] and explaining the reasons to outsource in SaaS mode [19],[20]. Software vendors viewpoint has been addressed in papers depicting archetypal SaaS business models [6],[21],[22], [23] comparing SaaS to other business models [2],[18],[24] and papers examining distinct aspects of SaaS business [25], [26]. Software-as-a-Service business model has also received attention in the closely related forums. In the following, we shall introduce and discuss relevant literature on SaaS business model.

Software-as-a-Service business model first seems to be close to the traditional model for selling software products. Only single set of functionalities is provided to all customers with limited possibilities for customer-specific alterations, and vendors aim to achieve economies of scale [13]. However, delivery of software capabilities over the Internet, hence, outsourcing deployment and hosting to service provider changes the business model configuration essentially. Differences to software product business include more direct and continuous nature of customer relationship, subscription based pricing logic, combining both software development and hosting as key activities and required capabilities [23]. A well-known contemporary example of SaaS business model is that of Dropbox, which combines characteristic of both software product and as-a-service business models. Provisioning applications as a service has also been compared to business of supplying customer-specific applications. Schwarz et al. [2] finds application service providers targeting SMEs with one-to-many model for non-critical applications, as opposed to targeting large firms with customer-specific offering for critical applications. They also see difference in short-term and standard contracts of service provisioning and long-term and complex outsourcing contracts. Overall, the reviewed literature considers Software-as-a-Service as explicit and unique configuration of business model elements. This configuration is argued to be different from preceding software business models [6],[20].

Benlian and Hess [13] conducted a survey on the IT executives perceptions on benefits and risks of SaaS, and found cost advantages as the strongest adoption level, followed by flexibility and improved quality factors. They also found that IT executives are concerned by the security, economic and contractual risks. Similarly, Repschlaeger et al. [15] found costs, flexibility, trustworthiness, IT security as general selection criteria for SaaS. However, results of survey on SaaS adoption by Benlian et al. [20] suggest that criterion of decisions on SaaS-adoption vary between application types. Less specific and less strategically important applications are to a higher degree adopted as SaaS, than more complex, specific or strategically significant applications [20]. Also, comparing traditional software product, open source software or software provided on-demand, Benlian [18] observes a difference in preferences between buyers in SMEs who favored open source and on- demand software, as compared to large enterprises who favored the features of traditional software products. While standardized software product and combined IT outsourcing is attractive to some customers, others may require more IT support services or aim to achieve advantages over customizing their software systems. As the needs of small and larger customers are different, its likely that also SaaS vendors are differentiating themselves to fulfill the customer requirements, and there will be different types of SaaS offerings.

Whereas some authors aim at uniform definition of SaaS and definitive SaaS business model configuration, few papers [6],[22],[27], [28] introduce possible variations of the assumed pure-play SaaS. In addition to offering a standard, horizontal web- enabled application, offering industry-specific and complex business applications is also a viable option for the SaaS vendor [6]. Equally, Cusumano [27] suggests several potential variations of a software business model as combinations of different customer segments, revenue models and delivery models. In a recent study, Luoma et al. [28] classified 163 ASP and SaaS firms to uncover two main types of SaaS business models, a pure-play and an enterprise version. Their description of pure-play SaaS is in line with the established thinking about the SaaS business model. Moreover, the enterprise SaaS suggests a configuration with more complex application requiring support services, a combination of subscription fee and time and materials fee, more high-touch customer relationships and varying marginal costs. Salesforce.com could be considered as present-day example of such business model, especially if one takes in their extended enterprise delivering value-adding applications and services. We find two implications of such business model; SaaS could become a part of inclusive offering of the software firm, and enterprise SaaS could be the means for vendors supplying customer-specific applications to embrace the demand for SaaS.

Cusumano [27] highlights the importance of the shift of software firms revenues from software product to service. He finds a number of cases where software product firms evolve from selling product licenses, to a mixture of products and services and finally to mostly services. In the context of SaaS, Dsouza et al. [24] examines the SaaS transition from software product business, and pinpoint essential changes in both operations, revenue logic and structures. Given the major impact of the transition on both the industry-level and on individual firms level, we find the lack of studies on the transition somewhat surprising.

To summarize, the current studies have discovered that general and simple software applications delivered as a service as very cost-efficient alternative appeals to intended target segment of small and medium size enterprises. These studies have mainly described an invariable business model configuration. Thus, there is very little indication whether adoption and overall uptake of SaaS is affected by offering which combines SaaS and value-adding services. However, there are early evidence that varying configurations for SaaS exists. More studies on the types of SaaS business models and their effect on SaaS adoption is needed.

3 Research Method

This study examines the operations, revenue logic and organizational structures, i.e. business models of Software-as-a-Service firms, based on the empirical case study data collected from Finnish software companies. Focusing on these aspects enables us to fill the gap of missing empirical insights on the different types of SaaS firms. An emphasis is also put on how software firms have evolved to pursue the selected Software-as-a-Service strategy. This helps us in assessing the ongoing change in the supply of applications.

The study applies the interpretive case study approach [29] in producing new insights and information to understand and portray the SaaS phenomenon. Overall, case study was deemed a suitable approach as the study relies on the experiences of practitioners and attempts to capture the complexity and details of the phenomenon [30]. The present study is considered as a holistic case study with multi-case design [31], [32].

Regarding the frame of reference, the operations and revenue logic of case companies were examined by employing the concepts and visualization of a business model suggested by Osterwalder et al. [33]. In particular, the concepts include value propositions, customer segmentation, channel preferences, key activities and partnerships, revenue logic, cost structure. Their framework was used as an initial guide to design and data collection. The framework for examining integrated solutions and related organizational structure by Davies et al. [34] was later discovered useful in examining and depicting SaaS business. They divide organization into front-end unit performing customer-specific work, two back-end units producing standardized products and services, and a strategic centre coordinating activities between front-end and back-end units.

The cases were selected to this study through purposive sampling [35] and in two phases. The initial sampling frame had two conditions: Company provides Software-as-a-Service and focuses on business-to-business market. Attention was also paid in finding SaaS firms with varying background, complexity of software offering, size and age. After initial round of interviews with five SaaS firms, four of the companies were found vastly similar in terms of their age and software product core as the foundational offering. Only one firm was found with background in professional services and, additionally, this was the largest and oldest of the firms. In line with objectives of the study, a decision was made to compare the latter firm against one with highest variation of the attributes in the initial sampling frame. Thus, the two firms were selected for their similarity as well as their differences, to facilitate comparing the characteristics.

The present study was executed during autumn 2011 and the year 2012, using two main sources of information: public documents and interviews. We initiated the study by gathering general background information on the case companies from their web pages and publicly available company presentations. As suggested by Walsham [29], interpretive research uses interviews with case company representatives as the primary data source. The interviews were both focused interviews and in-depth interviews with informants. By focused interviews, we refer to a single interview [32], which in the present study usually took approximately two hours. By in-depth interview, we refer to an interaction with the informant over longer period of time involving at least two interview sessions [32]. This enabled asking more detailed questions and confirming initial observations. The criterion for determining interviewees was that they were involved in managing of the execution of the selected strategy and business model.

The interviews were conducted as semi-structured interviews consisting of both fixed and open-ended questions, but the researcher also allowed some new directions during the interview for the benefit of richness of data. An interview guide was developed and data collection focused on the current operations and revenue logic, their changes over time and on the quantifiable facets of the organizational structure, according to the selected frameworks. Particularly, question were asked on the elements suggested by Osterwalder et al. [33], changes in any single element or configuration, or possible problems in executing intended business model. Questions related to organizational structure included allocation of employees to front-end and back-end of the organization, share of value created by these parts and level of product and service standardization. Following the common practice, interviews were recorded and transcribed for analysis.

Data collection, coding and analysis were conducted in iterative fashion [36]. During the first round, interviews and analysis can be considered more relaxed. In the later phase, more structured interview procedures were used. Data analysis followed the principles of qualitative research on parallel data reduction, data display and drawing conclusions [35]. First, the data was organized by identifying unique patterns in each case on the basis of interview questions. Pattern matching [32] enabled analyzing whether observation matches with expected pattern within the cases. Next cross-case synthesis technique was employed, enabling comparing the cases and aggregating the data [32].

4   Findings within the Cases

4.1   Case: Sopima

Sopima Ltd. is a greenfield SaaS company founded in 2009. Company aims at being a "puritan SaaS company". Respondents included companys co-founder and sales director (in total four interviews). Firms core product is an application for managing contracts. The business case forms around enhancing contract document handling and improving contracting processes. With careful contract management, client companies would be able to improve their financial result. Company website introduces reference cases from multiple industries, indicating a horizontal focus.

Companys value proposition is based on enhancing customer processes through the features of the application. SaaS is used as competitive advantage, i.e. its cheaper, faster to deploy and more flexible. The overall solution consists of standardized web-native application that is deployed in single, multi- tenant IT environment, namely on top of Microsoft Azure. The initial solution has minimal value- adding features and services. This is in line with the attributes of pure-play

SaaS model aiming at highly standardized offering and solution-ready product and operational services.

"Our solution is a way to achieve good contract management practices. The fastest and the easiest. Very low investment for the customers, easy to acquire. No deployment project and costs. Value is achieved immediately."

"Our vision is that less is more. You cannot do tailoring.. Id say level of standardization on the application and the service delivery is more than 90 percent. You cannot ruin your value proposition, cause then youre doing implementation project and SaaS becomes merely a mode of delivery."

The respondents stressed an efficient mode of sales. The firm engages in high-pressure sales. This type of SaaS is also associated with online channels for marketing, sales and delivery that, in turn, entail high level of automation to these activities. Respondents emphasized the strict requirements for both sales activities and system maturity, which are likely to be associated with the small sales case size:

"The biggest problem for SaaS businesses is the sales channel. It s difficult push this to a channel partner since you cannot give him a decent share. We aim at that the whole sales and delivery process would work using the inside sales model. Its the opposite to field sales, where you go and meet the customer. But its too expensive to meet all the customers. You just have to close the deal with online tools and on the phone. We optimize this all the time."

As assumed, the respondents reported that the company is targeting SMEs and sell to middle management and end-users. They also described that business model development is about balancing the value proposition, the segmentation and the sales model.

"You have to find out where this works the best. First, you cannot sell to large enterprises with inside sales model, youd have to meet them... Then you have to think, to which kind of customers does your product and value proposition fit."

"We need to develop the application to empower the person, let him push it in the organization.. It needs to be easy and intuitive. Then with bigger firms, we might give some support, do some minimal adjustments."

Sopimas revenue streams are obtained through an entry fee and a recurring fee. Owing to the revenue logic, customer base becomes the most important asset. SaaS business model requires investments on customers behalf as the initial software and service development costs may be high. Once the service is launched, pure-play SaaS firm aims for minimal marginal costs per customer. However, as the firm has increased focus on customer acquisition and retention, generally a high investments on customer acquisition is required.

"The basic model is per user per month. But often we sell an annual subscription with slightly lower cost, in return to the longer commitment."

"Launching SaaS requires monstrous development investment before you start receiving anything. That is, cash flow comes so much slower, compared to software projects, and then you realize you can make a product. You have to make a product before you get money. You have to have a good investor and relationship.

Youre financing your customer, because the money only comes afterwards. You make the investments on customers behalf."

SaaS firms combine capabilities for both operational excellence and infrastructure management into their solution. In Sopimas case, the firm partners with software developers for implementing the product core and with service providers for infrastructure and support services. Reasons include cost- efficiency, faster time-to-market and flexibility.

"We have roughly two types of people, those who build the solution and those selling it. We have a direct sales channel. Close to 50 percent of budget goes to development. It used to be 80 percent, but now were pretty close to 50. And in the middle, we have what we call service owner, who oversees that the application, service produced and mode of sales and delivery are synchronized."

The company website indicates that Sopima partners with legal professionals, IT service providers and IT security professionals. Company is a Microsoft ISV partner and Cloud accelerate partner.

This type of SaaS demands delicate balance between business model elements: product attributes, pricing and revenue logic and sales channel. Respondent reported problems in sustaining this balance, causing the company to move towards Enterprise SaaS with professional services. While the company aimed for removing customer- specific activities altogether, the employees conducting sales activities were forced to take the responsibilities of a customer facing unit in providing support and performing small customizations.

"We tried to take our light-touch inside sales to self service mode, where the sales channel would go pull-oriented.. and the product would spread as in viral marketing. Instead, we ended up going toward high touch field sales. Small domestic market caused.. we had to do customizations. This caused major problems since the selected pricing logic didn't match the mode of sales. There were cases were we had high sales costs per customer but low revenues per customer. Better model would have then be to increase revenues per customer by providing professional services."

"We had to put more effort to customer-specific work that we wanted to. Our sales team was also helping our customer to get started, did some minor customization. This was problematic, since it raises the costs of customer acquisition."

4.2 Case: Qvantel

Qvantel Ltd. is a Scandinavian IT solutions company, established in 1995, with 180 people worldwide. Company has two business units: One focusing on IT SaaS solutions in a pay-as-you-grow business model to help service providers in telecommunication sector to respond quickly to with new products and service launches and provide better customer experience. The second unit, in Bangalore, focuses on software development and testing with offshoring business model. Informants were the firms chief operating officer, HR manager and director of the business unit focusing on SaaS development and provisioning (in total six interviews).

The overall offering can be labeled as business process outsourcing, a solution where Qvantel takes responsibility of parts of customer processes. Consequently, firm is focused on providing exactly what the customer wants and each customer solution is unique. The software core is very complex, often a combination of multiple applications. Firm aims to standardize the core, but customizations are a necessity and performing customer-specific tailoring is also usual. Typically, the core is integrated as part of existing system infrastructure, but vendor aims for pre-integration.

"The core product is a customer care and billing solution for the telecommunication operators. Rating and billing is the core, and then we have supplementing products depending on customer needs. Some customers want to use their own CRM system, some customers needs mediation and provisioning and order management and so on. Basically helps the customer to bundle the different products."

"The way we do the work, we do approximately 90 percent customized solution. We have customers with different levels of SLAs. We have standardized our operating services, but we don't have standardized software for those. Meaning, we're supporting for example standardized billing process, but for each customer we have combined the solution. We're naturally using standard cloud platform and the architecture may be modular, but solution, it's different for each customer."

"Our benefits to the customers are agility, time-to-market and cost efficiency. This flexibility is achieved through customer-specific implementations and then we don't have to think about the constraints, we deploy and tailor what software is needed."

The company is required to possess up-to-date domain expertise and to utilize an ecosystem around it as a resource. Product development is driven by multiple inputs. In addition, in providing the overall offering, respondents stressed understanding customers business. In order to simultaneously improve operational efficiency and to provide customer intimacy, organization has been transformed from customer silos into competence areas serving all customers and smaller on-site teams. Company is also in the course of improving their software architecture, to improve cost efficiency and flexibility.

"Source number one is the industry standardization, making visible basically the standards and trends that are actually driving the industry growth. Then the key inputs for us come from the different RFPs and RFQs that we get from the customers. Basically from there we pick up what is new, what is the innovation that the particular operator is looking for. If we see it can add significant value to our product, we want to take it as core feature in our product. Then, of course, we also have customer relationships where we get a lot of requirements. We are evolving the solution and the service for the customer. And nowadays all these inputs are implemented in one core product."

"Business understanding. We're not software vendors, but we're experts in understanding customers business. That's why we focus on certain domain, cause we really need to have unique knowledge and capabilities. Then, how we split the

work, we have customer-independent teams, supporting every customer. They're not just working on product platform, but supporting multiple customer teams. For example, one is doing software development, operating our common hosted environment, managing common customer business processes. So, 50 percent of employees are working on customer-specific solutions and 50 percent for all the customers."

"Now, we decoupled the pieces and a monolith database we had. And took the pieces that are actually stable, reused them and decided to use latest technology to support the architecture. Like enterprise service bus which gives us the possibility to create dynamic services. We use of course virtualization environments, but the architecture makes it easier for us to scale and meet the SLA requirements. And this granularity helped us reduce the TCO. And it is also most flexible in terms of.. most configurable.. the pieces which are common across all the systems and its also very easy to integrate."

Firm concentrates on long-term customer relationships with tailored contracts. Thus, marketing and sales is based on field sales targeting mainly larger enterprises, willing to outsource their non-core functions, and their executives. Respondents indicated that theyre building trust by committing to customers growth in the way they organize and also in their pricing model. Vendor charges according to volume-based pay-as-go model, enabling both tiered pricing logic and monetizing on larger business case. Revenue model has two components: service fee and possibility for time and materials charging.

"We're mainly focusing on our existing customers and long-term operations and relationships. So, the sales is focused on better supporting their business needs. It's field sales, face-to-face with customers."

"When initiating our SaaS business, we changed our sales tactics so that we wouldnt target the CIO or IT management, but we went to the sales manager or general management and asked whether they have pain points. They would say they cannot invest on IT. But we could respond that they wouldnt be investing on software, theyd buy a service."

"We want to help our customers to buy, on a mental level. Customer would argue that they cannot predict their future volumes. Here, we could say that they dont need to buy a software license, but we check at the end of each month how the volume has changed and we charge based on the actual volume. We share risk and act as true partner. This logic has major effect on customers mental level."

"It's hard to say but I would estimate approximately 70-80 percent of revenue is based on our portfolio of product and services. Tailored services we charge on time and material basis, based on how much the customer needs."

5   Cross-Case Analysis and Discussion

The two main objectives of the paper are to compare different SaaS business models and to examine changes in the business model. Accordingly, Table 1 below summarizes the findings of the introduced cases and enables highlighting contrasting business model configurations. Scope and aims refer to both the current focus of the business as well as the intended direction of changes. Analysis on the vendors business models using the framework by Osterwalder et al. [33] is reduced to foremost findings about operations and revenue logic. Analysis on the quantifiable aspects of organizational structure with framework by Davies et al. [34] populate the last row.

Table 1. Comparsion of the business models of case companies

	Case Sopima	Case Qvantel
Scope and aims	Horizontal focus Balanced business model Cost efficiency Maintain standardization Increase automation	From vertical to horizontal Integrated solution Customer intimacy Increase standardization
Operations	Target on SMEs One application to all customers 100% standard application Inside sales, low-touch	Target on key customer One platform to all customers 90% custom-tailored Long-term relationships Helping customers
Revenue Logic	Recurrent monthly fee Service fees 100% of total Tailoring 0% of total	Revenue share Service fees 70-80% of total Time and materials 20-30%
Structure	Approx. 60% in front office Approx. 40% in back office Sw implementation outsourced Infrastr. Services fully outsourced Value adding services outsourced	Approx. 80% in front office Approx. 20% in back office R&D 10%, Managed services 10%

The case of Sopima Ltd. demostrates a business model configuration with focus on providing as a service a standard software application suitable for multiple domain. Sopima targets SMEs with inside sales model and low-cost monthly fee, and work toward minimal marginal costs. The company has outsourced software development, infrastructure hosting and value-added services and most of the team focuses on marketing and sales activities. The management strive for balance in the business model configuration to maintain cost-efficiency. This low-cost strategy necessitates keeping the application simple and increase the level of automation. These conditions have been difficult to retain.

The business model configuration of Qvantel Ltd. is vastly different from what case Sopima and descriptions in the contemporary literature presents. Their background is in delivering tailor-made solution for one vertical. The solution comprises not only software application provisioned in SaaS mode, but also a variety of services to help their customers to be effective. This is attributed to the focus on key customers, long-term customer relationships and revenue share model. Services fees cover approximately 70-80 percent of the revenues and, in addition, company charges for time and materials for customer specific work. Qvantel has and further aims to make their offerings uniform, for both software components and common set of services. Reaching this objective would enable them to serve also other vertical markets.

In line with the empirical findings by Currie et al. [6] and Luoma et al. [28], our case study reveals two very different SaaS business model configurations. We interpret this finding as a possibility for various configurations to appear. Rather than been an invariable set of elements, SaaS business models can be seen as a continuum. The other extreme is where standard and ultra-simple software applications are provided for the masses with freemium model. (At this point, were thinking of Dropbox). At the opposite end, we have a software application for a specific set of customers with standardized infrastructure, but combined with support and value-adding services. We also suggest that taking different business model configurations into account would increase the reliability of studies on SaaS adoption.

With regards to the strategic aims and changes in the business models, we find that SaaS vendors like Sopima are trying to sustain their focus on cost-efficiency through avoiding customer-specific work and complexity in their software. Increase in complexity results in increasing marginal costs and, in such case, SaaS vendors would need to increase their recurring fee at the cost of disheartening their customers. Taking the software market perspective, we find it likely that the new SaaS start-ups and the software firms with standardized software products will aim at or change to similar business model as represented by case Sopima.

On the other hand, we suggest that software vendors currently embracing customer intimacy strategy could develop their own SaaS offering, by standardizing a parts of their software application or developing common support or value-adding services for all their customers. This would help them to match the price competition by existing SaaS vendors or to capture better margins.

6   Conclusions

This study contributes to the literature on Software-as-a-Service by recognizing the different characteristics of SaaS business models. To conclude on these characteristics (research question 1), we also find a possibility for various types of SaaS business model configurations to appear. Or, rather than being discrete types, we suggest different SaaS business models to appear as a continuum. The configurations can be observed by measuring the degree of standardization or customer-specificity of the offering, revenue logic and operations and, consequently, marginal cost per customer. The software firms design their business models according to the needs of their prospective customer segments.

First, as the previous studies describe, SaaS business model can be associated with provisioning of simple and non-specific software application in a very cost-efficient manner. Owing to the subscription-based revenue logic and target at low marginal costs, customer relationship tends to be continuous but low-touch. Companies opting for this kind of business aim for low-cost operations and maintaining simplified offering. Demonstration of this type, the "Pure-play SaaS" business model, has enabled distinguishing SaaS from preceding software business models.

Second, findings here reveal a different SaaS business model with complex software application for a vertical domain. Vendors may incorporate customer-specific services to their offering and charge both a subscription fee and other service fees. They may also target larger customers and aim at enduring, trust-enhancing customer relationships with tailored contracts. These "Enterprise SaaS" firms may have their background in business of supplying customer-specific applications and their business model is changing towards more standardized offering and operations. This observation could be seen as early indication of the existing software vendors attempts to embrace the transforming software business setting.

With regards to the changes in software vendors' business models (research question 2), it seems obvious that those aiming for SaaS business shall reduce the number customer-specific elements in their offering and operations. As the firms with "Pure-play SaaS" start off with simplified offering, their scope and aim is to *maintain* standardization across customers and segments, to avoid increase in marginal costs. In fact, a fatal risk for a SaaS company would be to increase customer-specificity and at the same time restrict themselves to fixed subscription-based revenue logic.

The "Enterprise SaaS" business model can be seen as potential strategic option to those software firms who do not want the radically change their business model or wish to focus on larger customers. These software firms may benefit from increasing the degree of standardization in their offering and scale economics, but also from maintaining as part of their offering the customer-specific features due to customer demand and additional revenues.

Recognizing the issue of generalizing from rare cases, we suggest a need for further empirical investigation of different Software-as-a-Service business models. We realize that the business model as unit of analysis has been criticized for giving a limited picture of the firms surroundings. In this study, we examined the intended adjustments in operations that the SaaS companies perform to match the changes in their environment. Future studies should nonetheless attempt to observe SaaS vendors business context in more detail and by more structured means. Further, limiting our case study to Finland may fall short of providing a representative illustration on SaaS business model in a global context. Although the business of SaaS is less limited to national borders, we would welcome insights from similar studies in other countries.

Acknowledgments. The research reported in this paper was carried out within the framework of the Cloud Software Program which is governed by TIVIT Oy nominated to organize and manage the programs of the Strategic Center for Science, Technology and Innovation in the field of ICT funded by the Finnish Funding Agency for Technology and Innovation (TEKES).

References

1. Mell, P., Grance, T.: The NIST Definition of Cloud Computing (2011)
2. Schwarz, A., Jayatilaka, B., Hirschheim, R., Goles, T.: A Conjoint Approach to Understanding IT Application Services Outsourcing. Journal of Association of Information Systems 10, 748–781 (2009)
3. Yang, H., Tate, M.: A Descriptive Literature Review and Classification of Cloud Computing Research. Communications of the Association for Information Systems 31, 35–60 (2012)
4. Marston, S., Li, Z., Bandyopadhyay, S., Zhang, J., Ghalsasi, A.: Cloud computing The business perspective. Decision Support Systems 51, 176–189 (2011)
5. Kern, T., Willcocks, L.P., Lacity, M.: Application Service Provision: Risk Assessment and Mitigation. MIS Quarterly Executive 1, 113–126 (2002)
6. Currie, W., Desai, B., Khan, N.: Customer evaluation of application services provisioning in five vertical sectors. Journal of Information Technology 19, 39–58 (2004)
7. Magretta, J.: Why business models matter. Harvard Business Review 80, 3–8 (2002)
8. Hedman, J., Kalling, T.: The business model concept: theoretical underpinnings and empirical illustrations. European Journal of Information Systems 12, 49–59 (2003)
9. Zott, C., Amit, R., Massa, L.: The Business Model:Theoretical Roots, Recent Developments, and Future Research, Working Paper (2010)
10. Porter, M.E.: Strategy and the Internet. Harvard Business Review 79, 62–76 (2001)
11. George, G., Bock, A.J.: The business model in practice and its implications for entrepreneurship research. Entrepreneurship Theory and Practice 35, 83–111 (2011)
12. Andriole, S.J.: Seven Indisputable Technology Trends That Will Define 2015. Communications of the Association for Information Systems 30, 61–72 (2012)
13. Benlian, A., Hess, T.: Opportunities and risks of software-as-a-service: Findings from a survey of it executives. Decision Support Systems 52, 232–246 (2011)
14. Janssen, M., Joha, A.: Challenges For Adopting Cloud-Based Software As A Service (SAAS) In The Public Sector. In: ECIS 2011 (2011)
15. Repschlaeger, J., Wind, S., Zarnekow, R., Turowski, K.: Selection Criteria for Software as a Service: An Explorative Analysis of Provider Requirements. In: AMCIS 2012 (2012)
16. Walther, S., Plank, A., Eymann, T., Singh, N., Phadke, G.: Success Factors and Value Propositions of Software as a Service Providers A Literature Review and Classification. In: AMCIS 2012 (2012)
17. Choudhary, V.: Comparison of Software Quality Under Perpetual Licensing and Software as a Service. Journal of Management Information Systems 24, 141–165 (2007)
18. Benlian, A.: Is traditional, open-source, or on-demand first choice? Developing an AHP-based framework for the comparison of different software models in office suites selection. European Journal of Information Systems 20, 542–559 (2011)
19. Susarla, A., Barua, A., Whinston, A.: A Transaction Cost Perspective of the Software as a Service Business Model. Journal of Management Information Systems 26, 205–240 (2009)
20. Benlian, A., Hess, T., Buxmann, P.: Drivers of SaaS-Adoption An Empirical Study of Different Application Types. Business & Information Systems Engineering 1, 357–369 (2009)
21. Lyons, K., Playford, C., Messinger, P.R., Niu, R.H., Stroulia, E.: Business Models in Emerging Online Services. In: Nelson, M.L., Shaw, M.J., Strader, T.J. (eds.) AMCIS 2009. LNBIP, vol. 36, pp. 44–55. Springer, Heidelberg (2009)

22. Katzan, H., Dowling, W.: Software-As-A-Service Economics. Review of Business Information Systems 14, 27–38 (2010)
23. Stuckenberg, S., Fielt, E., Loser, T.: The Impact Of Software-As-A-Service On Business Models Of Leading Software Vendors: Experiences From Three Exploratory Case Studies. In: PACIS 2011 (2011)
24. Dsouza, A., Kabbedijk, J., Seo, D., Jansen, S., Brinkkemper, S.: Software-As-A-Service: Implications For Business And Technology In Product Software Companies. In: PACIS 2012 (2012)
25. Demirkan, H., Cheng, H., Bandyopadhyay, S.: Coordination Strategies in an SaaS Supply Chain. Journal of Management Information Systems 26, 119–143 (2010)
26. Katzmarzik, A.: Product Differentiation for Software-as-a-Service Providers. Business & Information Systems Engineering 3, 19–31 (2011)
27. Cusumano, M.: The Changing Software Business: Moving from Products to Services. IEEE Computer, 20–27 (January 2008)
28. Luoma, E., Rönkkö, M., Tyrväinen, P.: Current Software-as-a-Service Business Models: Evidence from Finland. In: Cusumano, M.A., Iyer, B., Venkatraman, N. (eds.) ICSOB 2012. LNBIP, vol. 114, pp. 181–194. Springer, Heidelberg (2012)
29. Walsham, G.: Interpretive case studies in IS research: Nature and method. European Journal of Information Systems 4, 74–81 (1995)
30. Bhattacherjee, A.: Social Science Research: Principles, Methods, and Practices (2012)
31. Benbasat, I., Goldstein, D., Mead, M.: The Case Research Strategy in Studies of Information Systems. MIS Quarterly 11, 369–386 (1987)
32. Yin, R.: Case Study Research: Design and Methods. Sage Publications (2009)
33. Osterwalder, A., Pigneur, Y., Tucci, C.: Clarifying Business Models: Origins, Present, and Future of the Concept. Communications of the Association for Information Systems 16, 1–25 (2005)
34. Davies, A., Brady, T., Hobday, M.: Charting a Path Towards Integrated Solutions. MIT Sloan Managment Review 47, 39–48 (2006)
35. Miles, M., Huberman, M.: Qualitative Data Analysis: An Expanded Sourcebook. Sage Publications (1994)
36. Glaser, B., Strauss, A.: The Discovery of Grounded Theory: Strategies for Qualitative Research. Wledenfeld and Nicholson, London (1967)

Cost Efficiency Strategy
in the Software-as-a-Service Market:
Modeling Results and Related Implementation Issues

Robert J. Kauffman and Dan Ma

Singapore Management University, Singapore
{rkauffman,madan}@smu.edu.sg

Abstract. We model competition between *software-as-a-service* (SaaS) ven-dors by focusing on several key features of SaaS. These include: differences in vendor offerings; incomplete information for the clients side about the vendor's capability to offer well-fitting services, and the clients' learning costs and op-tions to switch. Our findings suggest pricing strategies that will be effective for the SaaS vendor. High cost efficiency in the operations of the SaaS business model is key for the vendor to gain leverage to retain the client by making its switching costs too high, and to achieve high profitability in the process by im-plementing the appropriate strategies in the appropriate customer segments. We also extend the analysis by considering a broader set of implementation issues related to mechanism design choices in the SaaS market that arise around our modeling approach.

Keywords: Competition, Economic Analysis, IT-Enabled Services, Pricing Strategy, Service Science, Software-as-a-Service, Strategy.

1   Introduction

Software-as-a-service (SaaS) is a business model that has been transforming the soft-ware industry's foundations. In 2012, Gartner [10] reported that global spending for SaaS would rise to US$14.5 billion and growth will remain strong through 2015 when total spending is expected to reach US$22.1 billion. Though there were all kinds of uncertainties, concerns, and doubts in the initial years of SaaS, today SaaS has devel-oped into a significant marketplace and attracted a lot of attention from practitioners and researchers. Existing research has investigated a variety of economic and business issues of the SaaS and cloud computing market, including workload scheduling [11], vendor pricing strategies and schemes [19, 22], *service level agreements* (SLAs) [20], contract design [3, 16, 25], and impacts on the traditional software market [9]. Firm-to-firm competition in the SaaS market is not well understood though. In this re-search, we try to address this gap. We propose a model of competition to explore how SaaS vendors can implement strategies for success based on game theory [17, 19].

Competition in the SaaS market deserves a close investigation because it exhibits unique characteristics. First, SaaS offerings consist of two parts: software application and related IT services. Software applications are *horizontally-differentiated*: different

J. Altmann, K. Vanmechelen, and O.F. Rana (Eds.): GECON 2013, LNCS 8193, pp. 16–28, 2013.
© Springer International Publishing Switzerland 2013

clients may prefer different software functionalities. IT services, contrast, are *vertical-ly-differentiated*: vendors can choose to deliver higher or lower service quality. Second, the *multi-tenancy structure* of SaaS makes customization difficult [14]. The client has to use standardized software applications offered by the vendor, and as a result, the client will incur disutility from not using ideal services. Third, the *experience good* feature of software applications makes a client's choice even more complicated. We only learn about the quality of an experience good after we use it. The client faces uncertainty about how the SaaS offering will fit its specific business requirements, and also how well the application can be integrated into its existing legacy systems. Such information only can be learned after trying the SaaS offering. Finally, the client faces non-negligible switching costs because typically the vendor will be in charge of its data management, maintenance and back-up. To switch from one vendor to another will be costly for the client. The model we explore will capture all the above features, and is able to deliver new results that have not been observed in other types of competition.

We also aim to deliver practical findings for the SaaS industry. To do this, we include a rich discussion of implementation and mechanism design issues that arise as a result of our modeling choices. Figuring out how to identify the appropriate pricing strategy in a competitive IT services marketplace is a *mechanism design problem*. So vendors need to consider multiple issues that will influence their capacity to success-fully implement SaaS in the marketplace:

- viewing IT services client decision-making as occurring in continuous time rather than at discrete times;
- identifying the willingness-to-pay, pricing and services contract valuation implications that arise when there is flexibility for the client to opt out of an IT services contract;
- understanding how to leverage cost efficiency to achieve different kinds of leverage to retain the firm's clients; and finally,
- managing clients that have different levels of switching cost, and pinpointing when it is necessary to co-invest to achieve retention through the implement beneficial approaches that enabled them to be locked into the relationship.

Section 2 presents our model of SaaS vendor competition. Section 3 analyzes the competition game and suggests pricing strategies for SaaS vendors. Section 4 discusses issues that relate to our modeling assumptions and choices, as well as to other issues that arise around the mechanism design that we have investigated. It is intended to enrich our understanding of competition in the SaaS market. Section 5 summarizes and concludes.

2   Model

Consider two SaaS vendors, *H* and *L*, competing in the market. Each delivers a bundle of software applications and IT services to clients. Their offerings differ in two ways. First, the software applications have different attributes and functionalities, and are *horizontally-differentiated*. We adopt the Salop [23] circle model to capture horizontal differentiation. The *service space* is a unit-length circle, and the two vendors' software applications are located on opposite sides of the circle with a distance of 0.5 between them. This set-up follows the *principle of maximum product differentiation* [6] in duopolistic spatial competition.[1] Second, the two vendors offer IT services at different quality levels: they are *vertically-differentiated*. Vendor H is the *high-quality vendor* that offers services of higher quality q_H, while Vendor L is a *low-quality vendor* that offers services of lower quality q_L, and $q_H > q_L$. In this study, we will assume that vendors can eliminate service quality uncertainty through the use of SLAs, in which all quality-related issues, including productivity, service quality metrics, problem resolution procedures, and provisions for system and data security, are defined in detail. As a result, q_H and q_L are public information for clients.

A vendor bears both the initial setup cost I and the service cost c for delivering services. Setup cost I is a one-time cost incurred when the vendor acquires a new client. It includes the vendor's efforts to build the relationship with the new client, move the client's data to a centralized location, and understand the technical architecture and business needs of the new client. Service cost c is a recurring cost. It includes the vendor's efforts to maintain client data and application code, provide supporting services, and manage data security. Delivering higher service quality requires the SaaS vendor to bear a higher service cost. We assume the quality of the vendor's IT service, q, is a function of c: $q = f(c)$. This function $f(\cdot)$ has no specific functional form. In addition, both vendors charge their clients a fixed subscription price in each period, p_H and p_L. These are the decision variables in our model.

The Salop circle model represents clients with heterogeneous tastes toward software features. All clients are evenly distributed on the circle, and a client's location represents its ideal service.[2] Each vendor only offers one standard version of the software, however; this is due to the multi-tenancy structure of the SaaS business model. A client will incur a utility loss of td for not using its ideal service. Here, d measures the distance between the client's ideal service and the vendor's offering in the circle, and t is the parameter for a client's unit *fit costs*. In addition, we assume that the two SaaS vendors' positions on the circle initially are unknown to their potential clients: they learn about their fit as they use them. So a client will not know its distance to a vendor's offering in the circle in advance: it has to figure this out by using the vendor's software. On the other hand, although all clients always prefer higher quality services, their willingness-to-pay is likely to be different. Our model considers two types of clients with this in mind: a *higher willingness-to-pay client* θ_h is willing to pay more for a higher level of service quality than a *lower willingness-to-pay client* θ_l, with $\theta_h > \theta_l$.

The utility function of Client j, when it uses services from Vendor i, is:

$$U(\theta_j, q_i, d_i) = \theta_j \cdot q_i - p_i - t \cdot d_i \tag{1}$$

where $i \in \{H, L\}$ indicates Vendor H or L, and $j \in \{h, l\}$ indicates the client's type, θ_h or θ_l. Here, q_i is the level of service quality, p_i is the price per period offered by

---

[1] Under the *principle of maximum product differentiation*, competing SaaS vendors differentiate themselves as much as possible in the service space to avoid head-to-head price competition.

[2] An *ideal service* would be an individually customized application. It will fit a client's technical and business requirements perfectly, and can be integrated with its legacy systems seamlessly.

Vendor i, and d_i measures the distance between the client's ideal software and Vendor i's offering on the circle. The last term, $t \cdot d_i$, is the client's utility loss due to not using an ideal application. We call it the client's *fit costs*.

3   Analysis

The competition proceeds in two stages. Prior to time 0, the vendors will post their prices p_H and p_L simultaneously. Their service quality levels, q_H and q_L, will be known publicly. The *fit costs* experienced by each client for using a specific vendor will not be known though. At time 0, facing incomplete information, the client will decide which vendor's services to use. The first stage, between time 0 and 1, is called the client's *FitCost Sampling Stage*, during which the client learns information about the fit costs. As a result, at time 1, the client will have updated information about the vendor's offering and will decide whether to remain with the same vendor or switch to another. Switching is costly though. The client will face a switching cost S, which includes the cost of discovering the other vendor, recovering data from the current vendor, and making new service arrangements. The second stage, represented by the period after time 1, is called the *Long-Term Partnership Stage*. It reflects the firming up of the service relationship between clients and vendors. By then, the market will have stabilized.

Throughout the analysis, we will assume that both SaaS vendors and their clients maximize long-run profits. Following the literature in two-stage competition games with switching costs [4, 8], we focus on the analysis of competition between two SaaS vendors competing for the marginal customer.

3.1   Analysis of the SaaS Client's Decision

We first analyze the client's decisions at times 0 and 1, taking the SaaS vendors' prices p_H and p_L as given. We use backward induction to solve the problem.

Consider a client's switching decision at time 1. If a client j, $j \in \{h, l\}$ indicating this client's type, θ_h or θ_l, has chosen the Vendor H at time 0, after the FitCost Sampling Stage, this client will have learned the true fit costs of using Vendor H: $t \cdot d_{Hj}$, where t is the unit fit cost parameter and d_{Hj} is the distance from this Client j to the Vendor H in the circle. When making a decision on whether to switch at time 1, the client will compare its utility of staying with the current Vendor H, which is $\theta_j \cdot q_H - t \cdot d_{Hj} - p_H$, with its utility of switching to the other Vendor L, which is $\theta_j \cdot q_L - 0.25 \cdot t - p_L - S$.[3] The latter case will incur a switching cost S. By equating the two utilities, we can find the *marginal switcher* for Vendor H, who is indifferent between switching to L or staying with H at time 1, given that the client has chosen to sample

---

[3] The number 0.25 was not chosen as a parameter; instead it is a logical outline of the factor that the vendors position their services offerings 180° away from each other on the Salop circle. The distance between these points, then, will be one-half of the unit length of the circle or 0.50. By the same logic a client will never be farther away in terms of its ideal services preferences than one-half of the distance between the locations of the two vendors' services locations. This is one-half of the half-circumference of the Salop circle or 0.25.

Vendor H at time 0. We denote the marginal switcher's distance to Vendor H by d_{Hj}^*, and d_{Hj}^* is given by

$$d_{Hj}^* = 0.25 + \frac{\theta_j \cdot \Delta q - \Delta p}{t} + \frac{s}{t}. \tag{2}$$

Similarly, we can define the marginal switcher for Vendor L and solve for the relevant value as:

$$d_{Lj}^* = 0.25 - \frac{\theta_j \cdot \Delta q - \Delta p}{t} + \frac{s}{t}. \tag{3}$$

Next, we return to time 0 to solve client j's decision of which vendor to try out. The client is forward-looking and has rational expectations with respect to vendor's actions. At time 0, the client will be able to correctly estimate the probability of switching to Vendor L, if it chooses to sample Vendor H, is $2d_{Hj}^*$, and the probability of switching to Vendor H, if it chooses to sample Vendor L, is $2d_{Lj}^*$. Thus, the client will compare its expected utility from sampling Vendor H, as Equation 4, and the expected utility of sampling Vendor L, as Equation 5, to make the decision.

$$E[U_H](\theta_j) = 2 \cdot d_{Hj}^* \cdot (\theta_j \cdot q_H - p_H - 0.5 \cdot d_{Hj}^* \cdot t) + (1 - 2 \cdot d_{Hj}^*) \cdot [(\theta_j \cdot q_L - p_L - 0.25 \cdot t) - S] \tag{4}$$

$$E[U_L](\theta_j) = 2 \cdot d_{Lj}^* \cdot (\theta_j \cdot q_L - p_L - 0.5 \cdot d_{Lj}^* \cdot t) + (1 - 2 \cdot d_{Lj}^*) \cdot [(\theta_j \cdot q_H - p_H - 0.25 \cdot t) - S] \tag{5}$$

In Equation 4, the first term is the client's expected utility from staying with Vendor H with a probability of $2d_{Hj}^*$.[4] In this case, the expected distance between this client and Vendor H will be $0.5 \cdot d_{Hj}^*$ since d_{Hj}^* is the marginal switcher's distance. The second term is the client's expected utility from using Vendor L that will happen with a probability of $(1 - 2 \cdot d_{Hj}^*)$. Here, the expected distance between this client and Vendor L will be 0.25 since the client has not tried Vendor L at the first stage, so it will not get updated information about Vendor L's offering. The role of Equation 5 is similar.

Thus, there are three outcomes after time 0:

- all clients will choose to sample Vendor H, if and only if $E[U_H](\theta_j) > E[U_L](\theta_j)$ for $j = h$ and l;
- all clients will choose to sample Vendor L if and only if $E[U_H](\theta_j) < E[U_L](\theta_j)$ for $j = h$ and l;
- θ_h-type clients will choose to sample Vendor H and θ_l-type clients will choose to sample Vendor L if and only if $E[U_H](\theta_h) \geq E[U_L](\theta_h)$ and $E[U_H](\theta_l) \leq E[U_L](\theta_l)$.

3.2   Analysis of the Vendors' Pricing Strategy

Vendors also are forward-looking with rational expectations. This means that they will expect clients to respond strategically to their prices. Vendors will set their prices, prior to time 0, to optimize their own profits. To begin our analysis, we assert:

---

[4] The analysis of a marginal switcher shows that, for all clients who are in the range of $(-d_{Hj}^*, d_{Hj}^*)$ around the Vendor H in the Salop circle, the marginal switcher will stay with H at time 1, while the other clients will switch. Since the product circle is of unit length, the *ex ante* switching probability for any client at time 0 is $2d_{Hj}^*$.

- **Proposition 1 (Threshold Value for Switching Costs).** *When $S \geq 0.25 \cdot t$, no clients will not switch from their current vendor.*

Proofs for propositions are omitted, but are available upon request.

Proposition 1 identifies a threshold value for switching costs. When a client faces high switching costs exceeding this threshold value, it will always choose to stay with its current vendor. In this case, a SaaS vendor will have absolute leverage to retain its existing clients. This is called *lock-in power*. Finding the related threshold is straightforward: it equals a client's *ex ante* expected fit costs, $0.25 \cdot t$. This makes sense because the client's decision to switch is driven by the fact that the vendor's software does not fit the client's needs very well. As a result, the client must balance its switching costs, if it does indeed switch, and its fit costs, if it does not.

The strategies for vendors will be different for $S \geq 0.25 \cdot t$ and $S < 0.25 \cdot t$. We will analyze them separately as Cases A and B.

Case A: $S \geq 0.25 \cdot t$. A vendor knows that its clients eventually will not be able to switch to the competing vendor once its clients try its services and build a business relationship. In this case, a vendor will have a strong incentive to attract new clients in the first stage and then lock in them at a later stage. Meanwhile, clients will be aware of the risk of being locked in by a vendor and will be conservative when making their initial vendor choice at time 0. Keeping these considerations in mind, we expect that the market competition will become intense. Both vendors will compete head-to-head on price to make sure they are attractive enough so clients will try them out at the first stage. This has the potential to trigger a price war between them.

This conjecture, however, may not be entirely correct though. We instead find that the outcome actually depends on the two vendors' *relative cost efficiencies*, measured by the ratio $\Delta c / \Delta q$. Here, Δc is the service cost difference and Δq is the service quality difference for SaaS vendors. The ratio $\Delta c / \Delta q$ provides a measure for cost efficiency in the SaaS business model. Our next proposition suggests that a price war may occur when the cost efficiency for offering SaaS is very high or very low. It may cause one vendor to fail due to severe price competition:

- **Proposition 2 (Conditions for a Price War).** *A price war will occur under two different circumstances:*

  o *when cost efficiency is high ($\Delta c / \Delta q < \theta_l$), Vendor H will be able to compete aggressively, and at $p_H = c_L + \Delta q \cdot \theta_l$, Vendor H will be able to drive Vendor L out of the market and serve all clients itself; and*

  o *when the cost efficiency of the SaaS model is low ($\Delta c / \Delta q > \theta_h$), Vendor L will be able to compete aggressively, and at $p_L = c_H - \Delta q \cdot \theta_h$, Vendor L will drive Vendor H out of the market and serve all of the clients.*

When cost efficiency is at a medium level $\theta_l < \Delta c / \Delta q < \theta_h$, however, no vendor will be able to undercut its competitor's price. So the two vendors will coexist in the market. More importantly, there will be no direct competition between vendors. To wit:

- **Proposition 3 (Conditions for a Monopolistic Outcome).** *When the SaaS business model has mid-range cost efficiency, $\theta_l \leq \Delta c / \Delta q \leq \theta_h$, both vendors will co-exist. The equilibrium prices will be $p_L = \theta_l \cdot q_L - 0.25 \cdot t$ and $p_H = \theta_l \cdot q_L + \theta_h \cdot$*

Δq - 0.25 · *t*. Vendor H will serve θ_h type clients and Vendor L will serve θ_l type clients, and they will not compete with each other directly.

The equilibrium prices will ensure there is no direct competition. The price p_L serves to extract all expected consumer surplus from θ_l type clients. On the other hand, the price p_H will be set at a level to ensure that θ_h type clients will not be attracted to try Vendor L. This segments the market with no direct competition between the two vendors. Instead, each vendor will only target and serve one client group, behaving like a monopolist in its market segment.

Case B: $S < 0.25 \cdot t$. As long as the switching cost is not so high that it gives vendors full lock-in power over clients, the two vendors will always coexist in the market. One vendor will not become dominant, even when its SaaS cost efficiency is very high or very low. In this case, three different types of equilibria may come about, depending on the values of switching cost S and cost efficiency $\Delta c / \Delta q$. However, when the cost efficiency of the SaaS model is at different levels, somewhat paradoxically, the vendors will benefit from switching costs in different ways. For example, in certain situations with high cost efficiency, Vendor H will be the only beneficiary of switching cost: with increases in switching cost, Vendor H will be able to raise its price to achieve higher profitability, and meanwhile, Vendor L will be forced to reduce its price but still will experience lower profit. The opposite will happen when cost efficiency is low: in this case, Vendor L will be the only beneficiary.[5]

Previous research has never documented this finding. Instead, switching cost always has been reported to affect the two competing vendors in the same way – either positively or negatively, but not with elements of both. We are observing a unique aspect of SaaS competition: there is *asymmetric influence of clients' switching cost* on the vendors. So switching cost may benefit one vendor but hurt the other, depending on their relative cost efficiencies.

4   Discussion: Recommendations on Modeling and Implementation

The real world of competition in the IT services market is more complicated than our game-theoretical model suggests. Nevertheless, our model captures a number of interesting and important features, including the vertical and horizontal differentiation of vendors, and the sampling of fit costs and switching costs. The model also has the added benefit of enabling us to draw insightful conclusions about the pricing strategies of service vendors. The most deeply insightful finding is our observation of the asymmetric influence of clients' switching cost. This will inspire others to think more

---

[5] The three types of equilibria are: (1) all clients will try out Vendor H in the Fit Cost Sampling Stage and some will switch to Vendor L at time 1; (2) all clients will try out Vendor L in the Sampling Stage and some will switch to Vendor H at time 1; and (3) θ_h type clients will try out Vendor H in the Sampling Stage and some will switch to Vendor L at time 1, and θ_l type clients will try out Vendor L at the Sampling Stage and some will switch to Vendor H at time 1. In equilibrium, clients' decision-making will follow our analysis, with *marginal switchers* defined by Equations 2 and 3.

deeply about the inner workings of the IT services market, and to reflect on the effectiveness of our modeling choices and the implementation issues that arise the strategies we have indicated.

We offer three recommendations to managers to build on our analytical results:

- **Recommendation #1:** *After the Sampling Stage concludes, offer your SaaS clients value co-creating contract flexibility to reflect their need to iteratively address their potentially changing fit costs for the vendor's services.*

In the SaaS market, many vendors have adopted a marketing strategy involving free sampling periods for potential clients, typically of one-month duration, and offering opt-out flexibility. For example, Salesforce (www.salesforce.com) allows new clients to test-run its CRM applications for thirty days for free. A client only needs to register on Saleforce's website, and after sharing a little information, it will be able to run the software and quickly gauge whether the fit costs are high and unacceptable.

Our modeling approach accords clients the flexibility of sampling a vendor's SaaS offering, and reaching a conclusion about whether the fit costs are acceptable, similar to Salesforce.com's approach. Although our model requires clients to make switching decisions at a certain point in time, different clients may need different lengths of time to learn about the fit costs of working with a given vendor. So a decision to switch by the client may happen at any time during the contract period. This makes the modeling setup different, since it will require a continuous-time decision-making approach for the clients. This may be modeled in a different way than we have so far: as an embedded option in the decision process [7]. The managerial implications of embedded option models are clear and compelling: including them tends to make any contract more valuable, and so the client will have a higher level of willingness-to-pay. The worst case with an option-bearing contract is that it will not be exercised under unattractive conditions.

The arrangements that we have considered with respect to SaaS offerings are *incomplete contracts*: not all of the details are always pre-specified. During the period of the use of the services, different kinds of risks and uncertainty have to be borne by the vendor and its client, so SaaS contracts should be designed with enough flexibility to accommodate the different stakeholders' concerns. Clients face downward price uncertainty in the SaaS market, for example. So there is a need to permit *benchmarking*, which allows clients to utilize a third-party auditor to conduct an analysis of the current market prices for SaaS services, and then to adjust the price during the period of the contract, after services sampling has finished and a longer-term relationship has been established [16]. Clients may also switch to another services vendor even after a longer-term contract has been established. The discovery of true fit costs also may be influenced by changes in a client's business activities and strategy.[6]

Based on how this market operates, SaaS vendor senior managers need to address two questions in their competitive market operations. How can a firm convince potential clients to try out its services, as opposed to those of others? And what can be done to increase the *conversion rate* from free to paid services and the likelihood that a

---

[6] In addition, when demand volatility exists for computing cycles in a market, or a client experiences a precipitous drop in demand, flexibility will be of value. Clients might be permitted to opt out; a front-loaded fee for this option may compensate the vendor for its expected costs [3].

client will not opt out after this period passes, but enter into a longer-term relationship with the vendor? According to Sixteen Ventures [21], an IT services metrics provider, 66% of SaaS vendors reported conversion rates to longer-term service sales of 25%, a disappointing level.

Based on our ongoing field study discussions with managers in the United States, Canada and Singapore, interactions with vendors around the world, and assessments of what market pundits have been saying, there seem to be no simple answers. We conjecture that, as time goes by, vendors may need to be more aggressive, even going to subsidized longer-term sampling period durations to create a more compelling value proposition to attract new clients. Vendors need to make investments to ensure that clients trying out their services will be satisfied, though they only bring an expectation of future profit – not a guarantee. Though the first image of a SaaS vendor may be as a pure *digital services market intermediary*, our expectation is that intermediaries will strategically morph to match the needs of their clients. So we encourage SaaS providers will do more to create service adoption consulting and business facilitation services involving domain experts, experienced clients in the same industries, and more effective initial support to serve them. It is costly to provide these kinds of flexibility and support to clients. Strategic necessity is likely to win out though. Plus, a vendor that does the right things at the right points in time will be able to turn flexibility and extensive service facilitation into a strongly profitable business in the long run:

- **Recommendation #2:** *Lock in your SaaS clients, but only with mutually-beneficial impacts that are understood in the marketplace to balance the related risks and rewards.*

For SaaS vendors, experience and knowledge learned from serving one client can be used to enhance efficiency and create value in serving other clients. This approach is practiced by the large accounting, IS and marketing consulting firms: many firms reuse the business logic associated with their service excellence – many times over, in fact. Potential SaaS clients may view this as a dangerous practice though, because it gives rise to *poaching and misappropriation* of sensitive business information [5]. A collateral concern is *knowledge lock-in*. This will occur when the vendor can leverage the threat of using experience with the client and the resulting business knowledge to engage with and provide services to other firms. Clients face lock-in, but we conceptualized it more narrowly as a switching cost that involves data recovery from the SaaS vendor, a limitation of our modeling approach.

Real-world business settings involve other hidden switching costs though. Consider a large SaaS client firm that has used a particular SaaS vendor for some time, and also is an industry leader in its business sector. The vendor will learn industry-specific knowledge from serving this client over time. It also will gain a deep understanding of the client's business operations, a key enabler of the client's competitive advantage. The client will worry that – if it opts out from the vendor's service – it may be subject to exploitation of its business information. This could harm its competitive position.

The potential for lock-in occurs due to the extent to which competitive advantage may be lost. Lock-in that arises due to the vendor's intimate knowledge of a client's business is *adverse lock-in*, and is undesirable in a long-term IT services relationship. Other outcomes are possible, including *beneficial lock-in* to vendors. Consider the case of IBM and General Motors, a client of IBM's IT services organization (www.ibm.com/ services). The firms have worked together to develop a CRM solution "to align [IBM's] technologies with GM's business processes." Leveraging its experience in the automotive industry, IBM was "able to provide industry-based intellectual capital" that few other firms could [15]. The idea, in beneficial lock-in terms, is that having a long-term relationship has deepened IBM's industry-based intellectual capital for automotive industry IT services, and will benefit GM more than its competitors. Here, the vendor co-invests in R&D, creates new innovations, and works as a partner with GM as its client. Knowledge is shared and value is created from a cooperative strategic alliance.

Senior managers also need to think about how to retain their clients by leveraging beneficial lock-in in different ways. One way may be to subsidize those who are likely to be profitable high service demand customers. This is appealing due to the visibility of the vendor's commitment to concentrate the attention of a somewhat larger, more expert IT services staff as a way of helping the client to minimize the fit costs of adopting the vendor's services. This is why, we think, some SaaS vendors are offering the capability to partially customize the services they offer to big clients – a subtle morphing of the way they define their roles as SaaS vendors beyond the constraints of multi-tenancy structure. Vendors, including Salesforce.com and Amazon EC2, claim they are willing to cooperate, co-invest, and co-customize their applications to satisfy a client's business needs. The outcome is that the vendors truly need to achieve high profitability in the longer term: clients should be locked into the vendor's services, but in a way that achieves mutual benefits.

Our findings show that the competitive outcome will be different for competing SaaS vendors under different levels of cost efficiency for the SaaS business model. As a result, we advocate the strategy of employing differential pricing tied to a vendor's knowledge of the relative cost efficiency of the competition. We assert:

- **Recommendation #3:** *Leverage your firm's SaaS cost efficiency for stronger market positioning.*

In duopoly competition, the two vendors are likely to have different cost functions for the production of high quality SaaS at the firm level. This enables us to generalize our findings and make it easier for a business strategist to observe the competition and decide what business policy actions to undertake.

A vendor's SaaS capabilities also are subject to under-investment and over-investment. These include over-investment in the ownership of interorganizational networks [2], under-investment in the enhancement of financial risk management systems forecast quality [12] and a spectrum of over-investment, under-investment and right-sized investments in customer-protecting information security capabilities [18]. The result in these cases is that the firms will not be efficient in the production of profit unless they can identify the proper levels of investment.

The same value maximization logic applies to SaaS vendors: over-investment and under-investment in appropriately high quality SaaS capabilities will be a source of competitive disadvantage. For highly-capable firms to gain advantage on other SaaS providers that sell lower quality services will not be about how service quality can be enhanced. Instead, it will be about what it costs to offer an appropriate difference in quality. This will be determined by the overall cost efficiency of the firm.

Vendors will benefit from economies of scale and best practices that strong management can bring. Serving many clients contributes to a vendor's capacity to deliver service quality enhancements too. In addition, quality-related investments, including training customer support staff and expanding database and IT infrastructure capabilities, will help in other ways. Paul Strassmann [24], a past-CIO of Xerox, the U.S. Department of Defense and the National Aeronautics and Space Administration, for example, has claimed that these kinds of things promote *managerial productivity*.

An important question remains to be answered though. What kinds of firms will be more likely to have the capabilities to enhance the quality of their SaaS offerings to match the clockspeed of the market's demand growth for higher quality? We observed that the firm-level cost functions of different firms will be different, but in what ways? Will a long-established software vendor be at an advantage compared to a start-up in the SaaS patch? Large vendors may be able to leverage expertise and experience in the packaged software market to provide reliable, high-quality IT services. In contrast, a new start-up may need to position itself as a market follower, by offering lower quality services at a lower price. A start-up may discover dramatic new ways to do business that a large firm may not. Salesforce.com has proven to be an outstanding example.

5   Conclusion

This research offers competitive strategy and economics analysis for the SaaS business model. The duopoly setting we used was helpful to support our development of some fundamental and useful insights. We have been able to make some relatively refined observations about competition between SaaS vendors, especially related to how switching costs affect the vendors' pricing strategies. We identified a number of conditions that may motivate a vendor to employ an aggressive pricing strategy aimed at driving another IT services competitor with relatively lower cost efficiency out of the market. We also saw the surprising usefulness of a non-competitive pricing strategy that encourages the vendors to find a way to share the market. We saw that the two vendors were best off by cooperating with one another to ensure that each only targeted SaaS clients with an appropriate level of willingness-to-pay, a unique insight into the inner workings of competitive markets that economic analysis can support. Based on our findings, we provided additional commentary on mechanism design choices in the SaaS market. We highlighted: the importance of offering clients value co-creating contract flexibility; beneficial lock-in practices by SaaS vendors; and the danger of over-investment and under-investment in vendor service quality. These represent practical strategies for SaaS vendors to adopt.

There are some other limitations in our approach that deserve final comment. First, we assumed that all clients have only a limited time to sample the fit costs of the vendor whose software services they select. In practice, different firms have different capabilities to acquire and process information to make value-maximizing decisions. Some learn fast, some slow, and some very little. Thus, in practice, there will not be a single time by which switching decisions must occur. Second, our assumption that clients make their switching decisions at some predetermined point in time eliminates the possibility of assessing a more realistic valuation problem with an option embedded in a client's decision-making process. Third, we assumed also that switching cost is exogenously fixed. More likely is that switching cost will vary over time, and may not be entirely exogenous. There are a variety of things that firms can do to create some degree of endogeneity of choice related to how large their switching cost becomes over time [1]. Investments in the adoption of services-oriented architecture is such an approach.

Finally, market competition and incentives are such that one can imagine some competitor in the future doing a contract buyout for a new client's commitment to a prior service vendor. This is similar to buyouts of sports stars' contracts. The new vendor might also be willing to absorb and share some of the switching cost, possibly in the manner of Shapley value-based assignment of value stream rights to different stakeholders, who will be better off figuring out some way to split them [13]. All these are interesting directions to consider enhancing the future richness of our understanding of IT services strategy and management.

References

1. Aron, R., Clemons, E.K., Reddi, S.P.: Just right outsourcing: Understanding and managing risk. Journal of Management Information Systems 22(2), 37–55 (2005)
2. Bakos, Y., Nault, B.R.: Ownership and investment in electronic networks. Information Systems Research 8(4), 321–341 (1997)
3. Benaroch, M., Dai, Q., Kauffman, R.J.: Should we go our own way? Backsourcing flexibility in IT services contracts. Journal of Management Information Systems 26(4), 317–358 (2010)
4. Cabral, L.M.B.: Switching costs and equilibrium prices. Stern School of Business, New York University, New York (2012)
5. Clemons, E.K., Hitt, L.M.: Poaching and misappropriation of information: transaction risks of information exchange. Journal of Management Information Systems 21(2), 87–107 (2004)
6. D'Aspremont, C., Gabszewicz, J.J., Thisse, J.F.: On Hotelling's stability in competition. Econometrica 47(5), 1145–1150 (1979)
7. Dixit, A.K., Pindyck, R.S.: Investment under Uncertainty. Princeton University Press, Princeton (1994)
8. Dubé, J.P., Gunter, J.H., Peter, E.R.: Do switching costs make markets less competitive? Journal of Marketing Research 46(4), 435–445 (2009)
9. Fan, M., Kumar, S., Whinston, A.B.: Short-term and long-term competition between providers of shrink-wrap software and software as a service. European Journal of Operational Research 196(2), 661–671 (2009)
10. Gartner: Forecast: public cloud services, worldwide (2010-2016). Report, Stamford, CT (2012)
11. Genez, T., Bittencourt, L., Madeira, E.: Workflow scheduling for SaaS/PaaS cloud providers considering two SLA Levels. In: Proceedings of the 2012 IEEE Network Operations and Management Symposium, pp. 906–912. IEEE Computer Society Press, Washington, DC (2012)
12. Han, K., Kauffman, R.J., Nault, B.R.: Information exploitation and interorganizational systems ownership. Journal of Management Information Systems 21(2), 109–135 (2004)

13. Han, K., Kauffman, R.J., Nault, B.R.: Relative importance, specific investment and owner-ship in interorganizational systems. Information Technology and Management 9(3), 181–200 (2008)
14. Hickins, M.: Oracle: On-demand is now on the grid. Enterprise (2007)
15. IBM Global Services: General Motors: customer-centric strategy drives IBM managed CRM services. Report, Somers, NY (2001)
16. Kauffman, R.J., Sougstad, R.: Valuation of benchmark provisions in IT services contracts. In: Bichler, M., Lau, H.C., Yang, C., Yang, Y. (eds.) Proceedings of the 14th Annual International Conference on Electronic Commerce, pp. 270–271. IEEE Computer Society Press, Washington, DC (2012)
17. Künsemöller, J., Karl, H.: A game-theoretical approach to the benefits of cloud computing. In: Vanmechelen, K., Altmann, J., Rana, O.F. (eds.) GECON 2011. LNCS, vol. 7150, pp. 148–160. Springer, Heidelberg (2012)
18. Lee, Y.J., Kauffman, R.J., Sougstad, R.: Profit-maximizing firm investments in customer information security. Decision Support Systems 51(4), 904–920 (2011)
19. Ma, D., Seidmann, A.: The pricing strategy analysis for the "Software-as-a-service" business model. In: Altmann, J., Neumann, D., Fahringer, T. (eds.) GECON 2008. LNCS, vol. 5206, pp. 103–112. Springer, Heidelberg (2008)
20. McKee, P., Taylor, S., Surridge, M., Lowe, R., Ragusa, C.: Strategies for the service market place. In: Veit, D.J., Altmann, J. (eds.) GECON 2007. LNCS, vol. 4685, pp. 58–70. Springer, Heidelberg (2007)
21. Murphy, L.: Average free trial conversion rates... and why they don't matter. White paper, SaaS Growth Strategies, Sixteen Ventures, Arlington, TX (2012)
22. Rohitratana, J., Altmann, J.: Agent-based simulations of the software market under different pricing schemes for software-as-a-service and perpetual software. In: Altmann, J., Rana, O.F. (eds.) GECON 2010. LNCS, vol. 6296, pp. 62–77. Springer, Heidelberg (2010)
23. Salop, S.: Monopolistic competition with outside goods. Bell Journal of Economics 10(1), 141–156 (1979)
24. Strassmann, P.A.: The Business Value of Computers: An Executive's Guide. Information Economics Press, New Canaan (1990)
25. Susarla, A., Barua, A., Whinston, A.: Understanding the service component of application service provision: An empirical analysis of satisfaction with ASP services. MIS Quarterly 27(1), 91–123 (2003)

How Much Does Storage Really Cost? Towards a Full Cost Accounting Model for Data Storage

Amit Kumar Dutta and Ragib Hasan

University of Alabama at Birmingham, Birmingham, Alabama 35294-1170
{adutta,ragib}@cis.uab.edu

Abstract. In our everyday lives, we create massive amounts of data. But how much does it really cost to store data? With ever decreasing cost of storage media, a popular misconception is that the cost of storage has become cheaper than ever. However, we argue that the cost of storing data is not equal to the cost of storage media alone – rather, many often ignored factors including human, infrastructure, and environmental costs contribute to the total cost to store data. Unfortunately, very little research has been done to determine the full cost of cloud based storage systems. Most existing studies do not account for indirect factors and determinants of storage cost. To fully determine the true cost of data storage, we need to perform full cost accounting – a well known accounting technique. In this paper, we present a *full cost accounting* model for cloud storage systems. We include all the hidden and environmental costs as well as regular costs to develop a comprehensive model for storage system costs. To the best of our knowledge, this is the first work on creating a full cost accounting model for cloud based storage systems.

1 Introduction

With the advent of modern technology, digital storage is getting cheaper every day. As storage cost is continuing to drop by roughly 50% every 18 months [1], we can observe two effects: storage appears to be free or very cheap, and there is an illusion of infinite storage. As costs of storage devices are negligible, a very popular misconception is to equate storage costs with the cost of storage media. This line of thinking leads system designers to ignore redundancies or inefficiencies in storage system design, under-optimize data storage, and underestimate the total cost of data storage. We argue that the conventional wisdom about storage cost is mistaken, and a full range of factors – both direct and indirect – need to be considered to determine the real cost of data storage.

The problem of finding total cost of storage is interesting and important from both business and computational perspectives. In the current era of Big Data, the demand for long term storage systems is increasing every day. Many startup companies have started digital storage business (e.g. DropBox, SugarSync). Technology giants such as Google, Microsoft, and Amazon have set up large infrastructures for storage. Therefore, they need to identify the actual cost of long term

J. Altmann, K. Vanmechelen, and O.F. Rana (Eds.): GECON 2013, LNCS 8193, pp. 29–43, 2013.

digital data preservation. Moreover, storage is not only getting cheap, but also the capacity of storage is increasing in a high volume. For a desktop computer, the largest available disk size has increased from 5 MB to 4 TB. [2]. Therefore, we are storing more data than ever before. In fact, in many cases, we are storing redundant and useless data, which are never accessed after their creation [3]. A proper cost model will allow us to determine the true monetary amount that we are paying for these storage systems. The model will also allow system designers to make informed design decisions, choose local or outsourced storage systems, and provide an incentive to optimize their storage management.

Designing a storage cost model is not trivial as many hidden, non-obvious costs are involved. There are several factors associated with the maintenance of the storage systems, that are often neglected while developing a cost model. Factors such as power, cooling, maintenance, management, and disposal costs are significant. A deeper thought reveals that storage media price is only a small portion of the overall cost. The total cost of storage also includes hidden factors such as environmental costs. Previously developed models are often simplistic and do not include all possible costs related to the storage systems [4]. We argue that we can effectively apply full cost accounting to develop an all-encompassing storage system cost model. In this paper, we take a holistic view of storage systems and develop an end to end accounting model for long term digital storage. By considering direct and indirect costs, environmental impact, and many other factors, we develop a full cost accounting model for cloud storage. In particular, our model can be used to determine the amortized cost of storing a byte of data in a storage system over a year. To the best of our knowledge, this is the first application of full cost accounting principles to determine storage system cost.

Contributions: The contributions of this paper are as follows:

1. We propose a full cost accounting model for cloud based storage systems and determine the cost of storing one byte over a year.
2. We apply the developed model in a real life data center to show how the model actually works.
3. We evaluate the proposed scheme with the pricing schemes of well-known cloud storage providers.

Organization: The rest of the paper is organized as follows: in section 2, we provide an overview of full cost accounting. In section 3, we discuss various determinants of storage system cost. We present our full cost accounting model in section 4, a case study in section 5 based on the developed model, comparison of costs with well-known cloud storage providers in Section 6, related research in section 7 and conclusion in section 8.

2   Background

In this section, we present the definitions of cost accounting, full cost accounting, issues in regular accounting systems, and discuss why we use full cost accounting technique to develop the cost model. Additionally, we illustrate why other accounting models do not fit well to identify storage system cost.

2.1 Cost Accounting

Cost accounting refers to the internal financial system to track expenditures and costs within an organization [5]. Such a system guides managers and decision makers in their actions as they show the profit or loss of the organization within a specific period of time.

Traditional accounting process considers only direct cost related to the product and skips many environmental and hidden costs. For example, if toxic materials are emitted during the development of a product, then it has a high environmental cost. Manufacturing processes that generate high amount of wastes will have a high disposal cost. These kind of costs need to be included in the accounting system to have a proper cost model of a particular product. To solve this, accountants have developed full cost accounting models that include all of these costs into the accounting system.

2.2 Full Cost Accounting

Full cost accounting is a systematic approach for identifying, summing, and reporting the costs involved in the complete life cycle of a product or process. In addition to obvious and direct costs, full cost accounting aims to include hidden and overhead costs involved in the system. Figure 1 displays a full cost accounting framework that deals with all kind of costs involved in the life cycle of a product or process development [6], [7].

Outside of computing, comprehensive *full cost accounting* models have been successfully developed for many real-life problem domains such as coal plants and waste disposal systems [8], [9]. For example, Florida local government uses full cost accounting for Municipal Solid Waste (MSW) Management. According to Florida law,

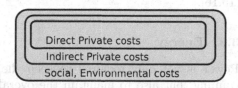

Fig. 1. Full Cost Accounting framework [6]

the local government needs to disclose the full cost of solid waste management services to public and the Department of Environmental Protection (DEP) annually. A book named "Municipal Solid Waste Management Full Cost Accounting Workbook" has been published for this purpose [10].

3   Determinants of Storage Cost

In this section, we study the determinants associated with the cost of a storage system. These factors are considered when we develop a full cost accounting model in the Section 4. Based on our analysis of Information Lifecycle Management models [11], we divide the determinants of storage cost into the following components: Initial, Floor rent, Energy, Service, Disposal, and Environmental cost. Different breakdown is also possible if we only consider costs of internal infrastructure of a storage service provider [4].

3.1 Initial Cost

Initial cost denotes all the costs related to infrastructure set up, including price of disks, networking equipment (e.g. router, switches, wires etc.), floor accessories (e.g. light, desk, furniture, security etc.), server racks, cooling fans, and other miscellaneous costs. Costs of these components decrease with time, therefore, we consider depreciated cost or current cost in our cost model.

3.2 Floor Rent

Floor rent is a very important determinant of storage cost and highly depends on the locality. In early 2013, the commercial property prices in San Francisco were almost double those in other places, such as Chicago [12]. Generally, floor rent is high in city and low in the less populated areas. For example, in Manhattan office space can be rented for up to tens of dollars per sqft per month; where data center can be had with $0.1 per sqft per month, which is much lower than the office rents [13], [14]. Small data center companies usually tend to rent spaces inside city for their services because building their own data center office require high capital cost. However, large technology companies usually build their own data centers outside of the city area, mainly in less populated areas. Therefore, per square feet cost is much lower and often the amortized cost is zero over time [15,16].

3.3 Energy

Power is not only required to keep the servers, networks, and disks up and running, but also to maintain the overall infrastructure, cooling, security and other accessories. We can divide the energy cost in four main parts: networks, infrastructure, cooling, and computation. Details of energy cost calculation are discussed in Section 5.

3.4 Service

The service cost depends on a number of components including software development, management, hardware repair, infrastructure and cooling maintenance, network set up, and power services [4]. The experience of the employees are often directly related to their remuneration and this needs to be considered in the cost model.

3.5   Disposal Cost

Storage service providers may decide to change their disks after a period of fixed interval. Physical destruction is the most effective way to dispose a disk [17]. With this process, it is not possible to recover the data. However, physical destruction of disks requires powerful and expensive machines. Sometimes organizations may outsource this task to other companies.

3.6   Environmental Cost

Storage service providers require massive amount of energy to keep the infrastructure up and running. Heavy diesel backup generators are used to keep the service smooth during any kind of unexpected incident (e.g. power failure, natural disaster etc.). Usually, the generators are turned off most of the time. However, it has been reported that backup generators emit exhausts even if there are no blackouts. This smoke pollutes air significantly. A number of major storage service providers have been accused for violations of air quality regulations in Virginia and Illinois. For example, in Northern Virginia, Amazon was cited with more than 24 violations over a three year period. As a result, they need to pay hefty fines to the government for this kind of issues, and also need to test their backup generators regularly [18]. At the same time, diesel emissions can be a potential cause of cancer. During 2008 and 2009, in California, Microsoft was under "Air Toxics 'Hot Spots' program" review for diesel emissions [19]. Many data centers use evaporative cooling [20]. Evaporative cooling process concentrates impurities in the remaining water, which might include anti-bacterials that were added to keep the cooling system clean. The remaining water can pollute the environment if not treated properly. Apart from these, the fuel or energy source used to generate electricity in data centers is the most significant factor in CO_2 emissions [21]. To nullify the effect of greenhouse gas emitted during physical destruction of disks, companies often need to donate amount proportional to their Carbon credit [22] to environment management authorities.

4   Cost Model

In this section, we derive equations for various costs associated to store a byte over a year in a data center. Total cost for a byte of data storage depends on initial cost, floor rent, energy, service, disposal, and environmental cost. We begin by providing the following equation for total cost per byte of data storage:

$$Total\ Cost = Initial + Floor + Energy + Service + Disposal + \\ Environmental \tag{1}$$

The following sections discuss how each of the above costs is calculated.

4.1   Initial Cost

Initial cost denotes all the costs related to infrastructure set up, including price of disks, networking equipment (e.g. router, switches, wires etc.), floor accessories (e.g. light, desk, furniture, security etc.), server racks, cooling fans, and other miscellaneous costs. We assume that there are N disks in one floor of the data center. We take cost for N disks, network equipment, floor accessories, server racks, cooling fans, and miscellaneous costs as $\$i_1$, $\$i_2$, $\$i_3$, $\$i_4$, $\$i_5$ and $\$i_6$ respectively. We assume straight line depreciation here. So, to calculate these costs, we divide the original cost by the corresponding lifetime. Thus the overall initial cost is:

$$Initial\ Cost\ for\ N\ disks = i_1 + i_2 + i_3 + i_4 + i_5 + i_6 \qquad (2)$$

Let us assume each disk contains m TeraBytes. The total bytes S is, $S = N \times m \times 10^{12}$. Therefore, using equation 2, we get initial cost for per byte:

$$Initial\ Cost\ Per\ Byte = \frac{Initial\ Cost\ for\ N\ disks}{S} \qquad (3)$$

4.2   Floor Rent

We assume that floor rent for one floor of a data center is $\$f$ per month and that the floor contains N disks. Therefore, for each byte, we can write:

$$Floor\ Rent\ Per\ Byte, F = \frac{12 \times f}{S} \qquad (4)$$

4.3   Energy

Total energy cost can be divided into the following parts: operational cost, computational cost, infrastructure maintenance cost (e.g. light, security etc.), and cooling cost.

Cooling Cost. In a data center, a significant part of energy is spent on cooling. Therefore, We can write:

$$Energy\ Cost = Network + Infrastructure + Cooling + Computation \qquad (5)$$

If for a floor with N disks has network, infrastructure and cooling maintenance cost e_1, e_2 and e_3 respectively for a month, then

$$Network,\ Infrastructure,\ Cooling\ Cost\ Per\ Byte = \frac{12 \times (e_1 + e_2 + e_3)}{S} \qquad (6)$$

Computation Cost. Computation cost depends on the number of reads, writes and deletion done on a disk. Disks that are always turned on; there is still some energy usage for data preservation. To calculate the computation cost, we can take the average current and voltage ratings of PDUs (Power Distribution Unit) of a server rack and calculate the average power (Watt) required to keep that rack running. Electricity bills are charged based on the energy spent. We compute the average energy consumption (in kilowatt-hour (kWh)) of a rack by multiplying its power with time period. Overall computational cost is calculated by multiplying combined energy usages (summation of energy usage of all server racks) with per killowatt-hour electricity price. We can write the following equation for this purpose:

$$Computation\ Cost\ Per\ Byte = \frac{Combined\ energy\ usage \times Electricity\ unit\ price}{S}$$

(7)

As we are computing energy cost, it is important to discuss how energy efficiency is measured in data centers. With the significant growth in demand for data centers, it is very important to reduce its overall energy cost and increase the operating efficiency. In this regard, The Green Grid Consortium (a non-profit, open-industry consortium) developed the concept of Power Usage Efficiency (PUE) which is a measure of the amount of the total power is used by computing equipments in contrast to cooling and other infrastructure overhead. PUE is defined as: PUE = Total Facility Power / IT Equipment Power [23]. A PUE value 2.0 denotes that, for every watt required to power a server, there is an additional watt consumed by the support infrastructure. As electricity bill is paid over the total amount of electricity used, reducing the overhead cost on support infrastructure will reduce the overall cost.

4.4 Service

We consider that n_4 system administrators and software developers are required for the installation and maintenance of N disks in a data center and their yearly remuneration is \$$r$ (on average). Therefore, service cost for each disk is:

$$Service\ Cost\ Per\ Byte = \frac{n_4 \times r}{S}$$

(8)

The software and licensing cost must also be applied to determine the overall Service cost. Software solutions usually require an initial cost for the first year and license renewal cost for the next years. If the initial cost is T, and license renewal cost is t for every year after the first year, and we amortize the initial cost over p years; then Software cost for any particular year is:

$$Software\ Cost\ Per\ Byte = \frac{T/p + t}{S}$$

(9)

4.5 Disposal Cost

If a data center needs to destroy its disks in every n_5 year, and cost to physically destroy N disks is s, then cost for N disks per year can be expressed as $\frac{s}{n_5}$.

$$Disposal\ Cost = \frac{s}{n_5 \times S}$$

(10)

4.6   Environmental Cost

We assume that a storage provider requires to spend U for different environmental issues in a year. Then, we can write:

$$Environmental\ Cost\ Per\ Byte = \frac{U}{S} \tag{11}$$

U is the summation of all the environmental costs. For example, storage providers need to spend $\$u_1$ annually to maintain backup generators properly. Evaporative cooling system also requires regular maintenance to prevent water pollution. Also, it uses wet pads, blades and nozzles to disperse water into the air. These surfaces can become breeding ground for bacteria if they are not cleaned regularly. Therefore, cooling system maintenance also contributes ($\$u_2$) in overall environmental cost. To control CO_2 emissions, storage providers may require to donate $\$u_3$ corresponding to their carbon credit. Therefore, we can write:

$$U = u_1 + u_2 + u_3 \tag{12}$$

At this point, we have detailed equations for all the items specified at equation 1. These equations include all private, direct, indirect and environmental costs to store a byte over a year for any kind of storage system.

5   Case Study: A Local Data Center

In this section, we apply the cost model we developed to the data center of Computer and Information Sciences (CIS) department at University of Alabama at Birmingham. This data center is very small as compared to the well-known data centers (e.g. Amazon, Google etc.). We decided to apply the cost model here because the internal infrastructure details and pricing for well-known data centers are not publicly available. However, the full cost accounting model for storage is applicable for any kind of data center and cloud storage systems.

5.1   Initial Cost

The CIS data center was developed in 2011. There are total 4 server racks and each rack contains 9 units. Each unit has the following configuration:

1. Supermicro 4U CSE-846E26-R1200B Rackmount Chassis / Rails
2. Supermicro X8DAH+-F Dual Xeon Server Board / Intel 5520 / IPMI
3. (2) Xeon X5650 CPUs 6 Core Westmere Processors
4. (16) WD2003FYYS 2TB 7200 rpm Hard Drives
5. 24 GB (6x4gb) DDR#-1333 ECCR Memory
6. (2) LSI 9212-4i4e HBAs
7. MegaRAID SAS 9280-4i4e with BBU's

Total cost of a unit is \$13630. Each rack also contains an UPS (\$5000 for each UPS), 2 Raritan Dominion PX (DPXS20A-30L6) Power Distribution Units (\$993 for each), 1 Cisco Catalyst 2960-24TC 24 port Switch (\$897 for each switch), network cables (\$150 per rack) and price of each rack is \$500. Total cost for development and setup of cooling infrastructure required \$17500. We calculate the initial major hardware cost using this data. We amortize the cost within the warranty period of the item and get the following equations:

$$Initial\ Cost = Rack + UPS + PDU + Unit + Switch + Cables + Cooling$$
$$= \frac{4 \times 500}{5} + \frac{4 \times 5000}{3} + \frac{8 \times 993}{2} + \frac{4 \times 9 \times 13630}{5} + \frac{4 \times 897}{3} + \frac{4 \times 150}{2} + \frac{17500}{5}$$
$$= 114170.67$$

$$(13)$$

Other than the major items, many miscellaneous items were also required for the data center. We add the costs of security system, security and environmental monitoring device (NetBotz 500), 2 Fire Extinguishers in 2 doors, 64 energy efficient daylights etc.

$$Miscellaneous\ Cost = Security + Monitoring + Fire\ Extinguishers + DayLights$$
$$= \frac{10000}{5} + \frac{1306}{5} + \frac{200}{2} + \frac{64 \times 30}{3}$$
$$= 3001.2$$

$$(14)$$

We get total initial cost \$117171.87 by adding equation 13 and 14. From the server rack unit configuration, we see that each unit contains 16, 2TB hard disks and there are 9 units in one rack. Therefore, these 4 racks contain 1152×10^{12} bytes ($S = 4 \times 9 \times 32 \times 10^{12}$). We calculate initial cost using equation 3:

$$Initial\ Cost\ Per\ Byte = \frac{117171.87}{S}. \tag{15}$$

5.2 Floor Rent

The CIS data center is L shaped and is 988 square feet in size. We take per square foot rent as \$45 for commercial locations at Birmingham, Alabama. Therefore, we use equation 4 for floor rent per byte:

$$Floor\ Rent\ Per\ Byte = \frac{12 \times 988 \times 45}{S} = \frac{533520}{S} \tag{16}$$

5.3 Energy

Cooling and Server rack energy consumption are the dominating factors in overall energy cost. Liebert Deluxe System//3^{TM} - DX is used as cooling unit and it has two main parts: Air Handlar (DH380A-HAAEI) and Condensing Unit (DCDF415-A). The average annual energy consumption by the cooling unit is 26504 kWhrs and overall annual operating cost is \$3469. We took current and voltage ratings from PDU to determine the average power required to keep a server rack up and running. Each PDU draws 10.08 Amps on average in a 220 voltage line. Therefore, PDU's power rating is 2217.6 watts[1]. There are two PDUs in every server rack and per rack average power rating is 4435.2 watts. The average price for electricity is about 12 cents per kilowatt-hour in USA. Therefore, average energy cost[2] for running a server rack for an hour is 532.224×10^{-3}. Energy cost for running one rack and four server racks are $4662.28[3] and $18649.12 respectively. Therefore, overall energy cost over a year is expressed by the following equation:

$$Energy\ Cost\ Per\ Byte = \frac{18649.12 + 3469}{X} = \frac{22118.12}{X} \qquad (17)$$

5.4 Service

Personnel cost may be calculated by determining how much time one system administrator is spending behind the set up and maintenance of the data center. Our example data center is maintained by two engineers; one senior system administrator and one mid-junior level engineer. The mid-junior level engineer works full time and the senior system administrator spends 20% of his time to guide junior engineers and maintain the data center. We collect the yearly remuneration data from http://www.indeed.com and perform the following calculation:

$$Personnel\ Cost\ Per\ Byte = \frac{20\% \times 80000 + 60000}{S} = \frac{76000}{S} \qquad (18)$$

Nexenta[4] Software is used at the UAB CIS data center for configuration and maintenance of software defined storage systems. Initial cost for each unit is $5000, for 36 units (4 racks, 9 units each) it is $180000. Every year license renewal price for each unit is $1000. Therefore, total renewal cost is $36000 ($36 \times 1000$). We amortize the initial software purchase cost over 5 years. We also include monthly internet connection bill ($250 per month) and apply equation 9:

$$Software\ Cost\ Per\ Byte = \frac{\frac{180000}{5} + 36000 + 250 \times 12}{S} = \frac{75000}{S} \qquad (19)$$

5.5 Total Cost per Byte

Now we add equations 15, 16, 17, 5.4, and 19 to get the overall cost to store a byte over a year at UAB CIS data center in picocents (1 $US\ picocent = \$1 \times 10^{-14}$):

$$Cost\ Per\ Byte = \frac{117171.87 + 533520 + 22118.12 + 76000 + 75000}{S}$$
$$= 71.51 \times 10^3 picocents. \qquad (20)$$

---

[1] Power = Voltage×Current, $220 \times 10.08 = 2217.6$
[2] Energy = Power×Time, $^{4435.2}/_{1000} \times 0.12 = 532.224 \times 10^{-3}$
[3] Energy cost for 1 year per rack = $532.224 \times 10^{-3} \times 24 \times 365 = 4662.28$
[4] http://www.nexenta.com/corp/index.php

We did not include environmental and disposal costs in the case study because those are negligible for small data centers. However, those should be considered for large data centers to apply full cost accounting model properly.

6 Comparison of Our Estimates with Amazon S3

The validity and effectiveness of the proposed accounting model depends on its applicability in the real world. In this section, we validate our results by exploring the pricing of Amazon Simple Storage Service (Amazon S3). Our calculation shows that the cost for storing one byte is 71.51×10^3 picocents. We compare this result with Amazon S3's advertised price available online[5]. Using AWS Simple Monthly Calculator[6], we get the monthly bill for storing 1152 TB at Amazon's US East/US Standard (Virginia) region is 88.37×10^3 picocents[7] per byte. While both prices are close to each other, below we discuss some important factors regarding the price difference:

Pricing: Amazon's price includes storage providers profit, environmental and disposal costs that are not applicable for UAB CIS data center. Amazon charges for data usage (i.e. PUT, GET, POST, LIST requests etc.) and data import/export[8]. Therefore, overall price to store data in Amazon S3 will increase if we incorporate the application usage. In our case study, we took the power usage directly from PDUs; therefore, any number of storage access cost is included in that price. The pricing of Amazon S3 also depends on the region we want to store data. For example, storing same amount of data in US-West (Northern California)[9] will cost 95.15×10^3 per byte. Apart from these, the hardware pricing that we have used in case study are from year 2011 and prices are much cheaper now a days compared to those. Open storage hardware projects built from commodity components demonstrate affordable and energy-efficient high-capacity storage servers[24], [25]. Hence, large data centers use these techniques internally to keep the hardware cost as low as possible.

Scale: To perform a proper comparison, Amazon's internal infrastructure details, energy management and many other information are required, which are not publicly available. Cloud providers like Amazon buy high volume of hardware at special discounted rate, build their own facilities, use different cooling techniques to keep power usage down, and apply many other schemes to reduce the overall cost. All these do not directly apply to small or medium scale data center like the one in our case study. For example, the total number of hardware at the UAB CIS data center is much lower compared to that of Amazon's, so there is a significant difference in buying price. Floor rent is almost constant for small or medium scale data center; whereas for large data centers amortized

---

[5] http://aws.amazon.com/s3/pricing
[6] http://calculator.s3.amazonaws.com/calc5.html
[7] $(84844.79 \times 12 \times 10 \times^{14})/(1152 \times 10 \times^{12}) = 88.37 \times 10^3$
[8] http://aws.amazon.com/importexport/
[9] $(91346.96 \times 12 \times 10 \times^{14})/(1152 \times 10 \times^{12}) = 95.15 \times 10^3$

cost is zero over time (Section 3.2). Also, only regular electrical cooling is used at UAB CIS data center, which is expensive.

Redundancy: Amazon S3 stores redundant copies for data durability and reliability. For example, triple mirroring [26], RAID-5, RAID-6 [27], and various types of erasure coding [28] are very common. Small fractions of departmental data of UAB data center are redundantly stored and most of the files are stored without any redundancy. Adding more redundant storage will increase the price for storing a byte for our case study.

We summarize that, the pricing difference between our case study and that of Amazon S3 is mainly due to the factors described above. However, the full cost accounting model we have developed addresses all the concerns and can be used as a framework to determine total cost of data ownership for any kind of cloud based storage systems. From the analysis, we believe the model will provide an accurate cost calculation for cloud based storage models given that internal details are available and very closely resemble the cost for large storage models (like Amazon S3, RackSpace etc.), where many exact internal features are somewhat unknown.

7 Related Work

As discussed in Section 2, full cost accounting has been used in various application domains. Paul et al. addressed the importance of full cost accounting in the context of life cycle impacts of coal plant [8]. Each stage in the life cycle of coal (extraction, transport, processing, and combustion) generates wastes that are hazardous for health and the environment. As these costs are not direct, coal industry often treat these as externalities and does not include these into their regular accounting model. The authors showed that the life cycle effects of coal and the generated waste stream costs the U.S public a significant amount of dollars annually. Moreover, including all these externalities will double to triple the price of electricity generated from coal. Similar to our case study, they focused on Appalachia (a coal mining area in the Appalachian Mountains) to determine the life cycle impacts of coal.

Full cost accounting has not been used to develop an economic model for digital storage. Patel et al. [29] addressed the importance of developing a model to identify the costs associated with housing and powering the computer, networking and storage equipment. They discussed costs related to real estate, burdened cost of power delivery, personnel as well as software and licensing with examples. Their report also included typical data center layout design and key to cost effective "smart" data center development. However, this work did not apply full cost accounting in the cost model and initial infrastructure cost, environmental and disposal costs were not discussed. While the report included brief examples of each type of cost, it did not calculate full cost of storing a byte in a specific period of time in a particular data center.

To determine when cloud computing is economically tenable, Chen et al., [30] developed a model to calculate the cost of a CPU cycle in cloud based systems. This model helps decide if the cloud computing platform is economically tenable for an organization. They considered several factors except disposal and environmental issues that contribute to the cost of CPU cycles inside a cloud. While we explore a similar problem domain in this paper, we provide a fine-grained cost model for full cost analysis of storage costs.

Another work by APC developed a method to measure the total cost of ownership of data center and network room physical infrastructure, and relates these costs to the overall information technology infrastructure [4] in a per rack basis. They showed the distribution of different costs such as project management, server racks, cooling equipment etc. However, their work did not include the disposal costs and did not break down the energy costs as we did in this paper.

Rosenthal et al. discussed the economics of long term digital storage with respect to Kryder's law, various storage business models, and the value of cloud for digital preservation [31]. They encouraged to develop an accounting model to properly recognize the long-term cost of ownership of preserved data, and utilized current low interest rates to invest on solid state technologies which despite of their higher capital cost, are likely to have a lower total cost than disk. At the same time, solid state technologies retain its fast rapid access. However, their work also does not include hidden and indirect environmental costs of data storage and disposal costs. Our work complements the limitations of these models by considering both direct and indirect determinants of storage cost.

8   Conclusion and Future Work

In-depth understanding of the full cost of data storage is very important to develop new storage business models and in many other computational purposes. The full cost accounting model developed here addresses all kinds of costs involved in long term digital storage services and provides a clear overview to the managers or decision makers about the full cost of this kind of systems. As a future work, we want to employ this model to determine the value of waste data in storage systems. Hasan et al. showed that a large amount of data have never been used for a long time after their creation or last modification [3]. These kinds of data are not different from regularly used data and contribute to the overall cost of the system. Thus, knowing the monetary value of digital waste will be very useful for the development of efficient file systems.

Acknowledgments. This research was supported by a Google Faculty Research Award, the Office of Naval Research Grant #N000141210217, the Department of Homeland Security Grant #FA8750-12-2-0254, and by the National Science Foundation under Grant #0937060 to the Computing Research Association for the CIFellows Project. The authors would also like to thank Larry Owen, Senior Systems Analyst at the Dept. of Computer and Information Sciences, UAB for providing access to data center details.

References

1. Intel: Moore's law inspires Intel innovation,
   http://www.intel.com/content/www/us/en/silicon-innovations/
   moores-law-technology.html (accessed February 5, 2013)
2. Farrance, R.: Timeline: 50 Years of Hard Drives,
   http://www.pcworld.com/article/127105/article.html
   (accessed February 12, 2013)
3. Hasan, R., Burns, R.C.: The life and death of unwanted bits: Towards proactive
   waste data management in digital ecosystems. CoRR abs/1106.6062 (2011)
4. APC: Determining total cost of ownership for data center and network room infrastructure, http://www.apcmedia.com/salestools/CMRP-5T9PQG_R4_EN.pdf
   (accessed March 5, 2013)
5. Horngren, C.T., Foster, G., Datar, S.M., Rajan, M., Ittner, C., Baldwin, A.A.:
   Cost accounting: A managerial emphasis. Issues in Accounting Education 25(4),
   789–790 (2010)
6. Conway-Schempf, N.: Full cost accounting,
   http://gdi.ce.cmu.edu/gd/education/FCA_Module_98.pdf
   (accessed January 2, 2013)
7. Popoff, F., Buzzelli, D.: Full-cost accounting. Chemical and Engineering News
   (United States) 71(2) (1993)
8. Epstein, P.R., Buonocore, J.J., Eckerle, K., Hendryx, M., Stout III, B.M., Heinberg,
   R., Clapp, R.W., May, B., Reinhart, N.L., Ahern, M.M., Doshi, S.K., Glustrom,
   L.: Full cost accounting for the life cycle of coal. Annals of the NY Academy of
   Sciences 1219(1), 73–98 (2011)
9. United States Environmental Protection Agency: Full cost accounting in action:
   Case studies of six solid waste management agencies,
   http://www.epa.gov/osw/conserve/tools/fca/docs/fca-case.pdf
   (accessed March 2, 2013)
10. United States Environmental Protection Agency: Wastes - resource conservation -
    conservation tools, http://www.epa.gov/osw/conserve/tools/fca/epadocs.htm
    (accessed March 2, 2013)
11. Brannon, K., Chen, Y., Mbogo, L., et al.: Information lifecycle management. WO
    Patent 2,008,058,824 (May 23, 2008)
12. Pienta, G., Van Ness, M., Trowbridge, E.A., Canter, T.A., Morrill, W.K.: Building
    a power portfolio. In: Commercial Investment Real Estate (A Publication of the
    CCM Institute) (March/April 2003)
13. Conrad, K.: Data centers hot once again in the bay area,
    http://www.insidebayarea.com/business/ci_5570458
    (accessed November 18, 2012)
14. Department of Administration. Records management fact sheet 13,
    http://www.doa.state.wi.us/facts_view.asp?factid=68&locid=2
    (accessed March 5, 2013)
15. Malik, O.: Googlenet going global (September 2007),
    http://gigaom.com/2007/09/21/googlenet-going-global/
    (accessed September 2, 2012)
16. Economie: Google wil energie eemshaven heeft het (December 2007),
    http://www.trouw.nl/nieuws/economie/article1247225.ece
17. Hard Drive Destruction in DC, MD, NY, OH and PA (July 2011),
    http://document-management-dc-md-ny-oh-pa.com/blog/9/
    hard-drive-destruction (accessed January 15, 2013)

18. Glanz, J.: Power, Pollution and the Internet (September 2012),
    http://www.nytimes.com/2012/09/23/technology/data-centers-waste-
    vast-amounts-of-energy-belying-industry-image.html?pagewanted=all&_r=0
    (accessed January 15, 2013)
19. Smith, M.: Microsoft data center pollutes, then wastes millions of watts to avoid
    paying fine (September 2012),
    http://www.networkworld.com/community/blog/microsoft-data-center-
    pollutes-then-wastes-millions-watts-avoid-paying-fine
    (accessed January 25, 2013)
20. Klots, C.E.: Evaporative cooling. The Journal of Chemical Physics 83, 5854 (1985)
21. APC: Estimating a data centers electrical carbon footprint,
    www.apcmedia.com/salestools/DBOY-7EVHLH/DBOY-7EVHLH_RO_EN.pdf (accessed
    June 2, 2013)
22. Show, K., Lee, D.: Carbon credit and emission trading: Anaerobic wastewater
    treatment. Journal of the Chinese Institute of Chemical Engineers 39(6), 557–562
    (2008)
23. Grid, T.G.: Green grid metrics: describing data center power efficiency (February
    2007), http://www.thegreengrid.org/~/media/WhitePapers/
    Green_Grid_Metrics_WP.pdf?lang=en
24. OpenStoragePod: Petascale storage for the rest of us!,
    http://openstoragepod.org/ (accessed March 2, 2013)
25. Nufire, T.: Petabytes on a budget: How to build cheap cloud storage (September
    2009), http://blog.backblaze.com/2009/09/01/petabytes-on-a-
    budget-how-to-build-cheap-cloud-storage/ (accessed March 2, 2013)
26. Leventhal, A.: Triple-parity raid and beyond. Queue 7(11), 30 (2009)
27. Chen, P.M., Lee, E.K., Gibson, G.A., Katz, R.H., Patterson, D.A.: Raid: High-
    performance, reliable secondary storage. ACM Computing Surveys (CSUR) 26(2),
    145–185 (1994)
28. Lin, W., Chiu, D.M., Lee, Y.: Erasure code replication revisited. In: Proceedings of
    the Fourth International Conference on Peer-to-Peer Computing, pp. 90–97. IEEE
    (2004)
29. Patel, C.D., Shah, A.J.: Cost model for planning, development and operation of a
    data center. Hewlett-Packard Laboratories Technical Report (2005)
30. Chen, Y., Sion, R.: To cloud or not to cloud? musings on costs and viability. In:
    ACM Symposium on Cloud Computing ACM SOCC (2011)
31. Rosenthal, D.S., Rosenthal, D.C., Miller, E.L., Adams, I.F., Storer, M.W., Zadok,
    E.: The economics of long–term digital storage. In: Memory of the World in the
    Digital Age, Vancouver, BC (2012)

Constraint Programming Based Large Neighbourhood Search for Energy Minimisation in Data Centres

Hadrien Cambazard[1], Deepak Mehta[2], Barry O'Sullivan[2], and Helmut Simonis[2]

[1] G-SCOP, Université de Grenoble; Grenoble INP; UJF Grenoble 1; CNRS, France
hadrien.cambazard@grenoble-inp.fr
[2] INSIGHT Centre for Data Analytics
Department of Computer Science, University College Cork, Ireland
{d.mehta,b.osullivan,h.simonis}@4c.ucc.ie

Abstract. EnergeTIC is a recent industrial research project carried out in Grenoble on optimising energy consumption in data centres. We study the problem formulation proposed by EnergeTIC. The problem focuses on the allocation of virtual machines to servers with time-variable resource demands in data centres in order to minimise energy costs while ensuring service quality. We present a scalable constraint programming-based large neighbourhood search (CP-LNS) method to solving this challenging problem. We present empirical results that demonstrate that the industrial benchmarks can be solved to near optimality using our approach. Our CP-LNS method provides a fast and practical approach for finding high quality solutions for lowering electricity costs in data centres.

1   Introduction

Data centres are a critical and ubiquitous resource for providing infrastructure for banking, Internet and electronic commerce. They use enormous amounts of electricity, and this demand is expected to increase in the future. For example, a report by the *EU Stand-by Initiative* stated that in 2007 Western European data centres consumed 56 Tera-Watt Hours (TWh) of power, which is expected to almost double to 104 TWh per year by 2020.[1] Nevertheless, as reported by the consulting firm McKinsey, only 6-12% of electricity used by data centres can be attributed to the performance of productive computation [1]. Therefore, one of the optimisation challenges in the domain of data centres is to keep servers well utilised so that energy costs can be reduced.

Many data centres have the infrastructure in place for load migration. There are several reasons for migrating the load of one or more virtual applications from their current servers to different ones. For example, if the load on a server is very high, or if the server is about to shut down, then one might want to move some or all the virtual machines from that server to others. Also, if there is a server where the energy cost per unit of computation is cheaper, then one might want to reassign some virtual applications to that server so that the overall cost of energy consumption is reduced. In general, the challenge is to consolidate machine workload intelligently to ensure that servers are well utilised so that energy costs can be reduced.

---

[1] http://re.jrc.ec.europa.eu/energyefficiency/html/
standby_initiative_data_centers.htm

J. Altmann, K. Vanmechelen, and O.F. Rana (Eds.): GECON 2013, LNCS 8193, pp. 44–59, 2013.

In this paper we describe a constraint optimisation model for energy-cost aware data centre assignment systems which allocates virtual machines with time-variable demands to servers where the energy cost per unit of computation can vary between different locations. The problem we consider is defined by a set of servers and a set of virtual applications to be run on those servers over a given operating horizon. Each server is associated with a set of available resources, e.g. CPU, RAM, DISK etc. Each virtual application is associated with an optional initial server on which it is running, and a set of required resource values, which might be different over different time slots in our operating horizon. The solution of the problem is an assignment of virtual machines to servers at each time-period which respects a set of hard constraints. The objective is to take advantage of differences in energy costs across the servers, the requirements of virtual applications, the transition costs of switching the states of servers from ON to STANDBY and vice-versa, and by reassigning virtual applications to servers within a given data centre.

The remainder of the paper is organised as follows. First we describe the overall project and in particular energy and demand models to give the context of our work on solving the optimisation problem addressed in this paper. We then describe the formal definition of the problem before presenting a constraint optimisation formulation of it. The size of the instances of this problem can be prohibitively large for standard optimisation techniques, but needs to be solved quickly. Therefore, the challenge is to search for a good quality solution of a very large problem instance in a very limited timeframe. We present a constraint programming-based large neighbourhood search (CP-LNS) for solving this problem which scales significantly beyond commercial optimisation tools such as CPLEX.[2] The key idea behind CP-LNS is to repeatedly consider a sub-problem of the overall problem and re-optimise it using constraint programming. We present a systematic empirical evaluation of our CP-LNS approach. Empirical results obtained on real benchmarks demonstrate the scalability of our CP-LNS approach, and show that it provides a practical basis for solving this very important and challenging real-world problem.

2 Related Work

A variety of studies on allocating data and workload amongst multiple servers have been reported [2,3]. A mixed integer programming approach to dynamically configuring the consolidation of multiple services or applications in a virtualised server cluster has been proposed [4]. That work both focuses on power efficiency, and considers the costs of turning on/off the servers. However, it is assuming homogeneous workloads, e.g. web searches, where there is little uncertainty around the duration of tasks or the current cost of energy.

Constraint programming based approaches have also been used previously to solve some related problems [5,6,7]. In [6] a data centre is viewed as a dynamic bin packing system where servers host applications with varying resource requirements and varying relative placement constraints. However, their work can be seen as a reactive approach where the servers are reconfigured when the current configuration is no longer viable.

---

[2] http://www-01.ibm.com/software/commerce/optimization/cplex-optimizer/

Therefore, their objective is to minimise the transition time for migrations of virtual machines, whereas we are concerned with minimising the energy consumption, and we plan the migrations for virtual machines in advance so that the configuration always remain viable.

A high-availability property for a virtual machine is defined in [7]. When a virtual machine is marked as k-resilient, as long as there are up to k server failures, it is guaranteed that it can be relocated to a non-failed host without relocating other virtual machines. The property of k-resiliency relies on static resource requirements of virtual machines whereas we are focusing on time variable resource demands.

Although in [5] an energy-aware framework is proposed for the reallocation of virtual machines in a data centre to reduce the power consumption, the goal is to find the best possible placement of virtual machines for a given time-period subject to service level agreements.

3   Energy and Demand Models

The problem studied in this paper comes from the EnergeTIC project which is accredited by the French government (FUI) [8].[3] EnergeTIC brought together four companies (Bull, Business & Decision Eolas, Schneider Electric, UXP) and several academic partners (G2Elab, G-SCOP, LIG). Its main objective is to control the energy consumption of a data centre and ensure that it is consistent with application needs, economic constraints and service level agreements. It focused on how to reduce energy cost by taking into account variable CPU requirements of the clients' applications, the wide range of IT equipment and virtualisation techniques. A tool was implemented and deployed in practice in a data centre designed by Eolas. The system developed by EnergeTIC is based on a model of the energy consumption of the various components in a data centre, a prediction system to forecast the demand and an optimisation component computing the placement of virtual machines onto servers. In the following we describe the energy and demand models of the system and in the remaining part of the paper we focus on the optimisation part.

3.1   Energy Model

Green data centres appeared as early as 2000 and focused on limiting the amount of energy that was not used for running the client's applications. The Power Usage Effectiveness (PUE) is a key indicator introduced by the Green Grid consortium [9] which measures the ratio between the total energy entering the data centre and the energy used by its IT systems (servers, networks, etc.). The power consumed by support equipment and infrastructure is regarded as an overhead according to this metric. A PUE value of 1 is a *perfect efficiency*. This indicator has been used to measure progress over the years. A value of 2.5 was common a few years ago whereas the current average in industry is around 1.7 with the most efficient data centres reaching 1.2 to 1.4.

---

[3] Minalogic EnergeTIC is a global competitive cluster located in Grenoble France and fosters research-led innovation in intelligent miniaturised products and solutions for industry.

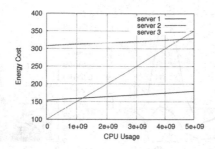

Fig. 1. Energy cost (Wh) vs CPU Usage (GHz) for 3 servers

The need to refine such metrics arose quickly, especially when considering that not all electrical power delivered by the IT equipment is transformed into value-adding computation. The Green Grid proposed a very fine-grained indicator called DCP (Data Center Productivity) for that purpose [9]. This metric, although very accurate, is not used in practice because of its complexity. The EnergeTIC project introduced two simple indicators related to usage efficiency. The first aims at checking the productive use of active resources while the second focuses on the energy consumed. This last energy indicator is defined as the ratio between the total energy consumed and the energy specifically used to run clients applications.

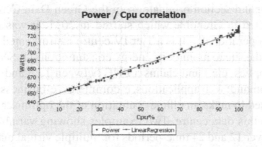

Fig. 2. Linear model of energy (courtesy to [8])

The energy indicator relies on a model of the energy consumption of each piece of equipment, e.g. ventilation units, power supplies, heating/cooling systems, etc., as well as a wide range of IT equipment such as servers, storage, etc. The characterisation of the energy consumption of each piece of IT equipment was performed on a cooled rack provided by Bull which was instrumented with sensors. The rack contained a dozen of heterogeneous servers based on three types of processors: quadri, bi and mono. Different energy behaviour were used in various scenarios to perform the measurements. As an example, the energy cost of the power consumption of three different servers at different CPU loads taken from one of the problem instances is shown in Figure 1. Reality is often quite complex as performance also depends on other parameters such as the room temperature or the shared resources where contention can occur. However, a

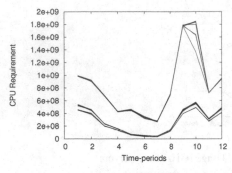
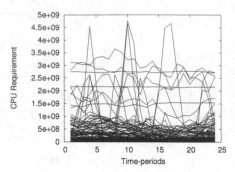

Fig. 3. Variable demands – Example 1   **Fig. 4.** Variable demands – Example 2

linear model was found accurate enough to model energy consumption of the servers. The model was computed by linear regression over the measures (see Figure 2). The measure of the CPU requirements of an application is more complex as it would need to be done on each possible server type. Therefore, in practice, a single measure was performed on a reference server [8].

3.2 Demand Model

The demands, i.e. the resource requirements, of the virtual machines in the benchmarks used in the experimental section originate from the Green Data Centre of Business & Decision Eolas located in Grenoble which started in 2011. It was used to study and validate the system operationally. It is a Tier IV centre instrumented with thousands of sensors spread over the site to monitor its energy consumption (IT, Security, monitoring, inverters, power supplies, etc.) and claims a PUE between 1.28 and 1.34. It deals with an heterogeneous demand: web applications, e-commerce, e-business, e-administration, etc. The data sets used to make an offline evaluation of the optimiser are obtained from historical data from this data centre. Two examples showing variable requirements of CPU usage (GHz) over 12 and 24 time-periods for multiple virtual machines taken from two problem instances is shown in Figures 3 and 4. An online evaluation of the optimiser was also performed in practice on a "sandbox" platform that reproduces the real environment with only three servers. Real applications were copied from the production environment to this restricted environment where the decisions proposed by the optimiser were implemented and evaluated.

4   Problem Description

We now describe the optimisation problem provided by EnergeTIC. The problem is to place a set of virtual machines on a set of servers over multiple time-periods in order to minimise the energy cost of the data centre. The CPU usage of a virtual machine changes over time. At each time-period, we must ensure that the virtual machines have enough resources (CPU and memory). Let $V = \{v_1, \ldots, v_n\}$ be the set of virtual machines, $S = \{s_1, \ldots, s_m\}$ be the set of servers and $T = \{p_1, \ldots, p_h\}$ be the set of time-periods.

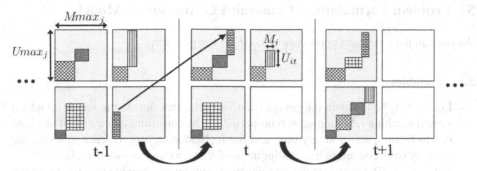

Fig. 5. A solution over three time-periods. Virtual machines migrate to turn off two servers at $t + 1$.

Virtual Machines. A virtual machine v_i is characterised by a memory consumption M_i independent of the time-period, a set $A_i \subseteq S$ of allowed servers where it can be hosted, and a potential initial server (for time-period p_0) denoted by $Iserv_i$ (which might be unknown). A virtual machine v_i has a CPU consumption U_{it} at time-period t.

Servers. A server s_j can be in two different states: ON=1 or STBY=0 (stand-by). It is characterised by: a CPU capacity $Umax_j$; a memory capacity $Mmax_j$; a fixed cost of usage $Emin_j$ (in Watt) when the server is ON; a unit cost τ_j per unit of CPU usage; a basic CPU consumption Ca_j when it is ON to run the operating system and other permanent tasks; an energy consumption $Esby_j$ when it is in state STBY; an energy consumption $Esta_j$ to change the state of the server from STBY to ON; an energy consumption $Esto_j$ to change the state of the server from ON to STBY; a maximum number $Nmax_j$ of virtual machines that can be allocated to it at any time-period; a set of periods $P_j \subseteq T$ during which s_j is forced to be ON; and a potential initial state $Istate_j \in \{0, 1\}$.

If a server is ON, its minimum cost is $Emin_j + \tau_j Ca_j$. Therefore, for the sake of simplicity, to compute the fixed energy cost of an active server we include the basic consumption Ca_j in $Emin_j$ and denote that by $Emin'_j = Emin_j + \tau_j Ca_j$. We also shift the CPU capacity of a server and denote that by $Umax'_j = Umax_j - Ca_j$.

Migrations. The maximum number of changes of servers among all virtual machines from one time-period to the next is denoted by N and the cost of a migration by $Cmig$.

This problem can be seen as a series of packing problems (one per time-period) in two dimensions (CPU and memory) that are coupled by the migration constraints and the cost for changing the state of a server. Figure 5 gives an overview of the problem. This example has four servers, each shown by a rectangle whose dimensions are representing the CPU and memory capacities of that server. A virtual machine is a small rectangle whose height (its CPU) varies from one period to the next. Therefore, the sum of the heights (CPU) must fit within the capacity (height of the rectangle), and similarly for the sum of the widths (memory) must fit within the available capacity (width of the rectangle). In this scenario, the CPU needs of some virtual machines decreases allowing us to find better packings and turn off two servers at $t + 1$.

5 Problem Formulation: Constraint Optimisation Model

We present the constraint optimisation model of the problem.

5.1 Variables

- Let $x_{it} \in A_i$ be the main integer decision variables that denote the server on which virtual machine v_i is running at time-period t. The constraint that a virtual machine has to be on a server at any time and the forbidden servers for each machine are trivially enforced through the assignment of x to a value from its domain.
- Let $cpu_{jt} \in [0, Umax'_j]$ be the non-negative continuous variable that measures the CPU consumption of server s_j at period t.
- Let $mem_{jt} \in [0, Mmax_j]$ be the non-negative continuous variable that measures the memory consumption of server s_j at period t.
- Let $nvm_{jt} \in [0, Nmax_j]$ be an integer variable that denotes the number of virtual machines running on server s_j at time t.
- Let $cs_t \in [0, N]$ be an integer variable that denotes the number of virtual machines that change servers from time-period $t-1$ to time-period t.
- Let $o_{jt} \in \{0, 1\}$ be a Boolean variable that is set to 1 if s_j is ON at time t, 0 otherwise.

The initial state is denoted by $t = 0$. For each server $s_j \in S$ and virtual machine $v_i \in V$ variables o_{j0} and x_{io} are also created.

5.2 Constraints

Capacity Constraint. The following constraints link the CPU and memory loads of a server to the virtual machines assigned to it.

$$\forall_{s_j \in S} \forall_{p_t \in T} : cpu_{jt} = \sum_{v_i \in V \wedge x_{it} = j} U_{it} \tag{1}$$

$$\forall_{s_j \in S} \forall_{p_t \in T} : mem_{jt} = \sum_{v_i \in V \wedge x_{it} = j} M_i \tag{2}$$

The constraint on the usage for CPU and memory on a server in any time-period must not exceed their capacities is trivially enforced through the upper bounds of the domains of cpu_{jt} and mem_{jt}, respectively.

Cardinality Constraint. The maximum number of virtual machines that can run on a server in any time-period is constrained:

$$\forall_{s_j \in S} \forall_{p_t \in T} : nvm_{jt} = |\{v_i | v_i \in V \wedge x_{it} = j\}| \tag{3}$$

Migration Constraint. The number of server changes over all virtual machines in any time-period is constrained:

$$\forall_{p_t \in T} : \quad cs_t = |\{v_i | v_i \in V \wedge x_{it-1} \neq x_{it}\}| \tag{4}$$

ON Constraint. A server is ON if it is hosting at least one virtual machine:

$$\forall_{v_i \in V} \forall_{p_t \in T} : \quad x_{it} = j \implies o_j = 1 \tag{5}$$

The following states the time-periods where a server has to be ON:

$$\forall_{s_j \in S} \forall_{p_t \in P_j} : \quad o_{jt} = 1 \tag{6}$$

When a server s_j is ON at two time-periods say t_a and t_c (where $t_c > t_a + 1$) it is better to leave it ON in between when it would cost more to switch it to STBY. The cost of putting s_j in ON state would be $(t_c - t_a) \times Emin'_j$ and the cost of putting s_j in STBY state would be $(t_c - t_a) \times Esby_j + Esta_j + Esto_j$. Thus, if $t_c - t_a < D$ where $D = \left\lceil \frac{Esta_j + Esto_j}{(Emin'_j - Esby_j)} \right\rceil$ then it is better to set $o_{jt_b} - 1$ for all t_b such that $t_c < t_b < t_a$. In other words in an **optimal** solution, any sequence of 0 values in the vector of variables $[o_{j1}, \dots, o_{jh}]$ should be of length at least D. If not the cost can be improved by turning ON the corresponding server in the corresponding time-periods. This dominance rule can be encoded using the following set of constraints:

$$\forall_{t_a \in T} \forall_{t_a + 1 < t_c \in T < t_a + D} \forall_{t_a < t_b < t_c} : \quad o_{jt_a} = 1 \wedge o_{jt_c} = 1 \implies o_{jt_b} = 1 \tag{7}$$

Similarly, for each server s_j we need to consider two special cases: the first time-period when the server s_j is ON and the last time-period when the server s_j is ON. If t_b is the first time-period when a server s_j is ON (where $t_b > 1$) it is better to leave it ON in all the time-periods before t_b if $t_b < D_f$ where $D_f = 1 + \left\lceil \frac{Esta_j}{(Emin'_j - Esby_j)} \right\rceil$.

$$\forall_{1 < t_b \in T < D_f} \forall_{1 \leq t_a < t_b} : \quad o_{jt_b} = 1 \implies o_{jt_a} = 1 \tag{8}$$

If t_a is the last time-period when a server s_j is ON (where $t_a < h$) it is better to leave it ON in all the time-periods after t_a if $t_a > D_l$ where $D_l = h - \left\lceil \frac{Esto_j}{(Emin'_j - Esby_j)} \right\rceil$.

$$\forall_{D_l < t_a \in T < h} \forall_{t_a < t_b \leq h} : \quad o_{jt_a} = 1 \implies o_{jt_b} = 1 \tag{9}$$

Initial State. If the initial configuration is given then the constraints $o_{j0} = Istate_j$ and $x_{i,0} = Iserv_i$ are enforced for each $s_j \in S$ and $v_i \in V$ respectively. Otherwise, the constraints $o_{j0} = o_{j1}$ and $x_{i0} = x_{i1}$ are enforced.

5.3 Objective Function

The objective is to minimise the sum of the following costs:

Migration Cost. The total migration cost is the total number of server changes over all virtual machines over all time-periods multiplied by the cost of migration:

$$Cmig \left(\sum_{t \in T} cs_t \right)$$

Transition Cost. The total transition cost is the sum of all the transitions of all servers from STBY state at time-period $t - 1$ to ON state at time-period t, and vice-versa over all time-periods:

$$\sum_{s_j \in S} \left(\sum_{t \in T \wedge o_{jt-1} < o_{jt}} Esta_j + \sum_{t \in T \wedge o_{jt-1} > o_{jt}} Esto_j \right)$$

CPU Usage Cost. The total CPU usage cost is the sum of all CPU costs incurred over all time-periods for all servers:

$$\sum_{s_j \in S} \left(\sum_{p_t \in T \wedge o_{jt}=0} Esby_j + \sum_{p_t \in T \wedge o_{jt}=1} \tau_j cpu_{jt} + Emin'_j \right)$$

6 Solution Method: Large Neighbourhood Search

An instance of the energy minimisation problem of data centre as described in the previous section can be very large. As it is an online problem, the challenge is to solve a very large instance in a very limited time. Constraint-based systematic search [10] has shown strong performance, but it does not scale well in terms of time and space for very large instances. Local Search (LS) and Large Neighbourhood Search (LNS) methods have shown remarkable performance on very large instances. A LS method moves from a solution to another by performing a small number of changes (and therefore small improvement) at each iteration, while a LNS method can allow a large number of changes (and possibly large improvement) at each iteration. A meta-heuristic is generally used with LS to escape from local minima, but it is generally unnecessary for LNS. LNS attempts to combine the power of systematic search with the scalability of local search.

In this section we describe a LNS approach for solving the problem formulated in the previous section. The overall solution method is shown in Figure 6. We first find the initial assignment of virtual machines to servers for all time-periods. We maintain a current assignment, which is initialised with the initial solution. At each iteration, we select a subset of the pairs of virtual machines and time-periods to be reassigned and, accordingly, create the sub-problem. We solve the resulting sub-problem with a threshold on the number of failures, and keep the best solution found as our new current assignment. The search stops when the total elapsed time is greater than the given time threshold. Notice that the decision variables can be restricted to the x variables as once an assignment of the virtual machines to the servers is known at all time-periods, the rest of the variables are assigned by propagation and the cost function is fully known.

6.1 Finding Initial Feasible Solution

The pseudo-code for finding an initial feasible solution is depicted in Algorithm 1. The algorithm requires problem $\mathcal{P}$ as input which is composed of Constraints (1)–(9) without any objective function as the task is to find any feasible solution. In the first phase (Lines 3–10) it iterates over a set of unassigned decision variables, denoted by

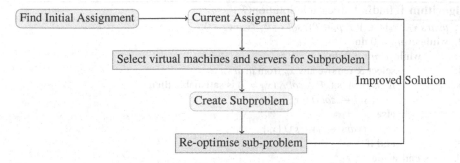

Fig. 6. Principle of the LNS approach

uvars, and tries to extend the current partial solution denoted by *sol*. If it succeeds then the current partial solution is updated, otherwise the set of variables, denoted by *fvars*, that failed to find any assignment is updated. In the second phase (Lines 10–21) it first resets the set of unassigned variables to the set of failed variables. For each failed virtual machine a server is selected and, until the assignment of the selected server to the selected virtual machine is consistent, it finds a constraint C that has failed, relaxes the current partial solution by removing a decision variable involved in the failed constraint, and updates the set of unassigned decision variables. The algorithm terminates when all the virtual machines over all time-periods are assigned servers, otherwise it repeatedly executes the first phase followed by the second phase.

6.2 Subproblem Selection

A key observation was that selecting a set of virtual machines from only some servers for reassignment works better than selecting them from many servers. Therefore, we first select a time-period t_b, and then select a number of servers, denoted by k_s, and then from each selected server we select a number of virtual machines that are assigned to them for the time-period t_b. The number of virtual machines that we want to reassign from each selected server is bounded by an integer parameter k_m. Each selected virtual machine that we want to reassign in time-period t_b is also selected from its servers for the time-periods ranging between t_a and t_c such that $t_a \le t_b \le t_c$ and $t_c - t_a$ is bounded by an integer parameter k_t. Notice that a virtual machine may not be necessarily running on the same server for all the time-periods between t_a and t_c inclusive. Initially k_s is set to 1, it is incremented as search progresses, and it is re-initialised to 1 when it exceeds 10. Similarly k_t is initially set to 1, it is incremented as search progresses, and it is re-initialised to 1 when it exceeds the maximum number of time-periods h. Depending on the value of k_s and k_t a fixed value of k_m is used. The total number of decision variables selected for reassignment for a sub-problem is bound by $k_s \times k_m \times k_t$.

6.3 Create and Re-optimise Subproblem

The conventional approach for creating a sub-problem would be to reset all the domains of the variables, reassign the servers to the virtual machines (for the appropriate time-periods) which are not chosen for reassignment, and perform constraint propagation

Algorithm 1. findInitialFeasibleSolution($\mathcal{P}$)

1:   $uvars \leftarrow \{x_{it}|v_i \in V \wedge p_t \in T\}; sol \leftarrow \emptyset; fvars \leftarrow \emptyset;$
2: **while** $uvars \neq \emptyset$ **do**
3:       **while** $uvars \neq \emptyset$ **do**
4:           select & remove any x_{it} from $uvars$;
5:           **if** $\exists s_j \in A_i$ s.t. $\mathcal{P} \wedge sol \wedge (x_{it} = j)$ is satisfiable **then**
6:               $sol \leftarrow sol \cup \{(x_{it} = j)\}$
7:           **else**
8:               $fvars \leftarrow fvars \cup \{x_{it}\}$
9:           **end if**
10:      **end while**
11:      $uvars \leftarrow fvars$
12:      **while** $fvars \neq \emptyset$ **do**
13:          select & remove any x_{it} from $fvars$;
14:          select any s_j from A_i
15:          **while** $\mathcal{P} \wedge sol \wedge (x_{it} = j)$ is not satisfaible **do**
16:             determine any constraint $C \in \mathcal{P}$ that is not satisfiable
17:             select any $x_{i't'}$ involved in C such that $x_{i't'} \in sol$
18:             $sol \leftarrow sol - \{(x_{i't'} = j')\}$
19:             $uvars \leftarrow uvars \cup \{x_{i't'}\}$
20:          **end while**
21:      **end while**
22: **end while**

before searching the resulting sub-problem. The reason for doing this is that existing solvers are typically designed for systematic backtracking search. However, in LNS one moves from one partial assignment to another in a non-systematic way and unfortunately no support is provided for updating the state of the problem domains incrementally. This way of creating a sub-problem can be a bottleneck for solving very large problems in a very limited time especially if the size of the sub-problem is considerably smaller than the size of the full problem. The reason is that the number of iterations that one would like to perform will increase as the size of the problem increases in which case the time spent in creating the subproblems will also increase. We therefore use the technique described in [11] for replenishing the domains via incremental recomputation. When a set of decisions are undone, the constraints are used explicitly to determine which removed values can be added back to the current domains. The advantage is that it is independent on the order in which the assignments are undone and, therefore, it can be very efficient for creating subproblems.

We use systematic branch and bound search with a threshold on the number of failures for solving a given sub-problem. At each node of the search tree constraint propagation is performed to reduce the search space. We use a random variable ordering heuristic for selecting decision variables. The value ordering heuristic for selecting a server for a given pair of virtual machine and time-period is based on the minimum increment in the objective cost, while ties are broken randomly.

7 Empirical Results

In this section we present empirical results to demonstrate the effectiveness of our large neighbourhood search approach for the constraint optimisation problem as described in Sections 4 and 5.

Approaches. We compare three approaches: the MIP formulation of the problem, the Temporal Greedy approach (TG), and large neighbourhood search (LNS) for the COP model. The detailed presentation of the Mixed Integer linear Programming (MIP) formulation is omitted due to lack of space. The Temporal Greedy (TG) is the currently employed approach in the platform of the industrial partners. It proceeds by decomposing time and is, therefore, more scalable than the MIP approach. It greedily solves the problem period by period using the MIP model restricted to one period (enforcing the known assignment of the previous period). Each time-period is used as a starting period as long as there is time left and, therefore, if required the assignment is extended in both directions towards the beginning and towards the end. In order to compare different upper bounds, we also computed lower bounds (LB) based on column generation with a 2 hour time-limit. The details of the lower bound computation is presented in [12].

Benchmarks. The industry partners provided 74 problem instances, where the maximum number of virtual machines, servers, and time-periods are 242, 20 and 287 respectively. All the instances are available online.[4] We observed on this benchmark that the CPU constraint is the tight one, as opposed to the memory constraint which is always satisfiable. Based on the original instances we also generated larger instances by just duplicating each virtual machine and each server. Out of 74 original instances, 2 instances then became unsatisfiable because of the migration constraints that restrict the movement of virtual machines to different servers over different time-periods. The result is that the increase in the total CPU requirements of the virtual machines running on a server for one or more time-periods exceeds the maximum capacity of the server, and hence the problem becomes unsatisfiable.

Evaluation. The time-limit is 600 seconds unless otherwise stated. If an approach fails to solve an instance within the time-limit then 600 is recorded as its solution time. All experiments were carried out on a Dual Quad Core Xeon CPU, running Linux 2.6.25 x64, with 11.76 GB of RAM, and 2.66 GHz processor speed. The MIP solver used is CPLEX 12.5 with default parameters. For the LNS approach we extended the solver used for the machine reassignment problem of ROADEF.[5] All algorithms were implemented in C.

For each problem instance LNS was allowed to run for 600 seconds. Therefore, we report the cpu time (denoted cpu) for only MIP and TG as in some cases they were terminated before the time-limit. For each approach we also report the number of instances (denoted by #nu) for which an approach failed to find a feasible solution. The *gaps* for upper bounds reported by different approaches are computed as $\frac{100 \times (ub - lb)}{lb}$

---

[4] http://www.4c.ucc.ie/~dm6/energetic.tar.gz
[5] http://www.sourceforge.net/projects/machinereassign/

Table 1. Summary of results obtained using MIP, LNS and TG approaches with 600 seconds time-limit over 74 original instances

	LNS	MIP		TG	
	gap	gap	cpu	gap	cpu
Mean	0.50	0.03	191.92	7.00	42.50
Median	0	0	2.67	0.05	1.45
Max	4.57	0.72	600	119.35	600
#nu	**0**	3		1	

Table 2. Comparison of upper bounds of the various approaches with 600 seconds time-limit on a few specific instances. The first part corresponds to the original instances while the second part corresponds to the generated instances.

n	m	h	LB lb	cpu	LNS ub	MIP ub	cpu	TG ub	cpu
32	3	96	25404.7	14.8	25586.7	**25575.7**	600	36049.7	112.3
36	3	287	126730.1	248.0	**127018.6**	127654.4	600	127036.6	600
242	20	24	38614.2	600	**40362.5**	-	600	43027.6	14.2
242	20	287	431703.9	600	**439926.2**	-	600	-	600
242	20	24	36890.8	56.1	37701.6	-	600	**36897.4**	600
90	7	8	12656.82	0.1	11728.2	**11435.3**	600	11435.5	1.5
64	6	15	7695.6	64.9	**8703.6**	9657.6	600	10233.6	5.74
64	6	96	48169.3	470.3	**53917.3**	-	600	66407.4	84.24
484	40	24	74098.1	600	**86748.8**	-	600	92006.2	63.5
484	40	287	848619.4	1200	**893463.6**	-	600	-	600
136	10	16	15529.3	74.72	15519.3	-	600	**15272.3**	70.52
484	40	24	73781.5	241.32	76240.9	-	600	**73791.44**	600
60	6	15	9857.76	104.82	**11302**	-	600	13407.7	4.18
72	6	287	232222.9	1200	**240679**	565145	600	250104.1	600
108	14	8	9094.86	164.33	**9555.49**	9720.67	600	-	600
72	10	16	18337.4	223.4	**18416.5**	35911.7	600	18556.21	2.57
60	12	24	25484.5	8.29	25535.3	62520.2	600	**25524.59**	5.85
66	6	1	30558.94	0.1	49013.31	**30558.94**	0.1	30558.94	0.1
180	14	8	22864.6	364.42	26427.47	-	600	**22971.3**	32.47

respectively. To compute mean/median/max values of gaps or time of a given approach, we exclude the instances where it fails to return any feasible solution.

Original Instances. Table 1 gives an overview of the results by reporting over the original 74 instances the average/median/max values of the gap to the best known lower bound, the *cpu* time, and the number of instances, *#nu*, where an approach fails to return any results within the time-limit. Out of 74 instances, MIP is able to find solutions for 71 instances within the time-limit out of which 54 are proved optimal. It thus failed for 3 instances where the space requirement for CPLEX exceeded 11GB. Notice that the largest instance in the original set has 1,389,080 decision variables. Clearly, MIP-based systematic search cannot scale in terms of time and memory. TG is able to find

Table 3. Summary of results obtained using MIP, LNS and TG approaches with 600 second time-limit over 72 instances which are generated by duplicating each virtual machine and each server of each original instance

	LNS	MIP		TG	
	gap	gap	cpu	gap	cpu
Mean	2.86	10.95	499	9.71	48.15
Median	0.20	0.08	600	0.18	5.59
Max	60.38	145.32	600	120.45	169.16
#nu	**0**	7		3	

Table 4. Comparison of LNS over 146 instances for 600, 300 and 150 second time-limits

	600s	300s	150s
Mean Gap	1.669	1.725	1.711
Median Gap	0.089	0.093	0.095
#nu	0	0	1

solutions for 73 instances (so it failed on one instance), out of which 26 are optimal. Its quality deteriorates severely when one should anticipate expensive peaks in demand by appropriately placing virtual machines several time-periods before the peak. This can be seen in Table 2 where the maximum gap is 119.35%. LNS succeeds in finding feasible solutions for all instances within 2 seconds, on average, but it was terminated after 600 seconds and for 41 instances it found optimal solutions. Its average gap to the best known lower bound is less than 0.5% showing that LNS scales very well both in quality and problem size. Table 2 also gives the results for a few hard original instances.

Larger Instances. For larger instances MIP failed to find solutions for 7 instances while TG failed to find solutions for 3 instances out of 72 satisfiable instances as shown in Table 3. The increase in the size of the instances has significantly deteriorated the performances of MIP and TG in terms of time and gap when compared to the original set of instances. LNS is the only approach that managed to find solutions for all instances. The maximum gap for LNS is for an instance for which both MIP and TG are able to solve it optimally. This instance has only one time-period but the packing part of the problem is harder because of the migration constraints. We note that when the number of time-periods is 1 both MIP and TG are equivalent. As we use a random variable selection heuristic for LNS, it could not perform as well as the systematic and complete search of MIP/TG on that particular instance. Table 2 also gives the results for a few larger instances.

Any-time Behavior. Having seen the good performance of LNS we also investigated the impact of different time-limits on LNS. The time-out limit of 600 seconds was defined by our industrial partners. We also solved all the 146 instances with 300 and 150 second time-outs. The results are summarised in Table 4. These results suggest that LNS has a very good any-time behaviour and it can find high quality solutions very quickly. When the time-limit is 150 seconds, it failed to find a solution for only 1 instance which has 5,556,320 decision variables. For this instance it requires at least 200 seconds to find an initial feasible solution and the majority of that effort is spent in the first phase of Algorithm 1, where it tries each choice at least once.

8 Conclusion

We presented a constraint optimisation formulation of the energy minimisation problem for data centres. We developed a tool that uses constraint programming and large neighbourhood search for solving large problem instances in very limited time. Empirical results on real benchmarks assert that our LNS approach is scalable, thus suited for solving large instances. The presented approach has good anytime behaviour which is important when solutions must be reported subject to a time limit. Currently, we are not taking advantage of multi-cores capabilities that might be available while solving the problem. We plan to explore this opportunity in the future.

Acknowledgments. The authors want to acknowledge the industrial partners: Bull, Schneider Electric, Business & Decision and UXP as well as public research institutions: G2Elab, G-SCOP and LIG. The authors from UCC are supported by Science Foundation Ireland Grant No. 10/IN.1/I3032.

References

1. Glanz, J.: Power, Pollution and the Internet (September 2012), http://www.nytimes.com/2012/09/23/technology/data-centers-waste-vast-amounts-of-energy-belying-industry-image.html
2. Lee, H., Park, T.: Allocating data and workload among multiple servers in a local area network. Inf. Syst. 20(3), 261–269 (1995)
3. Chase, J.S., Anderson, D.C., Thakar, P.N., Vahdat, A., Doyle, R.P.: Managing energy and server resources in hosting centres. In: SOSP, pp. 103–116 (2001)
4. Petrucci, V., Loques, O., Mosse, D.: A dynamic configuration model for power-efficient virtualized server clusters. In: Proceedings of the 11th Brazilian Workshop on Real-Time and Embedded Systems (2009)
5. Dupont, C., Giuliani, G., Hermenier, F., Schulze, T., Somov, A.: An energy aware framework for virtual machine placement in cloud federated data centres. In: 2012 Third International Conference on Future Energy Systems: Where Energy, Computing and Communication Meet (e-Energy), pp. 1–10. IEEE (2012)
6. Bin, E., Biran, O., Boni, O., Hadad, E., Kolodner, E.K., Moatti, Y., Lorenz, D.H.: Guaranteeing high availability goals for virtual machine placement. In: 2011 31st International Conference on Distributed Computing Systems (ICDCS), pp. 700–709. IEEE (2011)
7. Hermenier, F., Demassey, S., Lorca, X.: Bin Repacking Scheduling in Virtualized Datacenters. In: Lee, J. (ed.) CP 2011. LNCS, vol. 6876, pp. 27–41. Springer, Heidelberg (2011)
8. Efficience des data centers, les retombés du projet energetic. Technical report, EnergeTIC (2013), http://www.vesta-system.cades-solutions.com/images/vestalis/4/energetic_white%20paper.pdf
9. A framework for data center energy productivity. Technical report, The green grid (2008)

10. Rossi, F., van Beek, P., Walsh, T.: Handbook of Constraint Programming. Elsevier Science Inc. (2006)
11. Mehta, D., O'Sullivan, B., Simonis, H.: Comparing solution methods for the machine reassignment problem. In: Milano, M. (ed.) CP 2012. LNCS, vol. 7514, pp. 782–797. Springer, Heidelberg (2012)
12. Cambazard, H., Mehta, D., O'Sullivan, B., Simonis, H.: Bin packing with linear usage costs – an application to energy management in data centres. In: Schlte, C. (ed.) CP 2013. LNCS, vol. 8124, pp. 47–62. Springer, Heidelberg (2013)

A Study of Electricity Price Features on Distributed Internet Data Centers

Milan De Cauwer and Barry O'Sullivan

INSIGHT Centre for Data Analytics
Department of Computer Science, University College Cork, Ireland
{mdecauwer,b.osullivan}@4c.ucc.ie

Abstract. Many modern cloud services are provided using Internet Data Centers (IDCs), e.g. the Google search engine. A network of IDCs is implemented using a set of data centers that are geographically distributed over many locations. The energy requirements of these systems are considerable, and there is growing interest in minimizing the total cost of energy required to operate them either by making the hardware more energy efficient or by ensuring that opportunities to access low-cost energy are exploited. In this paper we present a methodology for studying the energy cost implications of minimizing IDC energy costs under different operational and energy cost prediction regimes. We systematically study the impact of the level of price variability, time lag between locations due to the geographical distribution, reconfiguration delay, and accuracy of price predictions, on the overall electricity cost associated with managing an IDC.

1 Introduction

For various operational and strategic reasons, such as speed and latency, redundancy of both equipment and data, networks of Internet Data Centers (IDCs) are engineered in a geographically distributed fashion [1, 2]. The cost per unit of computation can vary significantly between various locations due to regional specificities [3]. Considerable efforts, motivated by the importance of energy costs in operating a DC, which typically costs up to 15% of total capital investment [1], have been made to take advantage of these price differentials [4–7] and to design energy-aware routing protocols [8].

From a combinatorial optimisation point of view, we can formulate the problem of managing an IDC as an assignment problem where one tries to allocate workload to a set of data centers such that an overall cost function in minimized. This cost function should be a function of the various characteristics of the set of DCs and the forecasted electricity price at each location. Of course, factors such as geographical spread and the time needed to reconfigure the system should also be incorporated into the assignment problem. Some tools for analysing cloud infrastructure are available, for example *CloudSim* [9] is a rather complete solution for simulating Cloud Computing environments and building test beds for provisioning algorithms.

J. Altmann, K. Vanmechelen, and O.F. Rana (Eds.): GECON 2013, LNCS 8193, pp. 60–73, 2013.

In this paper we present an approach to studying energy management associated with an IDC under various energy price prediction regimes across a variety of geographically distributed locations. We present an approach to simulating realistic electricity prices using a time-series analysis technique. We provide an approach to studying the generic behavior of electricity prices on a wholesale electricity market. We will also introduce a simple approach to simulating errors while predicting prices over a short time-horizon. Finally, we study a variety of specific problems of interest in IDC management, using a framework to simulate instances of this routing problem. We investigate, in a systematic way, the impact of the level of price variability, time lag between locations (geographical distribution), reconfiguration delay, and accuracy of price predictions on the overall electricity cost associated with managing an IDC. Our electricity price forecasting models provide a useful tool for the development of policies for the location and management of IDCs.

2   Models for Electricity Prices

In order to study the electricity costs associated with managing an IDC, a realistic model for electricity price dynamics on a wholesale market is required. Figure 1(a) shows the weekly dynamics of the actual spot price of electricity on the Irish market over the first seven days of 2009 at 30 minute intervals. We study electricity price as a time-series in which each data points describes the price of electricity at a specific moment in time.[1]

There are various approaches to building a predictive model for real-time market electricity prices, for example GARCH models [10], wavelet models [11], artificial neural networks [12, 13], other machine learning-based methods [14], etc. We used a time-series analysis procedure referred to as the Box-Jenkins (BJ) method [15] to build an Auto-Regressive Integrated Moving Average (ARIMA) model characterizing the electricity price behavior over a day. We used features provided in R [16], a platform for statistical computing[2], to apply the BJ methodology, which is described in detail in [17].

The ARIMA model is a commonly used tool to understand, model and predict future values of a time-series P_t (see [18, 19]). The behavior of the series is expressed using two components. The first one is the autoregressive (AR) part,

$$AR(p) : P_t = \sum_{i=1}^{p} \varphi_i P_{t-i} + \epsilon_t$$

which states that values of the series are partially determined by its past values. The second part is the moving average (MA) part,

$$MA(q) : P_t = \epsilon_t + \sum_{j=1}^{q} \theta_j \epsilon_{t-j}.$$

---

[1] Our datasets can be found on-line as CSV files at
http://4c.ucc.ie/~gifrim/Irish-electricity-market/
[2] http://www.r-project.org

Combining these two components the model

$$ARMA(p,q) : P_t = \epsilon_t + \sum_{i=1}^{p} \varphi_i P_{t-i} + \sum_{j=1}^{q} \theta_i \epsilon_{t-j}$$

is a powerful tool that builds a rather simple model for a time-series. Note that ϵ_t is a set of independent variables identically distributed according to a Gaussian distribution $N(0, \sigma_{Price}^2)$ with σ_{Price}^2 being a measure of the variability of the price.

In order to grasp the seasonal nature of the series we used the generalized SARIMA$(p,d,q)(P,D,Q)[s]$ model. Where d and D are, respectively, the order of the ordinary and the seasonal differentiation, p and P are the orders of ordinary and seasonal AR processes, and q and Q the orders of the MA processes. Finally s is the frequency of the seasonality, which is 48 in our case representing a period of 24 hours at a fidelity of 30 minutes.

The BJ approach is a process that iterates over a set of candidate ARIMA models aiming to find the best fit, i.e. φ_i and θ_i, of a time-series to its past values. Figure 1 shows the various steps that were undertaken in what we considered as the best iteration of the BJ process. The first step is to ensure that the time-series under study is stationary, i.e. that the mean and variance over time is constant, and that we accurately model the seasonal effect, if any.

The actual series as seen in Figure 1(a) does not fulfill the stationary property, and shows a clear seasonality over a range of 48 time periods. Thus, the series was differentiated twice including a seasonal differentiation:

$$\nabla_{48} dP_t = dP_t - dP_{t-48}$$

with

$$dP_t = \nabla P_t = P_t - P_{t-1}.$$

As a result, Figure 1(b) shows that a stationary series was achieved by differentiating the time-series twice thus fixing the orders $d = 1$ for the regular and $D = 1$ for the periodic component.

The next step allows us to define the orders of both the AR and MA processes, p and q in our model, respectively. For doing so, we refer to the AutoCorrelation Function (ACF), illustrated in Figure 1(c), and the Partial AutoCorrelation Function (PACF), presented in Figure 1(d), of the differentiated series. The quick decay of values on the ACF suggests an $AR(p)$ process. The value of p should be read on the PACF as the last value significantly different from 0. Hence $p = 3$. Similarly, the order of the MA process is read on the ACF. Hence $q = 3$. Then, the same procedure is repeated for the seasonal component by taking into account a 48 period lag allowing us to fix $P = 1$ and $Q = 2$. Values of best fit for parameters θ_i and φ_i are listed in Table 1. The last step in the BJ method is to check that the residuals of the model are showing white noise properties. We performed checks for white noise, which were positive.

Figure 2 illustrates the range of situations that we are now able to simulate by varying the σ_{Price}^2 parameter. This parameter affects the amount of noise that

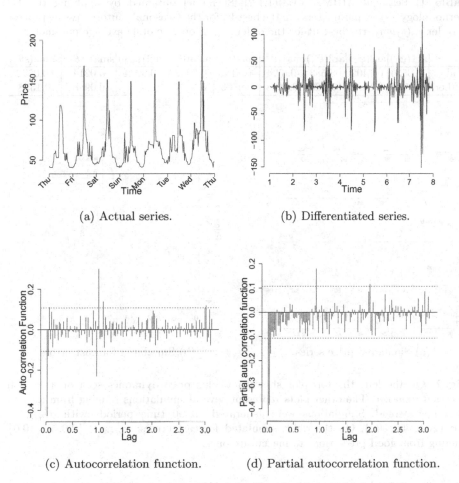

(a) Actual series.

(b) Differentiated series.

(c) Autocorrelation function.

(d) Partial autocorrelation function.

Fig. 1. An iteration of the Box-Jenkins method

the generated series shows against the theoretical ARIMA model. As the figure shows, even with highly fluctuating prices (e.g. $\sigma^2_{Price} = 500$) the trend over a day still appears. In the following, we will use σ^2_{Price} to conduct experiments in which price series are simulated with a controlled intrinsic variability.

3   A Model for Price Prediction Errors

One of the contributions of this paper is to provide an empirical insight into the impact of price prediction errors on the overall cost of the optimal assignment of workload in an IDC. To this end, we modelled forecasting errors for a particular time slot t as being distributed according to a Gaussian distribution centered on the actual value. Hence, let $P = \{p_1, \ldots, p_T\}$ be a price series and $\hat{P} =$

Table 1. Seasonal ARIMA(3,1,3)(1,1,2)[48] model obtained by applying the BJ methodology. $(s)ar_i$ parameters are the best fit for the (seasonal) autoregressive process of order i. $(s)ma_j$, the best fit for the order j (seasonal) mobile average parameters.

	ar1(φ_1)	ar2(φ_2)	ar3(φ_3)	ma1(θ_1)	ma2(θ_2)	ma3(θ_3)	sar1(sφ_1)	sma1(sθ_1)	sma2(sθ_1)
Val	-0.0536	0.7402	0.0583	-0.6738	-0.9145	0.5992	-0.5244	0.0214	-0.0772
std.er.	0.0578	0.1082	0.0788	0.0588	0.0763	0.1037	-	0.0988	0.1558

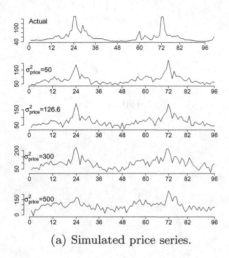

(a) Simulated price series.

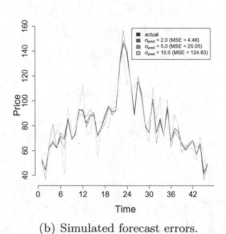

(b) Simulated forecast errors.

Fig. 2. On the left, the top plot shows a week's price dynamics seen on the Irish electricity market. The other plots represent several simulations ranging from a clean to a noisy trend. Simulations were generated on 96 time periods with $\sigma^2_{Price} \in \{50, 126.6, 300, 500\}$. On the right, simulated forecast errors: $\sigma_{pred} \in \{2.0, 5.0, 10.0\}$ ranging from good predictions to inaccurate ones.

$\{\hat{p}_1, \ldots, \hat{p}_T\}$ be a simulation of its forecasted values. Given P, we propose to build $\hat{P}$ such that $\hat{P}_t = \mathcal{N}(P_t, \sigma_{pred}), \forall t \in T$. Here σ_{pred} describes the standard deviation of the predictions.

Figure 2(b) shows an instance of a generated price series (in black) using the model discussed in the previous section. The figure also shows simulations of predicted prices for various σ_{pred} values. As a measure of the accuracy of the simulated predictions, we use the mean squared error (MSE) defined as $MSE(P, \hat{P}) = \frac{1}{T} \sum_{t \in T} (P_t - \hat{P}_t)^2$. Values of MSE for those particular simulations are also reported in the figure. Small values (e.g. 4.46) of MSE suggest that the overall predictions are good. As the accuracy of predictions degrades, the value of MSE rises (e.g. 124.83). Throughout the remainder of the paper we will be using the σ_{pred} parameter to simulate situations ranging from perfect ($\sigma_{pred} = 0$) to highly inaccurate price forecasts with bigger values of σ_{pred}.

Table 2. Notations of parameters and decision variables

N	Number of Locations
M_i	Number of servers available at $i \in L$
μ_i	Request rate handled by a server at $i \in L$
Po_i	Power used by a working server at $i \in L$
$WL(t)$	Amount of requests for period t
$P_i(t)$	Electricity Price at i during time slot t
$\hat{P}_i(t)$	Forecasted Price at i during time slot t
TR	Time needed to reconfigure
TL	Time lag between two consecutive loca-tions
m_i	Number of turned on servers at $i \in L$
λ_i	Number of requests assigned to $i \in L$

4   Minimizing IDC Electricity Cost

We formalize the problem of finding the minimum total electricity cost for a network of IDCs. The formulation is adapted from the problem described in [5]. Our intention, however, is to give a systematic characterization of price properties on the cost of running a network of IDCs. Table 2 summarizes the parameters and the decision variables needed to formulate the problem.

We first assume that each IDC is in a location where electricity price $P_i(t)$ on the wholesale market varies every 30 minutes; this is the case in Ireland where energy can be purchased from the Single Energy Market Operator.[3] We thus consider a set L of locations spread geographically so that there is a time lag of $TL \in \{0, 1, 2, \ldots, 24\}$ half hours between two consecutive locations. This time lag parameter actually controls how the price signals at the various locations will be shifted with respect to each other; it has been suggested that energy prices become less correlated between two locations as the distance between them increases, i.e. the further away two locations are, the less correlated are their energy prices [3]. Using the model defined in previous section, we also define $\hat{P}_i(t)$ as a vector of predicted prices of $P_i(t)$.

Each IDC has a number M_i of servers that can be switched on or off in order to handle the workload WL at location i. At each period the decision is thus to turn on a subset $m_i \in \{0, \ldots, M_i\}$ of servers at each location i. We assume that each server in location i has a capacity factor μ_i, expressed in terms of processing requests, and will consume an amount Po_i of electricity if running. For each time interval t we can express the expected total energy cost of running N IDCs as:

$$C_t = \sum_{i=1}^{N} m_i \times P_i(t) \times Po_i.$$

---

[3] http://www.sem-o.com

Therefore, we can define the cost over all time periods as $C = \sum_{t \in T} C_t$. The decision of the assignment of workload at a particular time t is computed in order to minimize overall expected energy cost. The optimization process is thus based the forecasted prices $\hat{P}_i(t)$. This quantity is given by:

$$\hat{C}_t = \sum_{i=1}^{N} m_i \times \hat{P}_i(t) \times Po_i.$$

In some of the experiments shown in the next section, we assume a perfect prediction accuracy ($\sigma_{pred} = 0$), and solving the problem with $\hat{P}$ is equivalent to solving the problem with P. A solution to this problem requires that all the workload is distributed among the locations. Thus we can express the workload constraint as $\sum_{i \in L} \lambda_i = WL(t)$. On the other hand, the assigned load to an IDC at location i should not exceed its processing power (requests): $\lambda_i \leq m_i \times \mu_i$.

Solving this problem requires finding the assignment of the workload to the IDCs λ_i, and subsequently the number of servers, m_i, that are turned on. The mathematical model can be written as follows and will be solved for each time interval $t \in T$ considered in the problem:

$$\min_{\lambda_i, m_i} \sum_{i \in L} m_i \times \hat{P}_i(t) \times Po_i$$

$$s.t.$$

$$\lambda_i \leq m_i \times \mu_i \qquad \qquad \forall i \in L$$

$$\sum_{i \in L} \lambda_i \leq WL(t)$$

$$m_i \in \{0, \ldots, M_i\} \qquad \qquad \forall i \in L$$

$$\lambda_i \in \mathbb{N} \qquad \qquad \forall i \in L$$

Finally, our model provides a way to simulate various levels of inertia in the system. The parameter TR specifies the number of time slots needed to reassign the workload. When TR is set to 0, we assume that the assignment for time t is performed instantaneously at the beginning of the period. For positive values of TR, a new assignment done at time t will be held over TR times slots before a new assignment is allowed to be performed. We simulate this by solving the optimization program on every time period divisible by TR and keeping the assignment in between those time periods.

5   Empirical Analysis

We consider the impact of factors such as price volatility, forecasting errors, time lag between locations, and time needed to reconfigure the system on the optimal energy cost required by a network of IDCs. For doing so, all experiments were conducted with the same set of fixed parameters for both the set of locations

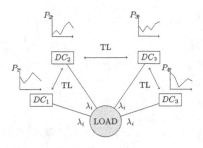

Fig. 3. A representation of the assignment problem

Table. 3. Data centers setup for each of the four locations

	IDCs			
l	1	2	3	4
Po	100	110	120	110
μ	0.9	1.1	1.5	1.2
M	50000	40000	20000	40000

and the workload. We simulated instances of the problem with 4 IDCs such that the total maximum processing power was fixed at $\sum_{i \in L} \mu_i \times M_i = 167000$. On the other hand, the load was fixed at $WL_t = 100000, \forall t \in T$ requests. We thus have the guarantee that the problem always admits a feasible solution.

The individual IDC configurations are summarized in Table 3. Those features form the static part of the model. We can see that IDC 3 has the most efficient configuration with a cheaper cost per unit of computation ratio. Despite the fact that we can order IDCs by efficiency, finding an optimal assignment for a particular time period requires one to further investigate price behavior features. We thus discuss these parameters in the remainder of this section.

5.1 Exploring Two Specific Scenarios

Figures 4 illustrates with two scenarios how the overall system behaves over time. Figure 4(a) shows how many servers (m_1 on top to m_4 at the bottom) were set to run in each of the 4 IDCs over the 48 time intervals. In this particular scenario we defined a 4 hour (8 intervals of 30 minutes) timezone difference between each location causing price peaks to be shifted across the day. The workload distribution was computed assuming that price forecasting was perfect (i.e. $\sigma_{pred} = 0$). The price levels for each individual location are also reported on the right axis. Despite the fact that some IDCs are more efficient than others, we see that none of the IDCs are constantly working at full capacity. In fact, none of the four IDCs are producing any work while local electricity prices are at their highest. Due to its superior configuration, IDC 3 is running all its servers over most of the day but is still powering down during time slots 39, 40 and 41, where local energy costs are highest.

We further note that the assignment over time is very sensitive to price variations. This is due to the fact that the cost per unit of computation in the various locations are always relatively close to each other. This ratio favors, in turn, different locations only because of the price differentials occurring within a day.

Let us explore another scenario involving errors in price prediction for both IDC 3 and IDC 4. For Figure 4(b) errors were simulated with a $\sigma_{pred} = 10$ level such that $\hat{P}_t = \mathcal{N}(P_t, 10), \forall t \in T$ and are represented with the solid gray line.

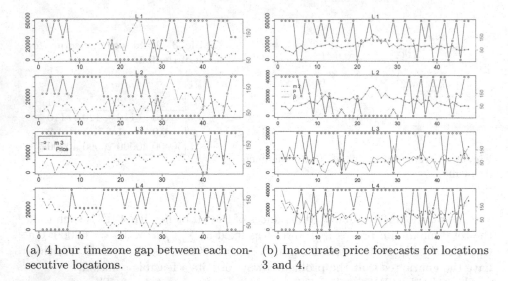

(a) 4 hour timezone gap between each con-   (b) Inaccurate price forecasts for locations
secutive locations.   3 and 4.

Fig. 4. Number of servers running m_i (in black) and price levels (in gray) at each
locations. In Figure 4(b) we also plot the electricity price forecasts (solid gray line).
Since σ_{pred} was set to 0 for IDCs 1 and 2, actual and forecasted prices are strictly
overlapping at these locations.

In this scenario we observe that forecasted prices can be significantly departed
from the actual price. Since workload distribution is computed from the predicted
prices $\hat{P}_t$, we can clearly see that this assignment is not optimal. For instance,
the workload assignment at $t = 29$ seem to be erroneous as IDC 1 and IDC 2 are
both in a quite high-priced period but are still carrying workload. This is due
to a large overshooting of the price forecast in location 3 at that particular time
causing IDC 3 to turn all its servers down and thus shifting the load to other
IDCs. Looking more closely at the dynamics of this scenario, one can observe
this faulty behavior taking place over the 24 hour period, e.g. $t = 16$, $t = 24$.

5.2   General Behaviors

We report on systematic experiments that sought to gain insights into how various features of the problem would affect the overall energy cost. Unless specified,
the configuration mentioned above was used. Each experiment was run 10 times.
In the following figures, we systematically fit curves to the data to help demonstrate the trend in the results.

Price Variability. The first two experiments that were conducted aim to characterize the impact of variety amongst prices on the overall assignment cost. To
this end we increase, in turn, the number of locations considered in the problem.
The underlying assumption here is that the number of opportunities to reduce
electricity costs occur more frequently as the number of locations increases. Price

P_i were all generated with $\sigma^2_{price} = 126.6$ and their forecast were set to be perfect (i.e. $\sigma_{pred} = 0$). Neither time lags nor reconfiguration times were used. One should note that the capacity M_i of each IDC was tuned in order to keep the total processing power constant (i.e. 167000).

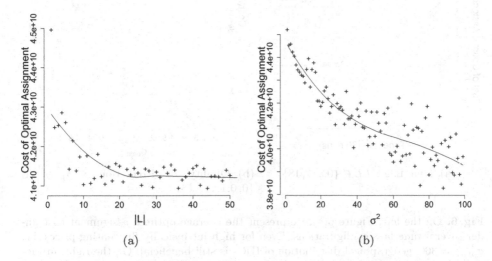

(a)   (b)

Fig. 5. On the left, Figure 5(a), we show the effect on optimal energy cost associated with increasing the number of locations. On the right, Figure 5(b), we show the effect associated with intrinsic price fluctuation with $\sigma^2_{price} \in \{0, 5, \ldots, 500\}$. Both factors can be seen as opportunities to exploit price diversities in order to reduce overall operating costs.

As Figure 5(a) shows, the cost of the optimal assignment quickly decreases with the cardinality of L. In fact, it dropped by almost 10% from a situation in which there is no possibility to take advantage of price differentials ($card(L) = 1$) to a situation in which price differentials are induced by a larger number of locations ($card(L) = 20$ and above). This effect seems to level off for more than 20 locations in this particular setup.

To further test the impact of price variety on total energy cost, we can also generate prices that are intrinsically more or less fluctuating as shown in Figure 2(a) by varying the σ^2_{price} parameter. Figure 5(b) shows how the level of fluctuation amongst prices affects the cost of the optimal assignment. For low values of σ^2_{price}, prices at distant locations will not deviate much from each other. As σ^2_{price} rises, prices are more and more noisy, and thus exhibit more intrinsic diversity. We see the impact of that diversity by the decreasing cost of the optimal assignment. In the best cases, it appears that energy costs can be reduced by almost 15% if prices at the different locations show a reasonable level of variability. Finally, we note that it is not clear if this effect would level, but we clearly see that as σ^2_{price} progresses the cost displays more variance.

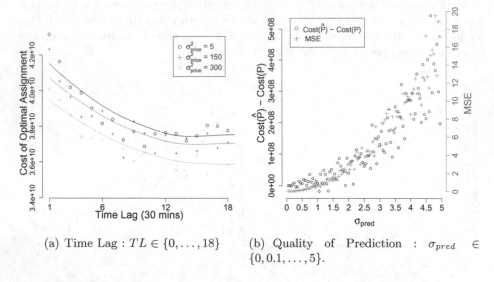

(a) Time Lag : $TL \in \{0, \dots, 18\}$ (b) Quality of Prediction : $\sigma_{pred} \in \{0, 0.1, \dots, 5\}$.

Fig. 6. On the left, Figure 6(a), we present the average optimal assignment cost under several time lags configurations. Even for high intrinsically fluctuating prices, i.e. $\sigma^2_{price} = 300$, geographical distribution of IDCs is still beneficial. On the right, in Figure 6(b), we show how the quality of price prediction is correlated to the suboptimal decision making by measuring the gap of assignment made under perfect prediction (i.e. $\sigma_{pred} = 0$) and several levels of uncertainty.

Timezone Effect. The timezone effect was illustrated in the first scenario (Figure 4(a)) discussed in the previous section. We conjecture that, given the particular daily shape of real-time electricity prices, spreading IDCs over distant locations would allow substantial electricity cost savings. To test this hypothesis, we assumed perfect prediction on prices generated with a $\sigma^2_{price} \in \{5, 150, 300\}$ and varied the TL parameter to set the time lag between each consecutive locations. Thus, $TL = 0$ means that prices are perfectly in phase and $TL = 2$ means that each consecutive location is separated by an hour, slightly shifting the price signals.

As Figure 6(a) suggests, in this configuration a time lag of 12 30-minute intervals (6 hours) is giving the best results. This is not surprising since with $TL = 12$ prices at the four locations are perfectly out of phase. This gives the opportunity to route the load away from locations showing high price levels (midday) to locations where electricity is cheaper (night time). In this particular setup, a perfect geographical spread could account for up to 15% in electricity cost savings. We further note that the price variability effect does not contradict the time lag effect since the observed trends are quite similar.

Price Forecast Quality. As the "bad forecast" scenario depicted in Figure 4(b) suggested, low prediction accuracy can lead to non-optimal assignments. To gain an insight into how the quality of price forecasting affects the cost of assignment, we varied the parameter σ_{pred} in the range $0, \ldots, 5$ by steps of 0.1. Predictions will thus be fuzzier as σ_{pred} rises. Prices at the various locations were generated with a standard variability level $\sigma^2_{price} = 126.6$. Recall that when $\sigma_{pred} = 0$, predictions are perfect and thus the assignment will be optimal.

Figure 6(b) shows that the difference between the assignment cost computed with $\hat{P}$ and the same solution evaluated with the actual price P. This difference can be interpreted as a penalty cost induced by bad decision-making due to the uncertainty while predicting prices. We show that this penalty cost is quadratically rising with the level of uncertainty σ_{pred}. Furthermore, this difference seems to be strongly correlated with the MSE indicator measuring the accuracy of predictions. For $\sigma_{pred} = 0$ the penalty cost represent about 10 % of the overall cost.

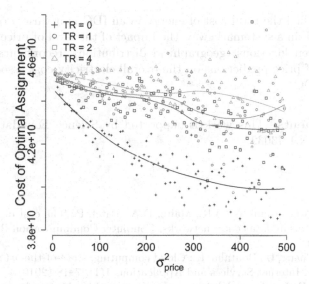

Fig. 7. Time to reconfigure $TR \in \{0, 1, 2, 4\}$. As there is more and more inertia in the system, the expected gain from highly fluctuating prices vanishes.

Reconfiguration Time. The last feature that was tested is the speed with which the IDC can be reconfigured. Until now, we assumed that the system could be configured instantaneously at the beginning of a given time period. For realism sake, we defined scenarios in which the time needed to reconfigure the system was set to $TR \in \{0, 1, 2, 4\}$. For instance, when TR is set to 2 the system will need an hour to reassign the workload.

As can been in Figure 7, the reconfiguration time dramatically affects the cost of the assignment. For $TR = 0$ we assumed that reconfiguration for period t is done at the beginning of period t, thus we have the same behavior as shown in Figure 5(a). For $TR = 4$, we see that the gain induced by more variability within prices is almost null. In fact, several runs are indicating a degradation of the cost of assignment. This could be explained by the fact that introducing latency in the system prevents one from taking immediate advantage of price differentials. We can derive from this that the more that prices fluctuate, the more flexible and responsive the system must be in order to benefit from it.

6 Conclusion

We have presented an approach to studying the energy costs associated with an IDC under various energy price prediction regimes across a variety of geographically distributed locations. The basis of our analysis is an approach to forecasting on the basis of a time-series representing energy prices over time, and an approach to controlling the effect of forecast errors. An assumption has been that the more distant a pair of IDCs, the less correlated are their local energy prices.

We have studied the total cost of energy in an IDC in a variety of scenarios. We investigated, in a systematic way, the impact of the level of price variability, time lag between locations (geographical distribution), reconfiguration delay, and accuracy of price predictions on the overall electricity cost associated with managing an IDC.

Acknowledgments. This work is supported by Science Foundation Ireland Grant No. 10/IN.1/I3032.

References

1. Greenberg, A.G., Hamilton, J.R., Maltz, D.A., Patel, P.: The cost of a cloud: Research problems in data center networks. Computer Communication Review 39(1), 68–73 (2009)
2. Zhang, Q., Cheng, L., Boutaba, R.: Cloud computing: state-of-the-art and research challenges. J. Internet Services and Applications 1(1), 7–18 (2010)
3. Qureshi, A., Weber, R., Balakrishnan, H., Guttag, J.V., Maggs, B.V.: Cutting the electric bill for internet-scale systems. In: SIGCOMM, pp. 123–134 (2009)
4. Li, J., Li, Z., Ren, K., Liu, X.: Towards optimal electric demand management for internet data centers. IEEE Trans. Smart Grid 3(1), 183–192 (2012)
5. Rao, L., Liu, X., Xie, L., Liu, W.: Minimizing electricity cost: Optimization of distributed internet data centers in a multi-electricity-market environment. In: INFOCOM, pp. 1145–1153 (2010)
6. Shang, Y., Li, D., Xu, M.: Energy-aware routing in data center network. In: Green Networking, pp. 1–8 (2010)
7. Berl, A., Gelenbe, E., Girolamo, M.D., Giuliani, G., de Meer, H., Quan, D.M., Pentikousis, K.: Energy-efficient cloud computing. Comput. J. 53(7), 1045–1051 (2010)
8. Qian, H., Li, F., Medhi, D.: On energy-aware aggregation of dynamic temporal demand in cloud computing. In: COMSNETS, pp. 1–6 (2012)
9. Calheiros, R.N., Ranjan, R., Beloglazov, A., De Rose, C.A.F., Buyya, R.: Cloudsim: a toolkit for modeling and simulation of cloud computing environments and evaluation of resource provisioning algorithms. Softw: Pract. Exper. 41(1), 23–50 (2011)

10. Hua, Z., Li, X., Li-zi, Z.: Electricity price forecasting based on garch model in deregulated market. In: The 7th International Power Engineering Conference, IPEC 2005, pp. 1–410 (2005)
11. Tan, Z., Zhang, J., Wang, J., Xu, J.: Day-ahead electricity price forecasting using wavelet transform combined with arima and garch models. Applied Energy 87(11), 3606–3610 (2010)
12. Yamin, H., Shahidehpour, S., Li, Z.: Adaptive short-term electricity price forecasting using artificial neural networks in the restructured power markets. International Journal of Electrical Power & Energy Systems 26(8), 571–581 (2004)
13. Hippert, H.S., Pedreira, C.E., Souza, R.C.: Neural networks for short-term load forecasting: A review and evaluation. IEEE Transactions on Power Systems 16(1), 44–55 (2001)
14. Ifrim, G., O'Sullivan, B., Simonis, H.: Properties of energy-price forecasts for scheduling. In: Milano, M. (ed.) CP 2012. LNCS, vol. 7514, pp. 957–972. Springer, Heidelberg (2012)
15. Box, G., Jenkins, G.: Holden-Day (1970)
16. R Core Team: R: A Language and Environment for Statistical Computing. R Foundation for Statistical Computing, Vienna, Austria (2012) ISBN 3-900051-07-0
17. Cryer, J.D., Chan, K.-S.: Time Series Analysis With Applications in R. Springer, New York (2009) ISBN 978-0-387-75958-6
18. Contreras, J., Espnola, R., Member, S., Nogales, F.J., Conejo, A.J., Member, S.: Arima models to predict next-day electricity prices. IEEE Transaction on Power Systems 1014–1020
19. Roken, R.M., Badri, M.A.: Time series models for forecasting monthly electricity peak-load for dubai

Quantifying Ecological Efficiency
in Cloud Computing

Gregory Katsaros and Pascal Stichler

FZI - Research Center for Information Technology, Berlin, Germany
{katsaros,stichler}@fzi.de

Abstract. Cloud computing is considered to be energy and ecological efficient, and is promoted as the environmental friendly computing solution. On the other hand, the massive development of the Cloud marketplace lead in an increase of the Data Centers globally and eventually in the increase of the CO_2 related footprint. The calculation of the impact of Virtual Machines (VMs) on the environment is a challenging task, not only due to the technical difficulties but also due to the lack of information from the energy providers. In this paper we present a methodology for the estimation of the ecological efficiency of Virtual Machines in Cloud infrastructures. We focus on the information management in relation with the energy production in a region as well as the ecological efficiency of a VM in a Data Center. To this end, we have designed and implemented a framework through which the ecological efficiency can be monitored. The presented framework is being evaluated through a private Cloud scenario deployed into infrastructure located in Germany.

Keywords: Ecological Efficiency, Cloud Computing, Virtual Machine, Energy Consumption, Monitoring.

1 Introduction

The rapid growth of ICT application services goes along with an increase in number and size of data centers (DCs) that host these services. Because data centers are massive energy consumers, the carbon footprint of application services is moving more and more into the focus. It is considered that ICT presently accounts for approximately 2% of global carbon emissions [1]. To give a concrete example, in 2011, Googles data centers alone were responsible for 1.43 million tons of carbon emissions, and this only accounts for about 1 percent of all data centers worldwide[1]. To this end, and as pointed out by 1,600 professionals during IBMs summit , ecological efficiency (a.k.a. eco-efficiency) of ICT application services will be the biggest economic game-changer for organizations during the next decades [2].

Nowadays, application services are increasingly provided using Cloud infrastructures. Its technological advantages (easy and fast access to heterogeneous

---

[1] www.google.com/green/bigpicture

J. Altmann, K. Vanmechelen, and O.F. Rana (Eds.): GECON 2013, LNCS 8193, pp. 74–89, 2013.

resources, flexible and powerful computing capacity etc.) as well as its economical advantages (e.g. pay-as-you-go model) made Cloud computing a common paradigm for developing and hosting application services. Such services compose resources on different layers, spanning physical and virtual infrastructure or other services, and can be deployed to different providers.

Ecological efficiency of a system is the amount of work that is delivered in relation to its CO_2 emissions. To assess the eco-efficiency of Cloud-based services, it becomes increasingly important to investigate the eco-efficiency of the Cloud resources that the service utilizes. To this end, there are several technical constraints and challenges [3]: virtualization technology, which is a major characteristic of Cloud computing, introduces a layer of intransparency between the consumers of Cloud resources and the physical infrastructure. The energy consumed by a service or a virtual machine cannot be directly metered and therefore must be estimated through certain modeling methodology. To what is more, the CO_2 footprint of the Cloud resources is directly related with the energy-mix that the respective data center consumes at the time of the Virtual Machine (VM) operation. Considering that the needed energy is provided by the local power providers, the calculation of ecological efficiency in Cloud computing is therefore a location and time relative figure.

The above-mentioned issues harden the effective calculation of ecological efficiency of Cloud services. To ecologically evaluate the resources that a Cloud-enabled application utilizes, providers require appropriate tools and methods that are still not there. Thus in this paper we aim at quantifying the environmental impact of Cloud resources and specifically estimate the ecological efficiency in the granularity of the Virtual Machine (VM).

As has been presented also in [4] there are many parameters that affect the cost (energy or financial) of Cloud resources. We ,though, selected to focus on the ecological efficiency of the VM as it is one very interesting variable parameter that is directly relates performance with power consumption of Cloud infrastructures, resulting in a highly dynamic metric. In our work, we have not considered the cost related with the static infrastructure (cooling of Data Center, management cost etc.) while those figures could be calculated separately and added on top of the parameters that we calculate dynamically. In addition, we assume that contemporary Cloud application topologies are consisted of multiple application components installed in different VMs. Therefore, the power consumption and eventually the ecological efficiency could be investigated in the level of the VMs.

In the following sections we will present the proposed methodology and corresponding implementation for calculating ecological efficiency of VMs considering the location and time constraints of the operation. In section 2 we present the state-of-the-art and the related work in the respective fields of research. In section 3 we elaborate on the proposed solution: a monitoring system that allows for the calculation of eco-efficiency of VMs. Finally, in section 4 we proceed in a proof of concept of the implemented solution with several deployment scenarios within Germany, while in section 5 we conclude and summarize our findings.

2 State of the Art and Related Work

In order to reduce the carbon footprint of a system or a service we need first of all to monitor and analyze the performance as well as energy related information of our computing infrastructure. In Cloud computing, it is important to know how much energy a specific service or a VM consumes, rather than the consumption of the physical infrastructure. However, measuring the energy consumption of a single or even several VMs is challenging task. While VMs, from a consumer point of view, are a black box, their energy consumption can only be estimated [5]. In order to do so, power usage models are normally used where performance characteristics are being used for the modeling of energy consumption. [6] [7] [8] [9] It is pointed out that CPU utilization is the factor driving energy consumption of a computing system, with memory and disk resource utilization to play a secondary role.

To what is more, in [10] they make use of power usage metering for calculating and forecasting the energy efficiency level of VMs in order to optimize VM deployments in private Clouds. The methodology for the calculation of energy efficiency of all Cloud entities has been proposed using the CPU utilization of the VMs as the parameter to define the useful work performed and linear regression technique for the forecasting. To this end, there have been many discussions about measuring the useful work of a computer accurately [11]. Several benchmarks have been proposed [12], however, since every application has different requirements no universal formula can be determined. In the same context, power consumption modeling has been used for power-aware VM allocation using genetic algorithms [13] or through heuristic algorithms [14]. The definition of energy efficiency in Cloud computing has been playing an important role also for the application of VM consolidation strategies. [15] [16]

The term ecological efficiency is a rather generic description of the efficient use of ecological resources. In computing systems eco-efficiency can be seen as computing power delivered compared to the environmental resources needed to do so. And again, in this context the complete product or service life-cycle and its related impacts on the environment have to be considered. In the context of Cloud computing, there have been different approaches to define eco-efficiency. For example, Google publishes the carbon emissions per query (0.2 g CO_2) and per watched minute on YouTube (0.1 g of CO_2) [17]. Similarly, in [18] a charge-back model is presented, where the environmental impact of providing data center services to the service consumers is traced back to the consumer. The consumer receives information about the CO_2 intensity of each transaction as well as the overall CO_2 emissions produced by his transactions. The eco-efficiency is calculated by CO_2 emissions per data transaction executed on the service.

In [19], the authors have formulated the cost of VM migrations between private Clouds aiming at the reduction of the carbon footprint of a Cloud network. Furthermore, in [20] is presented a routing methodology for user placement in data centers, that generates minimum carbon footprint and therefore optimizes the ecological efficiency. Both research studies point out the significance of the geographic location of the Cloud infrastructure towards the increasing the eco-efficiency of a service deployment. In addition, in [21], a framework for optimizing the carbon efficiency in Clouds is being presented, which is based on the installment of a registry with offers from Cloud providers with data about CO_2 emission rate, average DCiE(data center infrastructure efficiency) and VM power efficiency, prices, etc.; all these information though have to be updated by the provider.

In our work, we evolve and combine the above-mentioned techniques concerning the modeling of the VM performance and the estimation of energy consumed. We introduce also a methodology for the mapping of energy consumption with the amount of CO_2 emitted and therefore calculate the ecological efficiency of VMs based on the location of deployment, the time of execution and the performance characteristics of each instance.

3   Monitoring Ecological Efficiency in Clouds

The goal of the Cloud ecological efficiency monitoring system which we present in this paper, is to calculate the eco-efficiency of the VMs taking into consideration their performance utilization as well as energy related information. The system includes two independent operations (Figure 1) that are necessary for the calculation of the eco-efficiency of each VM:

- Creation of the CO_2 Emission Registry: the amount of CO_2 emitted by a service is based on the energy resources mix (coal, wind, solar, nuclear etc.) and therefore is a location-specific (for example, 10KWh electricity produced in Athens results in 2Kg of carbon emission, while in Berlin it results in 3Kg of carbon emission) and a time-related (the energy-mix changes by the time) figure. The CO_2 Emissions Registry will maintain the emission factors (how much CO_2 is generated for the production of 1KWh electricity) per location and for every hour of the day. The required information will be gathered by invoking public energy data streams (e.g. European Energy Exchange[2]) and historical data-stores, transformed and placed in a database from where it will become available to the rest services.
- Calculation for eco-efficiency: the systems monitors in terms of energy as well as performance metrics the Cloud infrastructure. The interaction with the private Cloud infrastructure is being done through a plug-in mechanism that can support multiple Cloud middleware. The respective service calculates in real-time the ecological efficiency of each VM.

The first operation represents the data aggregation phase in which the data regarding the CO_2 emissions from the energy resources of all regions and countries are being collected and analyzed. On the other hand, the second operation represents the monitoring phase in which the performance and energy data from the Cloud infrastructure are being gathered and the eco-efficiency of each VM is being calculated.

In the following subsections we will describe in detail the design, implementation and operation of the two phases.

---

[2] http://www.eex.com/en/

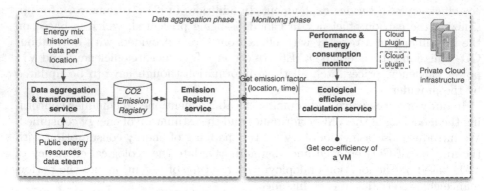

Fig. 1. High level architecture of the ecological efficiency monitoring system for Clouds

3.1   Aggregation Phase: Creation of the CO_2 Emission Registry

This phase aims at creating the CO_2 emission registry with region and time specific information about the carbon emission factor. As have been pointed out in [22], the location of a DC is of great importance. A DC and therefore the Cloud services (IaaS, PaaS, SaaS etc.) that it offers, is powered by energy sources of the local region. Transferring of energy in long distances is expensive and inefficient, thus, contemporary DCs are being constructed close to the energy sources and specifically close to "green" energy sources. Examples are Facebook's and Spotify's new DCs in Sweden where there is a big percentage of renewable energy production. In the following analysis, we assume that regardless of the existence of different power providers or utilities, all of them are consuming the same energy mix in the region. Therefore, for simplification reasons in the development of our methodology, we have extracted the complexity level of the power providers and we consider the regional energy mix when calculating the ecological impact of a DC and therefore a VM.

The challenge in this task was to discover public data streams that provide energy production information per country, region and per resource in a reliable manner. To succeed that we had to use energy information providers such as European Energy Exchange, that provide information for every country with an hourly refresh rate. We had also to combine that information with historical data regarding the energy mix of every region in order to come up with a real-time energy analysis of every region. We collected, analyzed and transformed those data by introducing a certain data structure and transformation logic which allows for the calculation of the CO_2 emission factors per region.

Data Structure. In order to efficiently manage the available information we designed a data model that captures all the above mentioned information and their interrelations. The gray boxes in Figure 2 represent the information that is collected from different sources and after certain processing and transformation is being aggregated in the CO_2 Emission Registry. The energy resources that we considered are split into the following categories: Coal, Gas, Lignite, Oil, Uranium, Water/Wind, Photovoltaic (sun), Others. The resource category "others" combines the energy produced from resources, not covered in the list, such as geothermal energy. In order to transform the energy mix to carbon emissions data, we need information about the CO_2 emissions of each energy category.

For the calculation of the different CO_2 emission factor we must also consider the complete life cycle of the respective power plants (construction, operation, maintenance, disposal). In the literature there have been different attempts to estimate the factors accurately. One common approach is the process chain analysis in which the energy production process is divided into different steps and for each step the input and output factors are calculated. Wagner et al. [23] have performed a comparison of the major methodologies and summarized them into a minimal reasonable, maximal reasonable and average CO_2 emission factor for each resource. In order to make all the emissions factors (like CH_4, N_2O etc.) comparable, we transformed them into CO_2 equivalents. To do so, one unit of the respective gas is transformed into the amount of CO_2, which would have the same impact on the environment as one unit of the gas. In our work we adopted these factors as well as data from Lübbert [24] during the aggregation phase of our system.

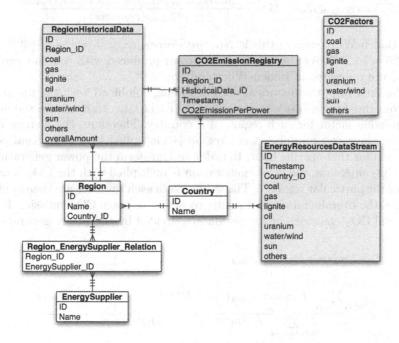

Fig. 2. Data model that captures the information used during the aggregation phase.

Transformation Logic. The raw information from the data streams is being transformed and combined to calculate the region and time specific CO_2 emission factor. The process is split into several steps. In the beginning, we work with the historical datasets and we calculate the overall amount of energy produced in a specific year for each resource in the region of interest. This is done by multiplying the share of the resource in the energy-mix of a region (E_Share) with the overall amount produced in the respective region. Then, the values from all regions are added up to get the overall amount for the country:

$$E_{country,resource} = \sum_{reg \in region} E\_Share_{res}(reg)\% * E_{total}(reg) \qquad (1)$$

For example in 2009 in Baden-Württemberg, region in Germany, 23 % of the energy was produced with coal as the energy source and the overall amount of energy produced was 61.792 million kWh. Hence, the amount of energy produced with coal in Baden-Württemberg was 14.212 million kWh. Added up with the corresponding values in all other regions, the overall amount of power produced with coal was 99.673 million kWh in 2009 in Germany.

In the second step, we calculate the energy share of each region in the country-wide power generation for each resource:

$$E\_Share_{region,resource}\% = \frac{E\_Share_{resource}(region)\% * E_{total}(region)}{E_{total}(resource)} \qquad (2)$$

For Baden-Württemberg this is $EnergyShare_{BaWu,coal} = \frac{14\ 212\ million\ kWh}{99\ 673\ million\ kWh}$ $= 0.1426 = 14.26\%$. As a result, from all power produced with coal in Germany, 14.26 % are generated in Baden-Württemberg.

In the final step, the historical data are being combined with the up-to-date data from the *EnergyResourcesDataStream* (ERDData) to calculate the actual CO_2 emission factor for each region of a country. Therefore, the historical energy share in power production per region is multiplied with the actual power production for that specific hour. In order to transform the power generation to actual CO_2 emissions, the power generation is multiplied with the CO_2 emission factor of the particular resource. The values from each resource are then summed up to get the overall emissions. Finally, to get an average CO_2 emission factor, the overall CO_2 emissions of the region are divided by the power generation of the region.

$$CO_2EmissionFactor_{region,time}$$

$$= \frac{\sum\limits_{r \in resources} E\_Share_{region}(r) * ERDData_T(r) * CO_2Factor(r)}{\sum\limits_{r \in resources} E\_Share_{region}(r) * ERDData_T(r)} \qquad (3)$$

If we look at the example February 13, 2013, from 10 am - 11 am in Baden-Württemberg: The overall energy production was 5.38 million kWh resulting in overall CO_2 emissions of 2.14 million kilogram. This leads to an average CO_2 factor for this time period of $397\frac{g}{kWh}$.

The detailed process is described in the pseudocode in Algorithm 1.

Algorithm 1. Algorithm 1: Transformation

Require: $ERDData, HistoricalData, CO_2Factors$
Ensure: CO_2 emission factor for each region of a country by energy sources

STEP 1
for $r \in resources$ do
  for $reg \in regions$ do
    $E_{total}[r] = E_{total}[r] + E\_Share[r][reg] * E_{total}[reg]$
  end for
end for

STEP 2
for $r \in resources$ do
  for $reg \in regions$ do
    if $E_{total}[r] > 0$ then
      $Eshare[r][reg] = \frac{E\_Share[r][reg]\% * overallAmount[reg]}{overallAmount[r]}$
    end if
  end for
end for

STEP 3
for $t \in EEXData$ do
  for $reg \in regions$ do
    for $r \in resources$ do
      $CO_2Emission[t][reg] \quad - \quad CO_2Emission[t][reg] + (E\_Share[reg][r] * ERDData[t][r]) * Co2Factor[r];$
      $energyProd[t][reg] \quad = \quad energyProd[t][reg] + (E\_Share[reg][r] * ERDData[t][r]);$
    end for
    $CO_2EmissionFactors[t][reg] = \frac{CO_2Emission[reg][t]}{energyProd[t][reg]}$
  end for
end for

3.2 Monitoring Phase: Calculation of Eco-efficiency

In this operational phase of our system the monitoring of the Cloud resources and the calculation of the eco-efficiency in being performed. As has been presented in Figure 1, the monitoring phase involves two separate processes: (a) the monitoring of the Cloud infrastructure, and (b) the calculation of eco-efficiency for each active VM resource of the private Cloud environment. As we mentioned before, we are examining the ecological footprint and efficiency of a VM from a computing system perspective, in the sense that we do not consider environmental, maintenance or installation costs. Those parameters are not directly related with the performance of the application that is being executed within the VM and therefore such static figures could be calculated and considered independently.

For the first process, the *Performance and Energy Monitor* interacts with the hypervisor of the Cloud infrastructure and collects the list of the active VMs. For each VM, our system monitors the status, the performance metrics (such as CPU, disk and memory utilization) as well as power consumption of the Cloud server that hosts those VMs. In this paper we will not discuss the methodology of energy metrics collection while in [10] we have presented more details about that issue. The methodology that we followed for the calculation of eco-efficiency in Clouds is based on a more low level approach from the ones we presented in section 2 to compare the useful work to the amount of carbon dioxide emitted.

The work performed by a computing system relies on three performance modules: CPU, memory and disk. The performance capacity of the CPU can be measured either by million instructions per second (MIPS) or in order to make it even more comparable by million whetstone instructions per second (MWIPS). In the same context, the memory capacity by the amount of allocated memory (measured in bytes) and the disk disk performance by the number of input and output operations per second (IOPS).

However, the absolute numbers are not comparable since they are calculated in different units. In addition, literature research as well as experimentation proved that the main factor that relates with the energy consumption of a computing system is CPU utilization [5] [6]. Hence, in this work we will consider as the useful work performed by a VM as the product of CPU utilization of a VM over the Cloud host, multiplied with the maximum capacity of operations of the same Cloud host. As a result, the formula for the real-time calculation of the eco-efficiency will be:

$$
\begin{aligned}
Eco-Efficiency &= \frac{MWIPS_{capacity,\ Node} * CPU_{util,VM}}{CO_2(g)} \\
&= \frac{MWIPS_{capacity,\ Node} * CPU_{util,VM}}{CO_2\ factor * PowerConsumption_{VM}}
\end{aligned}
\tag{4}
$$

In our implementation, the eco-efficiency is being calculated using the information deriving from the Cloud infrastructure (CPU utilization of every VM, power consumption of the VM), the CO_2 Emission Registry (CO_2 factor) and the static number of the MIPS capacity which is provided beforehand after having benchmarked the infrastructure. The unit of the eco-efficiency is defined as $\frac{billion\ whetstone\ instructions(BWI)}{CO_2(g) * s^2}$. The billion whetstone instructions represent the useful work that can be done per gram of carbon dioxide emitted. In the following the transformation steps to get to this unit will be shown. As it can be seen the result has to be multiplied by 3600 to transform the unit into the desired format.

$$\frac{1 \; MWIPS}{1 \; Watt * 1 \; \frac{CO_2(g)}{kWh}} = \frac{1 \; \frac{MWI}{s}}{1 \; Watt * 1 \; \frac{CO_2(g)}{1000 \; Watt}}$$

$$= \frac{1000 \; \frac{MWI}{s}}{1 \; CO_2(g) * h} = \frac{1000 * 3600 \; MWI}{1 \; CO_2(g) * s * s} = \frac{3600 \; BWI}{1 \; CO_2(g) * s^2} \tag{5}$$

In order to calculate the eco-efficiency of a VM as accurate as possible, we consider the CO_2 factor available in the CO_2 Emission Registry, that has the closest timestamp with the current time of monitoring. While the variation of the CO_2 emission factor has a certain pattern within a day for every region, we use the value for the same time period of the previous day. For example, if it 11:30 a.m., the eco-efficiency of a VM will be calculated considering the emission factor of the 11:00 to 12:00 a.m. of the previous day for that specific region. Hence, the eco-efficiency is calculated based not only on region but also time specific values for the CO_2 emission factors.

4   Proof of Concept

For the evaluation of the proposed system we performed a series of experiments using a private Cloud infrastructure located in Germany. The information sources that have been aggregated and transformed into the CO_2 Emission Registry are from the statistics platform *Statista* [3] through which we acquired data regarding the energy mix of each federated state in Germany, and from the European Energy Exchange Transparency Platform (EEX) which provided us the daily production and energy mix for every country.

By triggering the data aggregation and transformation service the CO_2 Emission Registry is being populated with information for every state in Germany, using the refresh interval that is available in the EEX dataset. Therefore, in Figure 3 we present the intra-day CO_2 emission factors for the German states based on the EEX dataset of 23rd of April, 2013. The significant variation between the values of the German states is a result of the type of the energy resources available in each state. For example, in Bavaria which the CO_2 emission factor is around 131gr/kWh, the 56% of the energy is produced by nuclear resources, while in Saxony where the CO_2 emission factors is around 1087gr/kWh, the 80% of the energy is produced by coal plants. In addition, we notice an important variation of the values within the day. This phenomenon is very interesting while could allow us to synchronize the VM scheduler with this distinctive pattern.

For the Cloud monitoring testing we instantiated one small VM instance (VM1) of 1vCPU and 1024MB memory and one big instance (VM2) of eight vCPUs and 2048 MB memory. The CPU capacity on the physical host (Cloud server) has been benchmarked through the UnixBench tool at 3560.0 MWIPS.

Assuming that within the VMs we execute some CPU intensive applications and considering also the fact that CPU is the driver of energy consumption

---

[3] http://www.statista.com/

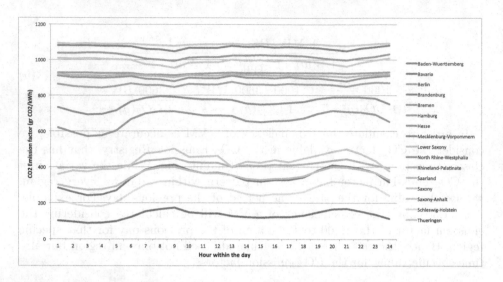

Fig. 3. Intraday CO_2 emission factors for all German states

into computing systems [25] [26] [27], in the following experimentation we have
monitored and analyzed the CPU workload in comparison with the eco-efficiency.

By applying variable CPU load to VM1 when it has being deployed in a private
Cloud in Berlin and the same load when it is deployed in Baden-Würtemberg
state, we collected the results shown in Figure 4. As expected, the eco-efficiency
of the VM in Berlin is worse than the one in Baden-Würtemberg, following the
pattern of the CPU utilization. The big spikes in the beginning and the end of the
chart are caused due to the small latency of the energy metric that is reported
(big and fast changes of CPU utilization cause increased energy consumption
that is reported with a small latency) and therefore the changes in the CPU
load are reported faster than the changes in energy metrics.

In Figure 5 we compare the ecological efficiency of the two different VMs, which
are deployed in the same infrastructure (Berlin). Even though they have different
specification and are subjected into different CPU load, the eco-efficiency level
during operation is very similar. The spikes in the chart are caused for the same
reason as mentioned before and the zero eco-efficiency is when a VM is inactive.

The relation of CPU utilization on a VM with it's eco-efficiency which is
depicted in Figure 6 brought some interesting results: as the CPU utilization
increases, the eco-efficiency increases as well. The threshold of 40% CPUutil
seems critical while above that the eco-efficiency seems stable at around 1.5
$\frac{billion\ whetstone\ instructions(BWI)}{CO_2(g) * s^2}$. That finding should be exploited by a VM resource allocation policy that would place VM resources into server trying to keep
the utilization above 40%.

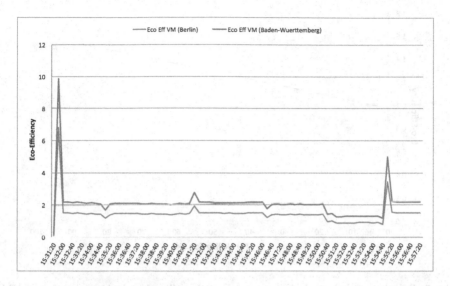

Fig. 4. Ecological efficiency comparison of a VM in Berlin and in Baden Württemberg state.

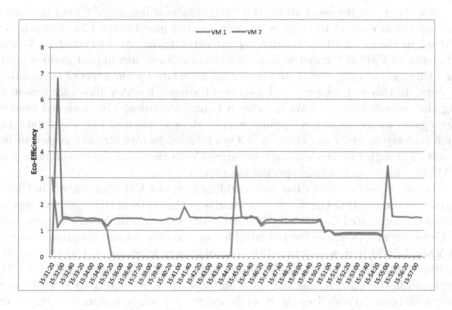

Fig. 5. Ecological efficiency comparison of two VMs in Berlin state.

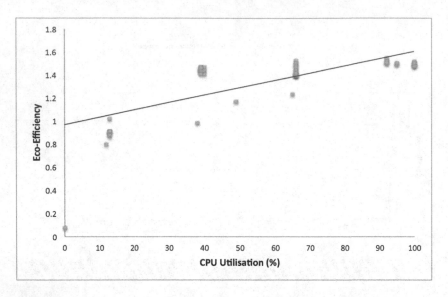

Fig. 6. Relation of ecological efficiency with CPU utilization during operation of VM1 in Berlin state

5 Conclusions

In this paper we discussed about the environmental impact of Cloud resources and specifically about techniques to measure and monitor the CO_2 footprint of virtual machines in Cloud computing infrastructures. We identified ecological efficiency of VMs as the metric that effectively defines such impact and we modeled this metric using energy and performance related parameters of the hosting system. To this end, we proposed a service framework which allows for monitoring the eco-efficiency of VMs in private Cloud scenarios. The designed system aggregates information from public energy data-stores and historical data for each country in order to define the CO_2 emission factors for each region of interest. Through this methodology we are able to calculate the eco-efficiency of VMs in a location and time specific manner.

The proposed framework has been validated against VM deployments in Cloud infrastructures within Germany. The results gathered from the executed experiments demonstrated the intra-day variation of CO_2 emission factors in each state of Germany and therefore the potential for an eco-efficient resource management of VMs. In addition, we captured the eco-efficiency levels for: (a) identical VMs deployed in different locations (Berlin, Karlsruhe), and (b) different size of VMs deployed in the same infrastructure. Finally, we noticed that a CPU utilization over 40% tends to stabilizes the eco-efficiency level, where bellow that threshold it drops significantly.

The targeted users of the toolkit are Cloud providers that can use services developed to monitor the eco-efficiency of their own infrastructure. They can use this information, for example, either for internal management or to offer new green services and therefore attract eco-concerned customers. Thus, the establishment of ecological efficiency as an important factor of ICT services and Cloud resources does not only have an environmental impact but also innovative market potentials.

As future steps of this research we are aiming at extending the eco-efficiency calculation formula by considering also the activity of the memory and disk resources when estimating the performed work of a VM. Contemporary production servers [4] that have been developed with the last generation CPU cores have significantly improved the power consumption and therefore resources like memory, network and disk must be considered as well. In addition, we would like to extend the data model and methodology of calculating the CO_2 Factors taking into account the energy providers too. Even if the energy resources of a region are the ones that the power providers are consuming, there can be significant variations in the energy mix that each company uses and therefore that could affect eco-footprint of the consumers. Finally, having completed with this work an analysis of the energy and ecological efficiency at the level of the VM, we now will focus our efforts towards a holistic ecological modeling of Cloud resources considering the cooling costs, environmental parameters and migration capabilities.

References

1. Gartner: Gartner Report for ICT Industry (2009),
   http://www.gartner.com/it/page.jsp?id=503867
2. Dirks, S., Gurdgiev, C.: The emergence of the eco-efficient economy. Technical report, IBM (2010)
3. Berl, A., Gelenbe, E., Di Girolamo, M., Giuliani, G., De Meer, H., Dang, M.Q., Pentikousis, K.: Energy-efficient cloud computing. The Computer Journal 53(7), 1045–1051 (2010)
4. Greenberg, A., Hamilton, J., Maltz, D.A., Patel, P.: The cost of a cloud: Research problems in data center networks. SIGCOMM Comput. Commun. Rev. 39(1), 68–73 (2008)
5. Chen, Q., Grosso, P., Veldt, K.V.D., Laat, C.D., Hofman, R., Bal, H.: Profiling Energy Consumption of VMs for Green Cloud Computing. In: 2011 IEEE Ninth International Conference on Dependable, Autonomic and Secure Computing, pp. 768–775 (December 2011)
6. Kansal, A., Zhao, F., Bhattacharya, A.A.: Virtual Machine Power Metering and Provisioning. In: Proceedings of the 1st ACM Symposium on Cloud Computing, pp. 39–50 (2010)
7. Stoess, J., Lang, C., Bellosa, F.: Energy Management for Hypervisor-Based Virtual Machines (2007)

---

[4] e.g. http://www.supermicro.com/products/system/1U/

8. Husain Bohra, A.E., Chaudhary, V.: VMeter: Power modelling for virtualized clouds. In: 2010 IEEE International Symposium on Parallel & Distributed Processing, Workshops and Phd Forum (IPDPSW), pp. 1–8 (April 2010)
9. Basmadjian, R., Ali, N., Niedermeier, F., de Meer, H., Giuliani, G.: A methodology to predict the power consumption of servers in data centres. In: Proceedings of the 2nd International Conference on Energy-Efficient Computing and Networking, e-Energy 2011, pp. 1–10. ACM, New York (2011)
10. Katsaros, G., Subirats, J., Fitó, J.O., Guitart, J., Gilet, P., Espling, D.: A service framework for energy-aware monitoring and VM management in Clouds. Future Generation Computer Systems (December 2012)
11. Vandierendonck, H., De Bosschere, K.: Many benchmarks stress the same bottlenecks. In: Workshop on Computer Architecture Evaluation Using Commercial Workloads, pp. 57–64 (2004)
12. Phansalkar, A., Joshi, A., Eeckhout, L., John, L.: Measuring program similarity: Experiments with SPEC CPU benchmark suites. In: 2005 IEEE International Symposium on Performance Analysis of Systems and Software, pp. 10–20 (2005)
13. Quang-Hung, N., Nien, P.D., Nam, N.H., Huynh Tuong, N., Thoai, N.: A genetic algorithm for power-aware virtual machine allocation in private cloud. In: Mustofa, K., Neuhold, E.J., Tjoa, A.M., Weippl, E., You, I. (eds.) ICT-EurAsia 2013. LNCS, vol. 7804, pp. 183–191. Springer, Heidelberg (2013)
14. Beloglazov, A., Abawajy, J., Buyya, R.: Energy-aware resource allocation heuristics for efficient management of data centers for Cloud computing. Future Generation Computer Systems 28(5), 755–768 (2012)
15. Hsu, C.H., Chen, S.C., Lee, C.C., Chang, H.Y., Lai, K.C., Li, K.C., Rong, C.: Energy-Aware Task Consolidation Technique for Cloud Computing. In: CLOUD-COM 2011: Proceedings of the 2011 IEEE Third International Conference on Cloud Computing Technology and Science. IEEE Computer Society (November 2011)
16. Lin, C., Liu, P., Wu, J.: Energy-efficient virtual machine provision algorithms for cloud systems, 81–88 (2011)
17. Google: Google Green Products (March 2013),
    http://www.google.com/green/bigpicture
18. Curry, E., Hasan, S., White, M., Melvin, H.: An Environmental Chargeback for Data Center and Cloud Computing Consumers (April 2012)
19. Moghaddam, F., Cheriet, M., Nguyen, K.K.: Low carbon virtual private clouds. In: 2011 IEEE International Conference on Cloud Computing (CLOUD), pp. 259–266 (2011)
20. Gao, P.X., Curtis, A.R., Wong, B., Keshav, S.: It's not easy being green. In: Proceedings of the ACM SIGCOMM 2012 Conference on Applications, Technologies, Architectures, and Protocols for Computer Communication, SIGCOMM 2012, pp. 211–222. ACM, New York (2012)
21. Garg, S.K., Yeo, C.S., Buyya, R.: Green cloud framework for improving carbon efficiency of clouds. In: Jeannot, E., Namyst, R., Roman, J. (eds.) Euro-Par 2011, Part I. LNCS, vol. 6852, pp. 491–502. Springer, Heidelberg (2011)
22. Greenpeace: Campain Report, How Clean is Your Cloud (2012),
    http://www.greenpeace.org/international/en/publications/
    Campaign-reports/Climate-Reports/How-Clean-is-Your-Cloud/
23. Wagner, H.J., Koch, M., Burkhardt, J., Böckmann, T., Feck, N., Kruse, P.: CO 2 -Emissionen der Stromerzeugung. BWK 59(10), 44–52 (2007)

24. Lübbert, D.: CO 2 -Bilanzen verschiedener Energieträger im Vergleich. Technical report (2007)
25. Zhang, Z., Fu, S.: Profiling and analysis of power consumption for virtualized systems and applications. In: 2010 IEEE 29th International Performance Computing and Communications Conference (IPCCC), pp. 329–330 (2010)
26. Viswanathan, H., Lee, E.K., Rodero, I., Pompili, D., Parashar, M., Gamell, M.: Energy-aware application-centric vm allocation for hpc workloads. In: 2011 IEEE International Symposium on Parallel and Distributed Processing Workshops and Phd Forum (IPDPSW), pp. 890–897 (2011)
27. Chen, Q., Grosso, P., van der Veldt, K., de Laat, C., Hofman, R., Bal, H.: Profiling energy consumption of vms for green cloud computing. In: 2011 IEEE Ninth International Conference on Dependable, Autonomic and Secure Computing (DASC), pp. 768–775 (2011)

Cost Evaluation of Migrating a Computation Intensive Problem from Clusters to Cloud

Sergio Hernández, Javier Fabra, Pedro Álvarez, and Joaquín Ezpeleta

Aragón Institute of Engineering Research (I3A)
Department of Computer Science and Systems Engineering
University of Zaragoza, Spain
{shernandez,jfabra,alvaper,ezpeleta}@unizar.es

Abstract. Cloud has emerged as an alternative to clusters and grids. Its adoption as an execution environment capable of supporting the high requirements of scientific computations is still an open question. In a previous work, the authors conducted successfully a practical experience of taking advantage of clusters and grids to solve a semantic annotation problem in 178 days. In this work, the authors analyse the cost of solving that problem and compare it with the cost of solving it in a pure Cloud scenario. For this last, a detailed cost estimation is conducted according to the data extracted from the actual execution of a reduced dataset on Amazon EC2. As a result, the suitability of using Cloud-based solutions to solve large and complex scientific problems is discussed.

Keywords: Computing Resource Management, Grid and Cloud Computing, Cloud Cost Estimation and Analysis, Large-scale Semantic Annotation.

1 Introduction

Grids and clusters have been, until recently, the way of dealing with large scale application execution. This approach may not be economically viable when the needs for such executions are rather spurious: acquiring and maintaining grids and clusters is expensive. Cloud computing emerges as a solution to that problem [1–3]. There are different definitions for the Cloud computing term, depending on which aspect one focuses on. Let us adopt the one proposed in [2] that conforms the concept of Infrastructure as a Service (IaaS): "A large-scale distributed computing paradigm that is driven by economies of scale, in which a pool of abstracted, virtualized, dynamically-scalable, managed computing power, storage, platforms, and services are delivered on demand to external customers over the Internet". Therefore, Cloud avoids the need of constantly maintaining a pool of computing resources, allowing acquiring and releasing them as the needs appear and just paying for their use, in a pay-as-you-go way. This makes Cloud an ideal execution environment to increase the computational power of clusters and grids when demand peeks appears and to carry out large scale scientific experiments.

J. Altmann, K. Vanmechelen, and O.F. Rana (Eds.): GECON 2013, LNCS 8193, pp. 90–105, 2013.
© Springer International Publishing Switzerland 2013

In a previous work, we conducted the problem of semantically annotating a Universia [4] repository composed of more than 15 million of educational resources [5]. The annotation process required both computing complex structures (semantic graphs) as well as interacting with external resources (DBpedia [6]), becoming a very expensive task in computational terms. To solve this, the process was programmed to be executed over a resource management framework able to integrate several heterogeneous computing resources. Three cluster infrastructures were used to solve the problem in about 178 days.

In this paper, we evaluate the economic cost of executing the same process using the Amazon Elastic Compute Cloud (Amazon EC2) [7] in the same time (178 days). For that purpose, Cloud-related costs are experimentally measured, analysed, and compared to the ones of the previous approach. The main goal of this work is to evaluate if Cloud computing can be an alternative environment to deploy the management framework and solve the annotation process.

The remainder of the paper is organized as follows. Section 2 presents the related work. Section 3 describes the semantic annotation problem and the solution approach. Section 4 analyses the cost of the annotation process using clusters and grids. Section 5 depicts an alternative Cloud-based deployment to solve the problem. Section 6 analyses the cost of the Cloud approach. Finally, Section 7 concludes the paper with a discussion of the suitability of Cloud to solve scientific problems.

2 Related Work

The current availability of Cloud computing has made the discussion about its integration with clusters and grids to become a hot topic. All the three approaches have common elements and also important differences. [2] compares them from different points of view, describing the essential characteristics of each approach. Concentrating on the same topic, [3] describes the main existing projects related to the three paradigms, as well as the challenges they must face.

Another relevant topic is the integration of Cloud-based resources with local clusters or grids. [8] integrates Cloud resources into a private grid, by extending the Askalon enactment engine to consider Cloud resources. By means of some experimental executions of real-world applications, the authors show the interest and viability of adding external Cloud-based resources to improve computing capabilities of grids. [9] investigates whether the use of Cloud computing infrastructures can provide with some benefits when added to local computing ones. For that, they evaluate six different scheduling strategies with the aim of finding a good balance between performance and usage costs. Studying the viability of Amazon S3 as the storage option for large scale science projects, from the performance, cost, and availability points of view is the objective of [10]. The study also suggests some recommendations that any storage service for the scientific community should provide. The conclusion is that, despite of Amazon S3 being successful for many usual applications, its security is not adequate for supporting complex collaborative scenarios, which are usual in scientific environments.

However, the use of Cloud resources can impact the performance of the system. [11] studies how virtualization overhead impacts on performance in High Performance Computing (HPC). The study is based on the use of standard benchmarks for HPC applications, being the main conclusion that virtualization can have, at least, a 60% performance penalty. [12] compares the performance of EC2's Cluster Compute instances (the Amazon's virtual HPC infrastructure) and NASA's Pleiades supercomputer when executing a wide range set of benchmarking applications. As a result, the authors conclude that the HPC offerings of Amazon cannot currently compete with specific HPC systems, particularly for tightly coupled applications where communication performance is important. [13] examines the performance of existing Cloud computing infrastructures, providing with a mechanism for their quantitative evaluation. By means of real executions of up to eight HPC applications, authors report and conclude that Amazon EC2 is six times slower than a Linux cluster and up to twenty times slower than a modern HPC system.

Finally, the cost of Cloud and Grid infrastructures has been analysed, modelled and compared by several authors. On the one hand, [14–16] focus on comparing the cost of Grid and Cloud infrastructures. In [14], the authors analyse the total cost of owning a computational Grid and they estimate the cost of two real life Grids. The analysis shows that the cost per processor and hour is highly influenced by the resource load. They also analyse the cost of commercial Clouds and they identify potential cost savings if the private Grid is underutilised. [15] analyses the financial suitability of Cloud for enterprises by comparing its cost to that of acquiring in-house resources. They conclude that the cost-effectiveness of the Cloud depends on the usage duration and intensity. In [16], the monetary cost-benefits of using Cloud computing for scientific applications are analysed by comparing Amazon EC2 and several BOINC-based projects. They determine that Clouds are advantageous for small projects with low bandwidth requirements whereas they are expensive for large projects. They also demonstrate that hybrid approaches can save between 40-95% depending on resource usage.

On the other hand, [17–19] focus on modelling the cost of hybrid approaches to assist in the decision process of migrating applications to Cloud. In [17], a service able to estimate the cost of migrating scientific applications to Clouds is presented. The service monitors the application performance, data transfers and data storages, and it uses this information to estimate the cost of several hybrid deployments. Thus, the service allows users to compare the cost of different deployments in order to select what part of a workflow should be executed in a Cloud to minimize the cost. [18] explores the benefit of migrating enterprise applications to Clouds. The authors build a model that takes into account both performance and cost implications of Cloud migration to find the best hybrid deployment. Through actual evaluations they show the importance of planning which components should be migrated to Cloud in order to take advantage of the potential cost savings of Clouds. In [19], the authors propose a comprehensive cost model for hybrid Clouds. The authors review and categorize the cost factors that a large enterprise must take into account to migrate some of its services to a Cloud environment. The cost model focuses on hybrid Clouds and it can be used to evaluate the economic impact of different configurations. Its main contribution is a model that includes all possible cost factors allowing to obtain a more accurate cost estimation improving the decision making.

3 Problem Description and Solution Approach

The Universia [4] repository is composed of a huge collection of educational resources in different languages and domains, totalling more than 15 million academic resources. These resources must be semantically annotated in order to facilitate the access to its contents. The ADEGA algorithm is used for this process [5]. The ADEGA algorithm consists of first identifying a set of relevant terms (or keywords) of each resource and, then, annotating each term by means of a Resource Description Framework (RDF) graph created from those instances of the DBpedia that were relevant in the resource domain. The resulting RDF graphs (a graph for each specific term) are then used to classify the considered educational resources facilitating the search and retrieval of information.

For each academic resource, around 10 terms are identified as relevant. Thus, the annotation process involves the execution of about 150 million computational tasks resulting in several CPU-years. The extremely high computational cost of annotating all resources stored in the repository was achieved by means of the use of a framework for the flexible deployment and execution of scientific workflows in heterogeneous clusters, grids, and Clouds [20].

Figure 1 depicts the general overview for the deployment of the annotation process using this framework. As shown, the integration model is based on a *message bus*. More specifically, the cornerstone of the proposal is DRLinda, a bus implementation inspired by the Linda coordination model [21]. The architectural design of the framework relies on the integration of two different types of components. On the one hand, management components are related to the functionality and capabilities of the framework. Some important components are the Meta-Scheduler to select a target computing infrastructure for each job, the Fault Management component to handle job failures, or the Data Movement component to move data among infrastructures in a transparent manner. On the other hand, mediation components encapsulate the heterogeneity of the computing resources providing a transparent interface to the underlying set of middleware systems that manage the infrastructures. A more detailed overview of the framework design and its components can be found in [20, 22].

For the annotation process, we developed a workflow that manages job submission and result retrieval. Thus, jobs are sent to the framework via the message bus. Next, the Meta-Scheduler retrieves each job, selects the target computing infrastructure where the job will be executed and writes a new message with that decision in the bus. The appropriate Mediator retrieves that message, submits the job to the computing infrastructure and collects the results when the job finishes. Additionally, it may request the Data Movement component to retrieve the input data from the specified Data Storage and store the output data afterwards. On the one hand, if the job has ended successfully, the Mediator puts a result message in the bus so that the annotation workflow can read it. On the other hand, if the job has failed, the Mediator writes an error message and the Fault Management component retrieves it and handles the failure taking the appropriate corrective action.

For the execution environment, three computing infrastructures were used in the problem resolution: the HERMES cluster hosted by the Aragón Institute of Engineering Research (I3A, http://i3a.unizar.es/) and two research and production grids hosted by the Institute for Biocomputation and Physics of Complex Systems (BIFI, http://bifi.es/en/), namely AraGrid (http://www.aragrid.es/) and PireGrid (http://www.piregrid.eu/). Furthermore, Amazon EC2 [7] was used to execute some jobs that suffered a lot of failures in the previous infrastructures, as we will depict in Section 4. Integrating these resources, the annotation of the 15 million of academic resources was solved in 178 days.

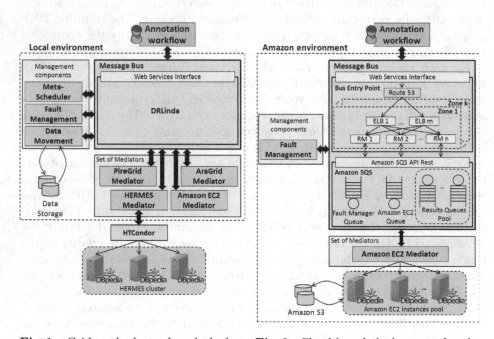

Fig. 1. Grid and cluster-based deployment for the semantic annotation process with detail of HERMES.

Fig. 2. Cloud-based deployment for the semantic annotation process on Amazon.

4   Economic Cost of the Grid-Based Implementation

Let us now describe the cost of solving the problem using the infrastructures at our disposal: HERMES, AraGrid, and PireGrid. The main difference compared to other analysis available in the literature [15, 14] is that this study is carried out from an user point of view. The prices of using these infrastructures were mainly based on a model of pay per CPU hour: €0.012 pay-per-CPU-hour in HERMES, and €0.03 in AraGrid and PireGrid. In order to establish these rates, the following internal costs had been considered by Grid-resource providers: software and hardware maintenance and updating, energy consumption, staff cost, data communications, resource usage and resource economic redemption. Additionally, users also had to pay for data storage into HERMES resources: €0.015 per GB-month of data stored. Data storage in AraGrid and PireGrid is included in the previous fee.

Top of Table 1 describes the cost of the first term computation: the terms are submitted to the infrastructures. As a result, some of them terminate properly, while others fail. Since we do not have data to estimate at which point in the processing a term fails, we assume that terms consume CPU time as if they will succeed. The cost is composed of:

Cost of Computation: The columns in the table correspond, respectively, to the cluster, the number of terms submitted to the cluster, the mean execution time for each term, the CPU cost in euros per hour, the total cost of processing all the submitted terms in euros, and the failure rate (which will require a later processing, as described in the following, increasing the real cost).

Cost of Data Storage: Only the HERMES cluster appears since the CPU consumption and data storage (DBpedia in each node and input/output data) are billed in a separated way, while in the case of AraGrid and PireGrid the storage is not considered in the pricing policy.

As shown in the last column, there is an important number of faults, which have to be solved (our objective is to annotate every term). These faults appear due to different reasons: hardware failures, software malfunction, middleware problems, etc. [22]. For fault management, a hierarchical three phases recovery policy is applied, whose real costs are shown in the second, third and fourth parts of Table 1, respectively. The recovery process is as follows. Each faulty term is first resubmitted to the same infrastructure (First Fault Handling Policy); if it fails again, the term is submitted to AraGrid (Second Fault Handling Policy), which in our initial experiments shown to be the most reliable computing infrastructure; if the term still fails, it is then sent to Amazon EC2 (Third Fault Handling Policy). This way, we have succeeded in processing the whole set of terms. For the Third Fault Handling policy we chose Amazon *m1.medium* instances, deployed in Ireland. Some experiments convinced us that this was a very appropriate configuration [5].

In general terms, processing $149,427,907$ terms costed €$36,446.02$, being €0.000243904 the mean cost per term. Let us now concentrate on the following question: How much cost every term initially submitted to HERMES, AraGrid and PireGrid? For the set of terms submitted to a computing infrastructure, we must consider the cost of the initial execution, plus the cost of the First Fault Handling Policy (for the percentage of faulty terms) and plus the cost of the

Table 1. Cost of solving the annotation problem

Executing the application				32,163,19	euros
Cost of Computation				31,791.74	euros
Execution environment	Terms processed	Exec. time sec/term.	CPU Price euros/h	Cost euros	% Faults
HERMES	35,274,419	71.18	0.012	8,369.44	19.87
AraGrid	74,483,721	23.84	0.03	14,797.43	2.98
PireGrid	39,669,767	26.09	0.03	8,624.87	3.45
Cost of Data Storage				371.45	euros
Execution environment	GB of data stored	Months	Euros per GB-month	Cost euros	
HERMES - DBpedia	2,862.58	5.93	0.015	254.77	
HERMES - I/O Data	7,778.69	1.00	0.015	116.68	

First Fault Handling Policy				2489.49	euros
Cost of Computation				2401.47	euros
Execution environment	Terms processed	Exec. time sec/term.	CPU Price euros/h	Cost euros	% Faults
HERMES	7,009,000	71.18	0.012	1663.00	45.00
AraGrid	2,219,600	23.84	0.03	440.96	33.72
PireGrid	1,368,400	26.09	0.03	297.51	34.99
Cost of Data Storage				88.02	euros
Execution environment	GB of data stored	Months	Euros per GB-month	Cost euros	
HERMES - DBPedia	2,862.58	1.51	0.015	64.84	
HERMES - I/O Data	1,545.61	1.00	0.015	23.18	

Second Fault Handling Policy				870.40	euros
Cost of Computation					
Execution environment	Terms processed	Exec. time sec/term.	CPU Price euros/h	Cost euros	% Faults
AraGrid	4,381,200	23.84	0.03	870.40	11.28

Third Fault Handling Policy				922.94	euros
Amazon EC2 - Cost of Computation					
Execution environment	Terms processed	Exec. time sec/term.	CPU Price euros/h	Cost euros	% Faults
EC2 (4 m1.medium)	494,412	61.55	0.09	786.95	0
Amazon EBS - Cost of Data Storage					
Execution environment	GB of data stored	Months	Euros per GB-month	Cost euros	
EC2 (4 m1.medium)	280	5.93	0.0776	128.89	
Amazon EBS - Cost of I/O Requests					
Execution environment	Terms processed	I/O per term	Euros per millon of I/O	Cost euros	
EC2 (4 m1.medium)	494,412	185.20	0.0776	7.10	

Second and Third Fault Handling (in a proportional way according to the number of faulty terms provided to these policies). Considering all these elements, the average processing cost per term in HERMES, AraGrid and PireGrid was €0.000334036, €0.000208700 and €0.000229857, respectively.

As it can be seen in the corresponding part of the table, the First Fault Handling Policy is not efficient (in all the three cases, more than a third of the terms failed a second time), which means that this intermediate step could be avoided, directly jumping to the Second Fault Handling Policy.

5   A Cloud-Based Deployment of the Annotation Process

We have decided to migrate the annotation process to the Amazon Cloud [7] due to the benefits described below. Cloud elasticity allows us to automatically vary the number of resources. Thus, the framework computational power can be increased to meet hard deadlines, deal with load peaks and provide good Quality of Service. In the same way, replication techniques can be easily incorporated to improve the framework performance and reliability. Also, decoupling the computing and storage resources is useful to recover from failures in virtual machines. Another key advantage is the increase in the framework availability (Amazon SLA guarantees a 99.95% availability), a must on a long-time experiment. Finally, Amazon provides a wide range of highly scalable and reliable services that can be used to enhance the framework capabilities.

For the deployment, some framework components have simply been hosted in an Amazon virtual instance while others have been modified in order to take advantage of some Amazon services and features. Figure 2 depicts the Cloud-based deployment. As depicted in the top of the figure, the user submits the annotation jobs via the message bus using the same annotation workflow as in the previous deployment. These jobs will be executed in the Amazon EC2 instance pool located at the bottom.

The message bus has been completely redesigned. The Cloud version consists of two decoupled components: the Bus Entry Point (BEP), which implements the bus interface, and the Amazon Simple Queue Service (Amazon SQS), which effectively implements the message bus. On the one hand, the BEP has been designed to be highly available, reliable and scalable by using different Amazon services. Amazon Route 53 is used as DNS Server to redirect requests to alive Elastic Load Balancers (ELBs) placed in different availability zones. The ELBs route the requests to the Request Managers (RMs), hosted by Amazon EC2 instances, that handle each request and interact with Amazon SQS to store and retrieve messages. On the other hand, Amazon SQS has been used for the implementation due to its high availability, reliability and scalability. Each framework component and each job submitted has an associated queue where messages addressed to them are placed. Thus, clients write messages to the Mediator queue of the infrastructure where the job will be executed or in the Meta-Scheduler queue if the job does not have a target infrastructure and read the job results from the appropriate results queue. Meanwhile, framework components retrieve messages from its associated queue and write the response messages to the right queue. In any case, the process is managed by the RMs, being transparent to users. More details on the design and operation of the message bus can be found in [23].

Therefore, messages submitted by users, are retrieved by the Amazon EC2 Mediator that acts as the Cloud Broker and manages the jobs execution in the resource pool. The Mediator is deployed using a virtual instance and it has been modified to acquire the resource pool at the beginning rather than on-demand. The same approach has been used to host the Fault Management component responsible of applying the appropriate corrective action when a job fails.

Finally, each virtual instance forming the computing resource pool uses its own local DBpedia database to improve the application performance and to avoid communication delays. Besides, the application has been slightly modified to download/upload input/output data using the specified location in the job description (Amazon S3 is used for this purpose).

6   Deployment on Amazon Services: A Cost Estimation

Let us now discuss about the cost of the Cloud-based deployment. First, we present the method we followed for selecting the most appropriate Amazon instance type for the execution environment. Then, we detail the cost estimation of applying the Cloud-based deployment presented in Section 5 to the semantic annotation problem. The deployment is proposed with the aim of solving the problem in the same time as described in Section 4: 178 days.

6.1   Instance Type Selection

To select the most appropriate machine instance from the wide range offered by Amazon, we have experimentally computed the mean time required to annotate a term using different Amazon instance types. Based on these results, we have chosen the instance type that provides the best performance/cost ratio. Then, we have estimated the number of resources required to solve the problem meeting the deadline of 178 days.

In [23], we concluded that the US West (Oregon) Amazon region is the best location to deploy the framework and the computing instances also should be deployed in the same region. Then, a reduced collection of terms has been executed for a week using different instances in that region. The same Amazon Machine Image (AMI) has been used, independently of the instance type. For each instance, as many parallel tasks as the number of processors provided by the machine instance have been executed. Table 2 summarizes for each instance type its number of processors, its cost per hour, the average execution time observed in the experiments (including data movement and other management delays) and the number of terms that can be annotated per euro.

Results depict that the performance/cost ratio improves when using more powerful instances until a limit is reached. They also show that *m1.xlarge* instances are the best choice in terms of performance/cost ratio. Finally, based on

Table 2. Evaluation of the time required to annotate a term using different Amazon EC2 instances

Instance type	m1.small	m1.medium	m1.large	m1.xlarge	m3.xlarge	m3.2xlarge
Number of cores	1	1	2	4	4	8
Price (€/hour)	0.04655	0.0931	0.1862	0.3724	0.3879	0.7758
Execution time (sec/term)	152.38	59.03	41.39	38.97	38.04	37.69
Terms per €	507.52	655.06	934.01	992.25	975.89	984.96

the observed execution time, we estimate that a pool of 95 *m1.xlarge* instances will be necessary to meet the objective of solving the problem in 178 days.

6.2   Comprehensive Cost Analysis

Now, we analyse the cost of the Cloud-based deployment. In addition to the 95 *m1.xlarge* instances forming the computing resource pool, one *m1.xlarge* instance is used to host the Amazon EC2 Mediator since it has to manage thousands of job requests and one *m1.medium* instance is used to host the Fault Manager since that component is not used so frequently. Also, the Bus Entry Point is deployed in a single availability zone using two Elastic Load Balancers and five Request Managers hosted in *m1.micro* instances because this configuration is reliable and scalable enough, providing with a good performance [23].

Cost of Executing the Annotation Application. Table 3 summarizes the cost of executing the semantic application on Amazon. Let us analyse the cost of each Amazon service involved.

Amazon Elastic Compute Cloud (Amazon EC2). 149,427,907 terms must be annotated using 95 *m1.xlarge* instances. The mean time to compute a term is 38.97 seconds, while CPU price is 0.093 €/hour. Therefore, the total cost will be €150,491.04. For this estimation, we have considered that there are no failures because in our preliminary experiments every term was annotated successfully and we have no information on the expected failure rate.

Amazon Elastic Block Storage (Amazon EBS). Every computing instance is attached to an Elastic Block Store (EBS) of 70 GB to store the database and data to be annotated. Amazon bills depending on the provisioned storage and the number of input/output requests performed. On the one hand, 6,650 GB-month (considering the 95 instances) are provisioned for 5.93 months with a cost of €3,059.33. On the other hand, an average of 185.2 requests are performed to calculate each term (this value has been extracted from the experiments described in the previous section) generating a cost of €2,146.95. Therefore, the total EBS-related cost amounts to €5,200.91.

Amazon Simple Storage Service (Amazon S3). Amazon bills depending on the number of requests performed and the amount of data stored. On the one hand, each job gets the input data (terms to annotate and associated contexts) at the beginning of the experiment and store the output data (in one single compressed file) at the end. Also, the input data is deleted but these requests are free of charge. Thus, the cost of the API requests is €57.37: €51.26 for GET requests and €6.11 for PUT requests. On the other hand, 1, 413.51 GB are stored in Amazon S3 between input and output data. Input data is deleted when terms are processed and output data is gradually generated and retrieved, therefore, we estimate that the cost is equivalent to considered 1 month storing all data. Therefore, the cost of storing I/O Data in Amazon S3 is €104.18. As summary, the Amazon S3 cost will be €161.55.

Briefly, the total cost of executing the application on Amazon is €155, 858.87. The Amazon EC2 service represents a 96.56% of the total cost, whereas the Amazon EBS represents the 3.34% and the Amazon S3 represents the remaining 0.1%. Also, the mean cost per term is €0.00104304.

Table 3. Cost estimation of executing the application on Amazon

Executing the application				155858.87	euros
Amazon EC2 - Cost of Computation					
Execution environment	Terms processed	Exec. time sec/term.	CPU Price euros/h	Cost euros	% Faults
EC2 (95 m1.xlarge)	149,427,907	38.97	0.09304	150,491.04	0.00
Amazon EBS - Cost of Data Storage					
Execution environment	GB of data stored	Months	Euros per GB-month	Cost euros	
EC2 (95 m1.xlarge)	6,650	5.93	0.0776	3,059.33	
Amazon EBS - Cost of I/O Requests					
Execution environment	Terms processed	I/O per term	Euros per millon of I/O	Cost euros	
EC2 (95 m1.xlarge)	149,427,907	185.20	0.0776	2,146.95	
Amazon S3 - Cost of Data Storage				104.18	euros
Execution environment	GB of data stored	Months	Euros per GB-month	Cost euros	
S3 (Input Data)	618.88	1.00	0.0737	45.61	
S3 (Output Data)	794.63	1.00	0.0737	58.57	
Amazon S3 - Cost of Data Requests				57.37	euros
Execution environment	Number of requests	Euros per 10,000 requests	Euros per 1,000 requests	Cost euros	
S3 (GET Requests)	165,178,886	0.0031	-	51.26	
S3 (PUT Requests)	1,575,098	-	0.0039	6.11	

Cost of Deploying the Framework on the Amazon Cloud. Table 4 summarizes the cost of deploying the framework on Amazon. Let us describe each one of the used Amazon services and their impact on the deployment cost:

Amazon Elastic Compute Cloud (Amazon EC2). The total cost of the virtual instances used in the deployment is €2, 318.73: €331.24 correspond to the Request Managers, €397.5 to the Fault Manager and €1, 590 to the Amazon EC2 Mediator.

Table 4. Cost estimation of deploying the framework on Amazon

Framework				2,598.59	euros
Amazon EC2 - Cost of Computation				2,318.73	euros
Execution environment	Number of resources	Months	Price euros/h	Cost euros	
EC2 (5 m1.micro)	5	5.93	0.0155	331.24	
EC2 (1 m1.medium)	1	5.93	0.0931	397.50	
EC2 (1 m1.xlarge)	1	5.93	0.3724	1590.00	
Amazon EBS - Cost of Data Storage				64.40	euros
Execution environment	GB of data stored	Months	Euros per GB-month	Cost euros	
EC2 (5 m1.micro)	40	5.93	0.0776	18.40	
EC2 (1 m1.medium)	50	5.93	0.0776	23.00	
EC2 (1 m1.xlarge)	50	5.93	0.0776	23.00	
Amazon EBS - Cost of I/O Requests				21.09	euros
Execution environment	Average I/O per second	Months	Euros per millon of I/O	Cost euros	
EC2 (5 m1.micro)	3.97	5.93	0.0776	4.73	
EC2 (1 m1.medium)	4.18	5.93	0.0776	4.98	
EC2 (1 m1.xlarge)	9.54	5.93	0.0776	11.38	
Amazon Simple Queue Service				7.33	euros
	Jobs executed	Requests per job	Euros per millon of I/O	Cost euros	
Requests	1,575,098	12	0.3879	7.33	
Amazon Elastic Load Balancer				172.81	euros
	Number of resources	Months	Price euros/h	Cost euros	
Computing	2	5.93	0.0194	165.66	
	Total messages	Total GB	Euros per GB	Cost euros	
Data Transfer	18,901,176	1,153.64	0.0062	7.15	
Amazon Route 53				14.23	euros
	Hosted domains	Months	Euros per month	Cost euros	
DNS Domain	1	5.93	0.3879	1.20	
	Number of Load Balancers	Months	Euros per month	Cost euros	
DNS Failover	2	5.93	0.3879	4.60	
	Total requests	Millions of requests	Euros per million requests	Cost euros	
DNS Requests	18,901,176	18.90	0.3879	7.33	

Amazon Elastic Block Storage (Amazon EBS). We have determined that 8 GB are attached to the Request Manager instances and 50 GB to the Fault Manager and Amazon EC2 Mediator instances. Furthermore, considering the average number of input/output operations per second obtained from the preliminary experiments, the total storage-related estimated cost is €85.49: €64.40 correspond to the provisioned storage and €21.09 to the I/O requests.

Amazon Simple Queue Service (Amazon SQS). The queueing service bills for the number of API requests and data transfer. However, data transfer cost is €0 since the exchange stays inside the same Amazon region. Regarding the number of API requests, each job involves writing and reading a submission message in the Mediator queue and writing and reading a results message in the right results queue. The write operation involves 2 API requests (get queue URL and send message) while the read operation involves 3 API requests (get queue URL, read message, and delete message). Furthermore, every job involves two additional requests (create and delete the results queue). Therefore, 12 requests per job are performed. As $1,575,098$ jobs must be executed and Amazon bills €0.3879 per each million of requests, the total cost is €7.33.

Amazon Elastic Load Balancer (Amazon ELB). Amazon bills according to the number of hours each ELB is active and the amount of data processed by the service. On the one hand, the computational cost is €165.66. On the other hand, the total number of requests handled by the Load Balancers matches the number of API Requests in the Amazon SQS. In order to calculate the amount of data processed, we assume a worst case scenario where the size of each request is 64 KB (the maximum size of message supported by Amazon SQS). Thus, the cost of data processed is €7.15 and the total cost will be €172.81.

Amazon Route 53. The DNS Service involves the cost corresponding to the zone where the framework is hosted, the DNS Failover mechanism over 2 Elastic Load Balancers (this mechanism checks the health of the Load Balancer and routes requests to the alive ones) and the number of DNS queries. The first two are fixed costs whereas the third one depends on the number of requests performed, being equal to the number of messages moving through the ELBs (we assume that the DNS information is not cached in any case). The total estimated cost of the Amazon Route 53 service amounts to €14.23.

Therefore, the total cost of deploying the framework on Amazon is €2,598.59. Most of this cost (89.23%) is due to the virtual machines hosting the framework components and the Bus Entry Point. The two Elastic Load Balancers represent a 6.38%. Finally, the Amazon EBS, SQS and Route 53 services together with the data processed by the Load Balancers represent the remaining 4.39%.

7   Conclusions and Future Work

In summary, the cost of solving the annotation problem with the grid approach is €36,446.02 while the estimated cost of the Cloud approach is €158,457.46. In both cases, the cost is mostly due to the computational resources and not to storage or I/O operations. In the cluster/grid approach, that cost represents 98.87% of the total while in the Cloud approach it is 94.97%. The Cloud approach is 334.77% more expensive and, therefore, it is not a good option if we simply want to solve the annotation process in the same time as the cluster/grid approach

(178 days). However, it can be useful if our goal is to reduce the required time, since using twice resources would reduce the time by half without increasing the computational cost. For example, if we want to solve the problem in 30 days, we estimate that *562 m1.xlarge* instances would be necessary, being the total cost about €157,589.15. This is even cheaper than solving the process in 178 days due to the savings when deploying the framework for a shorter time. Obviously, increasing the size of the resource pool has some implications one should pay for and are not considered in the previous estimation: it increases the complexity of the resource management, it impacts the performance of the whole framework, it may delay the acquisition and management of virtual machines, etc. In the future, we will further analyse this issue.

Let us now briefly sketch some lessons learned, whose value must be constrained to the problem domain we have been working on. Firstly, the use of Cloud is more suitable for handling some specific situations (fault recovery and dealing with demand peaks, for instance) than for providing all the required computing resources. This result is in accordance with other research works [16, 17] that show the benefits and potential savings of hybrid approaches. Secondly, Cloud vendors provide different instances with different capabilities, performance and cost. Therefore, selecting the most appropriate instance for each application is a challenging task because of the great variety of possible deployments and the inability to estimate the performance of each type of instance a priori. We have used an experimentation-based approach to simplify this preliminary stage, but alternative simulation based methods could also be put into practice. Also, in order to improve the accuracy of the cost estimation, we should measure the performance impact of the virtualization of a same type of instance in different hardware configurations. This could lead to performance variations depending on the physical resource used and, consequently, cause a change in the most appropriate instance type to compute the annotation process. Finally, Cloud gives the opportunity of increase the reliability of scientific computations. Cloud vendors guarantee 99.99% availability of their resources/services, which is much higher than what real-world cluster and grids provide [24]. Also, it provides the opportunity of running applications in a customized environment and without external interferences allowing higher reliability [22]. However, at this point, it is difficult to establish failure metrics in public Clouds as well as the impact of these failures in large-scale computations because of the impossibility to carry out these experiments due to the high cost involved.

As future work, we are interested in extending the analysis to other Amazon instances looking for new techniques to reduce the cost of the Cloud-based approach. Specifically, we are interested in the cost/performance ratio of the HPC Amazon instances because, although recent studies have shown that its performance is rather poor compared to local clusters [12], we consider them as an interesting/necessary solution for users without their own powerful computing resources who need to perform intensive computations. Additionally, we will explore the use of spot and reserved instances. On the one hand, spot instances have a lower price because they correspond to the unused Amazon capacity.

Besides, their price may vary, so they can be interrupted if it exceeds the user's bid. According to Amazon specifications, using spot instances can reduce the cost by about 50%. On the other hand, reserved instances are leased for 1 or 3 years with an initial payment and have a lower hourly price. A quick estimation is that using reserved instances for the considered annotation process could save about €35, 225.

Acknowledgments. This work has been supported by the research project TIN2010-17905, granted by the Spanish Ministry of Science and Innovation, and the regional project DGA-FSE, granted by the European Regional Development Fund (ERDF).

References

1. Buyya, R., Yeo, C.S., Venugopal, S.: Market-oriented cloud computing: Vision, hype, and reality for delivering it services as computing utilities. In: Proceedings of the 10th IEEE International Conference on High Performance Computing and Communications, HPCC 2008, pp. 5–13 (2008)
2. Foster, I., Zhao, Y., Raicu, I., Lu, S.: Cloud computing and grid computing 360-degree compared. In: Proceedings of the Grid Computing Environments Workshop, GCE 2008, pp. 1–10 (2008)
3. Sadashiv, N., Kumar, S.: Cluster, grid and cloud computing: A detailed comparison. In: Proceedings of the 6th International Conference on Computer Science Education, ICSE 2011, pp. 477–482 (2011)
4. Universia (2013), http://www.universia.es/ (accessed June 27, 2013)
5. Fabra, J., Hernández, S., Otero-García, E., Vidal, J.C., Lama, M., Álvarez, P.: A practical experience concerning the parallel semantic annotation of a large-scale data collection. To appear in the 9th International Conference on Semantics Systems, I-SEMANTICS 2013 (2013)
6. DBpedia (2013), http://dbpedia.org/ (accessed June 27, 2013)
7. Amazon Web Services (2013), http://aws.amazon.com (accessed June 27, 2013)
8. Ostermann, S., Prodan, R., Fahringer, T.: Extending grids with cloud resource management for scientific computing. In: Proceedings of the 10th IEEE/ACM International Conference on Grid Computing, pp. 42–49 (2009)
9. de Assuncao, M.D., di Costanzo, A., Buyya, R.: Evaluating the cost-benefit of using cloud computing to extend the capacity of clusters. In: Proceedings of the 18th ACM International Symposium on High Performance Distributed Computing, HPDC 2009, pp. 141–150 (2009)
10. Palankar, M.R., Iamnitchi, A., Ripeanu, M., Garfinkel, S.: Amazon s3 for science grids: a viable solution? In: Proceedings of the 2008 International Workshop on Data-aware Distributed Computing, DADC 2008, pp. 55–64 (2008)
11. Ramakrishnan, L., Canon, R.S., Muriki, K., Sakrejda, I., Wright, N.J.: Evaluating interconnect and virtualization performance for high performance computing. In: Proceedings of the Second International Workshop on Performance Modeling, Benchmarking and Simulation of High Performance Computing Systems, PMBS 2011, pp. 1–2 (2011)
12. Mehrotra, P., Djomehri, J., Heistand, S., Hood, R., Jin, H., Lazanoff, A., Saini, S., Biswas, R.: Performance evaluation of amazon ec2 for nasa hpc applications. In: Proceedings of the 3rd Workshop on Scientific Cloud Computing Date, Science-Cloud 2012, pp. 41–50 (2012)

13. Jackson, K.R., Ramakrishnan, L., Muriki, K., Canon, S., Cholia, S., Shalf, J., Wasserman, H.J., Wright, N.J.: Performance analysis of high performance computing applications on the amazon web services cloud. In: Proceedings of the 2010 IEEE Second International Conference on Cloud Computing Technology and Science, CLOUDCOM 2010, pp. 159–168 (2010)
14. Opitz, A., König, H., Szamlewska, S.: What does grid computing cost? J. Grid Comput. 6(4), 385–397 (2008)
15. Risch, M., Altmann, J.: Cost analysis of current grids and its implications for future grid markets. In: Altmann, J., Neumann, D., Fahringer, T. (eds.) GECON 2008. LNCS, vol. 5206, pp. 13–27. Springer, Heidelberg (2008)
16. Kondo, D., Javadi, B., Malecot, P., Cappello, F., Anderson, D.P.: Cost-benefit analysis of cloud computing versus desktop grids. In: Proceedings of the 2009 IEEE International Symposium on Parallel & Distributed Processing, IPDPS 2009, pp. 1–12 (2009)
17. Truong, H.L., Dustdar, S.: Composable cost estimation and monitoring for computational applications in cloud computing environments. In: Proceedings of the International Conference on Computational Science, ICCS 2010, pp. 2175–2184 (2010)
18. Hajjat, M., Sun, X., Sung, Y.-W.E., Maltz, D., Rao, S., Sripanidkulchai, K., Tawarmalani, M.: Cloudward bound: planning for beneficial migration of enterprise applications to the cloud. In: Proceedings of the ACM SIGCOMM 2010 Conference, SIGCOMM 2010, pp. 243–254 (2010)
19. Kashef, M.M., Altmann, J.: A cost model for hybrid clouds. In: Vanmechelen, K., Altmann, J., Rana, O.F. (eds.) GECON 2011. LNCS, vol. 7150, pp. 46–60. Springer, Heidelberg (2012)
20. Fabra, J., Hernández, S., Álvarez, P., Ezpeleta, J.: A framework for the flexible deployment of scientific workflows in grid environments. In: Proceedings of the Third International Conference on Cloud Computing, GRIDs, and Virtualization, CLOUD COMPUTING 2012, pp. 1–8 (2012)
21. Carriero, N., Gelernter, D.: Linda in context. Commun. ACM 32(4), 444–458 (1989)
22. Hernández, S., Fabra, J., Álvarez, P., Ezpeleta, J.: Using cloud-based resources to improve availability and reliability in a scientific workflow execution framework. In: The Fourth International Conference on Cloud Computing, GRIDs, and Virtualization, CLOUD COMPUTING 2013, pp. 230–237 (2013)
23. Hernández, S., Fabra, J., Álvarez, P., Ezpeleta, J.: A reliable and scalable service bus based on Amazon SQS. To appear in the 2nd European Conference on Service-Oriented and Cloud Computing, ESOCC 2013 (2013)
24. Javadi, B., Kondo, D., Iosup, A., Epema, D.: The failure trace archive: Enabling the comparison of failure measurements and models of distributed systems. Journal of Parallel and Distributed Computing 73(8), 1208–1223 (2013)

Incentives for Dynamic and Energy-Aware Capacity Allocation for Multi-tenant Clusters

Xavier León and Leandro Navarro

Distributed Systems Group, Department of Computer Architecture
Universitat Politècnica de Catalunya, Barcelona, Spain

Abstract. Large scale clusters are now being used in shared, multi-tenant scenarios by heterogeneous applications with completely different requirements. In this scenario, it's useful to explore the intersection of two complementary goals. On one side, energy efficiency is an important factor to consider in this world with increasing operating costs related to energy consumption. On the other side, heterogeneous applications emphasize the problem of distributing the execution capacity among competitive users in a shared setting. In this paper, we address the combination of these two goals by introducing an incentive mechanism to make users report their actual resource requirements, allowing them to dynamically scale-up or down as necessary. In turn, this information is used by the infrastructure operator to shut down resources without reducing the QoS provided to users and effectively reducing energy costs. We show how our mechanism is able to meet the performance requirements of applications without over-provisioning physical resources, which in turn translates into energy savings.

1 Introduction

Energy consumption is a key concern in networked computing systems, including service overlays, content distribution networks, and many other distributed systems. One of the main usages of large scale clusters is data analysis and manipulation using distributed computation models like MapReduce [1]. In this context, all data centers or cloud computing providers face the problem of a changing resource demand by applications over time and high energy costs that makes low server utilization a luxury.

Hoelzle and Barroso looked at the average CPU utilization of 5000 Google servers during a six-month period. It was shown that, on average, servers spend relatively little aggregate time at high load levels, but that they spend most of the time at the 10-50% CPU utilization range, where server efficiency in terms of energy is the lowest [2]. Given that, energy efficiency should be considered a first-order metric when designing data centers and the software they run.

From a different perspective, large scale clusters are used in shared, multi-user settings in which submitted applications may have completely different requirements. For this paper, we assume that applications are heterogeneous in terms of space (number of simultaneous running tasks) and time (duration of the execution), from small almost interactive executions, to very long programs

J. Altmann, K. Vanmechelen, and O.F. Rana (Eds.): GECON 2013, LNCS 8193, pp. 106–121, 2013.
© Springer International Publishing Switzerland 2013

that take hours to finish. This situation makes task scheduling, by which jobs are assigned a set of resources, even more relevant.

For example, Hadoop (the MapReduce implementation of computation supported by the Apache foundation) provides two different schedulers for multitenant scenarios: the *fair share* scheduler and the *capacity* scheduler. The former focuses on delivering a similar share of resources to all running applications targeting fairness as their main objective while the latter focuses on accommodating heterogeneous applications with different share requirements. However, both approaches are highly static in the sense that shares are granted by high-level policies decided by the infrastructure operator, and end users must negotiate a change in case the allocated shares are not enough. Besides, none of the approaches considers energy efficiency as a metric on the scheduling decisions.

To better understand the rationale behind our design, we start with a set of properties that scheduling policies try to satisfy: *social efficiency*, the allocation should maximize the utility or satisfaction (quality of experience, QoE) perceived by users; *capacity differentiation*, it should be capable of provisioning different capacity to different applications depending on their needs; *fairness*, each application should have a chance to obtain resources proportional to its assigned capacity; *elasticity*, or high utilization, a job should not be delayed or not executed if there are free or spare resources in the infrastructure due to an imbalance of execution capacity among users; *dynamically adaptive*, application capacity should be allowed to change or adapt dynamically depending on an application's needs without (or with minimal) intervention of administrators to increase responsiveness; and *energy efficient*, in today's world where energy operating costs are an important share of the total costs, the scheduling algorithm should consider energy costs as a first-order metric to optimize the energy consumption of operating the infrastructure.

Current schedulers already consider capacity differentiation, fairness and elasticity as important elements on its design. Thus, in this paper we focus and explore the intersection of two additional lines of research: i) energy costs awareness of big data clusters through resource scheduling policies and ii) enabling dynamic capacity allocation on shared multi-tenant clusters. In this context, our mechanism handles and manages the potential excess of allocated capacity to applications in relation to their QoS to achieve these goals.

From the energy efficiency perspective, it's risky for resource provides to simply power down a portion of the infrastructure without breaking service level agreements (SLAs) usually described as deadlines, given the heterogeneity of running applications and their changing requirements over time. Thus, we propose an incentive mechanism to maximize progress at an acceptable rate minimizing power consumption or unnecessary resource usage by *promoting* users to report their actual requirements in terms of resources instead of deadlines.

From the scheduling perspective, our goal is to move from operator-oriented static allocation policies to a user-oriented dynamic allocation to provide guarantees to users depending on their global or instant needs, without the intervention of the infrastructure operator.

This paper is organized as follows. Section 2 introduces some technical concepts related to map-reduce to situate the context of our mechanism. Section 3 and section 4 present our incentive mechanism and associated algorithms respectively. Section 5 presents the simulation results that support the contribution of our work. Finally, section 6 shows related work and we conclude in section 7.

2   Background

The MapReduce [1] model of computation was originally designed by Google to exploit large clusters to perform parallel computations on extremely large sets of data. It requires the programmer to implement two functions: a *map* function, which processes fragments of input data to produce intermediate results, usually in the form of key-value pairs, then feed a *reduce* function to combine the intermediate results to create the final output.

All nodes in the cluster execute these functions on different subsets of data. The MapReduce runtime divides and distributes the data across nodes and collects the results once nodes finish their calculations.

Although there are different implementations of this model for different purposes and architectures [3][4], we focus on Hadoop [5], one of the most widely used frameworks by companies like Yahoo!, Facebook or Amazon.

One of the core components of Hadoop is the job scheduler which allocates resources to jobs. Currently, there are three different scheduling policies implemented on Hadoop. The *FIFO* scheduler which pulls jobs from the work queue, oldest first. This scheduling policy has no concept of the size or resource requirement of a job, but the approach was simple enough to implement at first. The *fair share* scheduler –developed by Facebook– assigns resources to jobs in a way that on average, each job obtains a similar share of the available resources over time. This scheduler is able to interleave low consuming jobs with short time spans with jobs that require more resources and more time to complete, providing a more responsive system and avoiding starvation of small jobs in favor of larger ones. Finally, the *capacity* scheduler –developed by Yahoo!– shares some of the principles of the fair share scheduler in the sense that a certain amount of shares can be assigned to different users or applications. However, it was defined for large clusters with multiple, independent users and target applications, providing greater control over the capacity guarantees among users.

An important factor about the operation efficiency of Hadoop is how the data is spread among nodes. It is usually replicated over different nodes as to improve data availability in case some of the replicas are busy or just failed. Without digging into details, the aforementioned schedulers already deal with such issues related to data replication. Current research is dealing with data placement policies to overcome the problem of shutting down nodes to save energy costs as well [6][7][8].

As we will see, enhancements over data placement policies are orthogonal to our work since our mechanism is in fact an extension of the fair share or capacity schedulers and any improvement on that matter would be applicable to our solution as well. Thus, we will leave out the issues related to the mapping of jobs and data for simplicity and it will allow us to simplify our model. It will remain future work stating the impact of our solution considering data placement as another variable to consider.

3 Dynamic Allocation Based on Incentives

In this section we present the design, operation and objectives of the incentive-based allocation mechanism introduced in this paper. The mechanism consists of two elements: an incentive for users to report their actual resource requirement, and the strategy to allocate available resources.

3.1 Design Goal

The goal of the incentive mechanism presented in this paper is twofold. From the application perspective, users should have an incentive to report their actual resource requirement in order to allocate only those resources necessary to complete the task within their completion goal, and no more. This way, we may be able to aggregate unused resources that are not necessary to satisfy the Quality of Service (e.g. SLAs) of users and, therefore, put strategies in place to shut-down such resources to reduce energy costs. In contrast with current mechanisms which use the maximum amount of resources available to complete the task, targeting job runtime as a primary goal, we propose a more rational way to share resources by making explicit the cost of using such resources and giving users the option to scale up and down their resource allocation.

From the infrastructure operator perspective, the allocation of resources is usually static because of the complexity of the allocation decision. For example, the Hadoop fair share scheduler always allocates the same amount of resources to each application regardless of application requirements and the Capacity scheduler is able to allocate a specific share of resources to each application but requires the infrastructure operator to manually change such allocations in case of a change on the priority of different applications. Our mechanism simplifies the decision on the amount of resources to allocate to each user – because now users are in charge of such decisions – and allows reducing energy costs by shutting-down unused resources without breaking the QoS commitments with users.

Therefore, this may lead us to a win-win situation in which users are able to finish their tasks within a given time goal and infrastructure operators are able to reduce energy costs by shutting-down unused resources and simplify their allocation decisions.

3.2 System Model

While MapReduce was originally used for batch data processing, it is now also being used in shared, multi-tenant environments in which submitted jobs may have completely different priorities depending on resource requirements and completion time: from small, almost interactive, executions, to very long programs that take hours to complete. This shift in the initial paradigm makes the associated resource allocation even more relevant. In this multi-tenant scenario, each user has a guaranteed resource capacity according to different strategies implemented by different schedulers. For example, the fair share scheduler allocates $1/n$ of the available slots to each application and the Capacity scheduler allocates a fixed amount of resources to each application according to high-level policies –e.g. 5% to application A, 25% to application B and 70% to application C. Our mechanism can be considered an hybrid of these two in the sense that an application has a fair share of the resource guaranteed but is free to hand out spare resources to other applications or ask for more resource when necessary – this is the essence of dynamic allocation.

Through out this paper, we will indistinctly refer as user or application a piece of software running in the cluster to perform data intensive computations. These applications are modeled as a MapReduce job characterized by an upper (r_{max}) and lower (r_{min}) bound on resource requirements in the form of a percentage or share of the cluster capacity. This information is considered in principle unknown to the resource provider and private to the user.

This simple model allow us to specify the minimum share to meet a certain time goal to complete the job. Thus, the utility function of a user will be computed as a function of the share allocated by the scheduler (s_i) and the share requirement (r_{min}) in the following way:

$$U(s_i, r_{min}) = \begin{cases} 1 & \text{if } s_i \geq r_{min} \\ \frac{s_i}{r_{min}} & \text{if } s_i < r_{min} \end{cases} \quad (1)$$

In a few words, this utility function is in the range $[0, 1]$ and models the fact that users will not obtain more benefit if they obtain more than their minimum requirement, which is the minimum share to meet the deadline of the job. In case the allocated share is less than the share requirement, the utility obtained by the user will decrease linearly.

3.3 Making Private Information Explicit through Incentives

The basic principle behind our mechanism is a *use your assigned resources now or better save them for later* approach. Our goal is to provide users an incentive to truthfully declare their actual resource requirements (r_{min}). This way, the infrastructure operator can decide which minimum portion of the cluster is necessary to provide jobs with enough resources to complete their tasks in time.

As we stated in the model above, applications are given a fair share ($1/n^{th}$ where n is the number of concurrent applications) of the time slots available for execution. Sometimes applications will need more than this fair share, and sometimes applications will need less. The incentive we propose is a simple market in which users sell their spare allocations when not needed to the operator to obtain a certain amount of credits, and buy resources with these credits from the pool of unused resources when they need more than their fair share. Credits used in this mechanism are an abstract representation of the capacity which is used to exchange resources among users and the operator. In a few words, it's an enhancement over the fair-share scheduler in which users can dynamically decide which is their actual share allocated as a function of their requirements.

The benefits of such mechanism are two-fold: i) applications are able to scale up (buy) and down (sell) their allocations based on their requirements which provides a dynamic environment to adapt to changing conditions according to the workload (*dynamic capacity allocation*); and ii) if at any point in time, the aggregated demand is less than the total capacity, the infrastructure operator can decide to reduce costs by powering down (or switch resources to a low power consumption state) without breaking application's SLAs (*energy efficiency*).

4 Algorithms for Trading Unused Capacity

Throughout this section, we will detail the procedure to allocate resources to applications according to their requested share. The allocation mechanism presented in this work consists of two main components: i) an algorithm to update

---

Algorithm 1. UPDATECAPACITYALLOCATION – main algorithm to compute capacity allocation

---

Require: $\phi = \langle \phi_1, \ldots, \phi_n \rangle$ ▷ users' share request
Require: $C = \langle c_1, \ldots, c_n \rangle$ ▷ users' current credits
  $Q \leftarrow \{\emptyset\}$ ▷ greater than ϕ_i set
  $S \leftarrow \{\emptyset\}$ ▷ lower than ϕ_i share set
  $p \leftarrow 0$ ▷ pool of free resources
  $r \leftarrow 0$ ▷ extra capacity requested
  for all request ϕ_i **do**
   if $\phi_i \leq 1/n$ **then**
     $s_i \leftarrow \phi_i$ ▷ sellers
     $S \leftarrow S \cap \{s_i\}$
     $p \leftarrow p + (\frac{1}{n} - \phi_i)$
   else
     if $c_i > 0$ **then**
       $q_i \leftarrow \phi_i - \frac{1}{n}$ ▷ buyers
       $r \leftarrow r + q_i$
       $Q \leftarrow Q \cap \{q_i\}$
     end if
   end if
  end for
  if $r < p$ **then**
   for all request $q_i \in Q$ **do**
     $s_i \leftarrow \frac{1}{n} + q_i$
     $Q' \leftarrow Q' \cap \{s_i\}$
   end for
  else
   $Q' \leftarrow$ ALLOCATEUNUSEDCAPACITY(Q, C, p)
  end if
  return $S \cap Q'$

---

the capacity allocated to each application which is executed every time a new allocation request is made (Algorithms 1 and 2) and, ii) a procedure to recompute the credits earned by selling spare resources, or the credits spent (virtual money) by buying extra capacity required to accomplish the QoS needed (Algorithm 3).

Dynamic Capacity Allocation. Every time an application sends a request to obtain a specific set of resources, Algorithm 1 is executed. It recomputes the shares assigned to all running jobs taking into account the new request. Basically, we are given a set of share requests submitted by users (ϕ), which are the shares (percentage of the cluster) needed by an application to complete within a specific deadline and a set of budgets or credits for each user.

First, we divide all requests in two groups by looking if each request is lower (set S) or greater (set Q) than its fair share ($1/n$). In the first case, we directly grant the request (ϕ_i) and add the spare capacity not planned to be used ($1/n - \phi_i$) to the pool of free resources (p). In the second case, we add this extra capacity requested to a counter (r) for later use and include it on the second set (Q), always checking that the application has enough credit to spend on extra resources. Notice that the set S is the set of applications *selling their spare capacity*, and the set Q is the set of applications *buying extra capacity*.

Thereafter, if the amount of extra capacity required is lower than the pool of free resources or, in economic terms, demand is lower than supply, we allocate

---

Algorithm 2. ALLOCATEUNUSEDCAPACITY – ... among users

Require: $Q = \langle q_1, \ldots, q_m \rangle$ ▷ users' extra share request (above fair share)
Require: $C = \langle c_1, \ldots, c_m \rangle$ ▷ users' current credits
Require: p ▷ % of free resources
  for all $i \in Q$ **do**
$$X \leftarrow \sum_{i=0}^{m} c_i$$
    for all $c_i \in C$ **do**
      $x_i \leftarrow c_i / X$
      $y_i \leftarrow (x_i * p)/q_i$
    end for
    Sort set Q by y_i in decreasing order   ▷ if $y_i > 1 \rightarrow$ request < capacity

    if $y_i > 1$ **then**
      $a_i \leftarrow q_i$
    else
      $a_i \leftarrow (x_i * p)$
    end if
    $s_i \leftarrow 1/n + a_i$
    $p \leftarrow p - a_i$
  end for
  return $S \leftarrow (s_1, \ldots, s_m)$

Algorithm 3. UPDATECREDITS – update the amount of credits

Require: $S = \langle s_1, \ldots, s_n \rangle$ ▷ allocations by UpdateCapacityAllocation
Require: $C = \langle c_1, \ldots, c_n \rangle$ ▷ users' current credits
Require: t ▷ time since last updateCapacityAllocation
  for all $s_i \in S$ **do**
    $c_i \leftarrow c_i + t * (\frac{1}{n} - s_i)$
  end for
  return $C \leftarrow \{c_1, \ldots, c_n\}$

---

this extra capacity to applications buying resources – which will be charged for this extra use and accomplish the *elasticity* criteria presented on section 1. On the other hand, when resources are scarce and demand is higher than supply, we allocate these extra requests proportional to the credits earned previously –which accomplish the *fairness* criteria presented also on section 1– following Algorithm 2 which is a loosely-based proportional share allocation algorithm.

On algorithm 2, we take into account the set Q of extra capacity requests and the budget in credits owned by each application. Following our goal of allocating only the necessary (and no more) resources to applications, we first compute for each application the theoretical share of resources proportional to their budget (x_i) and compute the ratio y_i which will be greater than 1 for applications requesting less than their theoretical proportional share and lower than 1 for applications requesting more than their theoretical proportional share. Given that, by sorting the set Q by the ratio y_i in decreasing order, we first allocate the extra requested capacity to applications requesting less than their theoretical proportional share to accumulate their spare capacity to subsequent applications. In case $y_i < 1$, the theoretical proportional share is the upper bound on the amount of resources an application can obtain given the credits. This procedure is repeated until no application requests are left in the set Q.

It is important to note that users are always awarded a minimum resource allocation equal to a fair share $-1/n$ of the computational time, where n is the number of active users. If a user under-predict the actual resource requirements of the application to earn credits but do not make enough progress to meet the deadline, the user can always request more capacity up to its fair share, or more if enough credits are available.

Accounting of Credits. Before the actual allocation is made, algorithm 3 is processed to update the credits each application owns based on the previous execution. The current budget of credits for each application is computed as a function of the current allocation provided by algorithm 1 at time t-1. Therefore, if the application bought extra resources $(s_i \geq \frac{1}{n})$ on the previous round of the algorithm, the term $t * (\frac{1}{n} - s_i)$ will be negative and the corresponding amount of credits will be discounted. On the other hand, if the application sold spare resources $(s_i < \frac{1}{n})$, the term $t * (\frac{1}{n} - s_i)$ will be positive and the equivalent number of credits will be added to the current budget.

114   X. León and L. Navarro

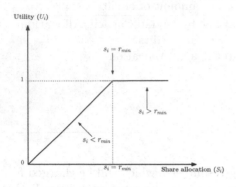

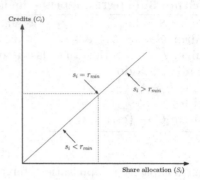

Fig. 1. User Utility comparing r_{min} and s_i

Fig. 2. Credits earned/spent comparing r_{min} and s_i

Analysis of Incentive Compatibility. A key factor of our mechanism is its *incentive compatibility*. A mechanism is incentive compatible if all the participants consider their best interest to truthfully reveal any private information inquired by the mechanism.

In our case, the private information that the mechanism asks users is their actual resource requirement in terms of shares to finish the job within a deadline. To perform the analysis, we will consider the case in which a user declare a share request below, above or exactly equal to its actual share requirement and observe how our mechanism reacts to these values and the utility function described in Equation 1.

An informal proof of incentive compatibility is as follows. Given a user i, a minimum share requirement for a job r_{min} and the outcome of our mechanism which is an actual share allocation s_i, we can observe these situations considering a user reports r_i:

- **case $r_i \leq 1/n$.** Request share is lower than fair share (potential earnings). In this case, $s_i = r_i$ because all requests less than the granted fair share are accepted without charges. Users have no incentive to report $r_i < r_{min}$ because it will not obtain its minimum share to complete the job ($U_i(s_i, r_i) = \frac{s_i}{r_{min}} < 1$), as shown in Figure 1. Reporting a r_i above its requirement r_{min} will grant the user more shares and maximize utility ($U_i(s_i, r_i) = 1$) but with the drawback of earning less credits to spend in the future without gaining any utility out of it. Therefore, the best response of the user is to report a $r_i = r_{min}$.
- **case $r_i > 1/n$.** Request share is higher than fair share (potential payments).
  - **case $r_i = r_{min}$.** Request share is equal to requirement. This is the ideal situation in which users truthfully report their requirements. In this case, $s_i \leq r_{min} = r_i$. Because the user is requesting more resources than its fair share, it will pay up to c_i credits which is proportional to $s_i - \frac{1}{n}$ or, in the best case, proportional to $r_{min} - \frac{1}{n} = r_i - \frac{1}{n}$. Looking at the utility function $U_i(s_i, r_i) = 1$ because $s_i = r_{min}$ in the best case. In the

following cases, we will see that this is the best possible situation and, thus, the users have no incentive to misreport r_i.

- **case** $r_i > r_{min}$. Request share is higher than requirement. In this case, $r_{min} \leq s_i \leq r_i$. Again, user will pay up to c_i credits which is proportional to $s_i - \frac{1}{n}$ or, in the best case of allocating the whole request, proportional to $r_i - \frac{1}{n}$. The request in this case is greater than the request in case ii-i, so the total amount of credits to pay will be higher ($s_i > r_{min}$ in Figure 2). Given that the outcome of our algorithm $U_i(s_i, r_i) = 1$ is the same as the case above because $s_i > r_{min}$, it will end up paying more credits for the same utility.

- **case** $r_i < r_{min}$. Request share is lower than requirement. In this case, the utility obtained $U_i(s_i, r_i) = \frac{s_i}{r_i} < 1$ because $s_i < r_{min}$ and it will be lower than in the previous two cases because our algorithm allocates a maximum number of shares equal to the request.

Following that, we can conclude that our mechanism always maximizes the utility $U_i(s_i, r_i) = 1$ while minimizing the amount of credits to pay in case of buying resources, and also maximizes the amount of credits to earn in case of selling resources.   ∎

5   Evaluation

We use simulation to evaluate the long-term impact of our system. To determine the effectiveness of our incentive mechanism in reducing the cluster usage without reducing the QoS perceived by users, we compare our algorithm   *cooperative* label in the figures – with the outcome of a widely used scheduler – the fair share scheduler used in Hadoop. We also use for comparison purposes an *optimum* allocation mechanism which always allocates the share requirement r_{min} to jobs effectively maximizing user utility and minimizing resource usage, independently of the market of resources (credits earned and spent). This *optimum* scheduler however has an unbound resource pool so it can always allocate the optimum shares regardless of the load.

The set-up of the simulations consists in varying the number of simultaneous users n (from 2 to 100) to assess the scalability of the solution as more users (and, therefore, more load) are added to the system. In addition, each user is assigned a set of jobs to execute in the cluster. Specifically, each job is represented by a tuple (t, r_{min}, r_{max}) where t is the deadline for completing the job, r_{min} is the minimum share necessary to finish the job before time t and r_{max} is the maximum number of shares the job is able to use taking into account that the level of parallelism is bounded or, in other words, we model the fact that depending on the nature of the job, it cannot use the whole cluster even if a single job is running on it.

Given the lack of public reliable MapReduce-like workloads, we simulate a synthetic workload that tries to mimic real world workloads as described by Zaharia et al. [9]. Thus, we assign r_{min} and t drawn from a log-normal distribution

$L \sim (1, 1.25)$ which produce a workload distribution in which most of the jobs have a rather short running time and share requirement (small to medium size jobs) and fewer jobs with higher running times and share requirements. r_{max} is derived from r_{min} by adding a variable k drawn from a uniform distribution $U \sim (0, 100)$. We normalize r_{min} and r_{max} in the range $[0, 100]$ as it represents the shares in percentage of a cluster and t is capped in the range $[0, 10000]$ which is an arbitrary number large enough to not misrepresent the random distribution but effective to avoid unrealistic or excessively large jobs.

To study the behavior of our mechanism, we consider the following metrics.

- *Cluster usage.* This is the average usage of the cluster in percentage over the whole simulation period. Although peak usage may differ over time depending on the actual jobs being run on the cluster, this is an indication of the overall usage over time, the time the cluster remains unused and the percentage of the cluster that could be shutdown to reduce power consumption on average.
- *Satisfaction.* Given a specific share request r_i for user i and a specific share allocation s_i, the satisfaction or efficiency is $\phi_i = s_i - r_i$. In other words, it is the difference between the share requirement of user i and the actual allocation made by the algorithm. This is a measure of the QoS the user perceives from the running time on the cluster considering their requests and their actual allocations. Given that this metric is measured as a difference, the lower the better.
- *Mean completion time.* Given a set of jobs for user i and its actual completion time (time elapsed between submitting the job and gathering the results), it is the mean time to complete each of the jobs. This measure is an indication of how well the scheduler is able to scale down the number of shares given to a job to save resources.

All figures are normalized in the range $[0, 1]$ for comparison purposes and because the actual numbers are actually meaningless because of the synthetic nature of our workload. Thus, we are only interested in the relative difference between our proposal and the widely used fair share scheduler.

Figure 3 shows the QoS perceived by users. Because satisfaction is measured as the difference between the share request (requirement) and the share allocated, the lower the number the better. We can see that our mechanism (label *cooperative* in the figures) is able to provide better QoS to users compared to the widely used fair share scheduler because it is able to allocate dynamically more resources to those jobs in more need instead of allocating the same fair share to all of them. It can also provide a QoS on par with the optimum up to the point where resources become scarce and the gap between share request and share allocation becomes noticeable (20-30 simulated users). However, we stress the importance of our incentive mechanism as users can buy more resources to improve their QoS even in high contention scenarios (more than 20-30 users).

If we now look at the cluster usage (Figure 4), we can observe that our algorithm consumes up to 50% less resources than the fair share scheduler with 20 simultaneous users. This lower resource consumption is possible because users

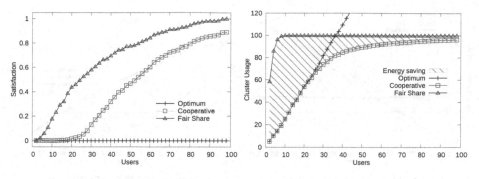

Fig. 3. User Satisfaction   **Fig. 4.** Cluster Usage

sell resources to the infrastructure operator when not strictly necessary to meet the job's deadline.

It's important to note that this lower cluster usage may allow the infrastructure operator to scale down the available nodes to reduce power consumption and, thus, increase the revenue obtained given the same workload. In contrast, the fair share scheduler always allocates the maximum amount of shares to a given job regardless of the actual minimum resource requirement. This is because the fair share scheduler is agnostic to the job characteristics – i.e. minimum share requirement and deadline. In contrast, our incentive mechanism is actually able to extract such information from the user and use it to the operator's benefit to maintain the resource usage to a minimum without impacting user efficiency.

However, these benefits (reduced resource consumption, lower energy costs, higher user's satisfaction) comes at a certain cost, namely a higher mean completion time (see Figure 5). Because our mechanism influences users to report the minimum share to meet a certain deadline, its easy to see that the mean completion time for the set of jobs a user must run will be higher than in the case of traditional schedulers, which one of the objectives is to finish a job as soon as the cluster capacity allows. However, this minor drawback is bearable considering that almost no deadlines are broken when there are less than 30 users. In fact, below this threshold its performance is comparable to the optimum allocation. As the number of concurrent users increases, our mechanism behaves almost exactly as the other schedulers. This fact comes from the algorithm design itself which awards at least a fair share of the cluster capacity at any time, regardless of workload conditions.

It's clear that our mechanism leads to a longer mean completion time and thus, resources are used for a longer period of time. However, the fact that we encourage users to scale down and report their actual resource requirements allows the infrastructure operator to make an informed decision on whether it is safe to shutdown spare resources without afecting the quality perceived by users. Therefore, we refer our mechanism as energy-aware in contrast to other scheduling policies which does not facilitate the problem of deciding whether a certain portion of the cluster is safe to shutdown considering the quality targets of users.

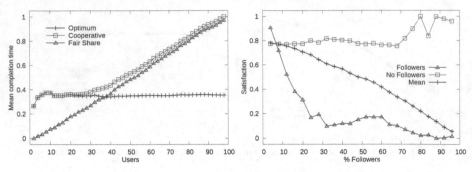

Fig. 5. Mean Completion Time   **Fig. 6.** Variable % of followers

Another important aspect is that users are free to follow our incentive mechanism by reporting the minimum share requirement and engaging in buying and selling resources, or reject it and just behave as a regular user receiving its fair share.

To state the effectiveness of our incentive mechanism, we observe the satisfaction of users depending on the opt-in ratio in our mechanism. Figure 6 shows the scalability of our mechanism with a variable ratio of opt-in users (label *followers*) and opt-out users (label *no followers*): the more users opt-in to collaborate through our mechanism the better the satisfaction (recall that a lower number is better by the definition of satisfaction). This is true because there will be more users selling resources which in turn can be used by other users in need of more resources effectively allowing a dynamic allocation of resources.

Although we evaluate and compare our mechanism against the vanilla fair share scheduler through out this paper, our proposal deals with scenarios where tasks have a sense of timeliness and therefore can observe an excess of resources or a potential need for additional capacity in the future. Therefore, our mechanism is easily applicable to other schedulers, as it focuses on handling excess and scarcity situations. For example, a FIFO scheduler may decide the order in which tasks are executed while our extension may allow users decide the amount of resources allocated.

6   Related Work

The focus of current schedulers in distributed processing frameworks is on high performance computations targeting job run time as a primary objective. However, the trade off between performance and the effect on data center energy efficiency has not been fully investigated. Our work is a step towards the reconciliation of quality of service allowing dynamic scale up and down of jobs and energy cost efficiency.

There are different strategies to address the problem of energy efficiency, most of them based on data replication strategies to allow shutting down a portion of the cluster safely. Jacob et al. [7] find that running Hadoop in fractional configurations by means of distributing data replicas over a covering set can save energy by shutting down idle fractions of the clusters at a cost of losing performance due to data contention. Kaushik et al. [6] makes use of hardware heterogeneity and different power consumption policies by dividing the cluster in two zones: the *hot* zone where highly popular data is placed and where servers run without any power saving policy and the *cold* zone where low spatial or temporal popularity data is placed but with an aggressive policy towards saving energy. Interestingly, their simulations were carried out using three month worth of traces from Yahoo! and found an impressing 26% savings in energy costs. Our proposal is orthogonal to such previous works in the sense that our focus is not on data placement strategies nor performance prediction but on scheduling decisions of the time slots allocated to each application and, as such, any improvement over data placement policies is complementary to our solution.

Lang et al. [8] proposes to use the entire cluster for a certain period of time to run a specific workload and then powers down the entire cluster until the next running period, certainly consolidating dispersed workload over a shorter period. Although an interesting analysis, the practicality of such mechanism remains to be seen as starting up and shutting down a large-scale cluster is not trivial and would need improvements on the hardware side between transition periods. From the economic standpoint, Sandholm et al. [10][11] already proposed a market for dynamically assigning resources of a shared cluster to multiple Hadoop instances. The priorities are assigned using high level policies like budgets similarly to our solution. However, they had to deal with the complexities of a "real" market like inflation and deflation or forcing the users to understand the mapping between currency and real resources. In our case, we simplify this complexity leveraging the share concept and applying a direct translation between shares, time and credits earned or bought, which help users understand how many resources they can buy or sell for a given share at any point in time.

It is important to note that, as previously stated on this paper, our mechanism relies on the users' knowledge about their jobs and quality targets. This knowledge could be acquired over time by learning from previous executions. In the literature, there are several works that propose learning from past executions [12][13][14] which could be integrated into our mechanism to aid users in their decisions or even implement high level policies to act on behalf of users using such predictions. However, it is important to note that learning or guessing resource profile needs from past executions is a different problem than the problem we are tackling in this paper, which is handling the excess and shortage of capacity of users at any point in time. It remains as future work to evaluate the impact of inacurate predictions about the requirements of applications.

7   Conclusions

In this paper we investigate the possibility of reducing energy costs by providing users an incentive to report their actual needs instead of over reporting the size of their jobs. Our mechanism is based on markets and could be implemented as an extension of the traditional Capacity Scheduler.

Our mechanism pursues two different goals. From the user perspective, we show how our incentive mechanism effectively encourages users to report their true share requirement for a given job. Thus, we are able to provide a *shares market* in which users engage to dynamically scale up (buy) or down (sell) the allocated time slots of a job without the intervention of the infrastructure operator, providing a more elastic and agile infrastructure. We also show that it's in the users' best interest to participate in the market to improve their QoS instead of default.

Furthermore, map-reduce computations are characterized by long, predictable, streaming I/O, massive parallelization, and non interactive performance. These computational services are often used in real-time data processing scenarios [15] and, as such, they can benefit from our mechanism as quality of service becomes more important than job run time.

From the infrastructure operator point of view, our mechanism is able to collect valuable information from users by providing them an incentive to truthfully report share requirements. In a scenario in which energy related costs is one of the single largest factors in the overall cost of operating a data center, this information can be used to shut down a portion of the cluster without reducing the quality of service provided to users, which in turn could reduce energy costs.

Looking at the results, we can conclude that our mechanism is a step towards a more rational use of the available resources. It is able to dynamically scale up and down the shares allocated to jobs with the aid of users and at the same time provide valuable information to the resource provider to shutdown spare resources without breaking SLAs or affecting QoS.

To the best of our knowledge, our work is the first to explore the problem of the intersection of ensuring users' quality of service providing dynamic allocation of resources based on user's requests and reducing energy costs together.

Acknowledgments. This work is supported by an FPI-UPC grant from the Universitat Politècnica de Catalunya (UPC) and partially supported by the Spanish government (DELFIN project under contract TIN2010-20140-C03-01). We thank the anonymous reviewers for their useful comments which helped to improve this work.

References

1. Dean, J., Ghemawat, S.: Mapreduce: simplified data processing on large clusters. Communications of the ACM 51(1), 107–113 (2008)
2. Barroso, L.A., Hölzle, U.: The datacenter as a computer: An introduction to the design of warehouse-scale machines. Synthesis Lectures on Computer Architecture 4(1), 1–108 (2009)
3. Rafique, M.M., Rose, B., Butt, A.R., Nikolopoulos, D.S.: Cellmr: A framework for supporting mapreduce on asymmetric cell-based clusters. In: IEEE International Symposium on Parallel & Distributed Processing, IPDPS, pp. 1–12. IEEE (2009)

4. He, B., Fang, W., Luo, Q., Govindaraju, N.K., Wang, T.: Mars: A mapreduce framework on graphics processors. In: Proceedings of the 17th International Conference on Parallel Architectures and Compilation Techniques, pp. 260–269. ACM (2008)
5. White, T.: Hadoop: The definitive guide. O'Reilly Media (2012)
6. Kaushik, R.T., Bhandarkar, M.: Greenhdfs: Towards an energy-conserving storage-efficient, hybrid hadoop compute cluster. In: Proceedings of the USENIX Annual Technical Conference (2010)
7. Leverich, J., Kozyrakis, C.: On the energy (in) efficiency of hadoop clusters. ACM SIGOPS Operating Systems Review 44(1), 61–65 (2010)
8. Lang, W., Patel, J.M.: Energy management for mapreduce clusters. Proceedings of the VLDB Endowment 3(1-2), 129–139 (2010)
9. Zaharia, M., Borthakur, D., Sen Sarma, J., Elmeleegy, K., Shenker, S., Stoica, I.: Job scheduling for multi-user mapreduce clusters. Technical Report UCB/EECS-2009-55, EECS Department, University of California, Berkeley (April 2009)
10. Sandholm, T., Lai, K.: Mapreduce optimization using regulated dynamic prioritization. In: 11th International Conference on Measurement and Modeling of Computer Systems, SIGMETRICS 2009, pp. 299–310. ACM, New York (2009)
11. Sandholm, T., Lai, K.: Dynamic proportional share scheduling in hadoop. In: Frachtenberg, E., Schwiegelshohn, U. (eds.) JSSPP 2010. LNCS, vol. 6253, pp. 110–131. Springer, Heidelberg (2010)
12. Yom-Tov, E., Aridor, Y.: A self-optimized job scheduler for heterogeneous server clusters. In: Frachtenberg, E., Schwiegelshohn, U. (eds.) JSSPP 2007. LNCS, vol. 4942, pp. 169–187. Springer, Heidelberg (2008)
13. Polo, J., Carrera, D., Becerra, Y., Torres, J., Ayguadé, E., Steinder, M., Whalley, I.: Performance-driven task co-scheduling for mapreduce environments. In: IEEE Network Operations and Management Symposium (NOMS), pp. 373–380. IEEE (2010)
14. Verma, A., Cherkasova, L., Campbell, R.H.: Aria: automatic resource inference and allocation for mapreduce environments. In: Proceedings of the 8th ACM International Conference on Autonomic Computing, ICAC 2011, pp. 235–244. ACM, New York (2011)
15. Chang, F., Dean, J., Ghemawat, S., Hsieh, W.C., Wallach, D.A., Burrows, M., Chandra, T., Fikes, A., Gruber, R.E.: Bigtable: A distributed storage system for structured data. ACM Transactions on Computer Systems 26(2) (2008)

Revenue Creation for Rate Adaptive Stream Management in Multi-tenancy Environments

José Ángel Bañares[2], Omer F. Rana[1],
Rafael Tolosana-Calasanz[2], and Congduc Pham[3]

[1] School of Computer Science & Informatics
Cardiff University, United Kingdom
o.f.rana@cs.cardiff.ac.uk
[2] Dpto. de Informática e Ingeniería de Sistemas
Universidad de Zaragoza, Spain
{rafaelt,banares}@unizar.es
[3] LIUPPA Laboratory
University of Pau, France
congduc.pham@univ-pau.fr

Abstract. With the increasing availability of streaming applications from mobile devices to dedicated sensors, understanding how such streaming content can be processed within some time threshold remains an important requirement. We investigate how a computational infrastructure responds to such streaming content based on the revenue per stream – taking account of the price paid to process each stream, the penalty per stream if the pre-agreed throughput rate is not met, and the cost of resource provisioning within the infrastructure. We use a token-bucket based rate adaptation strategy to limit the data injection rate of each data stream, along with the use of a shared token-bucket to enable better allocation of computational resource to each stream. We demonstrate how the shared token-bucket based approach can enhance the performance of a particular class of applications, whilst still maintaining a minimal quality of service for all streams entering the system.

1 Introduction

The increasing deployment of sensor network infrastructures has led to large volumes of data becoming available, which are often required to be processed in real-time. In addition, data from these sensors may be streamed in an unpredictable manner (i.e. the availability of data may not be known apriori) with potential bursty behaviour in data generation. Data source (sensor) can vary in complexity from smart phones to specialist instruments, and can consist of sensing, data processing and communication components. Data streams in such applications are generally large-scale and distributed, and generated continuously at a rate that cannot be estimated in advance. Scalability remains a major requirement for such applications, to handle variable event loads efficiently [1].

J. Altmann, K. Vanmechelen, and O.F. Rana (Eds.): GECON 2013, LNCS 8193, pp. 122–137, 2013.

Multi-tenancy Cloud environments enable such concurrent data streams (with data becoming available at unpredictable times) to be processed using a shared, distributed computing infastructure. This leads to challenges in offering Quality of Service (QoS) guarantees for each data stream, specified in Service Level Agreements (SLAs). SLAs identify the cost that a user must pay to achieve the required QoS, and the penalty in case the QoS cannot be met. Stream descriptions may, in some cases, provide placeholders in the SLA for data that will be generated at some time in the future. Assuming the maximisation of the revenue as the provider's objective, then it must decide which streams to accept for storage and analysis; and how many (computational / storage) resources to allocate to each stream in order to improve overall revenue. When the real-time requirements demand a rapid reaction, the dynamic provisioning of resource (i.e. from an elastic resource provider) may not be useful, since the delay incurred might be too high. Alternatively, idle resources that were initially allocated for other streams could be re-allocated, avoiding the penalisation.

This paper extends our previous contributions in this area; papers [2–4] describe a revenue-based resource management strategy for bursty data streams on shared Clouds. This contribution extends the token bucket model used previously to enable: (i) the re-distribution of unused resources amongst data streams; and (ii) a dynamic re-allocation of resources to streams likely to generate greater revenue for the provider. These extensions are provided by a direct addition of business rules in the token bucket behavior – as an alternative to using a rule engine alongside a token bucket model, which has a significant performance overhead. The remainder of this paper is structured as follows. Section 2 describes the revenue model and the resource requirements for QoS in data stream processing applications. Section 3 shows the system architecture based on the token bucket model and actions the provider can take to maximize revenue: using a rule-based approach with token bucket model extensions. Section 4 shows our evaluation and simulation results. In Section 5, related work is briefly discussed. Finally, conclusions and future work are outlined in Section 6.

2   Revenue Based Resource Management

We consider a provider centric view of costs incurred to provide data stream processing services over a number of available computational resources (e.g. a pool of virtual machines in an elastic infrastructure). A provider may use a (pre-agreed and reserved) posted price, a spot price (to gain revenue from currently unused capacity), or on an on-demand use (the most costly for the user) for resources, on a per-unit-time basis – as currently undertaken by Amazon.com in their EC2 and S3 services. In the case of data stream processing services, this cost may also be negotiated between the user and the provider using QoS criteria. How such a price is set is not the focus of this work, our primary interest is in identifying what are the performance objectives that can be established in a SLA, and what actions the provider can perform to guarantee the agreed QoS and maximize the revenue. A key distinction between batch-based execution on a Cloud infrastructure is that the query/computation and data are generally available before the execution commences. In a streamed application, a query is often executed continuously on dynamically available data. An SLA is therefore essential to identify what a user must pay the provider, often based on a previous estimation of resources required/used. Conversely, the provider can also utilize previously similar stream processing capability to identify resources required and any penalties paid in the past (for service degradation that violated the SLA). Due to the greater potential variation likely to be seen in stream processing applications, an SLA therefore protects both the user and the provider.

Defining QoS properties in an SLA is very application dependent. In applications such a commercial Web hosting, QoS levels specify parameters such as request rate, for example expressed as served URLs per period; and data bandwidth, that specifies the aggregate bandwidth in bytes per second to be allocated in the contract [5]. In other applications such as video-on-demand, QoS levels may represent frame rates and average frame sizes. In the context of data stream, the analysis can include min/max/avg calculations on a data or sample time window, an event analysis, a summarisation of data over a time window, etc. [6] provides a useful summary of the performance objectives of event processing and their associated metrics (see table 2).

Table 1. Performance objectives and their associated metrics for Event Processing [6]

Performance Objectives and their metrics	
Objective Name	Objective metrics
Max input throughput	Max. number of input events processed within an interval
Max output throughput	Max. number of derived events produced within an interval
Min average latency	Min. average time to process an event
Min Maximal latency	Min. the maximal time to process an event
Jitter	Min. value of the variance in processing times
Real-time	Min. of the deviation in latency from a given value

When a shared Cloud infrastructure is being used, a provider may serve multiple users using a common resource pool through a "multi-tenancy" architecture. This architecture is used to offer multiple functions over a shared infrastructure to one or more users. The revenue for the provider in this case is the total of all prices charged to users minus the cost of all required resources and the penalties incurred for degraded services.

We assume that the provider (client) monitor their offered (provided) QoS properties over fixed time intervals. The revenue obtained by the provider over a particular time interval is assumed to be constant, and determined by the price clients pay for allocated resources to process their data streams, minus the cost incurred by the provision of these resources (generally identified as operational expenditure (OPEX)). A sudden peak in data, due to sudden data injection or traffic burstiness can produce shortage of resources to process such bursts, over some time slots/intervals. The provider can either accept the penalty due to the unavailability of resources, or can provide additional resources in an elastic way. We define the benefit function for a provider over a particular a time interval for n clients (represented as Instant Revenue) as:

(Eq. 1) $Instant\ Revenue = \sum_{i=1}^{n}(CostPU_{client} - CostPU_{provider}) * \#PU$
$- \sum_{i=1}^{n} \#penalties_i * CostPenalties_i$
$- \Delta\#PU * CostPU_{provider}$

where $CostPU_{client}$ and $CostPU_{provider}$ are respectively the price of each processing unit (PU) for the client and the provider, $\#PU$ represents the number of resources (in PUs) provisioned by the provider for supporting the aggregated requests of n clients, and $\Delta\#PU$ the number of resources allocated to avoid penalties over bursty periods. The global revenue is the accumulated $Instant Revenue$ over time.

Eq. 1 can be extended to account for additional capabilities, for instance the cost of provisioning additional PUs ($\Delta\#PU$) – which can include the number of virtual machines executed on a single physical machine. Alternatively, the number of processing units can be a function of an estimated workload as a function of data size defined by a data window ($CostPU_{clienti} = f(operation, datasize)$), etc. We will consider Eq. 1 in this paper for sake of simplicity and we will assume for the same reason that data streams can be classified according to the benefit and penalty values of their respective QoS levels as: "Gold" – for high penalty and revenue; "Silver" – for medium penalty and revenue, and "Bronze" – for low revenue and no penalty [7]. This class approach for provisioning resource is commonly found in many commercial data centres and network providers today.

3   Dynamic Control of Resources under Revenue-Based Management

The revenue model can be used internally by a provider to decide what actions are the most "financially" suitable to dynamically manage resources on a near real-time basis. For instance, when a failure to meet the minimum QoS level for a given user is predicted or detected, a provider may perform the following actions:

– action (1): allocate new local resources or *buy* remote resources,
– action (2): redistribute unused resources by users,
– action (3): redistribute pre-allocated resources from less prioritized users to more prioritized users ("Bronze" to "Silver" to "Gold", or "Bronze" to "Silver").

Each of these actions could have a different cost or penalty for the provider. For instance, allocating new local resources is usually less costly than buying remote resources (using other providers' resources for instance), but may be more costly than redistributing pre-allocated resources from Silver users to Gold users. This could occur because the penalty for not satisfying these Silver users may be less than the cost of allocating new local resources, especially for a short period of time, or because this redistribution of resources may not impact the chosen Silver users due to statistical multiplexing of user needs. When redistributing unused resources, a typical SLA would indicate a negotiated mean data injection rate to be supported by the provider of the computational resource(s). Therefore, when the amount of injected data over a given time period is smaller than the predicted value, some pre-allocated resources are unutilized. In this case, the redistribution of these unused resources can be done at a low cost by the provider. Hence, we assume that due to the inherent variation in stream processing, it is often difficult to predict accurately the resource demand across multiple time frames. Consequently, this introduces a slack in the system, whereby unused resources may be reallocated to reduce penalties for other data streams in the system. We proposed in our previous work [3] an architecture that uses the token bucket model to perform traffic shaping on user data flows. We also defined how token bucket parameters can be controlled by a rule engine to prioritize data streams. In this paper, we will explain how self-controlled actions could also be directly implemented with different extensions of the token bucket model, introducing for instance an intermediate, shared bucket that will collect unused resources that can be later on be re-distributed across different user classes.

3.1 Dynamic Management of Resources

QoS requirements are often defined using the worst case scenario – i.e. the maximum number of resources required to achieve a particular QoS objective. However, some data streams may not use the resources that they have reserved and these unused resources could be used to process other streams to increase revenue. Hence, spare capacity in the system could be reallocated. This is particularly useful to handle periods of bursty behavior on some streams. The provider's objective is to maximize its revenue by the management of available computational resources (e.g. a pool of virtual machines in an elastic infrastructure) to process each data stream in accordance with its SLA, taking into account various costs and penalties. It is therefore necessary to regulate end-user's data injection rate according to an agreed SLA, to monitor whether enough resources have been provisioned, and to perform actions to redistribute resources when needed. We described in [3] a modular architecture (illustrated in Fig. 1) consisting of a *traffic shapping* component and a *QoS provisioning* component that provides a dynamic management of resources. We will quickly review the main features of this architecture.

The *traffic shapping* component provides a token bucket per data stream. Within a data stream, it is often useful to identify a "data acceptance rate", which is often different from the physical link capacity connecting nodes and which identifies the rate at which a client can send data to be processed by the server. The data stream processing service tries to maintain this acceptance rate as the output rate. We characterise it for each flow by means of three QoS parameters: (i) average throughput (average number of data elements processed per second), (ii) maximum allowed burst, and (iii) an optional load shedding (data dropping) rate. We make the first two parameters match R and b of the token bucket respectively. For each data stream, its associated token bucket will allow data elements to enter into the processing stage according to the R parameter. The token bucket can also accept a burst of b data elements. Subsequently, a data element is forwarded to a First Come First Serve (FCFS) queue buffer at a processing unit (PU). In addition to regulating access to the PU and enforcing QoS per data stream, the token bucket also achieves stream isolation, i.e. a data burst in one stream does not interfere with another. The load shedding mechanism acts at input buffers by discarding older data elements of a flow at a specified rate. It is only active, however, when triggered by the controller component.

The *QoS provisioning* component takes decisions about the allocation and redistribution of resources based on the monitoring of buffers and token buckets. For example, availability of data in buffers of a token bucket implies data injection over the agreed mean rate, which can trigger different actions based on occupancy thresholds: 1) dropping data from the buffers, 2) allocating additional resources to consume the burst of data, 3) reallocation of resources from other streams. The number of allocated resources for providing service to the aggregate demand may not be enough for a bursty period. In this case, the controller must detect data streams that require more resources. Data in the computational phase are stored in buffers associated with each data stream (we denote these as PU buffers to differentiate them from TB buffers). The PU buffer size can be used to detect when data are been buffered because there are not enough allocated resources. For instance, during each control interval T the maximum amount of data that can appear is $RT + b$. If the PU buffer size is greater than b, this suggests that not enough resources have been provisioned to sustain the QoS of this data stream. Note that during a time interval b data can be transferred to the processing phase if there are enough tokens in the TB.

The bottom part of Fig. 1 shows the control loop configuring the R parameter and the number of resources for each flow instance. For simplicity, the figure shows the regulation of one flow instance. Each flow instance monitors its input and output rates at each stage at a pre-defined sampling rate (magnifying glasses (a) in the figure). Using these initial parameter values, the control strategy is initiated, subsequently recording the TB (b) and PU (c) input queue buffer occupancies, and the number of resources in use at the PU (d). The size of each input buffer is chosen in accordance with the agreed requirements of the data flow. The controller must estimate the buffer size during execution. When the input buffer size reaches an established threshold, it triggers the controller to initiate one of two possible actions: (i) calculate the number of additional resources (PU) needed (based on those available) to process the additional data items generated above rate R; (ii) if there are free local resources (not being used by other data flows), they can be used to increase the rate R of flow associated with this instance. The amount of resources and the rate value will return to their previously agreed values when the input buffer size goes below the threshold. A detailed description of this control loop and validation scenarios can be found in [3].

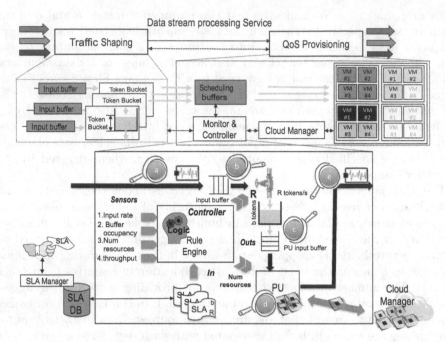

Fig. 1. Control loop for decision making

It appeared that allocating new resources, action (1), may not be suitable for handling short periods of resource shortage. The time required to get statistics and the inference process of the rule engine does not allow introduction of new resources in near real-time. In this paper, we propose to additionally investigate action (2), redistribute unused resources, and action (3), redistribute preallocated resources from less prioritized to more prioritized users. The choice of the final action will be determined by the revenue model using a cost, or penalty, associated with each action. We will describe how these actions can be easily implemented by the provider by extending the previous token bucket model.

3.2 Redistribute Unused Uesources by Users

When the real amount of injected data over a given time period is lower than the predicted amount, tokens can be saved by a user and they accumulate in its associated TB up to a maximum of b tokens (which is the bucket size). Normally, these excess tokens are dropped by the TB to avoid very large bursts of data in the future. However, it is possible for a provider to save these tokens in an additional shared bucket (of maximum size B_{max}) and to redistribute them at a low cost – as these tokens typical represent unused resources that have already been allocated. Figure 2 illustrates this behavior. These tokens in excess could also have a limited lifetime as symbolically represented by the clock in Fig. 2 in order to limit their usage within a few control intervals only.

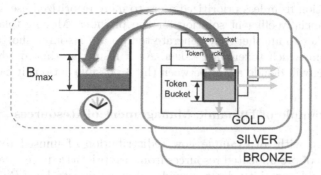

Fig. 2. Redistributing unused resources over a control period

Collecting tokens in excess and redistribution of tokens can be performed globally over all user classes. However, limiting token movement within the same class may be easier to support, e.g. excess tokens from Gold users can only be redistributed to other Gold users. Fig. 2 with the dashed box illustrates this solution where each user class should have their own additional bucket space. The B_{max} parameter can be different for each user class. For instance, $B_{max}^{gold} > B_{max}^{silver} > B_{max}^{bronze}$. The rationale behind different values for B_{max} is that unused resources from Bronze users could be considered more *volatile* than unused resources from Silver or Gold users for instance, as Bronze user resources may have been statistically allocated. It is possible to generalize this architecture for a higher number of classes where $B_{max}^{C_n} > B_{max}^{C_{n-1}} > ... > B_{max}^{C_2} > B_{max}^{C_1}$

3.3 Redistribute Pre-allocated Resources from Less Prioritized Users to More Prioritized Users

The case of redistributing pre-allocated resources is quite different from the unused resources case: tokens from a chosen user's bucket will be moved directly to another user's bucket. Figure 3 illustrates this redistribution process from a Bronze user to a Silver user.

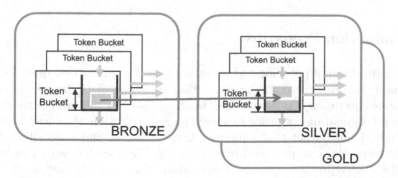

Fig. 3. Redistribution from low priority users to high priority users

Redistribution from less prioritized users to more prioritized users is typically the most financially efficient solution for the provider. Moving tokens directly from one bucket to another may generate temporary resource shortages for the data flow from which tokens are taken. As a result, at time of shortage, the revenue model will decide again between the 3 possible actions it can perform.

3.4   An Example of Dynamic Management of Resources

Let us explain with an example how redistribution of unused resources and redistribution of pre-allocated resources from less prioritized users could be used consistently and conjointly by a provider. Let us denote by $TB_u^{C_n}$ the token bucket of a user stream u in class C_n and by $TB_{unused}^{C_n}$ the shared bucket space in class C_n to keep unused resources (tokens) up to $B_{max}^{C_n}$.

Consider that a provider has under-estimated the resources that should be allocated to a user of class C_n (one reason could be a bursty injection period). When the system detects that this user does not have a sufficient processing rate according to its negotiated token bucket data injection rate, the provider can take unused tokens from $TB_{unused}^{C_n}$ that have been collected within class C_n, if any. If there are no unused tokens in class C_n, the provider will take tokens directly from $TB_u^{C_i}$ of a user u in a lower class C_i, with $1 \leq i \leq n-1$, and not from the shared bucket space $TB_{unused}^{C_i}$ of these lower classes C_i. The reason is that resources collected in $TB_{unused}^{C_i}$ represent more "volatile" resources than resources kept in $TB_u^{C_i}$ that normally could be somehow mapped to real resources in the current control interval.

By doing so, the class C_n user demand can be satisfied at minimum cost, therefore limiting the penalty for the provider. If the C_i class users, $1 \leq i \leq n-1$, from whom tokens have been taken away by users in class C_n have token/resource shortage, the system will first try to take tokens from the shared unused resource bucket space of the corresponding class, i.e. $TB_{unused}^{C_i}$, if any, and only then will try to take token directly from a token bucket of a lower class C_j, i.e. from $TB_u^{C_j}$, $1 \leq j \leq i-1$. This process could be repeated at each class C_i. We can therefore see how this 2-level token movement system can be used to optimally move resources (unused or pre-allocated) based on a maximum revenue strategy.

4   Evaluation Scenarios

The redistribution of pre-allocated resources from less prioritized users to more prioritized was illustrated in the evaluation scenarios of [3] by means of the rule engine controlling TB parameters. In this paper, we will present the results of different simulation scenarios to show the redistribution of unused resources by an additional bucket that collects tokens in excess and redistribute them over the same class, as proposed in section 3.2. We consider two scenarios: (i) using the rule-engine controller, which validates the shared bucket in an elastic provisioning approach with tokens representing reliable allocated resources; and

(ii) without use of controller actions, which validates the shared bucket with more *volatile* tokens.

The scenarios has been modeled using the *Reference net* formalism [8] to specify the decision making component. The models have been simulated in Renew (see http://www.renew.de), a Java-based editor and simulator based on reference nets that integrates the Petri net formalism, and the Java programming language. The Java Expert System Shell (Jess), is used to trigger actions based on threshold monitored values, such as token bucket and PU buffers, and input/output rates. For this work, the token bucket manager model that provides a token bucket for each new data stream presented in [2] has been extended with the common shared bucket. The modeled behavior moves excess tokens to the common bucket, and all data streams can make use of these tokens if their buckets are empty and there are no pending data items to be processed in the PU buffers. At the end of each control period, the common bucket is emptied: therefore the lifetime of collected unused resources is limited to a control interval.

4.1   Redistribution of Tokens in an Elastic Scenario

The first scenario considers data streams at the same priority level. We assume 4 Gold (i.e. high priority) customer streams with a period of control of T=1 second and all data streams have same requirements: R=20 and b=10. The maximum number of data to be processed is 120 data chunk/second and a token is required to process a data chunk. We assume that each resource can process 10 data chunk/s (therefore requiring in the worst case a maximum of 12 processing units). Input streams follow on ON-OFF process where ON and OFF periods follow a uniform distribution between 2 to 5 seconds and alternate each other. Data injection rates within the ON period follows an exponential law (Poisson distribution) therefore varying the data injection rate over time. On average about 4 resources are required for the 4 data streams (each stream sends on average 20 data/second half of the time). For the first set of simulations we compare the behavior of the system with and without the common bucket (of capacity $B_{max}^{gold} = 80$ tokens). These simulations are developed in combination with the use of the rule engine to provide enough resources throughout the simulation period. The rule engine triggers actions for dropping data when the TB buffer occupancy is over an established threshold, adding/removing resources in a elastic way (borrowing resources from low priority data streams) and tuning TB parameters to use the new added resources or available resources when PU buffers have accumulated data (which is an indication that not enough resources are available). All simulations reproduce the same input data injection rates for comparison purpose.

To calculate the revenue with Eq. 1 we assume a cost of 20 units/second per PU for clients and 15 units/second per PU for provider. We assume the client pays for having the processing rate R all the time. Taking into account that the data stream rates are irregular and the client send data at a rate R/2 on average, the provider will suffer from a high penalization, for example 30 times the price paid by the client, i.e. 600 units, if it does not provide enough resources.

A penalty occurs when the output rate is under the agreed rate R if there are data in the TB buffer. In this way, it is easy for the client to monitor whether the provider is allocating enough resources or not. If the buffer is full, the output rate should be at least equal to R. If the throughput is under this value, data in the buffer are being accumulated and will be delayed to be processed in the next control intervals due to the lack of resources.

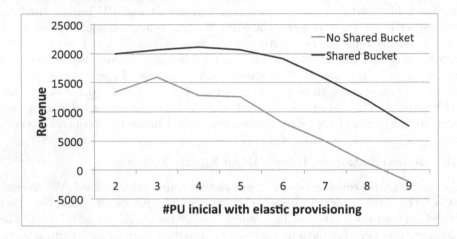

Fig. 4. Scenario I: Redistribution of tokens in an elastic scenario with different baseline PUs (horizontal axis) and using control loop to avoid penalties. Revenue is measured in an abstract unit, but can be mapped to a particular economic currency.

Figure 4 shows the provider's revenue for different number of initial PUs and an elastic provisioning of resources scenario. The x-axis represents the initial baseline number of resources and the y-axis the aggregated revenue over 300 seconds of simulation. These results show the maximum revenue when enough resources are available to satisfy the demand. Providing less resources than this baseline increases the number of penalties, and providing more resources as baseline increases the cost. The common bucket however does not improve significantly the aggregated throughput as shown in Figure 6, but the throughput of each individual data stream is improved as shown in the sample data stream output of figure 5. If we look at time interval 20s-40s, 70s-80s and 140s-150s we can see that the shared bucket allows the output throughput to closely follow the input data injection rate. This behavior can be more clearly seen with 9 PUs than with 4 PUs, i.e. when there are globally enough resources. Without the shared bucket the output throughput is clearly limited by the b parameter (maximum amount of tokens in the bucket) and a shortage of tokens limits the output throughput to R until the TB buffer is emptied.

The bottom of Figure 7 shows that the average number of PUs provisioned (their cost being represented by the last term in Eq. 1) in an elastic scenario is not affected by the use of the shared bucket. However the number of penalizations (second term in Eq 1.) is clearly reduced with the use of the shared bucket as illustrated in Figure 7(top).

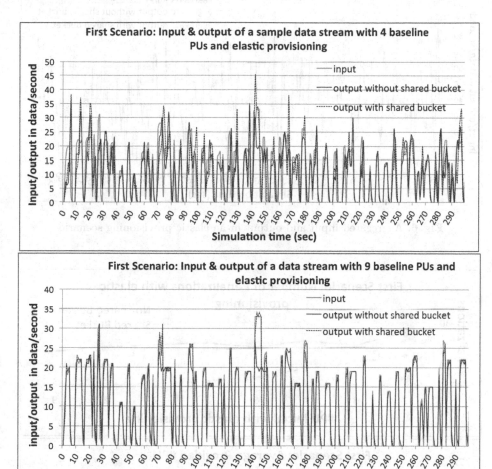

Fig. 5. Data stream input & output in an elastic provisioning scenario

4.2 Redistribution of Tokens in a Non-elastic Scenario

The second scenario uses the same number of data streams than previously but without rules to provide additional resources in an elastic way. Therefore, when there are shortage of resources, the benefit of the redistribution feature can be better seen. In this scenario data streams have a more sporadic behavior to enable greater usage of the shared bucket: ON and OFF period durations follow a uniform distribution between 1 to 3 seconds, but now an ON period have a probability of 1/3 to occur. Again, data injection rates follow a Poisson distribution. Therefore, for 4 data streams sending on average 20 data chunk/second

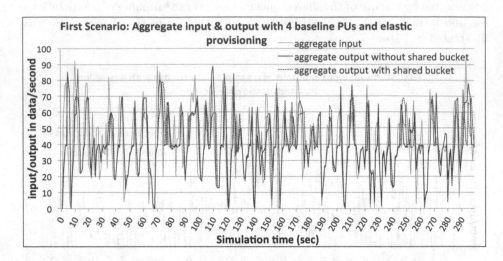

Fig. 6. Aggregated input and output in an elastic provisioning scenario

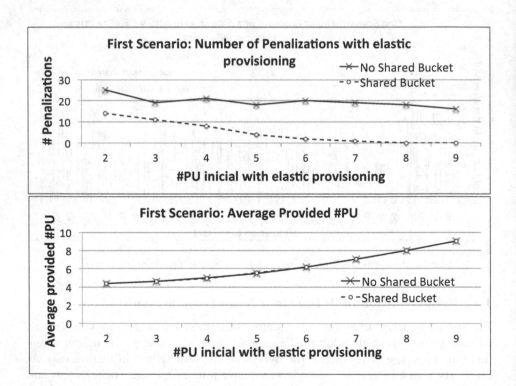

Fig. 7. Average number of PU in an elastic scenario and number of penalties

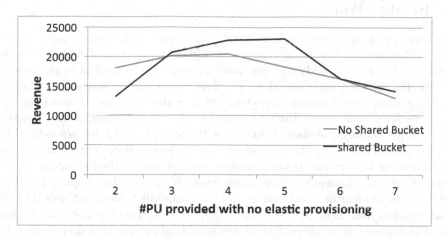

Fig. 8. Scenario II: Redistribution of tokens in a non-elastic scenario with different baseline PUs (horizontal axis)

the number of required resources is around 3. Figure 8 shows the provider's revenue with different number of initial provisioned PUs. With less than 3 PUs, the number of penalizations makes the revenue to decrease and the shared bucket gives a lower revenue when there is shortage of resources. Provisioning between 3 and 5 PUs makes the shared bucket very useful as a low cost solution to balance the usage of resources between classes. Figure 9 shows how throughput closely follows the input data injection rate at time interval 110s-120s and 210s-220s.

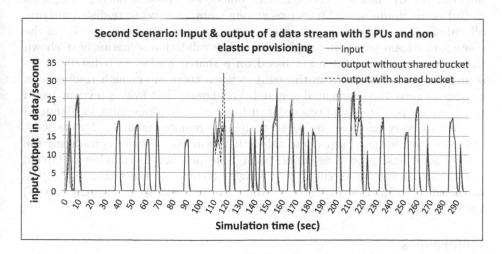

Fig. 9. Data stream input & output in a non elastic scenario

5   Related Work

Auto-scaling of resources has been identified as one of the main challenges for Cloud Computing. The main concern to optimize the use of resources is to automatically scale quickly up and down in response to load in order to save money, but without violating SLAs [1]. There is emerging interest in processing automated elastic resource provisioning over shared Cloud. Three main approaches have been pointed out to quickly scale resources [9]. First, reactive mechanisms, mainly use elasticity rules or threshold-based rules pre-defined by service providers [10, 7, 11]. Second, predictive mechanisms try to learn from previous data history and resource usage to construct mathematical models to forecast resource demands. These approaches are useful when regular behavior pattern can be identified, but can not forecast unpredictable burstiness [12, 13]. This problem has been considered in [14] to propose pattern matching scaling based algorithms as an alternative to mathematical models that do not consider arbitrarily-repetitive self-similarities. And third, hybrid approaches [15] that integrate the 2 previous approaches or, more recently, use theory of control [16]. A brief reference to related work on elastic resources provisioning of workflow, streaming and event processing have been presented in [3].

6   Conclusion and Future Work

We propose (i) an architecture that features a token bucket process envelop to support data throttling, (ii) a rule-based control loop to enable corrective actions to be triggered when QoS is violated: the control loop monitors QoS for each application and chooses an action that maximises revenue over a pre-defined control interval, and dynamic corrective actions embedded in token bucket extensions to (iii) re-distribute unused resources among users, and (iv) to re-distribute pre-allocated resources from less prioritized users to more prioritized users – in the context of stream processing applications. The validation scenarios have shown that the token bucket extension based on a shared bucket to redistribute resources increases data stream throughput when there are enough resources on average to serve the aggregated demand. We showed that from a revenue-based perspective, optimization of resources with low-cost solutions using local unused resources is very effective compared to buying remote resources. Future work will consider additional aspects to calculate the instant revenue considering the cost of additional processing units, taking into account the number of virtual machines that can be executed on a single machine, or the estimation of the workload as a function of historical data (using previous service executions) with different parameters (operation, data size, window size, etc.).

References

1. Armbrust, M., Fox, A., Griffith, R., Joseph, A.D., Katz, R., Konwinski, A., Lee, G., Patterson, D., Rabkin, A., Stoica, I., Zaharia, M.: A view of cloud computing. Commun. ACM 53(4), 50–58 (2010)

2. Tolosana-Calasanz, R., Bañares, J.Á., Pham, C., Rana, O.F.: Enforcing QoS in scientific workflow systems enacted over Cloud infrastructures. J. Comput. Syst. Sci. 78(5), 1300–1315 (2012)
3. Tolosana-Calasanz, R., Bañares, J.Á., Pham, C., Rana, O.F.: Revenue-based resource management on shared clouds for heterogenous bursty data streams. In: Vanmechelen, K., Altmann, J., Rana, O.F. (eds.) GECON 2012. LNCS, vol. 7714, pp. 61–75. Springer, Heidelberg (2012)
4. Tolosana-Calasanz, R., Bañares, J.Á., Rana, O., Papadopoulus, P., Pham, C.: A Distributed In-Transit Processing Infrastructure for Forecasting Electric Vehicle Charging Demand. In: DPMSS Workshop Alongside 13th IEEE/ACM Int. Symp. on Cluster, Cloud and Grid Computing, CCGrid 2013, Delft, Netherlands, May 13-16 (2013)
5. Abdelzaher, T., Bhatti, N.: Web server QoS management by adaptive content delivery. In: 7th Int. Workshop on IWQoS 1999, pp. 216–225 (1999)
6. Etzion, O., Niblett, P.: Event Processing in Action, 1st edn. Manning Publications Co., Greenwich (2010)
7. Macías, M., Fitó, J.O., Guitart, J.: Rule-based sla management for revenue maximisation in cloud computing markets. In: CNSM, pp. 354–357. IEEE (2010)
8. Kummer, O.: Referenznetze. Logos Verlag, Berlin (2002)
9. Jiang, J., Lu, J., Zhang, G., Long, G.: Optimal Cloud Resource Auto-Scaling for Web Applications. In: 13th IEEE/ACM Int. Symp. on Cluster, Cloud and Grid Computing, CCGrid 2013, Delft, Netherlands, May 13-16, pp. 58–65 (2013)
10. Amazon Auto Scaling
11. Copil, G., Moldovan, D., Truong, H.-L., Dustdar, S.: SYBL: An Extensible Language for Controlling Elasticity in Cloud Applications. In: 13th IEEE/ACM Int. Symp. on Cluster, Cloud and Grid Computing, CCGrid 2013, Delft, Netherlands, May 13-16, pp. 112–119 (2013)
12. Tsoumakos, D., Konstantinou, I., Boumpouka, C., Sioutas, S., Koziris, N.: Automated, Elastic Resource Provisioning for NoSQL Clusters Using TIRAMOLA. In: 13th IEEE/ACM Int. Symp. on Cluster, Cloud and Grid Computing, CCGrid 2013, Delft, Netherlands, May 13-16, pp. 34–41 (2013)
13. Morais, F., Brasileiro, F., Lopes, R., Araújo, R., Satterfield, W., Rosa, L.: Autoflex: Service Agnostic Auto-scaling Framework for IaaS Deployment Models. In: 13th IEEE/ACM Int. Symp. on Cluster, Cloud and Grid Computing, CCGrid 2013, Delft, Netherlands, May 13-16, pp. 112–119 (2013)
14. Shen, Z., Subbiah, S., Gu, X., Wilkes, J.: CloudScale: Elastic resource scaling for multi-tenant Cloud systems. In: Proceedings of the 2nd ACM Symposium on Cloud Computing, SOCC 2011, pp. 5:1–5:14. ACM, New York (2011)
15. Iqbal, W., Dailey, M.N., Carrera, D., Janecek, P.: Adaptive resource provisioning for read intensive multi-tier applications in the Cloud. Future Gener. Comput. Syst. 27(6), 871–879 (2011)
16. Padala, P., Hou, K.Y., Shin, K.G., Zhu, X., Uysal, M., Wang, Z., Singhal, S., Merchant, A.: Automated control of multiple virtualized resources. In: Proceedings of the 4th ACM European Conference on Computer Systems, EuroSys 2009, pp. 13–26. ACM, New York (2009)

Scheduling Divisible Loads
to Optimize the Computation Time and Cost

Natalia V. Shakhlevich

School of Computing, University of Leeds, Leeds LS2 9JT, U.K.
n.shakhlevich@leeds.ac.uk

Abstract. Efficient load distribution plays an important role in grid
and cloud applications. In a typical problem, a divisible load should be
split into parts and allocated to several processors, with one processor
responsible for the data transfer. Since processors have different speed
and cost characteristics, selecting the processor order for the transmission and defining the chunk sizes affect the computation time and cost.
We perform a systematic study of the model analysing the properties
of Pareto optimal solutions. We demonstrate that the earlier research
has a number of limitations. In particular, it is generally assumed that
the load should be distributed so that all processors have equal completion times, while in fact this property is satisfied only for some deadlines; for many optimal schedules this property does not hold. Moreover,
fixing the processor sequence in the non-decreasing order of the cost-
characteristic may be appropriate only for Pareto-optimal solutions with
relatively large deadlines; optimal schedules for tight deadlines may have
a different order of processors. We conclude with an efficient algorithm
for finding the time-cost trade-off.

Keywords: Scheduling, Divisible Load, Time/cost Optimization.

1 Introduction

Parallel computer systems have given rise to new scheduling models that go
beyond the classical scheduling theory. While in a traditional scheduling model
a task can be processed by one machine at a time, a new feature of multiprocessor
computations is the ability to split tasks into several parts and to process them
simultaneously by different processors, see, e.g., [8,14]. An additional feature of
modern Grid computing and cloud computing systems is the introduction of the
cost factor, see, e.g. [4,11,16]. This study is motivated by the lack of theoretical
research in the area and some inaccuracies which can be found in the earlier
research.

We consider the network model described in [13]. There is a set $\mathcal{P} = \{P_1, P_2,$
$\ldots, P_m\}$ of m processors connected via a bus type communication medium. One
processor of the set $\mathcal{P}$ is selected as a master processor to receive a divisible load
of size τ and to divide it into portions of size $\alpha_1\tau$, $\alpha_2\tau, \ldots, \alpha_m\tau$, $\sum_{k=1}^{m} \alpha_k =$
1, which are then transmitted to slave processors from $\mathcal{P}$ to perform required
computations.

J. Altmann, K. Vanmechelen, and O.F. Rana (Eds.): GECON 2013, LNCS 8193, pp. 138–148, 2013.

The processors have different computation speeds and for each processor $P_k \in \mathcal{P}$ the inverse of the speed w_k is given. This implies that the load of size $\alpha_k \tau$ allocated to processor P_k requires computation time $\alpha_k w_k \tau$.

If P_1 is selected as a master processor and the transmission sequence is P_2, P_3, ..., P_m, then P_1 can start processing its own load of size $\alpha_1 \tau$ at time 0 and at the same time it can start transmitting the relevant portions of the load first to P_2, then to P_3, etc., until the last portion is transmitted to P_m, see Fig. 1. If z is the time needed to transmit the whole load of size τ, then the communication time for transmitting the portion $\alpha_k \tau$ to processor P_k is $\alpha_k z$.

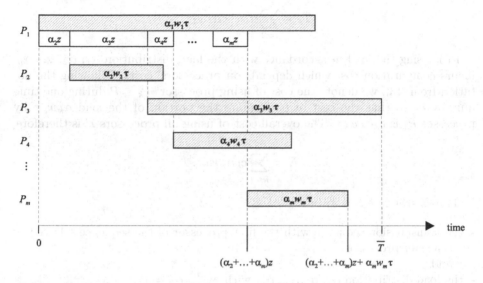

Fig. 1. An example of a schedule with master processor P_1 and transmission sequence $P_2, \ldots, P_m$

With the selected transmission order, processor P_1 completes its portion of computation at time

$$T_1 = \alpha_1 w_1 \tau. \tag{1}$$

Processor P_k, $2 \leq k \leq m$, receives its portion of the load at time $\sum_{i=2}^{k} \alpha_i z$ and immediately after that it can start computation, which takes $\alpha_k w_k \tau$ time. Thus processor P_k completes its portion of the load at time

$$T_k = \sum_{i=2}^{k} \alpha_i z + \alpha_k w_k \tau.$$

The finish time T of the load is defined as the *makespan* of the schedule; it is equal to the maximum completion time among all processors,

$$T = \max_{1 \leq k \leq m} \{T_k\}. \tag{2}$$

It is assumed in the described scenario that the master processor can perform data transmission and computation simultaneously. This usually happens if the processor is equipped with an additional front-end co-processor which takes care of all data transfer so that the master processor can perform computation as any other processor of the network. In the absence of a front-end co-processor, the master processor performs data transmission first and only after that it can start computing its portion of the load. In the latter scenario, Fig. 1 should be modified so that for processor P_1 the box "$\alpha_1 w_1 \tau$" is moved immediately after "$\alpha_m z$", and formula (1) should be replaced by

$$T_1 = \sum_{i=2}^{m} \alpha_i z + \alpha_1 w_1 \tau.$$

Processing the load in accordance with the load distribution $\alpha_1, \alpha_2, \ldots, \alpha_m$ incurs computation cost which depends on processors' costs. Following the notation from [13], we denote the cost of using processor $P_k \in \mathcal{P}$ during one time unit by c_k so that the cost of performing the portion of the load $\alpha_k w_k \tau$ by processor P_k is $c_k \alpha_k w_k \tau$. The overall cost of using all processors P is therefore

$$K = \sum_{k=1}^{m} c_k \alpha_k w_k \tau.$$

Thus a schedule S is given by

- the transmission sequence with the first processor of the sequence selected as a master processor
    and
- the load distribution $\alpha_1, \alpha_2, \ldots, \alpha_m$ with $\sum_{k=1}^{m} \alpha_k = 1$.

In this paper we assume that the processors are numbered so that

$$c_1 w_1 \leq c_2 w_2 \leq \cdots \leq c_m w_m. \tag{3}$$

The quality of a scheduled is measured in terms of the two characteristics: maximum completion time T and computation cost K. As a solution to a bicriteria problem we accept the set of Pareto optimal points defined by the breakpoints of the so-called *efficiency frontier*. In a pair of the associated single criterion problems,

$$\begin{aligned} &\min K \\ &\text{s.t. } T \leq \overline{T} \end{aligned} \tag{4}$$

and

$$\begin{aligned} &\min T \\ &\text{s.t. } K \leq \overline{K} \end{aligned} \tag{5}$$

one of the objectives is bounded while the other one is to be minimized. Here $\overline{T}$ and $\overline{K}$ are threshold values of the load finish time and computation cost, respectively.

Model (4) and its bicriteria counterpart have been under study since the 90s, see [13]. Over the last 20 years the research has been expanded to cover more complicated versions of the divisible load model which take into account additional features of real-world systems such as, e.g., the time needed for the transmission of the results back to the master processor, different transmission speeds dependent on a receiving processor (see, e.g., [2]), and generalized formulae for data transmission in which the transmission time is not proportional to the size of the computation chunk. Recently divisible load analysis has been extended to more complex networks [6,10], to the area of MapReduce distributed computations [3] and to cloud computing [1,9,12].

Although divisible load models have attracted much attention of researchers and the study expands now by incorporating additional features, there are still some optimization aspects which have not been addressed properly in the previous work. The flaws in the analysis of the basic problem (4) lead to some wrong conclusions in more recent research. Without re-solving those issues related to the simplest problem (4), the analysis of more complex models is questionable. In particular, in the early paper [13] the authors solve problem (4) under an unjustified assumption that in an optimal schedule all processors complete their computation chunks simultaneously. In addition, the processors' sequence is fixed in accordance with the non-decreasing order of the cost-characteristic, which does not necessarily hold in an optimal solution. The misconceptions from [13] are propagated to the subsequence research [6].

As we show in our study, there exist optimal schedules in which processors do not complete their chunks simultaneously and the processor order is different from the one proposed in [13]. A careful analysis of the divisible load model allows us to develop an efficient algorithm that solves the bicriteria problem of time-cost optimization and guarantees the optimality of the trade-off solutions it produces. Notice that until recently researchers have been working on heuristic approaches for solving single criterion problems (4) and (5), see, e.g., [7].

2 Finding the Efficiency Frontier

In the (T, K)-space, the set of Pareto-optimal points represents a time-cost efficiency frontier. We start with an overview of the main outcomes of [13] and then proceed with the description of additional steps needed to find a correct efficiency frontier.

It is claimed in [13] that all break-points correspond to the schedules of a special type: the processor sequence is the same for all break-points and it is $(P_1, P_2, \ldots, P_m)$; only a subset of the several first processors have a non-zero load, while the remaining processors are idle. Recall that processors are numbered in accordance with (3).

To represent the described schedules formally, introduce notation $(P_1^*, P_2^*, \ldots, P_k^*, -, \ldots, -)$ to indicate that processors $P_1, P_2, \ldots, P_k$ are fully loaded completing computation at time T, while the remaining processors $P_{k+1}, P_{k+2}, \ldots, P_m$ are idle. Then the set of the break-points established in [13] is of the form:

$$
\begin{array}{c}
(P_1^*, \ -, \ \ -, \ \cdots, \ -, \ \ \ -, \ \ \cdots, \ \ \ -, \ \ \ - \ ) \\
(P_1^*, P_2^*, \ -, \ \cdots, \ -, \ \ \ -, \ \ \cdots, \ \ \ -, \ \ \ - \ ) \\
(P_1^*, P_2^*, P_3^*, \cdots, \ -, \ \ \ -, \ \ \cdots, \ \ \ -, \ \ \ - \ )
\end{array}
$$

$$
\begin{array}{c}
(P_1^*, P_2^*, P_3^*, \cdots, P_k^*, \ \ -, \ \ \ \cdots, \ \ \ -, \ \ \ - \ ) \\
(P_1^*, P_2^*, P_3^*, \cdots, P_k^*, \ P_{k+1}^*, \ \ \ \ \ \ -, \ \ \ - \ )
\end{array}
$$

$$
\begin{array}{c}
(P_1^*, P_2^*, P_3^*, \cdots, P_k^*, \ P_{k+1}^*, \ \cdots, P_{m-1}^*, \ - \ ) \\
(P_1^*, P_2^*, P_3^*, \cdots, P_k^*, \ P_{k+1}^*, \ \cdots, P_{m-1}^*, \ P_m^* \ )
\end{array}
$$

The graphical representation of the efficiency frontier from [13] for the case of $m = 3$ processors is shown in Fig. 2. The three break-points, considered right to left, are $(P_1^*, -, -)$, $(P_1^*, P_2^*, -)$ and (P_1^*, P_2^*, P_3^*). When transition from $(P_1^*, -, -)$ to $(P_1^*, P_2^*, -)$ is performed, the load from P_1 is re-distributed to P_2 until both processors have equal completion time; the intermediate points belonging to that segment of the efficiency frontier are denoted by $(P_1^*, P_2, -)$, where notation P_2 in the schedule description indicates that processor P_2 is partly loaded. Similarly, when transition from $(P_1^*, P_2^*, -)$ to (P_1^*, P_2^*, P_3^*) is performed, the load from P_1 and P_2 is re-distributed to P_3 until all three processors have equal completion time; the intermediate points belonging to that segment are denoted by (P_1^*, P_2^*, P_3), where notation P_3 indicates that processor P_3 is partly loaded, while notation P_1^*, P_2^* implies that the corresponding processors are fully loaded completing their portions of the load simultaneously.

It appears that the efficiency frontier is more complicated than the one presented in [13]. In particular, it includes also the points with the processor order different from $(P_1, P_2, \ldots, P_m)$. In fact, the efficiency frontier can be found as the set of non-dominating segments of m curves $\mathcal{C}_\ell$, $\ell = 1, \ldots, m$. Each curve $\mathcal{C}_\ell$ consists of linear segments and corresponds to a processor sequence with a fixed master processor P_ℓ. As we demonstrate in the appendix, in the class of schedules with a fixed master processor P_ℓ, an optimal processor sequence is $(P_\ell, P_1, P_2, \ldots, P_{\ell-1}, P_{\ell+1}, \ldots, P_m)$. If $\ell > 1$, then the first $\ell - 1$ breakpoints (considered in the (T, K)-space from right to left) correspond to schedules in which the master processor P_ℓ performs only data transmission and does not perform ant computation; the next break-point involves all ℓ processors fully loaded, so that the master processor P_ℓ performs both, data transmission and computation; in the remaining $m - \ell$ schedules, ℓ first processors are fully loaded together with an increasing number of additional slave processors with indices larger than ℓ.

Formally, the break-points of the curve $\mathcal{C}_\ell$ with a fixed master processor P_ℓ are of the form:

$$
\begin{array}{l}
\textit{processor } P_\ell \\
\textit{does not perform} \\
\textit{any computation,} \\
\textit{only data} \\
\textit{transmission}
\end{array}
\left\{
\begin{array}{c}
(\underline{P_\ell}, P_1^*, \ -, \ \ -, \ \cdots, \ \ -, \ \ \ -, \ \ \cdots, \ \ -, \ \ \ - \ ) \\
(\underline{P_\ell}, P_1^*, P_2^*, \ -, \ \cdots, \ \ -, \ \ \ -, \ \ \cdots, \ \ -, \ \ \ - \ ) \\
(\underline{P_\ell}, P_1^*, P_2^*, P_3^*, \cdots, \ \ -, \ \ \ -, \ \ \cdots, \ \ -, \ \ \ - \ ) \\
\ddots \qquad\qquad\qquad -, \\
(\underline{P_\ell}, P_1^*, P_2^*, P_3^*, \cdots, P_{\ell-1}^*, \ -, \ \cdots, \ \ -, \ \ \ - \ )
\end{array}
\right.
$$

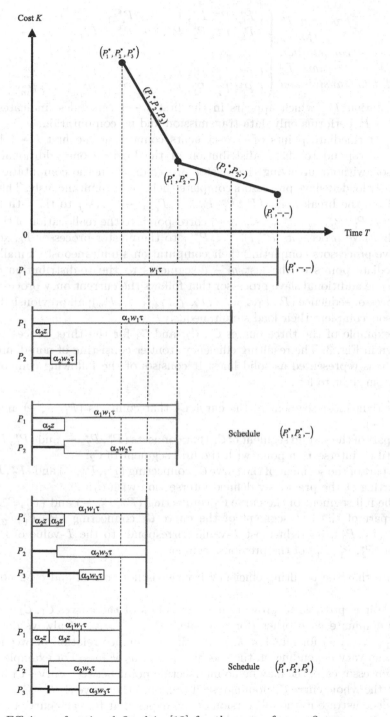

Fig. 2. Efficiency frontier defined in [13] for the case of $m = 3$ processors and the associated schedules (idle processors are omitted)

$$
\begin{array}{c}
\textit{processor } P_\ell \\
\textit{performs} \\
\textit{computation} \\
\textit{(until } T) \\
\textit{and data transmission}
\end{array}
\left\{
\begin{array}{l}
(\ P_\ell^*, P_1^*, P_2^*, P_3^*, \cdots, P_{\ell-1}^*, \quad -, \quad \cdots, \quad -, \quad - \ ) \\
(\ P_\ell^*, P_1^*, P_2^*, P_3^*, \cdots, P_{\ell-1}^*, P_{\ell+1}^*, \cdots, \quad -, \quad - \ ) \\
\qquad\qquad\qquad\qquad\qquad \ddots \\
(\ P_\ell^*, P_1^*, P_2^*, P_3^*, \cdots, P_{\ell-1}^*, P_{\ell+1}^*, \cdots, P_{m-1}^*, \ - \ ) \\
(\ P_\ell^*, P_1^*, P_2^*, P_3^*, \cdots, P_{\ell-1}^*, P_{\ell+1}^*, \cdots, P_{m-1}^*, P_m^* \ )
\end{array}
\right.
$$

Here notation $\underline{P_\ell}$, which appears in the first $\ell - 1$ schedules, indicates that processor P_ℓ performs only data transmission and no computation.

The intermediate points of the segments connecting the first $\ell - 1$ break-points correspond to the re-distribution of the load to one additional slave processor, without involving the master processor P_ℓ in the computation; the previously loaded slave processors complete their load simultaneously. The transition from the break-point $(\underline{P_\ell}, P_1^*, P_2^*, \ldots, P_{\ell-1}^*, -, \ldots, -)$ to the ℓ-th break-point $(P_\ell^*, P_1^*, P_2^*, \ldots, P_{\ell-1}^*, -, \ldots, -)$ corresponds to the reallocation of the load from the slave processors $P_1^*, P_2^*, \ldots, P_{\ell-1}^*$ to the master processor P_ℓ, keeping the slave processors completing their computation simultaneously. Finally, the intermediate points of the last $m - \ell$ segments to the re-distribution of the load to one additional slave processor that follows the current busy processors in the processor sequence $(P_\ell, P_1, P_2, \ldots, P_{\ell-1}, P_{\ell+1}, \ldots, P_m)$; all previously loaded processors complete their load simultaneously.

An example of the three curves $\mathcal{C}_1$, $\mathcal{C}_2$, and $\mathcal{C}_3$ for the three-processor case is shown in Fig. 3. The resulting efficiency frontier consisting of non-dominated solutions is represented as solid lines. It consists of the following components, listed from right to left:

(i) the right-most segment of the curve $\mathcal{C}_1$ that connects $(P_1^*, -, -)$ and $(P_1^*, P_2^*, -)$;

(ii) a part of the second segment of $\mathcal{C}_1$ that connects $(P_1^*, P_2^*, -)$ and (P_1^*, P_2^*, P_3^*) until its intersection point with the first segment of $\mathcal{C}_2$;

(iii) a part of the segment of the curve $\mathcal{C}_2$ connecting $(\underline{P_2}, P_1^*, -)$ and $(P_2^*, P_1^*, -)$ starting at the previously defined intersection with $\mathcal{C}_1$;

(iv) the full segment of the curve $\mathcal{C}_2$ connecting $(P_2^*, P_1^*, -)$ and (P_2^*, P_1^*, P_3^*);

(v) a part of the last segment of the curve $\mathcal{C}_3$ connecting $(\underline{P_3}, P_1^*, P_2^*)$ and (P_3^*, P_1^*, P_2^*); its right-most T-value corresponds to the T-value of the left end (P_2^*, P_1^*, P_3^*) of the previous segment.

Notice that the resulting efficiency frontier is not convex and even not continuous.

While it is possible to prove that some points of the curves $\mathcal{C}_1$, $\mathcal{C}_2$, and $\mathcal{C}_m$ always dominate each other (for example, $(P_1^*, -, -, \ldots, -)$ always dominate $(\underline{P_k}, P_1^*, -, \ldots, -)$ for any $1 < k \le m$), the dominance relation between other points can vary depending on the specific c_i- and w_i-values. For example in the three processor case, the may be no intersection point between curves $\mathcal{C}_1$ and $\mathcal{C}_2$, so that the whole curve $\mathcal{C}_1$ dominates all points of the curve $\mathcal{C}_2$.

We demonstrate in the full version of the paper that for each curve $\mathcal{C}_\ell$, all its break-points can be found in $O(m^2)$ time since each subsequent break-point can be defined from the previous one in $O(m)$ time by re-calculating the associated

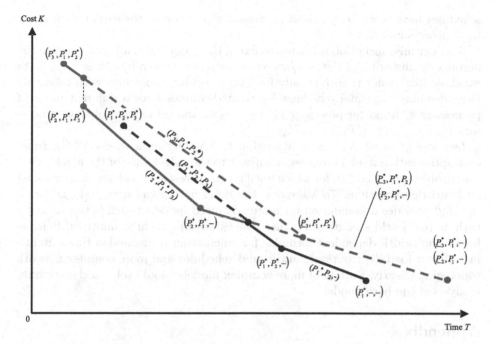

Fig. 3. Three curves
$\mathcal{C}_1$ coonecting $(P_1^*, -, -)$, $(P_1^*, P_2^*, -)$, (P_1^*, P_2^*, P_3^*)
$\mathcal{C}_2$ coonecting $(\underline{P}_2^*, P_1^*, -)$, $(P_2^*, P_1^*, -)$, (P_2^*, P_1^*, P_3^*)
$\mathcal{C}_2$ coonecting $(\underline{P}_3^*, P_1^*, -)$, (P_3^*, P_1^*, P_2^*), (P_3^*, P_1^*, P_2^*)
and the trade-off curve (in solid lines) consisting of non-dominating segments and their
parts

α_i-values, $1 \leq i \leq m$. Thus all break-points of the curves $\mathcal{C}_1$, $\mathcal{C}_2$, ..., $\mathcal{C}_m$ can be
found in $O(m^3)$ time.

Having constructed $m(m-1)$ segments of the curves $\mathcal{C}_1$, $\mathcal{C}_2$, and $\mathcal{C}_m$, the
required efficiency frontier is found as the lower boundary among the curves.

3   Conclusions

In this paper, we have performed a systematic analysis of the problem of scheduling a divisible load on m processes in order to minimize the computation time
and cost. An efficient algorithm for solving the bicriteria version of the problem defines optimal processor sequences for different segments of the efficiency
frontier and the corresponding optimal load distribution among the processors.

Our study demonstrates that some important underlying ideas in the divisible
load theory [6,7,13] have a number of limitations which result in incorrect major
conclusions. In particular, it is generally assumed in [6,13] that the load should be
distributed so that all processors complete their portions simultaneously. As we
show in our study, this property holds only for the break-points of the trade-off.
For the intermediate points that lie in-between the break-points, the associated

schedules have one partly-loaded processor which completes earlier than other busy processors.

Another misconception is related to fixing the sequence of all processors in the non-decreasing order of the cost/speed characteristic given by (3), see [7,13]. As we show, this order is correct only for Pareto-optimal solutions with relatively large deadlines; optimal schedules for tight deadlines have a different order of processors with master processor P_ℓ, $1 < \ell \leq m$, moved in front of slave processors $P_1, P_2, \ldots, P_{\ell-1}, P_{\ell+1}, \ldots, P_m$.

Developing an efficient exact algorithm for the bicriteria version of the time-cost optimization model provides an answer to the solvabilitiy of the single criterion problems (4) and (5), for which until recently, researchers have been working on heuristic algorithms [7]. Moreover, the described model with a single divisible load provides a foundation for more advanced models which better describe various real-world scenarios. Further generalizations include multiple divisible loads, bandwidth dependent formulae for calculating transmission times, multi-installment load distribution, multi-round schedules and more complex network topologies. Clearly, a study of more complex models should rely on the accurate analysis of the basic model.

Appendix

The validity of the described algorithm follows from a number of properties of optimal schedules. These properties are presented below for the single-criterion version of problem (4) for a fixed makespan parameter T; their proofs appear in the full version of the paper. Since parameter T may take different values, the properties are correct for all schedules of the efficiency frontier.

The first two propositions provide a justification for fixing a processor sequence in an optimal solution; the third proposition establishes how the load should be distributed in an optimal solution.

We assume that processors are numbered in accordance with (3). Initially we consider an arbitrary processor sequence which can be different from the sequences listed in Section 2.

Proposition 1. 'SWAPPING TWO NEIGHBOUR SLAVE PROCESSORS'
Consider schedule S in which two neighbour slave processors P_i and P_k in the processor sequence compute portions of load α_i and α_k and have finishing times T_i and T_k, respectively. It is always possible to change the order of P_i and P_k in the processor sequence so that in a new schedule S' the loads are α'_i and α'_k, processors' finish times are T'_i and T'_k and
(a) the loads are re-distributed so that $\alpha'_i = \alpha_i - \delta$ and $\alpha'_k = \alpha_k + \delta$ for $0 \leq \delta \leq \alpha_i$;
(b) the load on other processors remains the same;
(c) the maximum finish time of processors P_i and P_k does not increase:
$\max\{T'_i, T'_k\} \leq \max\{T_i, T_k\}.$

The next proposition justifies that the optimal sequence of slave processors corresponds to the non-decreasing order of the characteristic $c_i w_i$.

Proposition 2. 'NON-DECREASING SEQUENCE OF $c_i w_i$ FOR SLAVE PROCESSORS'
If the master processor P_ℓ is fixed, then an optimal processor sequence is $(P_\ell, P_1, P_2, \ldots, P_{\ell-1}, P_{\ell+1}, \ldots, P_m)$.

We next demonstrate that in an optimal solution all busy processors, except for possibly the last one, complete their computation chunks simultaneously; the last processor may have an earlier finish time.

Given a schedule, let T be its makespan, see (2). Depending on processors' completion times, we classify them as fully loaded, partly loaded or idle. Processor P_i is *busy* if $T_i \geq 0$, and it is *idle* otherwise. To be precise, we call processor P_i *fully loaded* if $T_i = T$ and it is *partly loaded* if $0 < T_i < T$. Notice that the master processor can be idle if its performs only data transmission and no computation.

Proposition 3. 'UNIQUE PARTLY LOADED PROCESSOR'
Consider a class of schedules with master processor P_ℓ and an optimal schedule with processor sequence $(P_\ell, P_1, P_2, \ldots, P_{\ell-1}, P_{\ell+1}, \ldots, P_m)$. Let k be the largest index among busy processors, $1 \leq k \leq m$. Then all processors with smaller indices $P_1, P_2, \ldots, P_{k-1}$ are fully loaded and all processors with larger indices $P_{k+1}, P_{k+2}, \ldots, P_m$ are idle.

It follows from Propositions 1-3 that in a class of schedules with a fixed master processor P_ℓ all optimal schedules have processor order $(P_\ell, P_1, P_2, \ldots, P_{\ell-1}, P_{\ell+1}, \ldots, P_m)$ and for a given makespan threshold value T, an optimal schedule can be constructed by loading in full processors in the order $P_1, P_2, \ldots, P_{k-1}$ until the remaining load can be processed by P_k. Varying the T-values we conclude that all optimal schedules in that class belong to the curve $\mathcal{C}_\ell$ defined in Section 2.

References

1. Abdullaha, M., Othman, M.: Cost-based multi-QoS job scheduling using divisible load theory in cloud computing. In: Proceedings of the 2013 International Conference on Computational Science (ICCS), pp. 928–935 (2013)
2. Beaumont, O., Legrand, A., Robert, Y.: Scheduling divisible workloads on heterogeneous platforms. Parallel Comput. 29, 1121–1152 (2003)
3. Berlińska, J., Drozdowski, M.: Scheduling divisible MapReduce computations, J. Parallel and Distrib. Comput. 71, 450–459 (2011)
4. Buyya, R., Abramson, D., Venugopal, S.: The grid economy. Proceedings of the IEEE 93, 698–714 (2005)
5. Charcranoon, S., Robertazzi, G.R., Luryu, S.: Parallel processor configuration design with processing/transmission costs. IEEE Trans. on Computers 49, 987–991 (2000)
6. Choi, K., Robertazzi, T.G.: Cost performance analysis in multi-level tree networks. In: Proceedings of the Ninth International Symposium on Parallel and Distributed Computing (ISPDC), pp. 41–48 (2010)

7. Chuprat, S., Baruah, S.: Real-time divisible load theory: incorporating computation costs. In: Proceedings of the 17th IEEE International Conference on Embedded and Real-Time Computing Systems and Applications, pp. 33–37 (2011)
8. Drozdowski, M.: Scheduling for Parallel Processing. Springer, London (2009)
9. Hu, M., Luo, J., Veeravalli, B.: Optimal provisioning for scheduling divisible loads with reserved cloud resources. In: Proceedings of the IEEE International Conference on Networks (ICON), pp. 204–209 (2012)
10. Jia, J., Veeravalli, B., Weissman, J.: Scheduling multisource divisible loads on arbitrary networks. IEEE Trans. on Parallel and Distrib. Systems 21, 520–530 (2010)
11. Kumar, S., Dutta, K., Mookerjee, V.: Maximizing business value by optimal assignment of jobs to resources in grid computing. European J. of Oper. Res. 194, 856–872 (2009)
12. Lin, W., Liang, C., Wang, J.Z., Buyya, R.: Bandwidth-aware divisible task scheduling for cloud computing. Software: Practice and Experience (accepted, available online, 2013)
13. Sohn, J., Robertazzi, T.G., Luryi, S.: Optimizing computing costs using divisible load analysis. IEEE Trans. Parallel and Distrib. Systems 9, 225–234 (1998)
14. Robertazzi, T.G.: Ten reasons to use divisible load theory. IEEE Computer 36, 63–68 (2003)
15. van Hoesel, S., Wagelmans, A., Moerman, B.: Using geometric techniques to improve dynamic programming algorithms for the economic lot-sizing problem and extensions. European J. Oper. Res. 75, 312–331 (1994)
16. Yu, J., Buyya, R., Ramamohanarao, K.: Workflow Scheduling Algorithms for Grid Computing. In: Xhafa, F., Abraham, A. (eds.) Meta. for Sched. in Distri. Comp. Envi. SCI, vol. 146, pp. 173–214. Springer, Heidelberg (2008)

Preference-Based Resource Allocation: Using Heuristics to Solve Two-Sided Matching Problems with Indifferences

Christian Haas[1], Steven O. Kimbrough[2],
Simon Caton[1], and Christof Weinhardt[1]

[1] Karlsruhe Service Research Institute, Karlsruhe Institute of Technology
{ch.haas,simon.caton,christof.weinhardt}@kit.edu
[2] The Wharton School, Philadelphia, PA, USA
kimbrough@wharton.upenn.edu

Abstract. The allocation of resources between providers to consumers is a well-known problem and has received significant attention, typically using notions of monetary exchanges. In this paper, we study resource matching in settings without monetary transactions by using a two-sided matching approach, e.g., in social and collaborative environments where users define preferences for with whom they may be matched. Whereas two-sided matching for strict and complete preference rankings (i.e., without indifferences) has been extensively studied, it is known that the matching problem is NP-hard for more realistic preference structures. We study, via simulation, the applicability of a heuristic procedure in settings with indiffernces in preferences, and compare its performance to existing algorithms. We study performance metrics like fairness and welfare in addition to the classic stability objective. Our results show interesting trade-offs between performance metrics and promising performance of the heuristic.

Keywords: Two-Sided Matching, Preferences with Indifferences, Multiple Objectives, Heuristics.

1 Introduction

Resource allocation is a well-known problem that occurs in many circumstances, ranging from technical applications such as job and VM scheduling on compute infrastructures to economic applications such as the allocation of products to consumers. In the field of Cloud computing, various types of market mechanisms have been suggested to facilitate efficient allocations. They range from monetary-based mechanisms like auctions or fixed-price markets (Infrastructure-as-a-Service, Software-as-a-Service) to dynamic negotiation that determines the details of the allocation and exchange of goods (e.g. B2B procurement). In most settings, allocation of goods involves monetary exchange based on (private) valuations that participants have for goods, and a mechanism that determines how the exchange price is calculated.

J. Altmann, K. Vanmechelen, and O.F. Rana (Eds.): GECON 2013, LNCS 8193, pp. 149–160, 2013.
© Springer International Publishing Switzerland 2013

Recently, electronic platforms have emerged that facilitate the collaborative sharing of resources based on non-monetary or voluntary exchanges. Unlike traditional Cloud platforms, participants (who can still be distinguished into resource providers and consumers) share and consume available resources without the immediate goal of monetary gain. One such approach is a Social Cloud [1,2] where social networks are leveraged as a means to construct Cloud platforms via sharing compute resources amongst socially-connected peers. A key characteristic of a Social Cloud and similar platforms is that users often do not require, expect or value monetary incentives, and instead value non-monetary incentives (such as reciprocity and altruism) more highly [3]. Based on the specific type of resource, users have preferences from whom they want to consume and to whom they want to provide resources, and the preferences are described by an ordinal ranking of users. For example, users might prefer users they know directly, rather than users with indirect connections such as a friend-of-a-friend. Consequentially, the question of how to efficiently allocate resources quickly arises. Leaving the allocation to users themselves through self-organization, for example via distributed communication protocols, e.g. [4], can lead to substantial overhead for the users and, in general, can lead to unpredictable and potentially inefficient allocations. In addition, Roth [5] also notes that many decentralized allocation systems can lead to market failure, which is why we address this problem using a *clearinghouse*: a centralized, managed market mechanism that considers the matching problem and the social context of participants. Social context, in our setting is critically important. It captures the basic parameters (user preferences) of social exchange: with whom does a user wish to interact, and to what extent, i.e. are some users preferred over others.

The field of two-sided matching markets is a successful and established means to allocate resources based on user preferences rather than monetary valuations, and therefore lends itself for our clearinghouse. The objective of the clearinghouse is to guarantee that the solutions given by a market mechanism satisfy certain desirable characteristics, such as stability, fairness, or optimal (social) welfare. Although literature with respect to preference-based matching has increased considerably over the past years, most of it considers the case of *strict* preferences: preference rankings are ordinal, transitive and there are no ties between any two ranked users. For this special case, several efficient algorithms exist that compute an optimal solution for certain objectives. However, in more realistic settings (such as a Social Cloud), even if users rank all other users they might be indifferent between some users they can be matched with. In this case, determining an optimal allocation is NP-hard for most of the previously mentioned objectives, and even difficult to approximate [6].

Although existing algorithms can be applied after transforming the preferences to a strictly ranked order, they cannot guarantee a good solution and their performance in the setting with indifferences is unclear as it depends on the way that ties are broken. Therefore, the contribution of this paper is the comparison of these algorithms with a heuristic approach, a Genetic Algorithm (GA), in the case of preferences with indifferences. GAs have been used for matching problems previously, such as in [7] in case of strict preferences, and [8] who emphasize fair solutions. In contrast to previous work in this field, we specifically consider the case of non-strict preferences. Hence, we use the GA with different objective functions to compute allocation solutions, and compare these with the solutions of other leading algorithms to address the following research questions:

1. For preferences with indifferences, can heuristics find better solutions than accepted algorithms?
2. Is there a relationship between the performance metrics, and how do they affect the selection of useful objective functions?

The structure of the paper is as follows. Section 2 overviews related work. Section 3 describes our model and defines performance metrics. Section 4 presents the simulation environment used to evaluate the algorithms. Section 5 presents our evaluation which shows that in many circumstances we can improve upon the standard solutions by using heuristics, especially for objectives such as welfare. Finally, section 6 discusses our findings and future work.

2 Related Work

The seminal paper on two-sided matching [9] introduced two of the standard problems in two-sided matching, the College Admissions problem and the Marriage Market, and provided the first description of the Deferred-Acceptance (DA) algorithm. Under the assumption of complete, strict (no ties) and independent (of preferences of other individuals) preference rankings, DA is able to find at least one and at most two stable matches rapidly (in polynomial time).[1] The literature on two-sided matching has grown considerably since [9] as have the applications of two-sided matching (see [5] for a survey of the latter). This section intends to provide an overview of topics related to this paper, yet does not claim to be a complete overview of the field. Considering this paper, the most relevant areas of research can be summarized as: (1) preferences, (2) alternative design objectives, and (3) computational complexity and heuristics.

Regarding preferences, most of the literature focuses on problems with strict and complete preference orderings, i.e., users are not indifferent between any two options (strict), and rank all users of the other side (complete). If either ties (indifferences) or incompleteness are introduced into the problem, certain characteristics of the algorithms can no longer be guaranteed. As the standard algorithms such as DA only allow strict preferences as input, the ties have to be broken first. Erdil and Ergin [10,11] introduced an extension to the DA that can cope with ties in preferences. Their algorithm tries to find cycles in a given solution which might Pareto-improve the solution (either for one, or both sides). Yet, as [12, page 219] note, many of the strong results for DA and related algorithms depend upon strict preference orderings, and characterizing stable matches under partial ordering remains a largely open problem.

---

[1] For incomplete preferences the DA will still yield stable matches, but not necessarily of maximum size.

Regarding design objectives for matching, other than stability, it was shown early on that DA is heavily biased as it finds the optimal stable match for one side, and the pessimal stable match for the other side [13]. This raises the question of finding stable matches (or matches with only a few unstable pairs of pairs) for the sake of other criteria, such as fairness and social welfare, however defined. For strict and complete preferences, [14] efficiently compute the welfare-best stable match. [15] discuss trade-offs between stability and welfare; [16] study (procedural) fairness and stability; [17] propose an algorithm that approximately yields the fairness-best stable matching; and [7] show that GAs can yield superior solutions for welfare and fairness if a certain instability is allowed.

The third area of concern, computational complexity, arises once we are forced to move beyond DA and closely related algorithms, as the first two issues mandate. On one hand, the number of stable matches can be large, sometimes exponential in the size of the problem [12,13], and it has been shown that the two-sided matching problem in general is #P-complete [12, page 157]. For strict and complete preferences, there are polynomial-time algorithms to compute the welfare-best [14] and approximately fairness-best solutions [17]. However, by introducing indifferences and/or incompleteness, the problem of finding the welfare-best, minimum-regret or fairness-best stable match becomes NP-hard, and sometimes even hard to approximate [6]. Due to this complexity, heuristics have been studied to obtain solutions to the matching problem, the GA being a prominent example. For example, [8] study whether a GA can yield stable matches with higher fairness than the DA solutions, yet do not consider indifferences or other objectives. [18] describe a GA to compute stable solutions from random initial assignments, with stability as the sole objective. Furthermore, both [7] and [19] compare a GA with multiple objectives to the standard algorithms, yet neither of them consider indifferences in preferences.

3   Model

3.1   Users, Preferences and Matches

Formally, in a two-sided matching problem we are given two sets of individuals, X and Y (in our case consumers and providers), and we are asked to produce a match μ (or $\langle X, Y \rangle$), consisting of pairs of individuals $\langle x, y \rangle$ where $x \in X$ and $y \in Y$ [20]. We consider users $i, i \in \{1, \ldots, n_X + n_Y\}$, as participants in the market who want to share and exchange resources, where n_X and n_Y are the number of users of the two sides. We assume that a user i cannot concurrently supply and demand the same resource type r, and for this paper only consider matching within the same resource type. Therefore it is possible to split the users into the set of providing users, X, and requesting users Y, thus $i \in X \vee i \in Y$.

Each user i has a preference ranking over users with whom they want to share resources. Preferences can either be strict, in which case $j \succ_{(i)} k$ denotes that user i strictly prefers to share with user j rather than user k, and indifferent, where $j \sim_{(i)} k$ denotes that user i is indifferent between user j and user k. We also require that the preferences are transitive. Hence, each user can represent their preferences by attributing an ordinal rank to the other users. Let $rank_{(i,j)}$ denote the ordinal rank of requester y_j for provider x_i, where $rank_{(i,j)} \in \{1, \ldots, n_J\}$, and $rank_{(i,j)} < (=) rank_{(i,k)}$ means that user i strictly prefers (is indifferent between) user j to (and) user k, and 1 counts as the highest rank. In general, users can also choose not to state a full preference ranking for all users of the other side of the market, in which case we would have incomplete preferences. This is, however, not focus of this paper, which considers complete preferences with indifferences. Given the representation of users' preferences and the supply and demand in the market, we now have to find a match $\langle X, Y \rangle$ to clear the market. $\langle X, Y \rangle$ consists of pairs $\langle x, y \rangle$ with $x \in X$ and $y \in Y$.

3.2 Stable Matching Algorithms

The algorithms found in the literature concentrate on finding stable matches under certain conditions. For strict preferences we can use the Deferred Acceptance (DA) algorithm by [9] which always yields a stable outcome. Additionally, in this case the welfare-optimal (WO) algorithm by [14] yields the welfare-best (or most egalitarian) stable solution in polynomial time, and for finding the most balanced (fair) solution we can use the approximation algorithm by [17] (henceforth called Fairness-Equal, FE). In the case of indifferences, which we are interested in, we have to first apply a tie-breaking rule in order to apply these algorithms. The tie-breaking rule greatly affects the goodness of the resulting match and, in general, tie-breaking and applying the algorithms does not guarantee a good solution. Therefore, we apply the Pareto-improvement cycles suggested by [10] to potentially increase the welfare of the solutions.

3.3 Matching Heuristics

In addition to the mentioned algorithms, we investigate the use of a GA [21] as an example of a heuristic to find solutions to the matching problem. Whereas much related work on GA's for two-sided matching focuses on finding (stable) solutions from random initial assignments (see e.g. [18]), we use the GA to improve an initial stable match by trying to retain stability and increasing other performance criteria.

The GA uses a population of chromosomes, each of which represents a solution to the matching problem (i.e., each chromosome describes a $\langle X, Y \rangle$). A chromosome consists of several genes, where each gene encodes a provider-requester match $\langle x, y \rangle$ of the solution. In other words, when a solution has m matches, the chromosome has m genes, and each gene consists of two identifiers, one for the provider, one for the requester. To determine the performance of a given chromosome, a fitness function is used. Common fitness functions for two-sided matching are the maximization of stability, welfare, fairness, or a combination thereof (see the next section for a definition of these metrics). In order to improve the fitness of the solutions, two genetic operators are applied after the fitness evaluation in order to derive new, potentially better-performing solutions. The cycle crossover operator [21], creates new potential solutions by combining two parent solutions. The mutation operator, given a certain mutation probability, randomly selects two genes (matched pairs) of a given chromosome and exchanges either the requester or provider identifiers to create a new chromosome. The population is evolved using these operators over a given number of rounds.

3.4 Performance Metrics

In standard two-sided matching scenarios, stability is often seen as the most important property. Further commonly addressed criteria are welfare and fairness. Hence, we consider the following *economic performance criteria*:[2]

Stability: Stability can be measured by the number of unstable (blocking) pairs in a solution. Given a match $\langle X, Y \rangle$ and a pair of matched users, $\langle x_1, y_1 \rangle$ and $\langle x_2, y_2 \rangle$, the pair is said to be unstable if x_1 prefers being matched with y_2 instead of y_1 and at the same time y_2 prefers being matched with x_1 than with x_2. The same argument holds if x_2 prefers y_1 over y_2 and y_1 prefers x_2 over x_1. If one of the previous statements holds, we count one unstable pair, in case both statements hold we count two unstable pairs.

Welfare: We define welfare, or equivalently the most "egalitarian" solution, as the average rank that each user is matched with, by summing the respective preference ranks of the matched users. Formally:[3]

$$\text{Welfare} = \frac{\sum_{x_i \in \langle X,Y \rangle} rank_{x_i, y_j} + \sum_{y_j \in \langle X,Y \rangle} rank_{y_j, x_i}}{n_X + n_Y} \tag{1}$$

Fairness: We use the definition of the "sex-equal"- match provided by [17]. Fairness is measured as the inequality in welfare distribution. Formally:

$$\text{Fairness} = \left| \frac{\sum_{x_i \in \langle X,Y \rangle} rank_{x_i, y_j}}{n_X} - \frac{\sum_{y_j \in \langle X,Y \rangle} rank_{y_j, x_i}}{n_Y} \right| \tag{2}$$

High scores reflect a high inequality between the two sides, whereas scores closer to 0 indicate a more equal distribution of welfare between the market sides.

4 Simulation

To evaluate the performance of the GA, we use simulation. Our simulator is implemented in Java and described in [23]. In all subsequently described simulation scenarios, randomly created sets of preferences for the users are used. In this paper we present scenarios where the two sides of the market are equally sized. Initial results show that in case of unequally sized market, the presented results are even stronger. We simulate scenarios with 10, 20, 50 and 100 consumers and providers (i.e., 20, 40, 100, 200 users in total). Each of the simulation scenarios was independently repeated 100 times with different user preferences in each repetition. Results refer to the averages of these runs.

---

[2] The definitions of welfare and fairness scores are adapted from [22] and [17].
[3] Note that lower numbers indicate better solutions.

As the focus of this paper is preferences with indifferences, we ensure that preferences are complete, i.e., each user has a complete ranking over all users of the opposite side. Each users' preferences contains indifference groups (i.e., users between which a user is indifferent) and the group size is randomly drawn from the interval [1,10]. In order to perform the algorithms which require strict preferences on indifference groups, randomized tie-breaking is performed to get a ordered preference ranking. For each scenario, the three performance metrics as described in the previous section are recorded.

The GA has a population of 50 chromosomes, a crossover probability of 0.6, and a mutation probability of 0.2 per chromosome. The GA uses DA, WO and FE to create initial (stable) solutions. We use 1000 evolution rounds and take the fittest chromosome for evaluation. The GA uses one of the following four fitness functions: (1) the number of unstable matches (S), (2) the welfare score (W), (3) the fairness score (F), and (4) an equally-weighted function of (1), (2) and (3) (EW). If we adjust the fitness function such that unstable solutions get a penalty on the number of unstable pairs, we add "P" for Penalty to the objective function description.[4] We indicate the GA fitness configuration in the form GA-S.x, where $x \in \{S, F, FP, W, WP, EW\}$.

5   Evaluation

In this section, we compare the performance of the GA and the algorithms developed for strict preferences. The third column of the table (PM) specifies the performance metric, stability (S), welfare (W) and fairness (F). The evaluation will compare results from the Deferred-Acceptance (DA), Welfare-Optimal (WO), Fairness-Equal (FE), and the GA's with the respective objective functions. Note that a score of 0 for stability means the solution is stable.

5.1   Optimization of Stability and Welfare

The goal of finding a stable solution with a best welfare performance is one of the standard problems in two-sided matching. Whereas for strict preferences we can use the welfare-optimal (WO) algorithm which runs in polynomial time, for more general preference structures this problem is NP-hard and also hard to approximate. Table 1 compares DA, WO and the GA with different objectives with respect to welfare performance. For all algorithms, the Pareto-improvement cycle described in [10] is applied on the algorithm's solutions to potentially find improvements in welfare. For the average performance of DA and WO, the welfare score is also shown in Figure 1a as the average rank of the matched partner of each user. As the GA is initialized with a population of 50 solutions, we report the average, best and worst solution out of 50 different tie-breakings of the DA and WO in order to evaluate the potential range of solution quality that can be expected. There are several interesting results that can be observed.

---

[4] In that case, unstable solutions have a much lower fitness than stable solutions, which discourages the creation of such solutions.

Table 1. Comparison of Welfare Optimization

Size	PM	DA-Avg (Best, Worst)	WO-Avg (Best, Worst)	GA-S-W	GA-S-WP	GA-S-EW
	S	0.00 (0.00, 0.00)	0.00 (0.00, 0.00)	0.00	0.00	0.00
10x10	W	1.24 (1.16, 1.47)	1.20 (1.16, 1.40)	1.16	1.16	1.21
	F	0.32 (0.20, 0.71)	0.23 (0.20, 0.54)	0.18	0.18	0.25
	S	0.00 (0.00, 0.00)	0.00 (0.00, 0.00)	0.13	0.00	0.00
20x20	W	2.16 (1.72, 2.84)	1.96 (1.69, 2.45)	1.72	1.72	1.99
	F	1.41 (0.51, 3.01)	0.69 (0.43, 1.22)	0.46	0.41	0.40
	S	0.00 (0.00, 0.00)	0.00 (0.00, 0.00)	1.01	0.00	0.00
50x50	W	5.52 (4.20, 7.07)	4.42 (3.88. 5.04)	3.91	3.99	4.50
	F	6.18 (2.10, 10.96)	1.42 (0.96, 2.04)	0.77	1.02	0.24
	S	0.00 (0.00, 0.00)	0.00 (0.00, 0.00)	2.64	0.00	0.00
100x100	W	10.33 (7.66, 13.20)	7.27 (6.70, 7.88)	6.66	6.78	7.41
	F	14.54 (5.62, 22.68)	1.85 (1.37, 2.41)	1.21	1.26	0.09

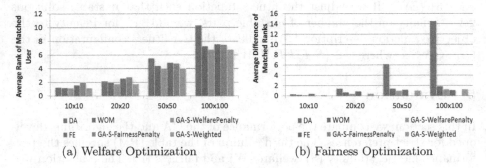

(a) Welfare Optimization   (b) Fairness Optimization

Fig. 1. Comparison of Algorithms

First, the GA with pure welfare optimization yields the best solutions welfare-wise, yet introduces a small number of unstable pairs (on average), which might not be desirable. In contrast, the GA with welfare optimization and penalty for unstable pairs (WP) essentially yields similar performance, yet enforces solutions that are completely stable. The GA with a weighted objective function seems to trade off fairness for stability, and yields similar results when it comes to welfare.

Comparing the GA with the DA and WO, we see that for the average solution quality, the GA-S-WP on average outperforms both algorithms for the studied problem sets. We can see that the welfare score of GA-S-WP is considerably better than the average welfare scores of DA and WO, and in most cases is similar to the best solutions of DA and WO. The relative welfare improvement of the GA-S-WP is 3-12% to WO-A and 7-34% to DA-A. The improvement to the average solutions is also statistically significant at the 0.1% level, using non-parametric paired Wilcoxon tests with Bonferroni adjustment. Another interesting result is the possible range of solution quality by using a random tie-breaking and applying the DA or WO with additional Pareto-improvement cycles. As can be seen in Table 1 this range can be quite large, and that one can end up with solutions that are particularly bad. Overall, given these results the use of GA-S-WP seems to be the most promising, yielding solutions which are superior to the other algorithms.

5.2   Optimization of Stability and Fairness

Finding the stable solution with the most equal welfare distribution between the two market sides is an NP-complete problem even for strict preferences, and the FE algorithm [17] approximates the optimal solution. For preferences with ties, the problem is NP-hard similar to the problem of finding the stable solution with best welfare score. Hence, we again apply the GA with pure fairness optimization (GA-S-F), additional penalty for unstable pairs (GA-S-FP) and a weighted function of stability, welfare and fairness (GA-S-EW).[5]

Table 2. Comparison of Fairness Optimization

Size	PM	DA-Avg (Best, Worst)	FE-Avg (Best, Worst)	GA-S-F	GA-S-FP	GA-S-EW
	S	0.00 (0.00, 0.00)	0.00 (0.00, 0.00)	4.41	0.00	0.00
10x10	W	1.24 (1.16, 1.47)	1.58 (1.56, 1.94)	2.90	1.98	1.19
	F	0.32 (0.20, 0.71)	0.43 (0.00, 1.63)	0.00	0.00	0.07
	S	0.00 (0.00, 0.00)	0.00 (0.00, 0.00)	48.83	0.00	0.07
20x20	W	2.16 (1.72, 2.84)	2.57 (2.48, 3.13)	7.75	2.76	1.86
	F	1.41 (0.51, 3.01)	0.89 (0.01, 3.38)	0.00	0.00	0.07
	S	0.00 (0.00, 0.00)	0.00 (0.00, 0.00)	479.85	0.00	0.86
50x50	W	5.52 (4.20, 7.07)	4.88 (4.74, 5.96)	22.64	4.76	4.15
	F	6.18 (2.10, 10.96)	1.21 (0.01, 7.44)	0.00	0.02	0.07
	S	0.00 (0.00, 0.00)	0.00 (0.00, 0.00)	1780.73	0.00	1.97
100x100	W	10.33 (7.66, 13.20)	7.57 (7.55, 8.84)	42.97	7.48	6.95
	F	14.54 (5.62, 22.68)	1.10 (0.02, 9.42)	0.00	0.03	0.06

Table 2 shows the average, best and worst solutions of the DA, FE and GA. Figure 1b compares the results for the average solution of DA, FE and GA. As before, the results in Table 2 show that the range of fairness scores for the DA and FE can be quite large, and the best solutions of the FE are stable and close to a perfect welfare distribution. The results also show that it seems to be always possible to find a completely fair solution in all scenarios, if fairness is the single objective (GA-S-F), yet this comes with a high penalty on stability and welfare performance. However, if we enforce stable solutions by adding penalties for unstable pairs (GA-S-FP), the GA yields almost completely fair solutions for most scenarios. Especially, these solutions are on average superior to the average FE solutions and also similar to the best FE solutions. In other words, this means that the GA-S-FP finds solutions that yield similar matched ranks for both sides, which also have (for larger market sizes) better welfare values. Using a non-parametric paired Wilcoxon test with Bonferroni adjustment reveals a significant improvement compared to the average FE solutions at the 0.1% level for the studied market sizes. The GA with weighted objective function yields very good results with respect to fairness, yet trades off gains in welfare (compared to GA-S-FP) for a certain number of unstable pairs.

---

[5] In this case, the Pareto-improvement cycles [10] are not applied, as they potentially decrease fairness of the solutions.

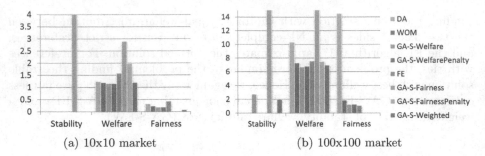

(a) 10x10 market   (b) 100x100 market

Fig. 2. Balancing Performance Metrics

5.3   Balancing Performance Metrics

We have seen that using heuristics to solve a two-sided matching problem with
indifferences is able to yield superior results to the best algorithms for strict
preferences coupled with Pareto-improvement cycles. Now, we study if trade-
offs between the performance metrics stability, welfare and fairness exist, and if
different algorithms yield similar trade-offs.

Figure 2 shows the comparison of the three performance metrics for a small
and a large problem instance. Several issues can be observed. First, the high
number of unstable pairs and the high welfare score in case of fairness optimization (GA-S-F) indicates that focusing solely on fairness has detrimental effects
on the other objectives. In contrast, focusing solely on welfare (GA-S-W) yields
solutions that are nearly stable (only 3 unstable pairs in a 100x100 market, on
average) and 0-2% better than the best stable solution (GA-S-WP) with respect
to welfare. Hence, the question is if such an increase in welfare justifies the introduction of unstable pairs into the system. Second, the penalty-based objective
functions (GA-S-FP and GA-S-WP) which are focusing on two out of the three
considered objectives yield solutions superior to the equally-weighted objective
function that tries to explicitly balance all three scores. Third, using the GA
objective functions with penalties for unstable pairs seems to yield the best,
i.e., most balanced solutions. The GA-S-WP optimization yields the best stable
solutions with respect to welfare and which are almost as fair as the average
FE solutions, whereas GA-S-FP optimization yields almost perfectly fair solutions without considerably decreasing the welfare score of the solution. Hence,
the choice of the proper objective function depends on the specific application
scenario, i.e., whether welfare or fairness are considered to be more important.

5.4   Summary

The results discussed in the previous sections give valuable insight in the gains
by using heuristics to solve two-sided matching problems with ties in preferences,

and the potential trade-offs between performance metrics. Given the research questions in section 1, we can derive the following statements:

1. The GA can find solutions that are significantly better than the average solutions provided by DA, WO and FE.
2. Optimizing only one metric can be detrimental to performance considering the other metrics, whereas objective functions focusing on two performance metrics yield the best, most-balanced results considering all metrics.

6   Conclusion and Future Work

With the widespread use of electronic platforms in various domains, the consideration of non-monetary allocation mechanisms becomes increasingly interesting and necessary. Such allocation mechanisms are particularly relevant for scenarios where users are embedded in a social network, which might elicit significant non-monetary incentives on sharing. In this paper we study two-sided matching for the allocation of resources based on preference rankings rather than monetary valuations. As the standard algorithms rely on the assumption of strict preferences and cannot guarantee the best solution(s) in the presence of preference ties, we studied the applicability of a Genetic Algorithm as a heuristic to compute potential solutions to the two-sided matching problem.

Our results show that heuristics with appropriate objective functions can yield superior solutions to the solutions of standard algorithms. Furthermore, that objective functions with a penalty for unstable pairs are effective in computing stable matches that simultaneously perform well with respect to welfare or fairness. Depending on the scenario, we could significantly increase the quality of a match, but still retain a computationally efficient procedure.

To increase the validity of the (simulation) results, firstly we will study the effect of real-life preferences on the robustness of the results by using friend-list-based preference groups from social network platforms (e.g. Facebook) and manually specified preferences for comparison to the random preferences in this paper. Secondly, we will investigate strategy-proofness to determine if users can benefit by misrepresenting their preferences. Thirdly, we will study additional heuristics and compare their performance with the results of the GA.

References

1. Chard, K., Caton, S., Rana, O., Bubendorfer, K.: Social Cloud: Cloud Computing in Social Networks. In: 2010 IEEE 3rd International Conference on Cloud Computing (CLOUD), pp. 99–106 (2010)
2. Chard, K., Caton, S., Rana, O., Katz, D.S.: Social Cloud Computing: A Vision for Socially Motivated Resource Sharing. In: The Third International Workshop on Data Intensive Computing in the Clouds, DataCloud 2012 (2012)
3. Fehr, E., Schmidt, K.M.: 8. In: The Economics of Fairness, Reciprocity and Altruism - Experimental Evidence and New Theories. Handbook on the Economics of Giving, Reciprocity and Altruism, vol. 1, pp. 615–691. Elsevier (2006)
4. Streitberger, W., Eymann, T.: A simulation of an economic, self-organising resource allocation approach for application layer networks. Computer Networks 53(10), 1760–1770 (2009)

5. Roth, A.: Deferred acceptance algorithms: History, theory, practice, and open questions. International Journal of Game Theory 36(3), 537–569 (2008)
6. Halldórsson, M., Iwama, K., Miyazaki, S., Yanagisawa, H.: Improved approximation results for the stable marriage problem. ACM Transactions on Algorithms (TALG) 3(3), 30 (2007)
7. Kimbrough, S., Kuo, A.: On heuristics for two-sided matching: Revisiting the stable marriage problem as a multiobjective problem. In: Proceedings of the 12th Annual Conference on Genetic and Evolutionary Computation, pp. 1283–1290. ACM (2010)
8. Nakamura, M., Onaga, K., Kyan, S., Silva, M.: Genetic algorithm for sex-fair stable marriage problem. In: 1995 IEEE International Symposium on Circuits and Systems, ISCAS 1995, April- May 3, vol. 1, pp. 509–512 (1995)
9. Gale, D., Shapley, L.: College admissions and the stability of marriage. In: American Mathematical Monthly, pp. 9–15 (1962)
10. Erdil, A., Ergin, H.: Two-sided matching with indifferences. Unpublished mimeo, Harvard Business School (2006)
11. Erdil, A., Ergin, H.: What's the matter with tie-breaking? improving efficiency in school choice. The American Economic Review 98(3), 669–689 (2008)
12. Gusfield, D., Irving, R.W.: The Stable Marriage Problem: Structure and Algorithms. MIT Press, Cambridge (1989)
13. Knuth, D.E.: Stable Marriage and Its Relation to Other Combinatorial Problems: An Introduction to the Mathematical Analysis of Algorithms. CRM Proceedings & Lecture Notes, Centre de Recherches Mathématiques Université de Montréal, vol. 10. American Mathematical Society, Providence, RI (1997); Originally published as Knuth, D.E.: Marriages Stables. Les Presses de l'Université de Montreal, Montreal Canada (1976)
14. Irving, R.W., Leather, P., Gusfield, D.: An efficient algorithm for the optimal stable marriage. Journal of the ACM 34(3), 532–543 (1987)
15. Axtell, R.L., Kimbrough, S.O.: The high cost of stability in two-sided matching: How much social welfare should be sacrificed in the pursuit of stability? In: Proceedings of the 2008 World Congress on Social Simulation, WCSS 2008 (2008)
16. Klaus, B., Klijn, F.: Procedurally fair and stable matching. Economic Theory 27, 431–447 (2006)
17. Iwama, K., Miyazaki, S., Yanagisawa, H.: Approximation algorithms for the sex-equal stable marriage problem. In: Dehne, F., Sack, J.-R., Zeh, N. (eds.) WADS 2007. LNCS, vol. 4619, pp. 201–213. Springer, Heidelberg (2007)
18. Aldershof, B., Carducci, O.M.: Stable marriage and genetic algorithms: A fertile union. Journal of Heuristics 5(1), 29–46 (1999)
19. Vien, N.A., Chung, T.C.: Multiobjective fitness functions for stable marriage problem using genetic algorithm. In: International Joint Conference on SICE-ICASE, pp. 5500–5503 (October 2006)
20. Royal Swedish Academy of Sciences: The Sveriges Riksbank prize in economic sciences in memory of Alfred Nobel for 2012. Word Wide Web (October 2012), http://www.nobelprize.org/nobel_prizes/economic-sciences/laureates/2012/advanced-economicsciences2012.pdf
21. Goldberg, D.E.: Genetic Algorithms in Search, Optimization and Machine Learning. Addison-Wesley Longman Publishing Co., Inc. (1989)
22. Gusfield, D.: Three fast algorithms for four problems in stable marriage. SIAM J. Comput. 16(1), 111–128 (1987)
23. Haas, C., Caton, S., Trumpp, D., Weinhardt, C.: A Simulator for Social Exchanges and Collaborations - Architecture and Case Study. In: Proceedings of the 8th IEEE International Conference on eScience, eScience 2012 (2012)

Advanced Promethee-Based Scheduler Enriched with User-Oriented Methods

Mircea Moca[1], Cristian Litan[1], Gheorghe Cosmin Silaghi[1], and Gilles Fedak[2]

[1] Babeş-Bolyai University, Cluj-Napoca, România
{mircea.moca,cristian.litan,gheorghe.silaghi}@econ.ubbcluj.ro
[2] INRIA, University of Lyon, France
gilles.fedak@inria.fr

Abstract. Efficiently scheduling tasks in hybrid Distributed Computing Infrastructures (DCI) is a challenging pursue because the scheduler must deal with a set of parameters that simultaneously characterize the tasks and the hosts originating from different types of infrastructure.

In this paper we propose a scheduling method for hybrid DCIs, based on advanced multi-criteria decision methods. The scheduling decisions are made using pairwise comparisons of the tasks for a set of criteria like expected completion time and price charged for computation. The results are obtained with an XtremWeb-like pull-based scheduler simulator using real failure traces from [1] for a combination of three types of infrastructure. We also show how such a scheduler should be configured to enhance user satisfaction regardless their profiles, while maintaining good values for makespan and cost.

We validate our approach with a statistical analysis on empirical data and show that our proposed scheduling method improves performance by 12-17% compared to other scheduling methods. Experimenting on large time-series and using realistic scheduling scenarios lead us to conclude about time consistency results of the method.

1 Introduction

The requirements of parallel applications in terms of processing power and storage capacities is continuously increasing, pushed by the gigantic deluge of large data volume to process. Meanwhile, scientific communities and industrial companies can choose between a large variety of DCIs to execute their Grand Challenge applications. Examples of such infrastructures are Desktop Grids or Volunteer Computing systems which can gather a huge number of volunteer PCs at almost no cost, Grids which assemble large number of distributed clusters and more recently, Cloud infrastructures which can be accessed remotely, following a pay-as-you-go pricing model. All these infrastructures have very different characteristics in terms of computing power, cost, reliability, power efficiency and more. Hence, combining these infrastructures in such a way that meets users' requirements raises several scheduling challenges.

J. Altmann, K. Vanmechelen, and O.F. Rana (Eds.): GECON 2013, LNCS 8193, pp. 161–172, 2013.

The first challenge concerns the middleware which allows the assemblage of hybrid computing infrastructures. The pull-based scheduler, often used in Desktop Grid computing, relies on the principle that the computing resources pull tasks from a centralized scheduler. Because of their desirable properties, such as scalability, fault resilience, low deployment cost, pull-based schedulers are widely used for assembling hybrid DCIs. For instance, GridBot [2] puts together Superlink@Technion, Condor pools and Grid resources to execute both throughput and fast-turnaround oriented BoTs.

The second challenge is the design of scheduling heuristics which efficiently use hybrid DCIs, given that computing resources are highly heterogeneous and infrastructures might be elastic and subject to failures. In our previous work [3], we proved that a multi-criteria non-parametric decision model like Promethee [4] can make a pull-based scheduler to be efficient, but for one infrastructure as target at a time: Internet Desktop Grid (IDG), Best Effort Grid[1] (BEG) or Cloud. However, up to now, we did not know whether such an approach would work with hybrid DCIs.

In this paper we introduce the work of investigating the performance of a pull-based scheduler employing a decision model like Promethee, considering a mix of several types of infrastructure. When working with Promethee, the challenge [4] is to properly define the preference function used by the decision model in order to incorporate both **the technical properties of the infrastructures** and the **user requirements**. We evaluate our approach by using the standard scheduling metrics - makespan and cost, and also by analyzing the user satisfaction gained at the completion of her BoT. We show how a system designer can empirically configure the scheduler to put more emphasize on criteria that are important from their own perspective.

The remaining of this paper is structured as follows. In section 2 we give the background for our work, in section 3 we discuss the evaluation methodology, then present the results obtained through a mix of experimentation and simulation. In section 4 we synthesize related work, then conclude and present interesting future work in section 5.

2   The Scheduling Context

In this section we describe the scheduling problem with hybrid DCIs, the architecture of the scheduler and the insights of the Promethee method.

2.1   The Scheduling Problem Definition

In our context we consider users submitting BoTs to a centralized pull-based scheduler, responsible with a mix of infrastructures: IDG, BEG and Clouds.

---

[1] BEG: an infrastructure or a particular usage of it (like OAR [5]) providing unused computing resources without guaranteing their full availability to user, during the complete execution of his application [6].

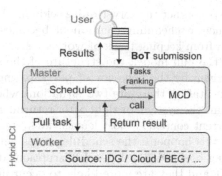

Fig. 1. Schematic architecture of a hybrid DCI with pull-based scheduler

Each computing resource from the above mentioned infrastructures have different characteristics in terms of computing power, reliability, cost, power efficiency, and trust. For instance, Internet volunteer desktop PCs could be considered as free of charge but insecure and unreliable, while a Cloud node can be costly but more secure and reliable.

Users usually expect good performance but they are also concerned about other issues like cost, confidence and environmental footprint of the infrastructure. Thus, the scheduling problem translates into finding the best usage of the infrastructures that meets user's preferences, expressed by multiple criteria.

2.2   Scheduler Architecture

Figure 1 depicts the schematic architecture of our scheduler for hybrid DCIs. In order to keep the discussion clear and simple, we omitted additional middleware-specific interfacing levels between users, the scheduling system and DCIs, which naturally occur in real systems. Hence, a user submits a bag of work units to the scheduler and receives after a while the corresponding results. During the execution, for each work unit, the scheduler creates at least one task and adds it to a priority queue. When a host from a particular type of DCI pulls work, the scheduler calls the multi-criteria decision component (MCD) to select a task. The scheduler maps this task to the pulling host, which, after completing the execution will return a result. The MCD component is responsible for the scheduling decisions by using the Promethee multi-criteria decision model.

Our scheduler is a centralized component, based on the **pull communication model** between the master and worker components. The rationale behind this design option is the requirement for elasticity and adaptability to structure disruptions that characterize IDG environments. This model allows complete independence of all system components [7]. The pull model allows clients to have the contact initiative, which overcome the real issue of connecting to volunteers residing behind firewalls [8] or other security components.

In our model, when a host becomes available (either because it (re-)joins the system or after completing a task execution) it contacts the scheduler in order to receive a new task. We denote with H_{pull} such a host. This approach is efficient

[9] since in IDGs, hosts contact the server quite seldom. More, if embedded into a real middleware, such a scheduling component becomes more scalable, since the master is relieved from keeping track of workers' state.

Due to the use of the pull model, the structure of the system and the scheduling process are driven by the behavior of participating hosts. As discussed above, in our implementation there are two situations when a host pulls work: either when it (re-)joins the system, or right after returning the result for a complete task. In the current context, a host leaves the system without preventing the scheduler. When this happens, the scheduler maps, after a while, the failed task to another pulling host. Obviously, such disruptions degrade the execution performance of a BoT and they are more likely to occur in IDGs.

2.3   The Promethee Method

Our scheduler relies on the Promethee method to map a task to a pulling host. When called, the MCD component computes a complete ranking of the tasks, from which, the scheduler maps the best ranked one to the current H_{pull}. In the following we shortly describe how the scheduler uses Promethee for task selection and highlight the challenges of this approach.

Promethee[10] is a multi-criteria decision model based on **pairwise comparisons**, which outputs a **ranking** of the tasks. This method considers a set of criteria $C = \{c_{i_c}; i_c \in [1, N_c]\}$ to characterize tasks. Such criteria can be host dependent or independent. In our case, we consider ECT (the expected completion time) of a task and the price charged by H_{pull} to execute the task. When designing a real system, one is free to put her own relevant criteria in C. In addition, we set weights of importance for each criterion, $W = \omega_{i_c}(c_{i_c})$, so that $\sum_{i_c=1}^{N_c} \omega_{i_c}(\cdot) = 1$.

For each task t_{i_t} and criterion c_{i_c} the method computes a real value a_{i_c, i_t}, representing the evaluation of the task within the respective criterion. To compare two tasks within a criterion the method inputs the tasks' evaluation values into a preference function which calculates a dominance (preference) relation between tasks. As indicated by the literature[4], we use the following preference functions $Linear, Level, Gaussian$, defined below:

$$P_{Linear}(d_{i_c}) = \begin{cases} \frac{d_{i_c}}{\sigma} & \text{if } d_{i_c} \leq \sigma \\ 1 & otherwise \end{cases} \tag{1}$$

$$P_{Gaussian}(d_{i_c}) = \begin{cases} 1 - e^{-\frac{d_{i_c}^2}{2\sigma^2}} & \text{if } d_{i_c} > 0 \\ 0 & otherwise \end{cases} \tag{2}$$

$$P_{Level}(d_{i_c}) = \begin{cases} 0 & \text{if } d_{i_c} < q \\ \frac{1}{2} & \text{if } q \leq d_{i_c} < p \\ 1 & \text{if } d_{i_c} \geq p \end{cases} \tag{3}$$

where:

- d_{i_c} is the deviation between the evaluations of two tasks within a criterion c_{i_c}: $d_{i_c}(t_1, t_2) = a_{i_c,1} - a_{i_c,2}$;
- σ is the standard deviation of all differences d_{i_c};
- q is the degree of indifference; any deviation below q leads to considering t_1 and t_2 equivalent;
- p is the degree of preference; any deviation greater than q gives a strict preference, either 0.5 (for deviations between q and p) or 1.

A criterion i_c can be considered either `max` or `min` in the sense that the scheduler will prefer a higher evaluation on that criterion to a lower one, or the viceversa. If a criterion i_c is max/min, and $d_{i_c}(t_1, t_2)$ is negative/positive, then $P_{(.)}(d_{i_c}(t_1, t_2))$ is 0. When comparing two tasks t_1 and t_2, the aggregated preference within all criteria is computed by applying the weights w_{i_c} to the values $P_{(.)}(d_{i_c})$.

When adapting Promethee to our scheduling problem with the *Level* preference function, we shall set the values for q and p in order to optimize the considered evaluation metrics of the scheduler. In subsection 3.2 we present a comprehensive discussion on this topic.

Further, Promethee computes the outranking flows, defined in [4] as: the positive outranking flows $\phi^+(a)$, representing how many times a task outranks (is preferred to) all others and the negative outranking flows $\phi^-(a)$, showing how many times a task is outranked by other tasks. So, the higher the $\phi^+(a)$, the better. Finally, the *net outranking flow* $\phi(a) = \phi^+(a) - \phi^-(a)$ gives the final ranking of the tasks. Thus, the higher the net flow, the better the task.

2.4   Tasks Evaluation Criteria

All tasks waiting in the priority queue at scheduler are evaluated against the following criteria:

ECT: the expected completion time of t_i, which is evaluated based on the computing power of H_{pull} and the number of instructions (NOI) of t_i, so

$$\text{ECT}(t_i) = \varepsilon \times \frac{\text{NOI}(t_i)}{\text{CPU}(H_{pull})} \tag{4}$$

We apply a *delay factor* $\varepsilon > 1$, in order to create realistic scenarios in which a fraction of all hosts complete later than expected. ε may have great values for IDG, or it can be 0 for Cloud.

Price: a task t_i is assigned a price 0 when H_{pull} is from IDG or BEG, meaning that the computation is free of charge; if the host is from Cloud, the evaluation is the price charged by H_{pull} for executing t_i.

Once the task evaluation phase is complete, the MCD component is executed, then the best ranked task is mapped to H_{pull}.

3   Experiments and Results

To validate the model presented in section 2 we implemented a scheduler, and tested it in a realistic XtremWeb-like simulator fitting the architecture depicted

Table 1. Computing power and price values for different types of infrastructure

DCI type	Computing power (instructions/ second)	Price charged by host (monetary units/sec., univ. distrib.)
IDG	$\{50, 100, 150, 200, 250, 300, 350, 400\}$	0
Cloud	$\{250, 300, 350, 400\}$	$\{0.001, 0.005, 0.0075, 0.01\}$
BEG	$\{50, 100, 150\}$	0

in figure 1. The scheduler accepts pull work requests from three types of infrastructure: IDG, Cloud and BEG. The behavior of these infrastructures is simulated by a component that *consumes* events created from real availability traces[11], downloaded from the public FTA repository [1]. In the following we describe the traces used in our experiments.

- **IDG**: For Internet Desktop Grid, we use BOINC failure traces, characterized by highly volatile resources. The traces contain 691 hosts observed during a period of 18 months, starting from 2010.
- **Cloud**: We use Amazon spot instance traces containing 1754 hosts observed during 2011. These resources are very stable.
- **BEG**: We use Grid5000 traces with host join/leave events for a period of 12 months during 2011 from the following sites: Lyon, Grenoble, Bordeaux and Lille, capturing the activity of 2256 hosts. Analyzing the trace files we observe that the resources are quite stable, only small groups of machines going off all a once for approximately a small number of hours.

In table 1 we describe the key parameters of the hosts for considered DCIs.

The workload used in all experiments is a bag of 2000 tasks with uniformly distributed size between 10^5 and 10^6 operations, lasting between $0.5 - 2$ hours on the various host types presented above.

3.1   Evaluation and Metrics

For the evaluation of the scheduler performance we use the following metrics: makespan, cost and Θ.

Makespan (M) denotes the time interval needed for the completion of a BoT, and it is computed as difference between the time of the last received result and the first task scheduling.

The **cost** (C) indicates the total cost in monetary units accumulated during the execution of a BoT.

To measure the user satisfaction, in eq. 5 we define the aggregated objective function Θ. Given that a system designer can configure the scheduler using a set S of configurations, Θ shows the relative satisfaction perceived by a user submitting for execution a BoT, for a scheduler configuration i from S.

$$\Theta_i(M, C) = w_m \times \frac{M_{max} - M_i}{M_{max} - M_{min}} + w_c \times \frac{C_{max} - C_i}{C_{max} - C_{min}} \qquad (5)$$

Table 2. Descriptive statistics of the makespan distributions for each method

Method	Mean (STDEV)	Difference (%)	The p-values[2]
Linear	367540,26 (104523,14)	0	0,190 ($> 10\%$)
Level	414840,79 (110604,18)	+12,86	0,466 ($> 10\%$)
FCFS	432419,97 (118178,69)	+17,65	0,831 ($> 10\%$)

where M_{max}, C_{max} represent the maximum value of makespan and cost obtained for the BoT execution in all configurations within S, M_{min}, C_{min} represent the minimum value of makespan and cost obtained for the BoT execution in all configurations within S, and w_m and w_c are the weights of importance from the user perspective over makespan and cost. While a higher w_m and a lower w_c denote a user which is more satisfied by a faster but costly execution, a lower w_m and a higher w_c indicate that the user wants a slower but cheaper execution.

3.2 Tuning the Scheduler to Enhance Performance

In this section we present the performance of our scheduler compared with other scheduling strategies and we show how Promethee can be configured to leverage the performance of the scheduler. Here we are interested in makespan and we do not consider the user-related metrics (cost and Θ).

First we compare our scheduler using *Level* and *Linear* preference functions described in subsection 2.3 and a $First-Come-First-Served$ (FCFS) scheduler. We omitted the *Gaussian* function as its performance is very close to *Linear*. Table 2 presents the descriptive statistics regarding makespan distribution after scheduling the same BoT 120 times with each method.

We note that in terms of average execution times, the *Linear* function obtains a 12,86% lower makespan than *Level*, and 17,65% lower makespan than $FCFS$. Figure 2 depicts the empirical cumulative distribution functions (CDFs) of the execution times for the three methods. The Y-axis depicts the values of the CDF function $F(M)$ of the makespan M, showing the probability that the makespan records values lower than the scalar on the abscissa. We observe that the *Linear* function strictly dominates the other two methods, in the sense that $F_{Linear} > F_{Level}$ and $F_{Linear} > F_{FCFS}$ for all values on the abscissa. We also tested the dominance of the *Linear* method over the *Level* and $FCFS$ using the $t-test$ for the equality of means in two samples and the *Levene*'s test for equality of variances in two samples with 99% confidence level, and the results are the same. Statistical tests show a weak dominance of *Level* over $FCFS$, therefore we conclude that the Promethee scheduling is superior to $FCFS$.

When using the scheduler with the *Level* function, an interesting and challenging issue is how to set the **indifference** and **preference** thresholds, q and p.

---

[2] P-values are computed for the Kolmogorov-Smirnov test of normality under the null hypothesis is that the distribution of makespan is Gaussian.

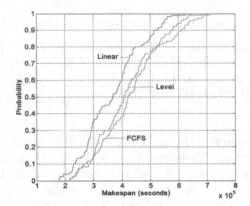

Fig. 2. Stochastic dominance of the *Linear* method with respect to the *FCFS* and *Level* methods

We observed that the values of q and p impact on makespan. Therefore, we conducted an empirical study to find values for q and p that minimize the makespan obtained with *Level*. If σ is the standard deviation of the evaluations of tasks (within criterion c_j) before making a scheduling decision, q and p can be mapped in a orthogonal space according with the following formulas: $q = p \times y$ and $p = \sigma \times x$.

Figure 3a depicts the makespan $surface$ resulted from scheduling the same BoT with different *Level* configurations, by varying x and y. Points of the surface are averages of 120 observations. Darker areas are obtained for low makespan values (darker areas) are obtained for particular values of x and y only. However, many other combinations of values from the solution search space yield a 20% higher makespan (see brighter surfaces and peeks). Consequently, when designing a scheduler, x and y seem to be worth optimizing. To sum up, we can say that such a preference function may be hard to use in practice because it needs optimization for a given context. It is out of the scope of this work to discuss a method of optimum search for the *Level* function. In all our experiments with the *Level* function we used q and p such that we obtain the best makespan.

In what follows, we are concerned about how overloaded is the scheduler when making the decision with various preference functions. In figure 3b we present real execution time measurements of the scheduling component captured during experimentation for the completion of a BoT, in the same experimental setup as above, with *Linear*, *Level* and *Gaussian* preference functions. The graph clearly shows that *Gaussian* is significantly more CPU-consuming, compared to *Linear* and *Level* functions. Consequently, although the *Linear* and *Gaussian* functions yield very similar performances in terms of makespan, when designing a real system one should consider the *Linear* function due to its efficiency in terms of execution time.

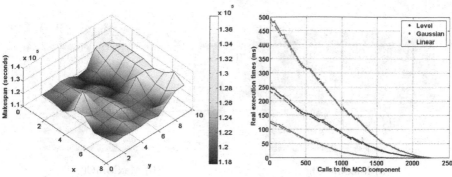

(a) Makespan *surface* for different configurations of the *Level* function.

(b) Real execution time measurements of the Promethee-based scheduling component during the execution of a BoT.

Fig. 3. Makespan and execution time measurements

3.3   Advanced Scheduling Scenarios

In this subsection we present how the scheduler should be configured to yield good values for the user satisfaction metric Θ. We aim at finding the combinations of importance weights ω_{i_c} for criteria ECT and price, and the scheduler configuration that maximizes user satisfaction regardless the user profile (w_m, w_c). We consider four configurations: MaxMaxCfg, MaxMinCfg, MinMaxCfg, MinMinCfg, in each, the scheduler is either interested in maximizing or minimizing the ECT or price. For each configuration we let ω_{ECT} and ω_P vary from 0.9 to 0.1 with a 0.1 step. We omit 1 and 0 values since this would not mean a multi-criteria decision any more. Thus, on each configuration we have 9 possible settings of the Promethee method by combining ω_{ECT} and ω_P.

Figure 4 presents the user satisfaction Θ for the considered configurations. On the X-axis we have 11 user profiles obtained by varying w_C and w_M from 1 to 0 (100% to 0%) with a 0.1 step. While the left-hand side of the figures depict cost-oriented user profiles, the right-hand side represent makespan-oriented profiles.

We notice that the best scheduler configurations are MaxMaxCfg and MaxMinCfg with $\omega_{ECT} \geq 0.7$, where high levels of satisfaction are obtained, regardless of the user profile. We notice that in MaxMinCfg we obtain the highest and more stable user satisfaction. Therefore, it is worth scheduling with higher priority the longer tasks and if possible on cheap infrastructures. We also notice that for the MinMaxCfg setup the scheduler yields worst performance. Analyzing the absolute values for this setup, we found the highest makespan and cost. In the MinMinCfg setup we observe that good satisfaction levels are obtained only for the cost-oriented user profile.

In this subsection we showed how can one select the best configuration of the Promethee method for a certain hybrid DCI, and these experiments should be repeated given that the parameters of the infrastructures change.

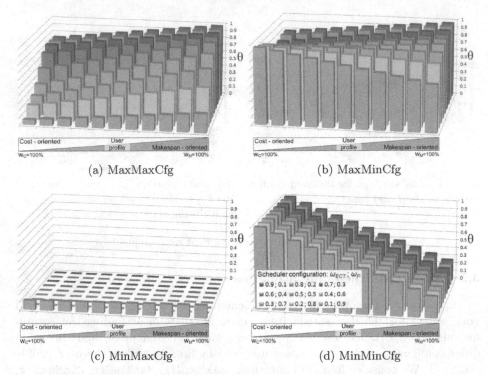

(a) MaxMaxCfg

(b) MaxMinCfg

(c) MinMaxCfg

(d) MinMinCfg

Fig. 4. User satisfaction for various user profiles and configurations of the scheduler

4   Related Work

The European FP7 projects EDGeS[12] and EDGI[13] are representative examples of hybrid DCIs which mixes Clouds, Grids and Desktop Grids. These projects have developed bridge technologies to allow BoT workflow to flow from Grid infrastructures to Desktop Grid. The SpeQuloS [14] system, developed in the context of EDGI, uses private Cloud resources to provide quality of service to BoT applications executed on Desktop Grid. In contrast, our work allows a broader range of usage optimization of hybrid DCIs such as cost minimization.

GridBot [2] represents a first solution to combine several grids in a *monolithic* platform for large-scale execution of grids, emphasizing on replication to handle the job failures on DCIs. GridBot scheduling is policy-based, but considers a fixed set of scheduling criteria.

Iosup et al. [15] employ a performance analysis of BoTs scheduling on large-scale cluster infrastructures, given that multiple users submit simultaneously BoTs to the system and the scheduling is driven by several policies. Kim [16] presents multi-criteria scheduling of bag-of-tasks in order to reduce the power consumption at the infrastructure level, while preserving the agreed SLA over the whole bag-of-tasks. Muthuvelu et al. [17] works on deciding the granularity of tasks composing the BoTs towards economically and efficient usage of grid resources, while satisfying the user QoS requirements. Users own a limited budget for the execution of the BoTs and they also have a deadline constraint. Dealing with cloud resources, Oprescu et al. [18] design a budget-constraint scheduler for BoTs, estimating the costs and the makespan for various scenario before executing the user-selected schedule.

However, the previously mentioned work only consider single DCI, while our work addresses the issues of using hybrid DCIs. In addition, because our evaluation include IDG, which suffer from a high volatility of the computing resources, we take into consideration fault tolerance in our scheduling strategies.

5 Conclusion and Future Work

In this work we introduced the work of investigating our pull and Promethee based scheduler for complex scenarios based on hybrid DCIs. We validated our scheduler using three types of infrastructure: Internet Desktop Grids, Cloud and Best Effort Grid. Our aim was to find the proper configurations of the Promethee method in order to minimize the makespan and cost for the execution of a BoT and increase user satisfaction. For this we conducted a statistical analysis in order find an efficient preference function in terms of makespan. Therefore, we found that the *Linear* function performs best, compared to other functions from the decision-models literature and First-Come-First-Served scheduling. We also found that *Linear* is less CPU-consuming compared to others (due to its lower complexity).

Analyzing the user satisfaction, we concluded that it is worth scheduling the longer tasks on more expensive and reliable infrastructures at the beginning of the BoT execution. This approach yields high and constant user satisfaction regardless the user profiles.

In future-work we plan to add new criteria in our scheduler (like the error rate of hosts) and make it more sensitive to other user requirements. We also intend to study the effectiveness of the scheduler by letting multiple users to simultaneously submit BoTs. We also plan to integrate the scheduler within the XtremWeb middleware, enlarging its infrastructure coverage.

Acknowledgments. This work was partly supported by grant POSDRU/89/ 1.5/S/63663. We also thank our colleague Darie Moldovan for his help concerning graphs and data interpretations.

References

1. FTA: Failure trace archive, inria, http://fta.inria.fr
2. Silberstein, M., Sharov, A., Geiger, D., Schuster, A.: Gridbot: execution of bags of tasks in multiple grids. In: Proc. of the Conf. on High Performance Computing Networking, Storage and Analysis, SC 2009, pp. 11:1–11:12. ACM Press (2009)

3. Moca, M., Fedak, G.: Using Promethee Methods for Multi-Criteria Pull-based scheduling on DCIs. In: 8th IEEE International Conference on eScience 2012. IEEE Press (2012)
4. Figueira, J., Greco, S., Ehrgott, M.: Multiple Criteria Decision Analysis: State of the Art Surveys. Springer (2005)
5. Capit, N., Da Costa, G., Georgiou, Y., Huard, G., Martin, C., Mounie, G., Neyron, P., Richard, O.: A batch scheduler with high level components. In: Proc. of the 5th IEEE CCGRID Symp., vol. 2, pp. 776–783. IEEE Computer Society (2005)
6. Delamare, S., Fedak, G., Kondo, D., Lodygensky, O.: Spequlos: A qos service for bot applications using best effort distributed computing infrastructures. In: Proc. of the 21st HPDC Symp., pp. 173–186. ACM, New York (2012)
7. Lodygensky, O., Fedak, G., Cappello, F., Neri, V., Livny, M., Thain, D.: XtremWeb & Condor sharing resources between Internet connected Condor pools. In: Proc. of the 3rd Intl. CCGRID Symp., pp. 382–389. IEEE Computer Society (2003)
8. Kondo, D., Fedak, G., Cappello, F., Chien, A.A., Casanova, H.: Characterizing resource availability in enterprise desktop grids. Future Generation Computer Systems 23(7), 888–903 (2007)
9. Tanenbaum, A.S., van Steen, M.: Distributed Systems Principles and Paradigms. Pearson Education (2007)
10. Brans, J., Vincke, P., Mareschal, B.: How to select and how to rank projects: The Promethee method. European Journal of Operational Research 2, 228–238 (1986)
11. Kondo, D., Javadi, B., Iosup, A., Epema, D.: The failure trace archive: Enabling comparative analysis of failures in diverse distributed systems. In: Proc. of the 2010 10th IEEE/ACM Intl. Conf. on CCGRID, pp. 398–407. IEEE Computer Society (2010)
12. Urbah, E., Kacsuk, P., Farkas, Z., Fedak, G., Kecskemeti, G., Lodygensky, O., Marosi, A., Balaton, Z., Caillat, G., Gombas, G., Kornafeld, A., Kovacs, J., He, H., Lovas, R.: EDGeS: Bridging egee to boinc and xtremweb. Journal of Grid Computing (2009)
13. EDGI: European desktop grid infrastructure (2010), http://edgi-project.eu
14. Delamare, S., Fedak, G., Kondo, D., Lodygensky, O.: SpeQuloS: a QoS service for BoT applications using best effort distributed computing infrastructures. In: Proc. of the 21st Intl. Symp. on HPDC, pp. 173–186. ACM Press (2012)
15. Iosup, A., Sonmez, O., Anoep, S., Epema, D.: The performance of bags-of-tasks in large-scale distributed systems. In: Proc. of the 17th Intl. Symp. on HPDC, pp. 97–108. ACM (2008)
16. Kim, K.H., Lee, W.Y., Kim, J., Buyya, R.: Sla-based scheduling of bag-of-tasks applications on power-aware cluster systems. IEICE Transactions on Information and Systems E93-D(12), 3194–3201 (2010)
17. Muthuvelu, N., Vecchiola, C., Chai, I., Chikkannan, E., Buyya, R.: Task granularity policies for deploying bag-of-task applications on global grids. Future Generation Computer Systems 29(1), 170 (2013)
18. Oprescu, A.-M., Kielmann, T., Leahu, H.: Budget estimation and control for bag-of-tasks scheduling in clouds. Parallel Processing Letters 21(2), 219–243 (2011)

Towards Sustainable IaaS Pricing

Philipp Berndt and Andreas Maier

Zimory GmbH, Berlin, Germany
`firstname.lastname@zimory.com`

Abstract Cloud computing has the potential to improve resource efficiency by consolidating many virtual computers onto each physical host.
This economization is based on the assumption that a significant percentage of virtual machines are indeed not fully utilized. Yet, despite the
much acclaimed *pay-only-for-what-you-use* paradigm, public IaaS cloud
customers are usually still billed by the hour for virtual systems of un-
certain performance rather than on the basis of actual resource usage.
Because ensuring and proving availability of defined performance for collocated multi-tenant VMs poses a complex technical problem, providers
are still reluctant to provide performance guarantees. In lack thereof, prevailing cloud products range in the low price segment, where providers
resort to overbooking and double selling capacity in order to maintain
profitability, thereby further harming trust and cloud adoption. In this
paper we argue that the predominant flat rate billing in conjunction
with the practice of overbooking and its associated mismatch between
actual costs and billed posts results in a substantial misalignment between the interests of providers and customers that stands in the way
of trustworthy and sustainable cloud computing. On these grounds, we
propose a hybrid IaaS pricing model that aims to avoid these problems in
a non-technical fashion by shifting to consumption based billing on top
of credible minimum performance. Requiring only measures that can be
obtained with a low degree of technical complexity as well as a moderate
amount of trust, the approach aspires to be more sustainable, practica-
ble and billable than common practice even without the use of complex
should-I verifiability.

1 Introduction

Virtualization enables cloud providers to run many virtual machines on each
physical host. Compared to running the same number of smaller physical machines, *unitizing*, i.e. selling portions of hosts, can already provide savings in
terms of power, space, hardware and maintenance costs. But even when, in absolute terms, a unitized host is booked out it may be far from busy. This is due
to the fact that a significant percentage of users do not utilize their purchased
CPU capacity to the full. The possibility to *overbook* hosts, i.e. optimistically sell
more compute capacity than is actually available, promises additional revenue.

On occasion, e.g. [8], this overbooking practice is compared to the kind of
overbooking exercised by airlines: Airlines sell more tickets than are seats available on the airplane, based on the assumption that a well predictable percentage

J. Altmann, K. Vanmechelen, and O.F. Rana (Eds.): GECON 2013, LNCS 8193, pp. 173–184, 2013.
© Springer International Publishing Switzerland 2013

of passengers will cancel or not show up. By way of overbooking, a higher utilization can be achieved. Yet, despite some similarities, there are distinct differences in overbooking practice between cloud providers and airlines:

- In the event that their prediction fails and not enough seats are available, the airline will first attempt to find volunteers that surrender their reservations in exchange for agreed benefits or failing that, refund or re-route as well as compensate passengers.
- If a flight was overbooked and not enough seats are available, this will become obvious during boarding at the latest.
- In many regions the rights (e. g. to compensation) of flight passengers are protected.

In contrast, a cloud customer cannot easily learn from resource shortages due to overbooking. Cloud providers are reluctant to share information about performance problems and rather have customers submit corroborated complaints [2,4]. Moreover, performance guarantees are commonly limited to mere reachability. A cloud customer may suspect degraded performance; but to be sure he would generally have to interrupt his workload and run a benchmark. But even then, he has no way to determine whether the host his VM is running on has been overbooked. Surprisingly, even for the provider, it is, for a virtualization host under full load and with overbooking in effect, non-trivial to tell which of the VMs receive their full nominal resource share: As long as the collective load of all VMs stays below the host's overall capacity, all VMs are sufficiently isolated from one another and overbooking may not necessarily induce substantial service degradation [18]. However, at the latest as soon as host capacity is utilized to the full, isolation breaks down and some customers will likely not receive their promised performance [15]. In this case it is hard to tell which VMs should have received more CPU and which ones were actually idle [22]. Although a mechanism for verifiable resource accounting has been proposed in theory, several practical issues (e. g. performance impact and overhead of the monitoring framework, accidental leakage of private information) remain unresolved [22].

Yet, despite these difficulties in determining whether a VM was offered a certain performance, the predominant IaaS billing model is still flat, i. e. time based, creating a mismatch between actual costs and billed posts that results in a substantial misalignment between the interests of providers and customers.

Instead of revealing their business models and adapting offered cloud products to match actual costs, providers do overbooking in the dark and pretend to not care about work loads. As a consequence they are very reluctant to giving any performance guarantees[1] despite this is what customers have desired for a long time [11]. Uncertainty and secrecy create a state of mistrust that further inhibits cloud adoption.

In this paper we propose an alternative cost model that tries to avoid several of these problems by aligning interests in the IaaS market and turning the current model into a more cooperative one.

---

[1] Commonplace statements, a virtual machine in a cloud product would match the performance of some reference system, are meaningless in lack of any guarantees.

The remainder of this paper is organized as follows: The following section takes a game theoretic approach to model the status quo as an asymmetric non-cooperative simultaneous game, exploring optimal strategies and global consequences. In Section 3, our new cost model is presented. Section 4 deals with the technical implementation of the model, particularly monitoring. Finally, Section 5 points out related work and Section 6 concludes the paper.

2   Status Quo Analysis

Starting from a brief discussion of flat rates and their application to cloud computing, we now model current billing practice from a game theoretic view to highlight the problems associated with this model.

2.1   Flat Rates

In order to maintain competitiveness of service providers of all trades, it has long been imperative to multiplex key resources between multiple customers. Hence, besides direct costs of operation (e. g. energy consumed in the process of serving a customer) specifically the proportional usage of means, e. g. expensive hardware, is a key factor for profitability. Clearly, the more customers can be served per monetary unit of means, the more profitable is the service provider. Where the cost varies significantly subject to customer behavior, it stands to reason to pass the usage associated costs on to the customer. Where the expected total utilization is self-limited or of subordinated economic impact a flat rate may be feasible instead. The latter particularly applies to services where human physiology limits consumption, e. g. all-you-can-eat buffets, free refills, or free phone calls[2]. In the last decade, Internet service providers (*ISPs*) have adopted the flat rate phone model for consumer Internet access. In the early years of the world wide web, consumer Internet traffic used to be dominated by the manual downloading of web pages ("surfing the web") and thus limited to human screen hours. However, with the advent of peer-to-peer file sharing, a large portion, temporarily even the lion's share of consumer Internet traffic, is non-interactive bulk traffic [21]. As such, it is not anymore limited by human physiology. Confronted with the consequences, ISPs are already starting to back away from the flat rate model[3].

---

[2] American phone companies have been offering flat rate service options effectively since the invention of the telephone in 1876, based on the rationale, that a human can spend only so much time on the phone. While in principle it is possible to establish a phone connection and then not use it, there is little benefit in it. On the contrary, not being able to receive other calls in the mean time constitutes a disadvantage that depreciates such practice. Accordingly, in [26] phone calls are associated with both a benefit, modeled as a logarithm of call duration, and an opposed opportunity cost, directly proportional to call duration.

[3] The breaking of the flat rate model can currently be observed in Germany, where the Deutsche Telekom has recently decided to cap its flat rate in response to soaring data demand [5].

Still public IaaS cloud providers are selling CPU flat fees as if they did not care about consumption while at the same time hiding overbooking practice. Customers are usually billed by the hour for virtual systems of specified performance, no matter how they utilize them. However, at the latest since the introduction of the decentralized currency *bitcoins (BTC)* [19], compute capacity has a direct (however small) minimum benefit in money's worth. Apart from that, by now there exist hundreds of volunteer computing projects, such as Folding@home [6], where excess compute capacity can be put to charitable use, providing a reputational benefit for corporates and individuals. But even without a direct reward, idling his virtual CPU may not be a cloud consumer's best option, as will be shown below.

2.2 Strategic Analysis

We now model this situation from a game theoretic view to determine what consequences can be drawn, both from the perspective of the cloud users and from that of the provider: Let r, c be the revenues and costs, respectively, of a cloud provider who lets her host, unitized to several consumers, initially without overbooking. Let x be the benefit the cloud consumers get from running their VMs unimpeded. This basic state is represented by the top-right cell (idle, don't overbook) of Table 1, showing a payoff matrix with all possible outcomes.

Table 1. Payoff matrix. The columns represent the provider's choice to overbook ($b > 1$) or not ($b = 1$); the rows represent the consumers' disposition of spare capacity, i. e. leaving it unused, monetizing it, or using it to verify VM performance.

		provider	
		overbook	don't
consumers	idle	$x - \delta,\ b_{\text{idle}} \cdot r - (c+u)$	$x,\ r-c$
	monetize	$x - \delta + \epsilon,\ b_{\text{busy}} \cdot r - (c+u)$	$x + \epsilon,\ r - (c+u)$
	benchmark	$x - \delta + \rho,\ b_{\text{busy}} \cdot r - (c+u) - \rho$	$x,\ r - (c+u)$

Since the consumers' workload is assumed to contain substantial idle times, the provider may decide to overbook her host by a factor of $b_{\text{idle}} > 1$, in which case her revenue is multiplied[4] and her expenditures are augmented slightly by additional resource usage dependent costs $u > 0$. In this case, the performance of the customers' VMs may be affected and their benefit x diminished by disturbance δ, $0 < \delta < x$, as shown in cell (idle, overbook).

On the other hand, the consumers may decide to use their idle capacity to perform other work, earning them additional profit $\epsilon > 0$. Because of the increased load the provider's ability to overbook is reduced to b_{busy}, $1 \leq b_{\text{busy}} < b_{\text{idle}}$, shown in cell (monetize, overbook).

---

[4] While in theory higher values of b result in higher profit for the provider, we note that there exists a limit as to what associated disturbance δ consumers will tolerate [10] and accordingly limit b in our analysis to some arbitrary tolerable value.

Alternatively, the consumers may run benchmarks that may prove they did not receive full performance, in which case the provider reimburses them with ρ, shown in cell (benchmark, overbook).

Irregardless of whether the provider overbooks, the consumers can always achieve an equal or better outcome by either monetizing or benchmarking, i. e. their strategy to idle is weakly dominated.

If the compensation ρ is higher than the additional revenue, i. e. $\rho > (b_{busy} - 1)r$, the provider is pressed to quit overbooking in case the consumers do benchmark. Otherwise, the provider's strategy to overbook is strictly dominant.

For $\epsilon \geq \rho$ the consumers strategy to monetize is strictly dominant.

For the more general case, the consumers' and the provider's best responses are interdependent. The provider's mixed strategy, specifically the probability to overbook, σ_o, that makes the consumers indifferent is determined by equating the expected utilities of monetizing, EU_m, and benchmarking, EU_b:

$$
\begin{aligned}
EU_m &= \sigma_o(x - \delta + \epsilon) + (1 - \sigma_o)(x + \epsilon) = x - \sigma_o\delta + \epsilon \\
EU_b &= \sigma_o(x - \delta + \rho) + (1 - \sigma_o)x \qquad = x + \sigma_o(\rho - \delta) \qquad (1) \\
EU_m &= EU_b \quad \Rightarrow \quad \sigma_o = \frac{\epsilon}{\rho}.
\end{aligned}
$$

Likewise, the consumers' mixed strategy, i. e. the probability to benchmark, σ_b, that makes the provider indifferent is determined by equating the expected utilities of overbooking, EU_o, or not, EU_d:

$$
\begin{aligned}
EU_o &= \sigma_b \left(b_{busy}r - (c + u) - \rho\right) + (1 - \sigma_b)\left(b_{busy}r - (c + u)\right) \\
&= -\rho\sigma_b + b_{busy}r - c - u \\
EU_d &= \sigma_b \left(r - (c + u)\right) + (1 - \sigma_b)\left(r - (c + u)\right) = r - c - u \qquad (2) \\
EU_o &= EU_d \quad \Rightarrow \quad \sigma_b = \frac{(b_{busy} - 1)r}{\rho}.
\end{aligned}
$$

This results in a mixed strategy Nash equilibrium at

$$
\left\langle \sigma_b = \frac{(b_{busy} - 1)r}{\rho}, \; \sigma_o = \frac{\epsilon}{\rho} \right\rangle. \qquad (3)
$$

This means, the lower the compensation ρ is, the higher is the probability of the provider overbooking and the more benchmarking the consumers must do to avoid the overbooking-incurred performance penalty δ. For $\rho \leq \epsilon$ the consumers cannot keep the provider from overbooking but should at least monetize their idle capacity. Note that under no circumstances the consumer is well advised to leave it unused because that would not only get him neither monetization nor compensation but also ensure the performance penalty from inevitable overbooking. In fact, even by keeping the CPU busy with arbitrary nonsensical computations, will he lower the probability of the provider further overbooking the busy machine, and may thus get better performance once he needs it.

Ironically, the strategy to idle is the only one that would make the cloud more resource efficient than classic computing. Instead, the billing practice, if purely

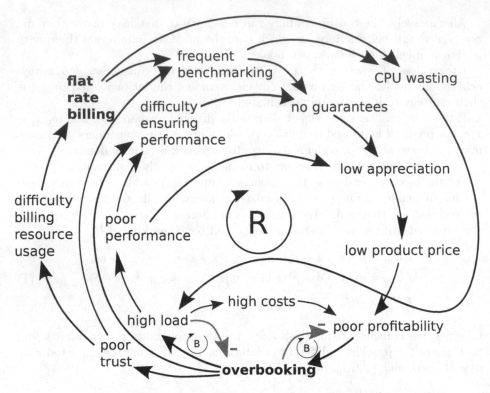

Fig. 1. Vicious circle of flat rate billing and overbooking

economically responded to, results in a situation where, rather than improving resource efficiency, the cloud is occupied by performing wasteful tasks that would not be performed without cloud computing. It is another instance of the tragedy of the commons [12], signifying that shared resources of value that can be utilized at no cost will reliably lead to exhaustion of these resources.

Unfortunately, the situation will likely not remedy itself, as the actions appear to be self-reinforcing. A causal loop diagram of the underlying vicious circle is shown in Figure 1. Following the notation of [24], "R" denotes a positive reinforcement loop whereas negative reinforcement (or "balancing") is labeled "B" and accompanied with green arrows annotated with a minus sign. As we have shown, the flat rate billing drives utility maximizing consumers towards exhausting their idle capacity, thereby increasing load and costs for the provider, and limiting her ability to overbook. The threat of free benchmarking, in conjunction with difficulties ensuring performance, described in Section 1, induces the provider to limit her guarantees to bare connectivity rather than performance, which suffers from high load and overbooking. This lowers the valuation of IaaS cloud products compared to dedicated servers. In order to maintain profitability she is forced resort to overbooking and double selling capacity. The inevitable loss of trust in conjunction with the enduring absence of workable solutions to strictly verifiable resource accounting leaves flat rate billing her only option.

3   Proposed Solution

Despite this dilemma, we believe it takes little more than a change in perspective and billing to align interest in the IaaS market and turn the current model into a more cooperative one. Our goal is to break the vicious circle by coming up with a sustainable economic model that is better balanced, technically realizable, and more transparent and trustworthy. To this end we target the issues flat rate billing, lack of guarantees, and overbooking.

Since it is, on the one hand, expensive to determine and prove whether a VM receives guaranteed performance, but, on the other hand, such guarantees cannot be avoided altogether, we propose to reduce the guaranteed performance to a minimum that is credibly attestable with simple technical means. A provider is thus able to collocate a high number of VMs with these minimum performance requirements without the need for (and suspicion of) additional overbooking. The main compute capacity is made available on a best-effort basis, billed by CPU time. Following this approach, the cloud product is composed of

1. a *flat rate part* in which a certain performance is guaranteed to the customer
2. a *flexible* (consumption based) *part* in which resource usage beyond the flat rate portion is billed.

This hybrid pricing model has several advantages:

– Consumers pay a flat fee only for the guaranteed minimum performance. All additional CPU work is billed on a pay-for-what-you-use basis.
– Guaranteed performance is a premium that justifies a higher price than current products, lacking SLAs, and thereby improves profitability and removes the need to double-sell capacity through overbooking.
– Through elastic billing, providers can fully utilize host capacity without breaching any SLAs and can thus avoid legal gray areas associated with traditional overbooking.
– Providers will be eager to provide sufficient performance in order to increase consumption. This alignment of interests removes pressure to expensively prove performance availability and builds up trust.
– No CPU time is wasted with uneconomical computations, enabling the originally aspired cloud efficiency.
– Instead of constantly surveilling the ongoing capability to provide a defined performance to all customers, monitoring is largely reduced to initial benchmarking, ensuring availability, and recording resource consumption.

Our approach requires, on the one hand, a measure of *performance* and, on the other hand, a measure of actual resource usage (*work*). The basis for both is the virtualization host's capacity, i. e. its abstract ability to perform a number of tasks within a certain time. It depends on a wide variety of factors, including CPU speed, architecture, memory access, storage and network bandwidths. Clearly, different configurations will perform better at different tasks. However, the utility and hardware abstraction aspects of cloud computing demand for different configurations to be made comparable, at least within application niches.

In [7] we present such a hardware independent performance measure and show how a virtualization host's compute capacity C can be determined by concurrent benchmarking. C determines the total performance $\sum P$ that can be guaranteed to the entirety of consumer VMs:

$$\sum P \leq C. \tag{4}$$

The common measure CPU time t_{CPU} denotes the cumulative time for which one CPU was occupied processing the customer's workload, including associated overheads. Assuming for now that capacity C is reached with n_{CPU} CPUs under full load, work can be computed as the product of performance and CPU time, divided by the number of CPUs

$$W = \int P\, \mathrm{d}t = \frac{C}{n_{\mathrm{CPU}}}\, t_{\mathrm{CPU}}. \tag{5}$$

4 Technical Considerations

Proving availability of performance for collocated multi-tenant VMs poses a complex technical problem [13,15,23,9]. Our proposed approach aims to avoid the issue by shifting the focus to consumption based billing on top of credible minimum performance, thereby requiring only measures that can be obtained with a low degree of technical complexity as well as a moderate amount of trust. The specific measures required to this end will be discussed below.

4.1 Benchmarking

Through benchmarking, the total virtual performance (capacity C) of a host is determined. In [7] we demonstrate how a hardware independent performance quantification can be accomplished in an IaaS cloud context. To this end, several scalable application benchmarks are run on multiple VMs simultaneously and competing for resources. For each benchmark the VM with minimum performance determines the benchmark score. One performance unit (PU) is defined as the minimum rating according to the weighted geometric mean of the individual benchmarks on the one hand, and any explicitly defined requirements on the other hand[5].

4.2 Quota Enforcement

Using virtualization technology specific methods it must be ensured that each VM is given its designated guaranteed amount of CPU time as well as IO and network bandwidths. For instance, starting with libvirt[6] version 0.9 it is possible

---

[5] For example, 1 PU could be defined as the conjunction of at least 2 GiB RAM, 20 GB storage space, 1 MB/s storage IO, 1 Mbit/s LAN bandwidth, 100 kbit/s Internet bandwidth, and a certain minimum application benchmark suite performance.

[6] http://www.libvirt.org/

to assign CPU shares and block IO weights that will determine how resources will be distributed in face of full host utilization. Note that unless VMs compete for resources, and the host is fully utilized, VMs are still allowed consume an arbitrary amount of resources.

4.3 Base Portion Accounting

The flat rate or base part of the contract foresees that rigid slices of host capacity are provisioned to the consumers. At this, the billable duration results directly from the contract, independent of actual VM usage. The host capacity is known from benchmarking, the proper resource allocation ensured through quota enforcement. All that remains is to verify availability of the VM during the appointed time span. In an IaaS context, availability could, for instance, be defined as error-free execution of the VM in conjunction with proper configuration of (virtual) network devices.

4.4 Elastic Portion Accounting

For the elastic portion, the resource usage beyond the amount included in the base portion must be recorded. This may include additional CPU time, storage space, RAM, and Internet transfer volume. While the measurement of these quantities is relatively straightforward and decidedly less costly than proving performance availability over a period of time, certain issues must nevertheless be regarded. [17] shows how, even without tampering with the operating system kernel or the VM processes, a provider can still easily mount various attacks to inflate the consumer's CPU usage. But even in absence of deliberate attacks, CPU time measurements of deterministic programs are sensitive to OS scheduling granularity. Resource contention, such as cache misses or network congestion may increase the computation footprint [22]. To maintain a comparable measure of work across different hardware and virtualization configurations it is therefore essential to also measure pessimistic CPU time overhead during host benchmarking.

4.5 Infrastructure Monitoring

Apart from the explicit measures describe above, the proper functioning and Internet connectivity of the cloud platform infrastructure must be monitored continuously. At this, conventional monitoring approaches can be applied.

4.6 Auditing

Several service aspects are not amenable to direct validation by the customer. In these cases the latter has to trust the statement of a certification authority signifying that the operation is indeed performed in accordance with regulations. One typical example is security. But obviously, all of the measures described above are only meaningful if performed honestly and properly, to which auditing can be the only assurance. However, because of the better alignment of interests, i. e. by billing work rather than performance time, the pressure to cheat, e. g. claim nonexistent performance, is greatly reduced.

5   Related Work

Various billing models are employed by cloud providers. In the AMAZON ELASTIC COMPUTE CLOUD (AMAZON EC2) [2] and for WINDOWS AZURE VIRTUAL MACHINES [4] the consumer is billed by the hour, irrespective of resource usage. Both provide only guarantees regarding external connectivity, not performance. Customer claims including sufficient evidence to support them will result in a partial credit of the service fee, if validated. AMAZON EC2 SPOT INSTANCES [1] facilitates resource utilization by selling their available capacity in a spot market fashion where supply and demand determine the instance price per hour. When the spot price exceeds a customer's bid his VMs will be terminated. In this way, the Spot Instances model more openly embraces resource utilization and consequent best-effort availability; however, instances are still billed flatly by the hour. [14] presents a pay-as-you-consume pricing scheme that, while still time based, compensates interference between VMs using a support vector machine (SVM) based machine learning approach. GOOGLE APP ENGINE [3] provides a platform for running web applications on Google's infrastructure. The consumer is billed by resource usage (CPU hours, data store usage, channels opened, API calls, etc.) exceeding a minimum quota. The SLA provides partial credit for internal server errors encountered. Their API usage based billing approach avoids many of the problems of CPU time billing but is limited to the PaaS model. The use of CPU time for billing a grid user is anticipated in the OGF Usage Record by including a `CpuDuration` field. However these values are incomparable if the performance of the respective resource is unknown. In [20] the need to normalize such resource consumption values across heterogeneous resources or platforms by way of some notion of processing power is embraced. As the first composite unit of measurement for the use of computing resources HP envisions the *computon* as "a bundle of processing power, storage, and bandwidth that can be sold and consumed" [25]. Originally intended for their TYCOON DISTRIBUTED MARKET-BASED RESOURCE ALLOCATION SYSTEM [16] the approach is independently pursued in [27]. A systematic study on the trustworthiness of conventional CPU usage metering is presented in [17]. [22] proposes a systematic approach for verifiable resource accounting by which cloud customers can be assured that (a) their applications indeed physically consumed the resources they were charged for and (b) that this consumption was justified based on an agreed policy. With ALIBI [9], a minimal, trusted reference monitor underneath the service provider's software platform is proposed that observes resource allocation to VMs and reports its observations to the customers, for verifiable reconciliation.

6   Conclusion

In this paper we have surveyed prevailing IaaS product pricing practice. We found that—despite long held public desire for *pay-only-for-what-you-use* billing and better performance certainty—CPU flat rate models are still the norm, whereas performance guarantees are still rudimentary to nonexistent. We have modeled the situation as an asymmetric non-cooperative simultaneous game and explored best strategies. Under given circumstances, consumers fare worst when *not* using left-over capacity. Assuming utility maximizing consumers, this leads to a situation where the clouds are occupied with wasteful computations, forestalling the promise of energy efficient cloud computing. Providers are reluctant to give performance guarantees and instead do overbooking, while at the same time suffering from poor trust, appreciation, and profitability, self-reinforced by a causal loop. On these grounds, we have presented an approach to break this vicious circle by switching to a hybrid pricing model comprised of a flat rate part in which a certain performance is guaranteed to the customer and flexible, consumption based part in which resource usage beyond the flat rate portion is billed. Because of the better alignment of interests the approach manages with simpler benchmarking, monitoring, and accounting measures instead of expensive *should-I verifiability*, as per [22].

Future work will focus on establishing a technical proof of concept as well as elaborating performance and work measures.

References

1. Amazon EC2 spot instances, http://aws.amazon.com/ec2/spot-instances/
2. Amazon elastic compute cloud (amazon EC2), http://aws.amazon.com/ec2/
3. Google app engine: Paid apps: Budgeting, billing, and buying resources, https://developers.google.com/appengine/docs/billing
4. Windows Azure virtual machines pricing, http://www.windowsazure.com/en-us/pricing/details/virtual-machines/
5. Deutsche telekom confirms new broadband data limits (April 2013), http://www.telecompaper.com/news/deutsche-telekom-confirms-new-broadband-data-limits-938900
6. Beberg, A.L., Ensign, D.L., Jayachandran, G., Khaliq, S., Pande, V.S.: Folding@home: Lessons from eight years of volunteer distributed computing. In: Proceedings of the 23rd IEEE International Symposium on Parallel Distributed Processing, IPDPS 2009, pp. 1–8 (2009)
7. Berndt, P., Watzl, J.: Unitizing performance of IaaS cloud deployments. In: Proceedings of the 9th World Congress on Services, SERVICES 2013, Santa Clara, pp. 356–362. IEEE (July 2013)
8. Birkenheuer, G., Brinkmann, A., Karl, H.: The Gain of Overbooking. In: Frachtenberg, E., Schwiegelshohn, U. (eds.) JSSPP 2009. LNCS, vol. 5798, pp. 80–100. Springer, Heidelberg (2009)
9. Chen, C., Maniatis, P., Perrig, A., Vasudevan, A., Sekar, V.: Towards verifiable resource accounting for outsourced computation. In: Proceedings of the 9th ACM SIGPLAN/SIGOPS International Conference on Virtual Execution Environments, VEE 2013, pp. 167–178. ACM, New York (2013)
10. Chen, J., Wang, C., Zhou, B.B., Sun, L., Lee, Y.C., Zomaya, A.Y.: Tradeoffs between profit and customer satisfaction for service provisioning in the cloud. In: Proceedings of the 20th International Symposium on High Performance Distributed Computing, HPDC 2011, pp. 229–238. ACM, New York (2011)
11. Gens, F.: It cloud services user survey, pt.3: What users want from cloud services providers (October 2008), http://blogs.idc.com/ie/?p=213

12. Hardin, G.: The tragedy of the commons. Science 162(3859), 1243–1248 (1968)
13. Hauck, M., Huber, M., Klems, M., Kounev, S., Müller-Quade, J., Pretschner, A., Reussner, R., Tai, S.: Challenges and opportunities of cloud computing. Technical Report 2010-19, Karlsruhe Institute of Technology (2010)
14. Ibrahim, S., He, B., Jin, H.: Towards pay-as-you-consume cloud computing. In: 2011 IEEE International Conference on Services Computing (SCC), SCC 2011, pp. 370–377 (2011)
15. Krebs, R., Momm, C., Kounev, S.: Metrics and techniques for quantifying performance isolation in cloud environments. In: Proceedings of the 8th International ACM SIGSOFT Conference on Quality of Software Architectures, QoSA 2012, pp. 91–100. ACM, New York (2012)
16. Lai, K., Huberman, B.A., Fine, L.: Tycoon: A distributed market-based resource allocation system. Technical report, HP Labs (February 2008), http://arxiv.org/abs/cs/0404013
17. Liu, M., Ding, X.: On trustworthiness of CPU usage metering and accounting. In: Proceedings of the IEEE 30th International Conference on Distributed Computing Systems Workshops, ICDCSW 2010, pp. 82–91 (2010)
18. Matthews, J., Hu, W., Hapuarachchi, M., Deshane, T., Dimatos, D., Hamilton, G., McCabe, M., Owens, J.: Quantifying the performance isolation properties of virtualization systems. In: Proceedings of the 2007 Workshop on Experimental Computer Science, ExpCS 2007. ACM, New York (2007)
19. Nakamoto, S.: Bitcoin: A peer-to-peer electronic cash system (2008), http://bitcoin.org/bitcoin.pdf
20. Piro, R.M., Pace, M., Ghiselli, A., Guarise, A., Luppi, E., Patania, G., Tomassetti, L., Werbrouck, A.: Tracing resource usage over heterogeneous grid platforms: A prototype RUS interface for DGAS. In: Proc. of the 3rd IEEE Intl. Conf. on e-Science and Grid Computing, E-SCIENCE 2007, pp. 93–101. IEEE Computer Society, Washington, DC (2007)
21. Schulze, H., Mochalski, K.: Internet study 2008/2009. Technical report, ipoque GmbH (2009), http://www.ipoque.com/resources/internetstudies
22. Sekar, V., Maniatis, P.: Verifiable resource accounting for cloud computing services. In: Proceedings of the 3rd ACM Cloud Computing Security Workshop, CCSW 2011, pp. 21–26. ACM, New York (2011)
23. Shue, D., Freedman, M.J., Shaikh, A.: Performance isolation and fairness for multi-tenant cloud storage. In: Proceedings of the 10th USENIX Conference on Operating Systems Design and Implementation, OSDI 2012, pp. 349–362. USENIX Association, Berkeley (2012)
24. Sterman, J.: Business Dynamics: Systems Thinking and Modeling for a Complex World. McGraw-Hill Education (2000)
25. Stuart, A., Huberman, B.: An economy of IT—allocating resources in the computing utility (October 2003), http://www.hpl.hp.com/news/2003/oct_dec/computons.html
26. Train, K.E., McFadden, D.L., Ben-Akiva, M.: The demand for local telephone service: A fully discrete model of residential calling patterns and service choices. RAND Journal of Economics 18(1), 109–123 (1987)
27. Yu, J., Chen, H., Liu, Y.: The computon in computing grid. In: Proceedings of the 5th WSEAS International Conference on Simulation, Modelling and Optimization, SMO 2005, pp. 89–94. World Scientific, Stevens Point (2005)

Towards a PaaS Architecture
for Resource Allocation in IaaS Providers
Considering Different Charging Models

Cristiano C.A. Vieira[1], Luiz F. Bittencourt[2], and Edmundo R.M. Madeira[2]

[1] Federal University of Mato Grosso do Sul - Faculty of Computing
Cidade Universitária, Campo Grande/MS - Brasil
[2] University of Campinas - Institute of Computing
Av. Albert Einstein, 1251 Cidade Universitária, Campinas/SP - Brasil

Abstract. With the increase in computing infrastructure commercialization through the pay-as-you-go model, competition among providers puts the user as a decision agent on which is the best provider to comply with his/her demands and requirements. Currently, users rely on instances offered as on-demand, reserved, and spot to decide which is the best resource allocation model over the time. In this work, we present substantial contributions to compose a PaaS architecture that leverages different charging models, where we propose the use of a new charging model called time-slotted reservation. Moreover, we developed an integer linear program (ILP) to perform the scheduling of incoming requests according to different QoS levels, proposing a mapping of those levels into the charging models offered by IaaS providers. Simulations show the applicability of the ILP in the proposed model, being able to maximize the number of requisitions executed following the user's QoS requirements.

Keywords: Cloud Computing, Architecture, PaaS, IaaS, Charging model, Scheduling.

1 Introduction

The increase in the pay-as-you-go model in Infrastructure as a Service (IaaS) cloud providers allowed corporations to reduce the initial capital needed for IT infrastructure. This popularization, not coincidently, comes as both higher bandwidth is available over the Internet and virtualization technologies maturates. In this sense, IaaS cloud providers such as Amazon, GoGrid, lixiscale, Windows Azure, and Ninefold, offer different charging models to commercialize different types of services. One of these services is the virtual machine (VM) leasing, where the user can choose to lease a VM from a variety of hardware configurations (processor speed, processor cores, RAM, storage, and so on). The main charging models currently available are *on-demand* (OD), *reserved* (RE), and *spot* (SP), which present differences in availability and charged price.

The competition among IaaS providers puts the user as a decision agent that selects the provider that best matches the application demands and requirements. When the user has many requests with different running times and

J. Altmann, K. Vanmechelen, and O.F. Rana (Eds.): GECON 2013, LNCS 8193, pp. 185–196, 2013.

quality of service (QoS) requirements, it is desirable to automate the decision-making process of choosing what type of VM, and with which charging model, should run each request.

In general, the resource allocation problem in IaaS providers can be tackled with two different objectives: reduce costs to the client [1][2][3] or increase the provider income guaranteeing the user satisfaction [4][5][6][7][8]. We are interested in the first objective, i.e., reducing the running costs for the client of public cloud providers. A good application scheduling can reduce the allocation costs, avoiding high budgets when running applications in the cloud.

In this work, we present substantial contributions to compose a PaaS architecture that helps customers to schedule VM requests on different public clouds. The architecture leverages different charging models, and we propose the use of a new charging model, called *time-slotted reservation*, which enables a better utilization for leased instances in the reserved (RE) charging model. The proposed platform supports two levels of SLA. The first SLA level governs the interaction between the user and the PaaS, while the second level governs the the interaction of the PaaS with a set of IaaS providers, and therefore contains charging models in use.

We consider that the platform belongs to an organization and receives requests for VMs to be allocated to public clouds. In this sense, the main contributions of this work are: a) a PaaS architecture with two SLA levels; b) a new charging model called "time-slotted reservation-TS"; c) a mapping proposal between the two SLA levels of the architecture; d) an Integer Linear Program (ILP) formulation for scheduling; and e) analysis of experimental results.

In the next section we give an overview of the related work. The background and problem formulation are provided in Section 3. A PaaS architecture is proposed in Section 4. A detailed discussion on simulation set-up, metrics, and experimental results is given in Section 5. Finally, Section 6 presents the conclusions and the future work.

2   Related Work

The utilization of public clouds to extend the locally available computing power has been widely explored recently [9][10]. Zhao et. al. [5] present CloudBay, a platform to offer resources from different public clouds utilizing auction strategies. Other auction strategies for marketing resources in clouds were proposed [11][12].

Cloud federation was proposed by Toosi et. al. [6], where a provider uses resources from other providers in the federation to meet the need for reserved instances. The provider can trade reserved instances but also sell them in the on-demand (OD) model. When the client wants to utilize the reserved instance, the provider can look for an instance in the federation to serve the user.

Chen et. al. [7] developed a new utility model for measuring customer satisfaction in the cloud. Based on the utility model, they designed a mechanism to support utility-based SLAs in order to balance the performance of applications and the cost of running them. They presented two scheduling algorithms that can effectively bid for different types of VM instances.

An ILP is presented by Genez et al. [2] to solve the scheduling problem for dependent services in SaaS/PaaS with two SLA-levels. They utilize both RE and OD models in the simulations. Similarly, but for a single SLA level, Bittencourt et al. [3] propose an algorithm to schedule workflows which considers costs and deadlines, to select VM configurations from public IaaS providers to expand the available computational power locally available.

Assunção et al. [1] investigated the benefits that organizations can reach by using cloud computing providers to increase the computing capacity of their local infrastructure. They evaluated the cost of seven scheduling strategies used by an organization that operates a cluster managed by virtual machine technology and seeks to utilize resources from a remote IaaS provider to reduce the response time of its user requests.

Although some work uses charging models, a few consider OD, RE and SP charging models in scheduling. It is interesting to consider the utilization of different charging models for different QoS categories. Besides, some work deals with the provider perspective only, i.e., they aim to increase the provider profit. In this work, we focus on decreasing the scheduling cost for the user.

3   Background and Problem Formulation

Users request VMs from an IaaS provider to run their applications, therefore we define the user need for a single VM as a *VM request*. A user can perform a number of requests to run applications that need different QoS levels. More specifically, considering execution time as the main QoS parameter, in this work we classify the VM requests into three QoS categories:

- Fixed-time request (FTRx): In this category, the start time is immediate and the VM cannot be interrupted (preempted) during its execution.
- Floating-time request: (FTRt): The request may not start immediately, but once it is started, it cannot be interrupted (preempted).
- Variable-time request (VTR): The request may not start immediately and it can be interrupted (preempted), i. e., the execution of requests in this category can be fragmented in smaller parts.

In the face of the wide availability of services offered by a variety of IaaS providers, the user has the burden of choosing which resources from which provider he/she should utilize. On the other hand, providers have SLAs composed of different charging models utilized to lease the resources, which regulates how and how much the user will pay for leasing a VM instance. In this context, a user must choose VMs and charging models according to requests with different QoS needs. We consider that VMs requests from the user must be allocated over VMs from IaaS providers with the objective of achieving a low scheduling cost. Moreover, the set of VMs considered during the scheduling process is already leased, thus we are dealing with a pre-determined set of already rented VMs from various providers. Optimizing the use of currently leased VMs allows the user/organization to determine which VMs are needed, reducing costs.

The problem tackled in this paper is stated as follows: *Compute a schedule S to a set $\mathcal{R}$ of VM requests over a set Ψ of VM instances from IaaS providers with the objective of achieving the smallest allocation cost without violating QoS.*

The $\mathcal{R}$ set is composed of n VM instance requests $r = \{k, d, d\alpha, qos\}$, where $r(k)$ represents the instance type, $r(d)$ represents the total time for which the instance must be available to the user, $r(d\alpha)$ represents a relaxing over d, and $r(qos) = \{$ FTRx | FTRt | VTR $\}$ corresponds to the QoS category of the request. By definition, we have $d = d\alpha$, $\forall\, r \in \mathcal{R}$ such that $r(qos) = \{FTRx\}$; and $d < d\alpha$, $\forall\, r \in \mathcal{R}$ such that $r(qos) = \{FTRt, VTR\}$.

Each provider has a set of VM instances available to the user. From the user perspective, it is necessary to verify how requests can be fulfilled, and at which costs, utilizing the VMs from the providers. A request must be fulfilled with the smallest cost without violating its maximum execution time. In this work, we assume that tasks have no dependency among them. Figure 1 presents the scenario we are considering in this work.

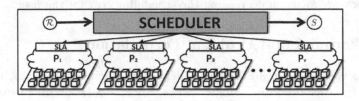

Fig. 1. Scenario for request submission

Given a set $\mathcal{R}$ of n requests, we must obtain a schedule $S = \{t, q, c, E\}$, composed, respectively, of: t, the total execution time of $\mathcal{R}$; q, the number of requests fulfilled; c, the lowest cost to the user and the scheduling containing the instance; and E, the time at which each request is to be allocated. Moreover, we denote, as follows, some definitions utilized in this paper. Let:

- $\mathcal{R} = \{r_1, r_2, ..., r_n\}$: set containing n requests;
- $\mathcal{P} = \{p_1, p_2, ..., p_v\}$: set of v providers;
- Ψ_i: set of instances available to the user in the provider p_i;
- $\Psi = \bigcup_{i=1}^{v} \Psi_i$:set of all instances available to the user;
- $\mathcal{B}^{s1}$: set of PaaS charging models;
- $\mathcal{B}_i^{s2}$: IaaS providers i charging models set;
- m: number of instances in Ψ.

4   Towards a PaaS Architecture

Considering the problem formulated in Section 3, we present substantial contributions to compose a PaaS that receives a set of VM requests and performs the scheduling of these requests over a set of instances available from IaaS providers. The objective is to compute a schedule that minimizes the execution costs to the user [1]. Next, we present the PaaS architecture, proposing a new charging model and a mapping between the two levels of SLA, and an ILP to compute the schedule in this architecture.

4.1 PaaS Architecture

The proposed architecture is composed of three layers: application, business, and infrastructure. Figure 2 presents the platform architecture. The application layer receives a set of requests $\mathcal{R}$ and performs their scheduling over the instances available to the PaaS utilizing a scheduling algorithm. The business layer is composed of the allocation strategies and the charging models, both of which utilized by the scheduler to allocate a request r in a provider p_i. The business models in this layer can be changed with no interference in the models made available by the IaaS providers. The infrastructure layer is responsible for maintaining information to manage and monitor the IaaS providers used by the PaaS. We consider all requests are allocated to the IaaS providers.

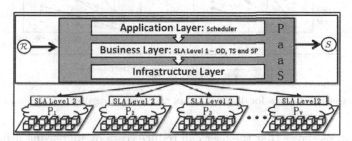

Fig. 2. Architecture utilized in the VM scheduling

Two SLA levels are present in the platform. The first level acts in the interaction between the user and the PaaS, while the second level is between the interaction among the PaaS and the IaaS providers. Charging models belonging to level 1 are located in the business layer, and charging models belonging to the second level refer to the models adopted by the IaaS providers.

4.2 Increasing Instance Utilization

An RE instance imposes the payment of an initial surcharge to offer a discounted price during the VM utilization. This strategy can be advantageous to the customer only if he promotes a high utilization of the reserved instance, otherwise

---

[1] The proposed PaaS can be extended to act as a Broker [13][8], where it could lease VMs from the IaaS providers and offer them to the users. However, it would be necessary to consider economic aspects to enable this broker to be profitable. At this point, we do not consider this implementation as a profitable broker.

the cost per time unit can end up larger than the one for the OD instance. For example, Fig. 3 presents scenarios where the customer utilizes 10%, 20%, 40%. 60%, 80%, and 100% of the time of RE instances for 1 and 3 years, considering prices and configurations from Amazon EC2[2]. A one year usage of an OD instance costs \$1,051.20, while for 100% of utilization for an RE instance would cost \$644.22, including the initial surcharge. On the other hand, utilizing the RE instance only 25% of the time would have a cost of \$368.98. The same use (2,190 hours) in the OD charging model would cost \$262.80. Therefore, low utilization makes the RE instance to be more expensive than the OD instance. Moreover, we can see from the *limit economy* line that, for current market prices, the customer should utilize more than 40% of an instance reserved for one year, and 20% for an instance reserved for three years to them to be worthless.

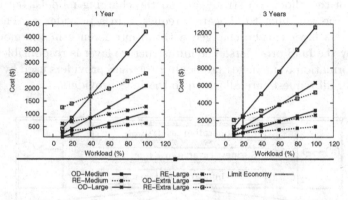

Fig. 3. Comparative costs for 1 and 3 years reservation against on demand instances

This analysis shows that the user can reduce costs by increasing utilization of RE instances. Following this, we propose a new charging model called "Time-slotted reservation - TS", where the user schedules a VM utilization in slots of time. In this model, requests cannot be interrupted. This enables better utilization of RE instances, minimizing the cost per time unit. We added the new TS charging model to $\mathcal{B}^{s1}$, as well as the OD and SP models. Thus, we have that $\mathcal{B}^{s1} = \{OD \mid TS \mid SP\}$ is placed in the business layer of the architecture.

4.3   A Mapping Proposal between the Two SLA Levels of the Architecture

As presented in Fig. 2, the platform is composed of two SLA levels. Considering the QoS categories (FTRx, FTRt, VTR), we define a conceptual model of interaction between these QoS categories, the level-1 SLA set $\mathcal{B}^{s1}$, and the level-2 SLA set $\mathcal{B}^{s2}$, as illustrated in Fig. 4(a). The conceptual model allows new charging models to be incorporated without interfering in the charging models currently available from IaaS providers.

---

[2] From: Amazon - http://aws.amazon.com/ec2/pricing/ in 05/2013.

Figure 4(b) presents a mapping proposal between the two levels in the conceptual model. Other possibilities can be explored, mainly with the appearance of new models. In this work we focused in the mapping from Fig. 4(b).

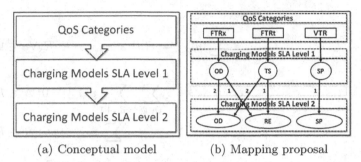

(a) Conceptual model   (b) Mapping proposal

Fig. 4. a)Model of interaction between QoS categories and SLAs at levels 1 and 2. b) Proposed charging model mapping between SLA1 and SLA2.

The presented mapping proposal has the objective of mapping a charging model from $\mathcal{B}^{s1}$ to another from $\mathcal{B}^{s2}$. The SP model at level 2 has low availability guarantee, and therefore it can receive only mappings from the SP model from level 1. The OD and TS models at level 1 can be mapped to both OD and RE models at level 2. However, there is a scheduling priority in the mapping of RE over the OD, aiming at higher utilization (and thus lower prices) using the RE charging model.

4.4 Requests Scheduling

The requests scheduling is obtained utilizing the ILP and two heuristics.

An Integer Linear Program (ILP) Formulation for Scheduling
   The integer linear program solves the scheduling problem through the binary variables w, x, y and z and the constants C, M and K as follows:

- w_r: binary variable that assumes the value 1 if request r is executing; otherwise it assumes the value 0;
- $x_{r,\psi}$: binary variable that assumes the value 1 if request r is executing in VM ψ on independent time t; otherwise it assumes the value 0;
- $y_{r,t,\psi}$: binary variable that assumes the value 1 if request r is executing in VM ψ on the time t; otherwise it assumes the value 0;
- $z_{r,t,\psi}$: binary variable that assumes the value 1 if request r with $r(qos) = \{FTRt\}$ starts executing on time t in VM ψ; 0 otherwise;
- $C_{t,\psi}$: constant that assumes the cost per time unit for using the VM ψ.
- $\mathcal{M}$: sufficiently large constant that assigns a weight for each request.
- $\mathcal{K}$: sufficiently large constant used to ensure FTRt requests start once.

We formulate the objective function $F = \sum\limits_{r \in \mathcal{R}} \sum\limits_{t \in T} \sum\limits_{\psi \in \Psi} (y_{r,t,\psi} \times C_{t,\psi}) - \sum\limits_{r \in \mathcal{R}} (w_r \times \mathcal{M})$ that computes the scheduling of $\mathcal{R}$ in Ψ aiming lower cost allocation. Thus, we want to minimize F subject to:

$$\sum_{t=1}^{r(d\alpha)} y_{r,t,\psi} = r(d) \times x_{r,\psi}; \forall r \in \mathcal{R}, \forall \psi \in \Psi \qquad (1)$$

$$\sum_{\psi \in \Psi} \sum_{t=d\alpha+1}^{T} y_{r,t,\psi} = 0; \forall r \in \mathcal{R} \qquad (2)$$

$$\sum_{\psi \in \Psi} x_{r,\psi} = w_r; \forall r \in \mathcal{R} \qquad (3)$$

$$\sum_{r \in \mathcal{R}} y_{r,t,\psi} \leq 1; \forall t \in \left[1, r(d\alpha)\right], \forall \psi \in \Psi \qquad (4)$$

$$\sum_{r \in R} y_{r,t,\psi} = 0; \forall t \in T; \psi \in \Psi; MF(r, \psi) = 0 \qquad (5)$$

$$r(d) - \mathcal{K} \times (1 - z_{r,t,\psi}) \leq \sum_{s=t}^{r(d)+t-1} y_{r,s,\psi} \leq r(d) + \mathcal{K} \times (1 - z_{r,t,\psi}) \qquad (6)$$

$$\forall r \in \mathcal{R}, \forall t \in \left[1, r(d\alpha) - r(d) + 1\right], \forall \psi \in \Psi, r(qos) = \{FTRx, FTRt\}$$

$$\sum_{t=1}^{\mathcal{L}} z_{r,t,\psi} = x_{r,\psi}; \forall r \in \mathcal{R}, \forall \psi \in (\Psi^{od} \bigcup \Psi^{re}) \qquad (7)$$

$$w_r, x_{r,\psi}, y_{r,t,\psi}, z_{r,t,\psi} \in \{0,1\}; \forall r \in \mathcal{R}, \forall t \in \mathcal{T}, \forall \psi \in \Psi \qquad (8)$$

The ILP utilizes the binary variables w_r, $x_{r,\psi}$, $y_{r,t,\psi}$, $z_{r,t,\psi}$ and constants $\mathcal{K}$, $\mathcal{M}$ and $C_{t,\psi}$ to compute a schedule that minimizes the cost, but also utilizing VM instances from the IaaS providers that guarantee the QoS of each request. Moreover, it is built over the mapping presented in Fig. 4(b).

The constraints (C-1) and (C-3) specify that a request, if executed, must be executed in $r(d)$ time units and in a single VM. The constraint (C-2) specifies that a request mustn't be executed in $t > r(d\alpha)$, while the constraint (C-4) specifies that a VM must perform one request per time. The constraint (C-5) specifies that a request must be executed considering the proposed charging model mapping between SLA1 and SLA2 presented in Fig. 4(b). The constraints (C-6) and (C-7) are used to ensure FTRt requests are executed so atomic. The constraint (C-1) ensures the atomicity for FTRx requests. The last constraint (C-8), specifies that the variables of this ILP, called w, x, y, and z, will only assume the binary values. MF() is a mapping function.

The schedule generated is the best schedule that can be achieved with the highest number of requests fulfilled. A request cannot be partially fulfilled. However, the number of VMs available may not suffice to run all requests. In this case, the ILP returns the schedule with the highest number of requests that can be fulfilled, and the smallest cost to run them.

The constant $\mathcal{M}$ is used to achieve the schedule with the highest number of requests, since it establishes a weight for the variable w_r. This means that the larger the number of w_r variables set to true, the smaller will be the ILP result. Let C_t be the total cost returned by the ILP. Then, $S.q = \lfloor \frac{-C_t}{\mathcal{M}} \rfloor + 1$ and $S.c = (S.q \times \mathcal{M}) - C_t$. Let d_m and ψ_m, respectively, be the largest execution time among all requests $r \in \mathcal{R}$ and the largest execution cost per time unit among all VMs $\psi \in \Psi$. Following this, $S.q$ and $S.t$ can be computed as stated before only if $\mathcal{M} > d_m \times \psi_m$. This is how the constant $\mathcal{M}$ must be defined, otherwise it would compromise the result obtained by the ILP.

Heuristics. We implemented two heuristic algorithms to compute the scheduling of $\mathcal{R}$ over VMs of Ψ: 1-FIFO (*First-in First-out*) and 2-DO (*Doubly Ordered*):

1. **FIFO**: Performs the request scheduling using the strategy of allocation the first request in the first VM possible, considering the time duration, the relaxation and the QoS category. Let l be the highest value of $d\alpha$ among all requests. The asymptotic complexity is $O(nml)$.

2. **DO**: Order $\mathcal{R}$ in non-increasing order of size (execution time) and Ψ in non-decreasing order of execution cost per time unit. Use the FIFO algorithm to compute the scheduling. This is a straightforward adaptation of the Max-Min algorithm [14], focusing on the execution of requests with greater duration in VMs with lower cost. Its asymptotic complexity is $O(nml + n \log n + m \log m)$.

5   Experimental Results

We implemented the platform proposed in this work using JAVA, and the scheduler using IBM ILOG CPLEX with default configuration. The mapping model proposed in Fig. 4 was utilized in the scheduling. The simulations were run in a dual-processor Xeon Quad-Core with 32GB of RAM. The metrics utilized were the number of fulfilled requests and the scheduling cost.

The number of VMs in some cases can be insufficient to fulfill all requests, when the execution cost of the R set must be analyzed considering only the fulfilled requests. To minimize the execution cost and maximize the number of fulfilled requests, we verified the scheduling result when relaxing the maximum execution time of each request in FTRt and VTR categories. The experiments were conducted with the requested time extended by 10%, 30%, 50%, and 100%. We do not extend $d\alpha$ for FTRx requests since this would violate the QoS.

5.1 Simulation Setup

We evaluated the number of fulfilled requests, execution costs, and we also assessed the behavior of the scheduler in the platform when $d\alpha$ is varied. The scenario has four providers with a total of $m = 25$ VMs, with characteristics distributed as shown in Table 1.

Table 1. VMs configuration available to the PaaS users

Provider	OD	$	RE	$	SP	$	Provider	OD	$	RE	$	SP	$
1	3	10.00	2	5.00	3	1.00	2	3	11.00	1	6.00	1	2.00
3	2	12.00	2	7.00	2	3.00	4	2	13.00	3	8.00	1	4.00

Three experiments, E_1, E_2, and E_3 were run, each one with 30 sets of requests, $E_i = \{R_1, R_2, ..., R_{30}\}$. $d\alpha$ was in the set $\{10\%, 30\%, 50\%, 100\%\}$. In each experiment, the number of requests in each set was E_1: $|R_j| = 30$, E_2: $|R_j| = 45$, E_3: $|R_j| = 60$, $1 \leq j \leq 30$. The $r(d)$ of each request in each set $R_j \in E_i$ is randomly taken from the $(1, 15)$ interval. The composition $r(d\alpha)$ is done by summing a value t_1 randomly taken from the same $(1, 15)$ interval: $r(d\alpha) \leftarrow r(d) + t_1$. The number of requests in the FTRx, FTRt, and VTR categories are, respectively, 20%, 40% e 40%. We defined $\mathcal{M} = 1.000$.

5.2 Results

We have run the simulations to compare the three approaches: ILP, FIFO, and DO. In the first experiment, E_1, the number of requests is close to the number of VMs available to the PaaS, while E_2 and E_3 have more requests than the number of VMs available. Figure 5 presents the results obtained by the three algorithms in the three experiments. The schedule cost found by the ILP is lower than the costs found by FIFO and DO. Moreover, the ILP was able to fulfill more requests than the other algorithms, satisfying the QoS of almost 100% of the requests with the original $d\alpha$.

Figures 5(g), 5(h) and 5(i), present the cost per fulfilled requests for the schedules found in experiments E_1 to E_3. The ILP results presented lower costs per request when compared to the FIFO and DO algorithms. In experiment E_1, the ILP reduced costs from 25% (0% relaxation) to 35% (100% relaxation) in relation to FIFO, and from 6% to 3% in relation to DO. This difference is enlarged with more requests, reaching 33% to 37% in relation to FIFO, and from 27% to 19% in relation to DO for experiment E_3 (60 requests).

Results showed in this section suggest that the presented charging model allows a better utilization of RE instances, reducing costs from the user perspective. Furthermore, the presented ILP was able to reduce costs and fulfill a higher number of requests than FIFO and DO algorithms in IaaS VMs within the PaaS proposal considering the TS charging model.

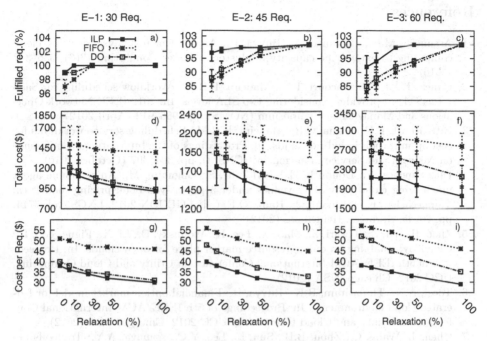

Fig. 5. Results for experiments E_1, E_2, and E_3

6   Conclusions and Future Work

We presented substantial contributions to compose a PaaS architecture and a platform to schedule requests on a set of leased VMs from IaaS providers. We proposed a mapping of currently existing charging models to three different quality of service requirements from the users requests, also introducing the *Time-Slotted Reservation* charging model. The objective of the proposal is to allow a better utilization of the leased VMs from a set of IaaS providers in order to reduce costs, avoiding the lease of new VMs and helping to determine if any leased VM contracts could be finished. Moreover, we propose an integer linear program (ILP) scheduler that considers the leased VMs, their costs, and the quality of service of requests to maximize the number of fulfilled requests and reduce costs. Indeed, the ILP presented better results than two heuristics used in the comparison, allowing more requests to be fulfilled without QoS violation with the use of the time-slotted reservation, but also reducing the cost per request. As future work we consider the development of dynamic mappings between the two SLA levels according to existing charging models and their prices.

Acknowledgments. We would like to thank FAPESP, FAEPEX, CNPq, and CAPES for the financial support.

References

1. Assunção, M.D., Costanzo, A., Buyya, R.: A cost-benefit analysis of using cloud computing to extend the capacity of clusters. Cluster Computing 13(3), 335–347 (2010)
2. Genez, T.A.L., Bittencourt, L.F., Madeira, E.R.M.: Workflow scheduling for SaaS / PaaS cloud providers considering two SLA levels. In: 2012 IEEE Network Operations and Management Symposium (NOMS), pp. 906–912 (April 2012)
3. Bittencourt, L.F., Senna, C.R., Madeira, E.R.M.: Scheduling service workflows for cost optimization in hybrid clouds. In: Proceedings of the International Conference on Network and Service Management (CNSM), pp. 394–397 (October 2010)
4. Díaz Sánchez, F., Doumith, E.A., Al Zahr, S., Gagnaire, M.: An economic agent maximizing cloud provider revenues under a pay-as-you-book pricing model. In: Vanmechelen, K., Altmann, J., Rana, O.F. (eds.) GECON 2012. LNCS, vol. 7714, pp. 29–45. Springer, Heidelberg (2012)
5. Zhao, H., Yu, Z., Tiwari, S., Mao, X., Lee, K., Wolinsky, D., Li, X., Figueiredo, R.: Cloudbay: Enabling an online resource market place for open clouds. In: Proceedings of 5th IEEE/ACM International Conference on Utility and Cloud Computing, UCC 2012, Chicago, USA (2012)
6. Toosi, A.N., Thulasiram, R.K., Buyya, R.: Financial option market model for federated cloud environments. In: Proceedings of 5th IEEE/ACM International Conference on Utility and Cloud Computing, UCC 2012, Chicago, USA (2012)
7. Chen, J., Wang, C., Zhou, B.B., Sun, L., Lee, Y.C., Zomaya, A.Y.: Tradeoffs between profit and customer satisfaction for service provisioning in the cloud. In: Proceedings of the 20th International Symposium on High Performance Distributed Computing, HPDC 2011, pp. 229–238. ACM, New York (2011)
8. Wu, L., Garg, S., Buyya, R., Chen, C., Versteeg, S.: Automated SLA negotiation framework for cloud computing. In: 2013 13th IEEE/ACM International Symposium on Cluster, Cloud and Grid Computing (CCGrid), pp. 235–244 (2013)
9. Konstantinou, I., Floros, E., Koziris, N.: Public vs private cloud usage costs: the stratuslab case. In: Proceedings of the 2nd International Workshop on Cloud Computing Platforms, CloudCP 2012, pp. 3:1–3:6. ACM, New York (2012)
10. Khajeh-Hosseini, A., Greenwood, D., Sommerville, I.: Cloud migration: A case study of migrating an enterprise it system to IaaS. In: Proceedings of the 2010 IEEE 3rd International Conference on Cloud Computing, CLOUD 2010, pp. 450–457. IEEE Computer Society Press, Washington, DC (2010)
11. Garg, S., Venugopal, S., Buyya, R.: A meta-scheduler with auction based resource allocation for global grids. In: 14th IEEE International Conference on Parallel and Distributed Systems, ICPADS 2008, pp. 187–194 (December 2008)
12. Mihailescu, M., Teo, Y.M.: On economic and computational-efficient resource pricing in large distributed systems. In: Proceedings of the 2010 10th IEEE/ACM International Conference on Cluster, Cloud and Grid Computing, Washington, DC, USA, pp. 838–843 (2010)
13. Raj, G.: An efficient broker cloud management system. In: Proceedings of the International Conference on Advances in Computing and Artificial Intelligence, ACAI 2011, pp. 72–76. ACM, New York (2011)
14. Ibarra, O.H., Kim, C.E.: Heuristic algorithms for scheduling independent tasks on nonidentical processors. J. ACM 24(2), 280–289 (1977)

Towards Incentive-Based Resource Assignment and Regulation in Clouds for Community Networks

Amin M. Khan, Ümit Cavus Büyükşahin, and Felix Freitag

Department of Computer Architecture
Universitat Politècnica de Catalunya, Barcelona, Spain
{mkhan,ubuyuksa,felix}@ac.upc.edu

Abstract. Community networks are built with off-the-shelf communication equipment aiming to satisfy a community's demand for Internet access and services. These networks are a real world example of a collective that shares ICT resources. But while these community networks successfully achieve the IP connectivity over the shared network infrastructure, the deployment of applications inside of community networks is surprisingly low. Given that community networks are driven by volunteers, we believe that bringing in incentive-based mechanisms for service and application deployments in community networks will help in unlocking its true potential. We investigate in this paper such mechanisms to steer user contributions, in order to provide cloud services from within community networks. From the analysis of the community network's topology, we derive two scenarios of community clouds, the local cloud and the federated cloud. We develop an architecture tailored to community networks which integrates the incentive mechanism we propose. In simulations of large scale community cloud scenarios we study the behaviour of the incentive mechanism in different configurations, where slices of homogeneous virtual machine instances are shared. Our simulation results allow us to understand better how to configure such an incentive mechanism in a future prototype of a real community cloud system, which ultimately should lead to realisation of clouds in community networks.

Keywords: Incentive Mechanisms, Cloud Computing, Community Networks, Distributed Resource Sharing.

1 Introduction

Community networks aim to satisfy a community's demand for Internet access and services using open unlicensed wireless spectrum and off-the-shelf communication equipment. Most community networks originated in rural areas which commercial telecommunication operators left behind when focusing the deployment of their infrastructure on urban areas. The lack of broadband access brought together different stakeholders of such geographic areas to team up and invest, create and run a community network as an open telecommunication infrastructure based on self-service and self-management by the users [1].

J. Altmann, K. Vanmechelen, and O.F. Rana (Eds.): GECON 2013, LNCS 8193, pp. 197–211, 2013.

These community networks are a real world example of a collective that shares information and communication technology (ICT) infrastructure and human resources. The ICT resources shared are the bandwidth of the wireless network formed by the networking hardware belonging to multiple owners. This bandwidth allows members of the community network obtaining access to the Internet or use services and applications inside of the community network. The human resources shared are the time and knowledge of the participants, needed to maintain the network and technically organize it for further growth.

Sharing of network bandwidth has early been identified as essential and is part of the membership rules or peering agreements of many community networks, which regulate the usage and growth of the network. The Wireless Commons License (WCL) [2] of many community networks states that the network participants that extend the network, e.g. contribute new nodes, will extend the network in the same WCL terms and conditions, allowing traffic of other members to transit on their own network segments. Since this sharing is done by all members, community networks successfully operate as IP networks.

Today's Internet, however, is more than bandwidth resources. Computing and storage resources are shared through Cloud Computing, offering virtual machine instances over infrastructure services, APIs and support services through platform-as-a-service, and Web-based applications to end users through software-as-a-service. These services, now common practice in today's Internet, hardly exist in community networks [3]. Services offered in community networks still run on machines exclusively dedicated to a single member. Community network members, however, do use commercial cloud solutions, for instance for network administration, where sometimes a commercial storage service is used for node data. Why have clouds not emerged inside of the community networks?

We argue that community cloud, a cloud infrastructure formed by community-owned computing and communication resources, has many technical and social challenges so that the main drivers of today's contribution to community networks, voluntariness and altruistic behaviour, are not enough to successfully cope with it. Our hypothesis is that for community cloud to happen, the members' technical and human contribution needed for such a cloud, needs to be steered by incentive mechanisms that pay back the users' contribution with a better quality of experience for them.

In this paper, we present an incentive mechanism tailored to community networks. The main contributions of this paper are the following:

1. From the analysis of the key socio-technical characteristics of community networks, we identify two scenarios for community clouds, the local clouds and federated clouds, for which a community cloud management system is proposed.
2. We design an incentive mechanism that is part of the community cloud architecture and evaluate its behaviour in simulations of community cloud scenarios.

We elaborate our contributions in the following way: In section 2 we present our system model and design. In section 3, we evaluate our incentive mechanism in a community cloud scenario. In section 4 we relate the work of other authors with our results. We discuss open issues in section 5 on future work and in section 6 we conclude our findings.

2   System Model and Design

Our incentive mechanism for community cloud targets real community networks so it must be integrated into an architecture, design and implementation which fits into these conditions and scenarios. In this section, we first analyse the topology of community networks from which we develop two main cloud scenarios we foresee for them. We then present the conceptual overview of a cloud management system suitable for community networks, of which we identify the resource assignment and regulation mechanism as a key component.

2.1   Topology of Community Networks

The community network generally has two different types of nodes, super nodes (SN) and ordinary nodes (ON). Super nodes have at least two wireless links, each to other super nodes. Most super nodes are installed in the community network participant's premises. A few super nodes, however are placed strategically on third party location, e.g. telecommunication installations of municipalities, to improve the community network's backbone. Ordinary nodes only connect to a super node, but do not route any traffic. A topological analysis of the Guifi.net community network [4] indicates that from approximately 17,000 analysed nodes of Guifi.net, 7% are super nodes while the others are ordinary nodes.

2.2   Community Cloud Scenarios

The scenario of *local community cloud* is derived from the topology of community network and the observed characteristics of the strength of the social network within community network zones. In the local community cloud, a super node is responsible for the management of a set of attached nodes contributing cloud resources. From the perspective of the attached nodes, this super node acts as a centralized unit to manage the cloud services.

Multiple super nodes in a community network can connect and form *federated community clouds* [5]. The super node connects physically with other super nodes through wireless links and logically in an overlay network to other SNs that manage local clouds. SNs coordinate among each other and the requests originating from one SN's zone can therefore be satisfied by the resources allocated from another SN's zone.

2.3   Community Cloud Manager

The option we foresee for enabling a cloud in a community network is deploying a cloud management system tailored to community networks on a super node.

We propose a conceptual overview for such a system in Figure 1 which consists of the following.

- The ordinary nodes of the community network provide hardware resources isolated as virtual machine (VM) instances and form the hardware layer of the cloud architecture.
- The core layer residing in the super node contains the software for managing the virtual machines on ordinary nodes.
- The cloud coordinator is responsible for the federation of the cloud resources which are independently managed by different local community clouds. The cloud coordinator components in different SNs connect with each other in a decentralized manner to exchange relevant information about managing the available resources.
- The front end layer provides the interface for accessing resources from the cloud as Infrastructure-as-a-Service (IaaS).

The core of cloud management system is virtual machine manager that is responsible for instantiating, scheduling and monitoring virtual machines on the nodes. There are some cloud management systems available to manage public and private clouds, for example OpenNebula [5] and OpenStack [6] are among the most consolidated and popular open source tools. Such cloud management systems are then tailored for community networks by extending them with implementing the cloud coordinator and its services on top of them, to address the particular conditions of community networks.

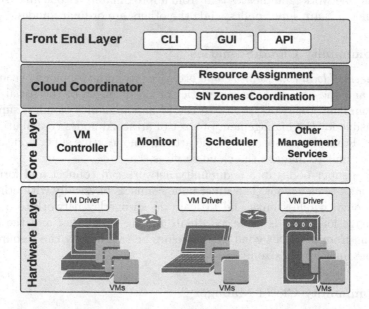

Fig. 1. Conceptual overview of the Community Cloud Manager

2.4   Incentive Mechanisms in Community Cloud

Participants in a community network are mainly volunteers that act independently and are not obliged to contribute. To ensure sustainability and growth of the community cloud, incentive mechanisms are needed that encourage members to contribute with their hardware, effort and time [7,8]. When designing such mechanisms, the heterogeneity of the nodes and communication links has to be considered since each member brings in a widely varying set of resources and physical capacity to the system.

Most peer-to-peer (P2P) systems implement incentive mechanisms based on contribution where nodes are rewarded according to resources they donate to the system [9]. We suggest an effort-based incentive mechanism for community cloud where effort is defined as contribution relative to the capacity of a node [10]. This mechanism is inspired by the *Parecon* economic model [11–13] which focuses on social welfare by considering inequality among nodes. Nodes with different capacity cannot have same contribution to the system but in this mechanism they get same reward if they share as much as possible of their capacity as we explain in the following.

Formulations. We first discuss here the criteria that a super node uses to evaluate requests from ordinary nodes. When a node asks for a resource from a SN, which in this case means to commit an instance of virtual machine for a given duration, the SN first checks whether the ON's credit is sufficient to cover the cost of the transaction. The cost is proportional to the number of resources requested R_i and the duration T_i for how long they are required.

$$transaction\_cost = \gamma R_i \times \rho T_i \tag{1}$$

where γ and ρ are nonzero coefficients for the amount and duration of resources shared respectively.

If the requesting node does not have enough credit, the request is rejected. Otherwise, the SN searches for nodes that have resources available. It selects as many nodes as possible from its local zone as providers. If the demand cannot be met locally, the SN forwards the request to super nodes in the federated community cloud.

Now we consider how the SN manages the credits of the nodes that take part in the transaction. For each node which contributed its resources to fulfil the request, the SN calculates the transaction cost as shown above and adds it to that node's credits. The cost is deducted from the credits of the node that consumed the resources. After the transaction is completed, the effort for each node involved in the transaction is recalculated as in [10] by:

$$E_i = \begin{cases} \frac{credit_i}{\epsilon C_i} & if \quad \frac{credit_i}{\epsilon C_i} < 1 \\ 1 & otherwise \end{cases} \tag{2}$$

where ϵ is nonzero coefficient for the capacity of the node. The effort of a node expresses its relative contribution to the system, since the mechanism considers the capacity C_i of a node as well. This means that a node with low capacity puts in more effort than a node with high capacity if they both donate same amount of resources to the system.

The total amount of resources available Ω in the system is sum of the resources ω_i shared by each node.

$$\Omega = \sum_i^{all\ nodes} \omega_i \tag{3}$$

And the maximum resource ΔR_i a node can consume depends on its effort.

$$\Delta R_i = E_i \times (\Omega - \omega_i) \tag{4}$$

Require: receive query from node i with the requested amount R_i and the time T_i
1: calculate(ΔR_i)
2: **if** $R_i <= \Delta R_i$ **then**
3:     call Decision(i, R_i, T_i)
4: **else**
5:     send("rejected", i)
6: **end if**
7: **function** DECISION(i, R_i, T_i)
8: **if** $R_i <= \Omega$ **then**
9:     $ProvidersList[n] \leftarrow$ high_score_first(ON_List, R_i)
10:     **for each** j in $ProviderList[n]$ **do**
11:         $CostOfTransaction_{j \rightarrow i} \leftarrow R_j^r * T_j^t$
12:         update_credits($CostOfTransaction_{j \rightarrow i}$)
13:         update_database(ON_List)
14:     **end for**
15: **else**
16:     $SN \leftarrow$ low_credit_first($SN\_List, R_i, reserved\_ratio$)
17:     forward(SN, i, R_i, T_i)
18: **end if**

Fig. 2. Algorithm for handling requests from ordinary nodes

Algorithm for Requests Processing. Figure 2 shows algorithm for how a SN handles request from a node in its zone. When SN receives request, it first calculates that node's allowance ΔR_i to confirm whether it has enough credit to fulfil the request. If not, the request is rejected, otherwise the algorithm calls *decision* function which searches for available resources (lines 1–5).

The *decision* function first checks if enough resources are available in the local zone (line 8), and selects the nodes that will provide the resources from its local zone using *high-score-first* policy (line 9). The idea is to give preference to the nodes that need credit the most for participating in the system. If SN cannot satisfy request from its local nodes, it forwards request to one of its neighbouring super nodes which is chosen using *low-credit-first* policy (lines 16–18). This allows the zone with depleted credits to earn more so its nodes can be active the system again. After the provider nodes commit resources, SN calculates cost of the transaction and updates the nodes' credits, deducting credits from the requester and increasing credits of the providers (lines 10–14).

Policies for Nodes Selection. When SN processes requests for resources, there may be multiple nodes that can be providers so SN applies a selection policy for prioritizing which nodes to choose. Similarly when SN forwards requests to other SN zones, it also has to select between multiple zones that have resources available. We evaluated a number of selection criteria that can be employed in above algorithm, and observed in experiments that *low-credit-first* and *high-score-first* policies were better in terms of efficiency of the system. In the following we explain these different policies and discuss the motivation behind them.

- **Low Credit First Selection.** When nodes consume resources, their credit gets spent and with time their credit may be too low to request any resources. Such nodes can provide their resources to other nodes and earn credit allowing them to participate in the system again. This policy gives priority to nodes with low credit with the aim to ensure that most nodes participate in the system and are not left out because of lack of credit.

  When multiple SN zones participate in the system, same problem exists since nodes in a particular zone may have all spent their credit and cannot request any more resources. So the algorithm above gives preference to such zones by applying low-credit-first policy when selecting other SNs to forward requests.
- **High Score First Selection.** One issue with the low-credit-first approach is that it does not differentiate among nodes with low credit. Some of the nodes may be inactive and not making any requests while others may be getting their requests rejected because of inadequate credit. In this policy, the SN tracks unsuccessful attempts by each node and assigns it a *score* calculated as follows. Nodes with higher score get preference so they can recover their credit.

$$score_i = \frac{attempts_i}{credit_i} \tag{5}$$

- **Other Policies.** We also considered following policies and compared their effect on efficiency of the system.
  - First-in-first-out (FIFO). In this simple policy, as soon as nodes have free resources, they register their availability with SN which keeps on adding them in a queue. When processing requests, the SN selects a node that has been in the queue the longest.
  - Random. In this policy, SN picks a node at random from the queue.
  - High credit first. This is the opposite of low-credit-first policy and here nodes with more credits are chosen first.

3   Evaluation

In the past work [10], we studied incentive mechanisms for resource regulation within a single SN zone which corresponds to local community cloud scenario. Here we extend our simulator to study resource regulation across multiple SN zones covering both local and federated community cloud scenarios. In addition to simulations, we also implemented and deployed a prototype of the regulation component of Cloud Coordinator on nodes of a real community network using the Community-Lab testbed [14] provided by the CONFINE project [15]. However, as only a handful of nodes are made available currently, the analysis of our proposed system on greater scale using the real prototype system is too limited. Therefore, we focus here on reporting results from the simulation experiments, where our scenario could be extended to a community cloud consisting of 1,000 nodes.

3.1   Experiment Setup

We simulate a community network comprising of 1,000 nodes which is divided into 100 zones and each zone has one super node and nine ordinary nodes. The zones are distributed in a small world topology where each zone is neighbour to 10 other zones. This approximation holds well for real world community networks as, for example, topology analysis of Guifi.net [4] shows that the ratio of super node to ordinary nodes is approximately 1 to 10. Each ordinary node in the simulation can host a number of VM instances that allows users' applications to run in isolation. Nodes in the zone have two main attributes, one is capacity which is the number of available VM instances, and other is sharing behaviour which is how many instances are shared with other nodes. Table 1 shows the different configurations for each of the nine ONs in each zone. Nodes with low, medium and high capacity host 3, 6 and 9 VM instances respectively and they exhibit selfish, normal or altruistic behaviour sharing one-third, two-thirds or all of their VM instances. For example, node ON2 has medium capacity with 6 instances and exhibits selfish behaviour reserving 4 instances for itself and contributing only 2 to the system.

Table 1. Configuration for each node in a zone with shared and total instances

Node Behaviour	Shared	Small capacity	Medium capacity	Large capacity
Selfish	33%	ON1 (1/3)	ON2 (2/6)	ON3 (3/9)
Normal	66%	ON4 (2/3)	ON5 (4/6)	ON6 (6/9)
Altruistic	100%	ON7 (3/3)	ON8 (6/6)	ON9 (9/9)

When the experiment runs, nodes make requests for resources proportional to their capacity asking for two-thirds of their capacity. For instance nodes with capacity of 3, 6 and 9 VM instances request 2, 4 and 6 instances respectively.

Table 2. Success ration of nodes for different configurations with effort and contribution based incentives

Node Behaviour	Incentives	Small capacity	Medium capacity	Large capacity
Selfish	effort-based	54%	53%	50%
	contribution-based	66%	59%	39%
Normal	effort-based	90%	91%	86%
	contribution-based	97%	77%	66%
Altruistic	effort-based	97%	94%	86%
	contribution-based	97%	85%	65%

Nodes request instances for fixed duration and after transaction is complete wait briefly before making further requests.

3.2 Experimental Results

We evaluate the impact of the effort-based incentive mechanisms in the system in simulation experiments and discuss the results below. We study the success ratio, i.e. number of requests fulfilled versus total requests, and the overall resource utilization in the system.

Ratio of Successful Requests. Table 2 shows the success ratio for requests made by different nodes analysed both with the effort-based and contribution-based incentive mechanisms. We first notice that the success ratio values decrease as the capacity of the nodes increases. This is explained by the fact that nodes with greater capacity request more instances and so have a higher chance getting rejected either because there are not many resources available in the system or because the requesting nodes do not have sufficient credit.

Moreover, when we compare success ratio for nodes as capacity increases, we observe greater variation in the case of contribution-based incentives. For instance, for the normal sharing behaviour the values range from 66% to 97% for contribution-based incentives, but from 86% to 90% for effort-based incentives. This is explained by the fact that contribution-based approach does not take heterogeneity of nodes into account and penalizes nodes with low capacity as they cannot contribute as much to the system as others. These results indicate that effort-based incentives ensure *fairness* in the system since the nodes with the same sharing behaviour are treated equally irrespective of their capacity.

Breakdown of Request Responses. Figure 3 shows the breakdown of successful and rejected requests. The success ratio is higher for effort-based incentives. Moreover, contribution-based mechanism has greater share of requests rejected because of lack of credit. This indicates that effort-based incentives

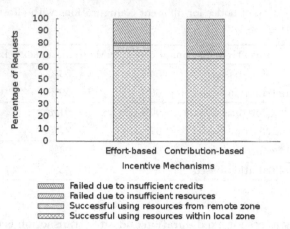

Fig. 3. Breakdown of outcome of requests with effort and contribution based mechanisms

result in better efficiency as more resources remain utilized. Another observation is that majority of requests are fulfilled using resources from local zone with very few requests forwarded to other zones.

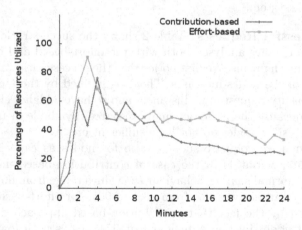

Fig. 4. Resource utilization along 24 minutes of the experiment

Resource Utilization. Figure 4 shows the proportion of resources utilized in the system along the execution of a 24 minutes experiment for effort and contribution based approach. In the start all nodes have enough credit and the resource utilization is high. Then it drops to below 60% at around the 12th minute. Then, since most of the nodes completed their transactions and consumed their credits, the utilization decreases significantly. The effort-based approach though achieve a higher resource utilization during that time.

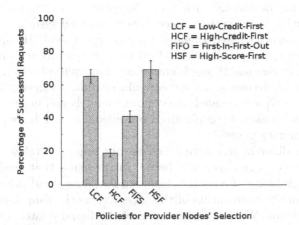

Fig. 5. Success ratio comparison of provider ON selection strategies

Nodes Selection Policies. Figure 5 shows the effect of different node selection policies on the success ratio when using effort-based incentives. High-credit-first and first-in-first-out policies perform poorly since they do not consider the credits of the nodes and so fail in ensuring a balanced distribution across the system. The low-credit-first and high-credit-first policies perform better since they give preference to nodes with low credit allowing them to earn more so that they can be successful with their future requests.

4   Related Work

After the prevalence of public clouds [16], there is now increasing interest in providing cloud services by harvesting excess resources from the idle machines connected to the Internet [17]. Having different service level requirements and conditions, different solutions for how resources are contributed to build clouds have been found. Commercial clouds have dedicated resources that are financed by the users who pay in hard currency to use the cloud services. Previous distributed multi-owned computing platforms like Seti@Home [18], HTCondor [19] and Seattle [20] have relied on altruistic contribution of volunteer users. PlanetLab [21] requires for granting resource usage a prior fixed contribution before the services are made available. None of these cases, however, correspond to the concrete situation of community networks. In order to build a cloud platform within a community network, there is a need to create incentives to encourage active participation from the members of the community.

Various incentive mechanisms have been studied for P2P and decentralized systems that address different requirements for ensuring a sustainable volunteer-based system [9]. P2P systems like BitTorrent [22] incentivize using reciprocity based schemes where users consume resources in proportion to their contribution. Most of these schemes do not take heterogeneity and varying capacity of different nodes into account so nodes with limited capacity are at a disadvantage because they do not benefit as much from the system even though they may be actively contributing to the system. Recent work in cloud systems have also employed similar reciprocity based schemes, for example, Cloud@Home project [23] envisages ensuring Quality of Service (QoS) using a rewards and credit system. Fixed contribution schemes [21] need centralized management which are not suitable and scalable for decentralized systems like community networks. Monetary based schemes [24–27] are founded on economic models and need careful micromanagement which makes it complicated to implement for a large decentralized system like community networks.

Regarding the different incentive schemes, our approach takes advantage of elements of the monetary-payment scheme, in the sense that credits are used to reflect the interchange of resources between consumers and providers. These credits are part of the components of the incentive mechanism that we propose for community clouds. We notice that none of the found related work focus on wireless community networks such as targeted by us.

5   Future Work

We have investigated incentive mechanisms for community clouds based on reciprocal resource sharing. Our results indicate their impact on the efficiency of the system and on regulating the resource assignments. The understanding gained from the different experimental results helps in the design of the policies that such incentive mechanism could follow in a future prototype of real community cloud system.

Our results, however, have revealed new issues that are to be addressed in the next steps towards a real cloud system. First, we have not yet investigated the behaviour of the incentive mechanism for extended periods of time. Further experiments are needed to study how the mechanism can be used for long durations. Secondly, we have not yet investigated the incentive mechanism in a prototype deployed in a real community network.

For the permanent operation of the cloud system with the incentive mechanism, the mechanism needs to be able to adapt to the system state in runtime. The mechanism will need to be able to take into account the evolution of the system with regards to users, resources, and different kind of behaviours. Therefore, parameters of the incentive mechanism will need to be defined as functions of the system state in order to account and decide correctly on the current situation. In order to further develop this runtime adaptability, a two-fold approach, which on one hand extends the simulations with refined system models and on the other hand evaluates the performance of deployed prototype components, is suggested to assure the realisation of an operative adaptive system.

A prototype of the incentive mechanism integrated in a cloud management platform is needed to be able to obtain performance results from real users and services. An operative modular system is needed that allows an easy modification of its components according to the simulation results. The transfer of the simulation results to the deployed system should be required, in order to assure that the simulated system model reflects the real system, and that the obtained findings can actually be brought into the real system in a feasible way.

Finally, the deployment of several federated clouds with real users and real usage should ultimately be undertaken. Such large-scale cloud deployments need to have an extended implementation of a communication middleware for the coordination in a network of super nodes, complemented by additional services, to fully achieve an incentive-based resource assignment. For such systems, additional work is needed to develop in detail the feedback loop between the user's contribution and the experience the user obtains from the cloud services, needed for the building and maintenance of a cloud in community networks.

6 Conclusion

Community clouds are motivated by the additional value they would bring to community networks. Deploying applications in community clouds will boost the usage and spread of the community network model as ICT infrastructure for society. This paper builds upon the topology of community networks to derive two community cloud scenarios, local community cloud and federated community cloud. A community cloud architecture is then proposed which fits into these scenarios. The need for an incentive mechanism in order to community clouds to happen is stated, since for the contribution of any resources the motivation of the users is needed. This incentive mechanism is specified and implemented in a simulator in order to be able to perform assessments for large scale scenarios. With simulation experiments we characterized the behaviour of different settings of the incentive mechanism and evaluated the success ratio of nodes and resource utilization. A deeper analysis of the behaviour allowed us to better understand the influence of the different configuration options. The incentive mechanism has been designed and evaluated taking into account the conditions of community networks. Therefore, we expect our results to be transferable to a prototype of a real community cloud system.

Acknowledgments. This work was supported by the European Community Framework Programme 7 FIRE Initiative projects Community Networks Testbed for the Future Internet (CONFINE), FP7-288535, and CLOMMUNITY, FP7-317879. Support is also provided by the Universitat Politècnica de Catalunya BarcelonaTECH and the Spanish Government through the Delfin project TIN2010-20140-C03-01.

References

1. Elianos, F.A., Plakia, G., Frangoudis, P.A., Polyzos, G.C.: Structure and evolution of a large-scale Wireless Community Network. In: 2009 IEEE International Symposium on a World of Wireless, Mobile and Multimedia Networks & Workshops. IEEE (June 2009)

2. Guifi.net: Commons for Open, Free & Neutral Network, OFNN (2010), http://guifi.net/es/ProcomunXOLN

3. Khan, A.M., Sharifi, L., Veiga, L., Navarro, L.: Clouds of Small Things: Provisioning Infrastructure-as-a-Service from within Community Networks. In: 2nd International Workshop on Community Networks and Bottom-up-Broadband (CNBuB 2013), within IEEE WiMob, Lyon, France (October 2013)

4. Vega, D., Cerda-Alabern, L., Navarro, L., Meseguer, R.: Topology patterns of a community network: Guifi.net. In: 2012 1st International Workshop on Community Networks and Bottom-up-Broadband (CNBuB 2012), within IEEE WiMob, pp. 612–619. IEEE (October 2012)

5. Moreno-Vozmediano, R., Montero, R.S., Llorente, I.M.: IaaS Cloud Architecture: From Virtualized Datacenters to Federated Cloud Infrastructures. Computer 45(12), 65–72 (2012)

6. OpenStack - Open Source Cloud Computing Software, http://www.openstack.org/

7. Biczók, G., Toka, L., Gulyás, A., Trinh, T.A., Vidács, A.: Incentivizing the global wireless village. Computer Networks 55(2), 439–456 (2011)

8. Bina, M., Giaglis, G.: Unwired Collective Action: Motivations of Wireless Community Participants. In: 2006 International Conference on Mobile Business. IEEE (December 2006)

9. Zhang, K., Antonopoulos, N., Mahmood, Z.: A taxonomy of incentive mechanisms in peer-to-peer systems: Design requirements and classification. International Journal on Advances in Networks and Services 3(1), 196–205 (2010)

10. Buyuksahin, U., Khan, A., Freitag, F.: Support Service for Reciprocal Computational Resource Sharing in Wireless Community Networks. In: 5th International Workshop on Hot Topics in Mesh Networking (IEEE HotMESH 2013), within IEEE WoWMoM, Madrid, Spain (June 2013)

11. Rahman, R., Meulpolder, M., Hales, D., Pouwelse, J., Epema, D., Sips, H.: Improving Efficiency and Fairness in P2P Systems with Effort-Based Incentives. In: 2010 IEEE International Conference on Communications, pp. 1–5 (May 2010)

12. Vega, D., Meseguer, R., Freitag, F., Ochoa, S.: Effort-Based Incentives for Resource Sharing in Collaborative Volunteer Applications. In: 2013 17th IEEE International Conference on Computer Supported Cooperative Work in Design (CSCWD 2013). IEEE (June 2013)

13. Vega, D., Messeguer, R., Ochoa, S.F., Freitag, F.: Sharing hardware resources in heterogeneous computer-supported collaboration scenarios. Integrated Computer-Aided Engineering 20(1), 59–77 (2013)

14. Neumann, A., Vilata, I., Leon, X., Escrich, P., Navarro, L., Lopez, E.: CommunityLab: Architecture of a Community Networking Testbed for the Future Internet . In: 2012 1st International Workshop on Community Networks and Bottom-up-Broadband (CNBuB 2012), within IEEE WiMob. IEEE (October 2012)

15. Braem, B., Baig Viñas, R., Kaplan, A.L., Neumann, A., Vilata i Balaguer, I., Tatum, B., Matson, M., Blondia, C., Barz, C., Rogge, H., Freitag, F., Navarro, L., Bonicioli, J., Papathanasiou, S., Escrich, P.: A case for research with and on community networks. ACM SIGCOMM Computer Communication Review 43(3), 68–73 (2013)

16. Armbrust, M., Stoica, I., Zaharia, M., Fox, A., Griffith, R., Joseph, A.D., Katz, R., Konwinski, A., Lee, G., Patterson, D., Rabkin, A.: A view of cloud computing. Communications of the ACM 53(4), 50 (2010)

17. Marinos, A., Briscoe, G.: Community Cloud Computing. In: Jaatun, M.G., Zhao, G., Rong, C. (eds.) Cloud Computing. LNCS, vol. 5931, pp. 472–484. Springer, Heidelberg (2009)
18. Anderson, D.P., Cobb, J., Korpela, E., Lebofsky, M., Werthimer, D.: SETI@home: an experiment in public-resource computing. Communications of the ACM 45(11), 56–61 (2002)
19. Thain, D., Tannenbaum, T., Livny, M.: Distributed computing in practice: The Condor experience. Concurrency and Computation: Practice and Experience 17(2-4), 323–356 (2005)
20. Cappos, J., Beschastnikh, I., Krishnamurthy, A., Anderson, T.: Seattle: A platform for educational cloud computing. In: Proceedings of the 40th ACM Technical Symposium on Computer Science Education (SIGCSE 2009), pp. 111–115. ACM Press, New York (2009)
21. Chun, B., Culler, D., Roscoe, T., Bavier, A., Peterson, L., Wawrzoniak, M., Bowman, M.: PlanetLab: An Overlay Testbed for Broad-Coverage Services. ACM SIGCOMM Computer Communication Review 33(3), 3 (2003)
22. Cohen, B.: Incentives build robustness in BitTorrent. In: Workshop on Economics of Peer-to-Peer Systems, vol. 6, pp. 68–72 (2003)
23. Distefano, S., Puliafito, A.: Cloud@Home: Toward a Volunteer Cloud. IT Professional 14(1), 27–31 (2012)
24. Punceva, M., Rodero, I., Parashar, M., Rana, O.F., Petri, I.: Incentivising resource sharing in social clouds. Concurrency and Computation: Practice and Experience (March 2013)
25. Roovers, J., Vanmechelen, K., Broeckhove, J.: A Reverse Auction Market for Cloud Resources. In: Vanmechelen, K., Altmann, J., Rana, O.F. (eds.) GECON 2011. LNCS, vol. 7150, pp. 32–45. Springer, Heidelberg (2012)
26. Petri, I., Rana, O., Cosmin Silaghi, G.: SLA as a Complementary Currency in Peer-2-Peer Markets. In: Altmann, J., Rana, O.F. (eds.) GECON 2010. LNCS, vol. 6296, pp. 141–152. Springer, Heidelberg (2010)
27. Toka, L., Maillé, P.: Managing a peer-to-peer backup system: Does imposed fairness socially outperform a revenue-driven monopoly? In: Veit, D.J., Altmann, J. (eds.) GECON 2007. LNCS, vol. 4685, pp. 150–163. Springer, Heidelberg (2007)

Towards Autonomic Cloud Services Engineering via Intention Workflow Model

Thar Baker[1], Omer F. Rana[2], Radu Calinescu[3], Rafael Tolosana-Calasanz[4],
and José Ángel Bañares[4]

[1] School of Computing & Mathematical Sciences
Liverpool John Moores University, Liverpool, UK
t.baker@ljmu.ac.uk
[2] School of Computer Science & Informatics
Cardiff University, Cardiff, UK
o.f.rana@cs.cardiff.ac.uk
[3] Department of Computer Science
University of York, York, UK
radu.calinescu@york.ac.uk
[4] Departamento de Infomática e Ingeniería de Sistemas
Universidad de Zaragoza, Spain
{rafaelt,banares}@unizar.es

Abstract. In recent years, the rise and rapid adoption of cloud computing has acted as a catalyst for research in related fields: virtualization, distributed and service-oriented computing to name but a few. Whilst cloud computing technology is rapidly maturing, many of the associated long-standing socio-technical challenges including the dependability of cloud-based service composition, services manageability and interoperability remain unsolved. These can be argued to slow down the migration of serious business critical applications to the cloud model. This paper reports on progress towards the development of a method to generate cloud-based service compositions from requirements metadata. The paper presents a formal approach that uses Situation Calculus to translate service requirements into an Intention Workflow Model (IWM). This IWM is then used to generate autonomic cloud service composition. The Petshop benchmark is used to illustrate and evaluate the proposed method.

1   Introduction

Over the last decade, the creation of value-added services by automating the composition of existing ones has drawn a significant attention, as they are playing an increasingly important role in application domains ranging from research and healthcare to defense and aerospace. Much research already exists for automating service compositions from both functional and non-functional requirements. Nevertheless, for a number of reasons, automating the composition of services is still a highly complex task: i) there is a growing number of services

J. Altmann, K. Vanmechelen, and O.F. Rana (Eds.): GECON 2013, LNCS 8193, pp. 212–227, 2013.

available, generating heterogeneity, and requiring the adoption of more sophisticated catalogue search tools with support for publishing of and searching for services; ii) some of the properties of services are required to be annotated with knowledge representation to support catalogue registration and subsequent lookup of services satisfying functional and non-functional requirements; iii) services, as belonging to third-party organisations, are subject to unexpected behaviours, such as failures or performance degradation. Overall, the automation of service composition requires the adoption of several mechanisms throughout the composition lifecycle, but compositions themselves need to be adaptive enough and amenable to changes in the environment.

In recent years, the rise and rapid adoption of cloud computing has acted as a catalyst for research in related fields: virtualization, distributed and service oriented computing to name but a few. This has –amongst other benefits– led to the adaptation of existing and emergence of new tools and techniques to support the cloud computational and architectural model. Whilst cloud computing technology is rapidly maturing; many of the associated long-standing technical challenges such as the dependability of cloud-based service composition, and services manageability and interoperability remain unsolved. In order to facilitate adaptive and elastic cloud service provisioning and management [2,1], autonomic sen self-* design principles [12] are increasingly being adopted. Whereby, for instance, policies are used to manage Quality of Service (QoS) enforcement [18], and/or user services management [13]. However, as argued by Sloman [15], policy-based autonomy has a number of limitations, including its lack of support for safe deliberation and adjustment to new situations encountered at runtime, which often culminate in human intervention and manual policy adaptation. The authors believe that addressing this particular limitation will accelerate the migration of serious business applications to cloud-based services.

For dynamic service compositions, most techniques developed in the past are based on the automatic generation of plans (composition of services), taken from AI planning theory, and deductive theorem proving. The general assumption of such kind of methods is that each service can be specified by its preconditions and effects in the planning context. For instance, a service can be seen as a software component that takes the input data and produces the output data. Thus, the preconditions and effects are the input and the output parameters of the service respectively. If the user can specify the preconditions and effects required by the composite service, a plan or process can be generated automatically by logical theorem prover or AI planners without knowledge of predefined workflow. During the planning, the business logic can provide constraints in the planning setting. Extensive work is also underway to adapt dynamic configuration. These approaches involve the use of autonomic computing principles, developing intelligent control loops that collect information about the current state of the system, make decisions and then adjust the system as necessary. For example, the SmartFrog [8] framework and the work by Calinescu et al. [5] support dynamic configuration to provide orchestration capabilities to start and stop sub-systems and resources automatically. However, these approaches do not offer a task-level description language that can be used to link tasks to available physical resources, process the output, and then make a decision accordingly. Moreover, the existing approaches require a high-level of programming and/or scripting skills, which pushes them beyond the skills set of any non-specialist users.

To this end, this paper proposes the Intention Workflow Model (IWM) [3], an autonomic service composition model designed for non-specialist users and cloud environments. Unlike previous approaches, IWM offers non-specialist users a front-end where both functional, and non-functional requirements can be specified without requiring any programming skill. Additionally, users can even change the requirements during the actual execution. IWM specifications, incorporating both functional and non-functional requirements, can be used to generate and deploy the desired autonomic cloud service composition or application. In particular, at runtime, an IWM specification is translated into Situation Calculus, a logic formalism designed for representing and reasoning about dynamic domains. Situation Calculus is used here to represent and reason about the possible situations and actions mappings of a given system [17]. This provides a reasoning framework that enables software service compositions and supports their dynamic self-management [11].

Whenever a user changes any of the requirements or in the event of violation of any non-functional requirement (i.e. triggered by monitoring the orchestration of services of an actual composition), the composition structure can be automatically modified in order to enforce requirements. For the non-functional ones, we focus on requirements related to economic cost and performance.

The paper is organised as follows. Section 2 provides a brief overview of research into methods for generating service compositions from requirements. Section 3 describes the new transformation approach proposed in this work. Section 4 presents the application of the proposed method to the widely used Petshop benchmark e-business application. This is followed, in Section 5, by general concluding remarks and a discussion of further work.

2   From Requirements to Cloud Service Composition

In Service-Oriented Architectures (SOA), complex systems are often composed from multiple Internet accessible software services, which can be distributed across many businesses and organisational domains and invoked via the ubiquitous SOAP and/or REST services invocation models.

2.1   Interoperability in Complex-Service-Oriented Architectures

The Web Service-Business Process Execution Language (WS-BPEL) [1] is emerging as a key web services orchestration language. By design, WS-BPEL has no support for formal or semi-formal modelling and analysis of a given process

---

[1] http://www.oasis-open.org/

execution. In addition, in WS-BPEL the mechanisms for the execution and deployment of a concrete service composition is left out of the standard and so is often the concern of the designer's implementation choice or his/her selection of a suitable BPEL execution engine. Thus, Van Sinderen et al. [14] adopt the Model Driven Engineering (MDE) approach to generate executable service compositions from high-level service requirements via a series of model transformations.

Along the same line of work, Spies et al. [16] presented an extended MDE method, which, as depicted in Figure 1, takes an intentions model describing system requirements in terms of actionable goals as its input. The Intention Model (IM) is a key to the required autonomic behaviour of a system since it defines normative principles (the ethics of the system), and not just reactive behaviour. An operable definition of these intentions, for autonomic service governance and regulation, is produced to provide the Platform Independent Autonomic Model (PIAM). The operable definition of an IM can, in general, be provided in several languages. A commonly used paradigm on this level is to use constraint and rule frameworks on computation specific (but platform independent) levels so as to enable model checking, verification and improvement for the subsequently generated PSMs. Accordingly a number of approaches can be used here, such as Object Constraint Language (OCL) or predicate transition networks.

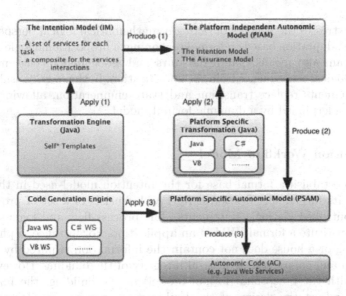

Fig. 1. A Generic Services Implementation Modelling Framework [16]

Viewed from the perspective of a business process, an example of a PIAM language is any declarative business process notation that primarily represents the constraints and rules governing a service composition.

Moving to the platform specific level, we need a modelling layer that is still somewhat beyond actual executable process scripts and program code –the Platform Specific Application Module (PSAM) layer. The reason for this is that PIAM models objects upon transformation to a platform specific level which are not specific enough to define executable behaviour. This has been addressed in the PIAM related literature –behavioural conditions of a given service are usually not sufficient to determine the necessary business execution properties in all practical situations. The solution to this platform specific and yet not fully executable modelling elements in our approach will be through the use of WS-BPEL and web service templates.

According to the MDA/MDE process, model transformations are used to compile a generic intention/assurance template model into a PSAM service description, which is not fully executable, but can become so given a specific context of data types and operational implementation. Upon a suitable transformation, we finally arrive at the executable stage of an Autonomic Computing (AC) level. AC is conveniently characterized by a set of self-management capabilities as introduced in [12] self-configuration, self-optimization, self-healing, self-protection. These capabilities are often referred to briefly as self-* properties.

3   Theoretical Foundation

This paper stresses the benefits of taking a mathematical logical perspective, for dependable adaptation based on formal reasoning; a propositional logic definition of the domain also means that behaviours and associated service invocations follow as a logical consequence from the specification. In this way, causal laws and logical statements replace transition and state enumeration, allowing runtime reasoning underpinned by a dynamic formal model.

3.1   Intention Workflow Model

In order to establish a formal base for the intention model used in this paper, we provide its formal specification here. IWM consists of a set of process flow, which is controlled via logic statements. The process flow and logic statement together constitute a formal IWM of an application. For instance, a photograph of a building or a house does not contain the information required by a builder to ascertain and enforce the structural integrity of the building. However, when provided with the blueprints (formal model) of the building, the builder can model and adjust the design of the building accordingly/ similarly here, for adaptation of a decision process to take place, its formal model is required to be abstracted and exposed. IWM, therefore, can be thought of as consisting of a flow sub-model and a logic sub-model. The flow sub-model provides the order in which decisions are made and the links among them, whilst the logic sub-model decides which path through the flow sub-model should be taken based on the inputs to the intention decision process.

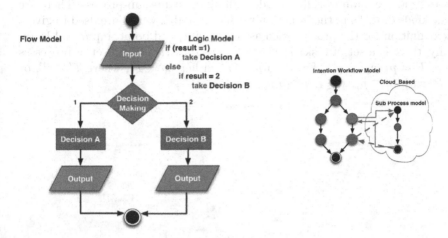

Fig. 2. Flow and logic sub-models example in IWM (left). Automatically generated workflow from IWM (right)

Figure 2 (left) describes the example of a decision process based on the sex of a patient. If male, then return result 1, and according to the current flow, the patient will be provided with treatment A, otherwise, if female, the returned value will be 2 and the patient is provided with treatment B. Here, the logic sub-model of the IWM forms the basis of the decision taken, and the flow is transferred to either A or B dependent on this decision. However, the logic sub-model itself has no reference to either A or B. Instead, the logic sub-model returns a result (1 or 2), which is interpreted by the flow sub-model to produce an action (move to A or B) accordingly. Consequently, adaptations can occur in the flow sub-model without having any impact on the logic sub-model. This level of independency between models means that both can be written and adapted separately, allowing the logic that powers the decision process to remain assured and tested, though the actions and consequences of the decision are open to change as well as allowing the IWM adaptation to be more flexible and achievable. In this case, the IWM can be defined suing 2-tuples structure: $P =< T, cp >$, where T represents a set of tasks, and cp represents a set of conditions required for a task to be selected for execution or implementation. In effect, T represents the flow sub-model of the process and cp represents the log sub-model of the process. Thus, a task t, such that $t \in T$, is defined as a 3-tuples structure: $T =< \Sigma, ct, \Omega >$

Where Σ represents a set of requirements that define the effect of the task, and ct represents a set of conditions required for the requirements to be instigated and selected, and Ω defines the set of instructions required to produce the effects given in Σ. To accurately do this job, IWM processes are composed/modularised of sub-processes that may include a task or a set of tasks that should be executed to achieve the desired behaviour. All the processes and sub-processes are loosely coupled, to support the insertion, deletion and re-direction of any of them at runtime. Figure 2 (right) highlights this characteristic, with two processes from the main workflow model calling the same sub-process. There are different kinds of tasks in the intention workflow model, which are used to give a precise definition for the process such as start point, end point, input and Data. Formally, there is a set of tasks T where $T = t_1, t_2, ..., t_n$, and a set of processes P where $P = p_1, p_2, ..., p_m$. For each $p_i \in P$, either $p_i = T'$, where $T' \subset T$, or $\exists p_j \in P$, with $p_i \subset p_j$, $1 \leq i, j \leq m$.

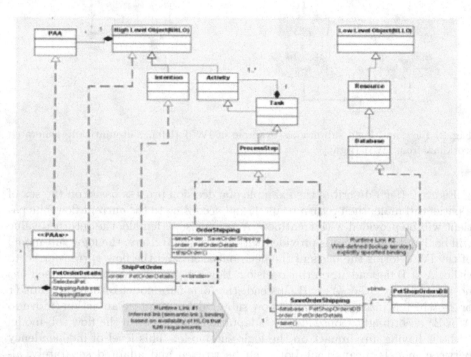

Fig. 3. Significant classes for Neptune PetShop Example

3.2 Situation Calculus

Situation calculus provides a logical approach to modelling dynamic systems [10], which views situations as action histories. Fluent values are initialised in the starting situation (S_0) and changed from situation to situation according to effect axioms for each action. So, an initial situation, S_0 is the start of the Situation Calculus representation. An action, a, then changes this situation from S_0 to $\rightarrow do(a, S_0)$ with the next action, a_1 say, changing the situation to $\rightarrow do(a_1, do(a, S_0))$ with a_2 giving $do(a_2, do(a_1, do(a, S_0)))$ and so on. Additionally in S_0 a set of fluents (predicates and functions) has an initial set of values. Precondition axioms, $poss(a, s)$, show when it is possible to perform action a in situation s.

3.3   Capturing Requirements

As depicted by Figure 3, to translate the formal model into executable requirements and ultimately compose and orchestrate a fully functional system, a pragmatic weaving approach is proposed, composed of two parts: the Intention Workflow Model (IWM), which exists as a separate concern within the system and is easily accessible and adapted, by the users at runtime, and the Provision, Assurance and Auditing (PAA) framework, which reads and executes the IWM and the emergent requirements expressed therein, using the logical model. The PAA is out of the scope of this paper and a full description on the framework can be found in [2,9,3].

The IWM encapsulates three main requirements within the two previously described models (flow and logic), to automate service provision/composition. Firstly, the workflow requirements in terms of *what* is happening; this is generally represented in XML using a flow attribute, which is embedded within each task to direct the execution to the next task. The flow has two main subclasses: move to and the decision. $< moveto >$ directs the task to the next task, whereas $< Decision >$ causes workflow to invoke a specific task arising according given requirements. Secondly, the business requirements are specified in the Neptune language [11] to describe the desired system behaviour: This approach describes *why* something has to happen according to the rules and requirements and automates the decision logic from the initial formal specification and uses a semantic description. The NeptuneScript is used in the intention model to describe and create executable functions that describe why something is done according to the requirements.

```
<neptunescript>
define OrderShipping as ProcessStep
{
        requires {
        saveOrder     : SaveOrderShipping
        order         : PetOrderDetails }

        features
        { feature shipOrder for order; }

        actuation    {
          order.ShippingDate = TODAY;
          onceValid : saveOrder(order);        }
}
</neptunescript>
```

Fig. 4. Neptune spec for Petshop example

Thirdly, there needs to be a technical requirement of the objects required to provide the desired behaviour: The *how* aspect of the specification. For instance, in a web services setting this may be the code, the name of the service, the type of the service, the URL of the service, the execution engine, etc.

3.4 Enacting the Computational Model

A computational model for Situation Calculus acts as a mechanism to allow software to enact the intention model for safe composition, based on deliberating on the effects of the service interactions and arrangements. The programming language Neptune is also used to represent Situation Calculus. The Concept-Aided Situated Prediction Action (CA-SPA) [17] policy format used in Neptune provides the requisite construct here. By providing a situation and a prediction of the required behaviour (or the state to move to), CA-SPA uses the introspective nature of Neptune to determine the actions that need to take place to provide the transition. The full description of Neptune language and CA-SPA are again out of the scope of this work but can be found in [17].

3.5 Sensing and Knowledge

The representation of knowledge and beliefs in the Situation Calculus is achieved by seeing the world states as action histories or situations with the concept of accessible situations. So if s_1 and s_2 are situations then $(s_1, s_2) \in K_i$ means that in situation s_2 service instance i considers s_1 a possible situation with K_i an accessibility relation for service instance i. That is, all fluents known to hold in situation s_2 also hold in s_1. So an accessibility fluent may be specified: $K_i(s_1, s_2)$ meaning in situation s_2 service instance i thinks s_1 could be the actual situation. So knowledge for service instance i ($knows_i$) can be formulated in a situation as: $knows_i(\varphi, s) \equiv \forall s_1(K_i(s_1, s) \rightarrow \varphi(s_1))[alternatively \forall s_1(K_i(s_1, s) \vee \varphi(s_1))]$

However to make any axiom complete, it is necessary to establish whether a sensing action has taken place [7]. That was the action that occurred, to change the situation to its successor, the perception of the value of a fluent. So the change was a change in the semantic state of the service. Thus, it is necessary to distinguish sensing actions by writing $SR(sense_\varphi, s)$ to denote that the action produced a result for φ. $SR(sense_\varphi, s) = r = value$ of φ in s from the context.

4 Case Study: PetShop

PetShop is an architectural blueprint developed by Microsoft based on the original Sun Microsystems PetStore benchmark for enterprise architecture and e-business [6]. The application produced by the PetShop blueprint builds a web-based service composition for browsing and purchasing pets, through a workflow outlined in the next Figure (left).

This section outlines the adaptation steps when a new interactive process or service is either injected to the above PetShop IWM or swapped at run-time with another processes. The standard Microsoft PetShop blueprint process model cannot be adapted at runtime (e.g. a new service cannot be added to the PetShop process model), thus, this is a good basis to highlight the new approach capability.

The procedures outlined in this paper have been applied to designing the PetShop using a PetShop IWM, as shown in Figure 6, which can be accessed

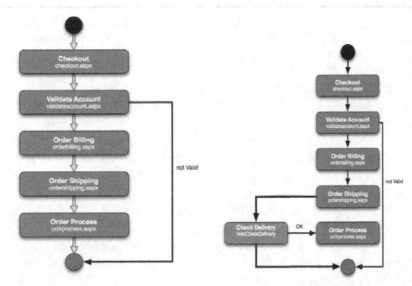

Fig. 5. Petshop examples: original workflow (left). Dynamically modified one (right).

and modified by the user via the PAA editor service [4]; this allows the user to modify the entire workflow model and upload the modified version at runtime in an assured manner, by following the Situation Calculus procedure described in Section 3. An intermediate model saves all the IWM information that is shown in the IWM meta-model (the IWM creator, IWM name, IWM owner, and the guide key). This information is used to differentiate the requested IWM from the other IWM models in the system. The agility behind this model is in providing important data in the form of adaptable XML tags. These tags can be adapted at runtime, by the user, using the PAA editor. Hence, the IWM model and the other information can be adapted at runtime depending on the location of the requested IWM.

4.1   Evaluation of Scalability

As previously stated it is possible to maintain assurance within a simple SOA or cloud-based service model. However, when the services and their orchestration become more complex, it is very difficult to automatically guarantee assurance. For this reason it is proposed to test the Petshop benchmark system to ascertain the scalability of this approach during its operation in comparison to the original Microsoft PetShop. By introducing a new assured behaviour to PetShop via IWM with PAA, the impact of the further interpretation of the new assured behaviour can be contrasted against the performance impact of the introduction of the same behaviour, performed manually, in the original Microsoft PetShop model. In this case CPU load is considered.

```
<IWMModelFileName>c:\inetpub\wwwroot\neptune\DecisionM
odel\PetShop.xml</IWMModelFileName>
    <Organisation>Liverpool JMU </Organisation>
    <Creator>Thar Baker</Creator>
    <DateAdded>20090507T13:56:17.81</DateAdded>
    <DateAccessed>20090507T13:56:17.81</DateAccessed>
<IWMModelStub>
        <Name>SimpleOrder</Name>
        <UID>f14821fe-a131-4a5f-b3c5-0b3a7b4fedf3</UID>
<IWMModelFileName>c:\inetpub\wwwroot\neptune\DecisionM
o del\swellingsimple.xml</IWMModelFileName>
        <Organisation>LJMU</Organisation>
        <Creator> Thar Baker </Creator>
        <DateAdded>20090507T09:44:45.91</DateAdded>
<DateAccessed>20090507T09:44:45.91</DateAccessed>
</IWMModelStub>
<IWMModelStub>
<Name>SimpleOrderExtended</Name> <UID>d537d371-ae1e-
4b09-9c7a-d48bae851282</UID>
<IWMModelFileName>c:\inetpub\wwwroot\neptune\DecisionM
o del\extended.xml</IWMModelFileName>
<Organisation>LJMU</Organisation>
<Creator> Thar Baker </Creator>
<DateAdded>20090507T09:51:06.47</DateAdded>
<DateAccessed>20090507T09:51:06.47</DateAccessed>
</IWMModelStub>
</ArrayOfIWMModelStub>
```

Fig. 6. IWM spec for Petshop example

Reasoning, using deduction, abduction, induction or inference, can then be performed on the logical representation to supply receptors for perceived signals. In this way new service interactions and compositions that cause no harm, and may be beneficial, are allowed. For example the action history represented by: $do(a, do(a_1, do(a, s)))$ with $SR(a, s) \neq SR(a, do(a_1, do(a, s)))$

Where $SR(a, s)$ and $a = sensef$ for some fluent f are as defined in Section 3 and a_1 is some deterministic action that can be used to provide a new prediction for the results of action a1 where the values of other fluents in situation s form the action precondition axioms for a a1 as a context. In this way, action a_1, executing in the context of situation s, provides semantic interoperability for f. So an event may be grounded by the system and a parameter for a safe response can be deduced, allowing assured adaptation at runtime. Thus, using the previously defined sensing and knowledge constructs from the Situation Calculus, the service usage may be monitored via a CPU load sensor: A fluent $heavyLoad(s)$ is true if the CPU is working at over 60% capacity:

$$cpuload(do(a, s)) = n \Leftrightarrow$$
$$[cpuload(s) = n \land a \neq sense_{CPULOAD}] \lor$$
$$[a = sense_{CPULOAD} \land SR(sense_{CPULOAD}, s) = n]$$
$$heavyLoad(do(a, s)) \Leftrightarrow$$
$$[heavyLoad(s) \land ((a \neq sense_{CPULOAD}) \lor$$
$$\neg (a = sense_{CPULOAD} \land SR(sense_{CPULOAD}, s) < 60))] \lor$$
$$[a = sense_{CPULOAD} \land SR(sense_{CPULOAD}, s) > 60]$$

Fig. 7. Situation Calculus spec for Petshop example

Thus an action a_1 may be assigned a predicted outcome via the construct: $do(a, do(a_1, do(a, s)))$ with $SR(a, s) \neq SR(a, do(a_1, do(a, s)))$ with $a = sense_{CPULOAD}$ to deduce: $knows(heavyLoad, s)$ and $knows(heavyLoad, do(a_1, s))$

In this way the action a_1 can form the action that returns a system to a required predicted state, based on a grounded signal for heavy CPU load. Additionally a mechanism needs to be included to determine the relevance of the response. In this way correct responses are reinforced whilst poor results lead to the perceived relevance of the deduced rule diminishing, eventually leading to the response losing all significance to the system, in cases where the semantic linking was detected in error. An example simple reward system, to ensure assured and most appropriate response may consist of, for instance as depicted in Figure 8.

$$reward(regenerateService(S), s) = r \Leftrightarrow$$
$$S = service_1 \land r = 80 \lor S = service_2 \land r = 60 \lor$$
$$service(S) \land S \neq service1 \land S \neq service2 \land r = 40$$
$$reward(sense_{CPULOAD}, s) = 10$$
$$cost(allocateMemory(n, S), s) = 0.1 * size(n)$$

Fig. 8. IWM spec for Petshop example

There may then be an action $regenerateService(S)$ representing a class of actions depending on the stimulus that caused the action to be considered for enactment. For instance, in the previous example, it may be the case that a new service instance is required because of either a heavy CPU load: regenerateService(S).heavyLoad or because of an unresponsive service: regenerateService(S).unresponsive. Additionally, the rewarding of the action needs to be moved to the successor state, as it is only here that the success of the prediction can be determined. Thus, for example it may be stated using a reward for the action performance to cumulatively influence a fitness function for the response, as shown in Figure 9.

$$reward(regenerateService(S).heavyLoad,do(a,s))=r_{\leftrightarrow}$$
$$a=regenerateService(S)\wedge[(r=10\wedge \neg heavyLoad(do(a,s)))\vee$$
$$(r=-10\wedge heavyLoad(do(a,s)))]$$

with
$$fitness(regenerateService(S).heavyLoad,do(a,s))=$$
$$reward(regenerateService(S).heavyLoad,do(a,s))+$$

Fig. 9. Reward of an action expressed in terms of Situation Calculus

In this formulation the more successful a prediction of response to stimulus is, the higher the fitness value of the successor state axiom. Thus axioms that fall below a certain threshold can be discarded whilst those with a higher fitness can be treated as first class axioms with a corresponding increase in their reward value compared to an axiom of equal merit but lower fitness. Thus the Semantic interoperability problem is addressed by providing preinstalled, human level, meaning to some initial signal set, which is then evolved through safe assured adaptation in the runtime system. This may lead to the automatic derivation of a script in Neptune as shown in Figure 10.

```
define service s
if (service.availableServices.likeMe.count = 0)
        service.s = regenerate(me,machineID)
else
        service.s =
        services.availableServices.likeMe[0]
end if
rerouteCalls (s)
```

Fig. 10. Example of an automately derived Neptune script

Figure 11 below shows two systems executed to produce the same behaviour over a timescale of cycles of a process execution. After 50,000 executions, a new service requirement is introduced in the IWM model, and a task description updated accordingly. As new semantic linking and the previously described deliberation takes place, performance is reduced and the time to complete the process increases. It should be noted, however, that, as only one new requirement is needed to be linked, the performance impact is less than that of the original initiation at cycle 0, where many new requirements are introduced at the same time. After the reconfiguration, linking and execution, performance returns to a new standard, slightly slower than the original behaviour from 10,000 to 50,000. This is due to the added time needed to execute the action. There is a slight increase in execution time of the original PetShop (the lower plot) from 50,000, due to the new behaviour introduced to the PetShop code to be executed. It can be noted that after the execution of the new behaviour, however, the execution

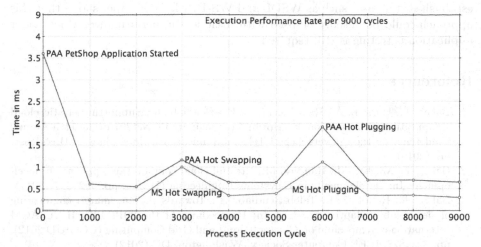

Fig. 11. Performance of dynamic assured PetShop system against benchmark

performance of PetShop, with assured service composition and integration, and the original Microsoft PetShop are similar.

A new Petshop IWM shown in Figure 5 (right) shows that a new service (Check Delivery) should be added and completed. The new service might be injected to the original IWM from a public cloud or from a local server if it is available there. The purpose of adding the new service to IWM is to ascertain whether the customer is shipping to a UK based address or not. If the customer is not UK-based, then the order-shipping task will be cancelled directly to the end of the process model without moving to the order produces task.

5   Conclusion and Future Work

As has been discussed, the use of situation calculus to provide a formalised model of both the enactment and specification of logic enables a powerful and rich intention model for assured behaviour to be provided for composition and arrangement of complex services configurations in Cloud-based systems or large scale SOA-based systems. Using the techniques introduced in this paper, situation calculus can be both effectively represented, and enacted using an open XML standard that is consumed by the IWM, Neptune and CA-SPA paradigms. By being able to adapt and re-implement the situation calculus behind a system, the intended adaptation can be safely and effectively produced, and enacted by the software. In many cases there will typically be competing actions to move from a situation to a predicted situation. The action that is preferred should be the one of most benefit to the system. This ought to also provide a reinforcing mechanism for certain rules and associated actions based on previous history and monitoring. Further work is also required to integrate with and support established standards such as WSDL and WS-BPEL. This paper shows that this approach could potentially be used with little loss in performance. Much wider application is testing is still required.

References

1. Baker, T., Hussien, A., Randles, M., Taleb-Bendiab, A.: Supporting elastic cloud computation with intention description language. In: PGNet2010: The 11th Annual Conference on the Convergence of Telecommunications, Networking & Broadcasting (2010)
2. Baker, T., Mackay, M., Randles, M.: Eternal cloud computation application development. In: Developments in E-systems Engineering (DeSE), pp. 392–397 (2011)
3. Baker, T., Randles, M., Taleb-Bendiab, A.: Towards the automated engineering of dependable adaptive services. In: Proceedings of the 2012 12th IEEE/ACM International Symposium on Cluster, Cloud and Grid Computing (CCGRID 2012), pp. 823–828. IEEE Computer Society, Washington, DC (2012)
4. Baker, T., Taleb-Bendiab, A., Randles, M.: Support for m-commerce software autonomy. In: Proceedings of the 2008 Conference on Techniques and Applications for Mobile Commerce: Proceedings of TAMoCo 2008, pp. 165–176. IOS Press, Amsterdam (2008)
5. Calinescu, R., Grunske, L., Kwiatkowska, M., Mirandola, R., Tamburrelli, G.: Dynamic qos management and optimization in service-based systems. IEEE Trans. Softw. Eng. 37(3), 387–409 (2011)
6. Corporation, M.: Implementing sun's java petstore using microsoft.net. Tech. rep., Microsoft Corporation (2001)
7. Darimont, R., Delor, E., Massonet, P., van Lamsweerde, A.: Grail/kaos: An environment for goal-driven requirements engineering. In: Proceedings of the 19th International Conference on Software Engineering, ICSE 1997, pp. 612–613. ACM, New York (1997)
8. Goldsack, P., Guijarro, J., Loughran, S., Coles, A.N., Farrell, A., Lain, A., Murray, P., Toft, P.: The smartfrog configuration management framework. Operating Systems Review 43(1), 16–25 (2009)
9. Karam, Y., Baker, T., Taleb-Bendiab, A.: Intention-oriented modelling support for socio-technical driven elastic cloud applications. In: 2012 International Conference on Innovations in Information Technology (IIT), pp. 42–47 (2012)
10. Levesque, H., Pirri, F., Reiter, R.: Foundations for the situational calculus. Linkoping Electronic Articles in Computer and Information Science 3, 14 (1998)
11. Miseldine, P., Taleb-Bendiab, A.: A programmatic approach to applying sympathetic and parasympathetic autonomic systems to software design. In: Proceedings of the 2005 Conference on Self-Organization and Autonomic Informatics (I), pp. 293–303. IOS Press, Amsterdam (2005)
12. Parashar, M., Hariri, S.: Autonomic computing: An overview. In: Banâtre, J.-P., Fradet, P., Giavitto, J.-L., Michel, O. (eds.) UPP 2004. LNCS, vol. 3566, pp. 257–269. Springer, Heidelberg (2005)
13. Randles, M., Taleb-Bendiab, A., Miseldine, P., Laws, A.: Adjustable deliberation of self-managing systems. In: 12th IEEE International Conference and Workshops on the Engineering of Computer-Based Systems, ECBS 2005, pp. 449–456 (2005)
14. van Sinderen, M., Spies, M.: Towards model-driven service-oriented enterprise computing. Enterp. Inf. Syst. 3(3), 211–217 (2009)

15. Sloman, M.: Policy driven management for distributed systems. Journal of Network and Systems Management 2, 333–360 (1994)
16. Spies, M., Taleb-Bendiab, A.: Requirements of Metadata Driven Dynamic Configuration of Business Processes. In: Electronic Business Interoperability: Concepts, Opportunities and Challenges, pp. 185–209. IGI Global (2011)
17. Taleb-Bendiab, A., Miseldine, P., Randles, M., Baker, T.: Programming support and governance for process-oriented software autonomy. In: Filipe, J., Cordeiro, J. (eds.) WEBIST 2007. LNBIP, vol. 8, pp. 3–18. Springer, Heidelberg (2007)
18. Tolosana-Calasanz, R., Bañares, J.A., Pham, C., Rana, O.F.: Enforcing QoS in Scientific Workflow Systems Enacted Over Cloud Infrastructures. Journal of Computer and System Sciences, 1–20 (2012) (to appear)

End-to-End Service Quality
for Cloud Applications

Karsten Oberle, Davide Cherubini, and Tommaso Cucinotta

Bell Laboratories, Alcatel-Lucent
{karsten.oberle,davide.cherubini,tommaso.cucinotta}@alcatel-lucent.com

Abstract. This paper aims to highlight the importance of End-to-End (E2E) service quality for cloud scenarios, with focus on telecom carrier-grade services. In multi-tenant distributed and virtualized cloud infrastructures, enhanced resource sharing raises issues in terms of performance stability and reliability. Moreover, the heterogeneity of business entities responsible for the cloud service delivery, threatens the possibility of offering precise E2E service levels.

Setting up proper Service-Level Agreements (SLAs) among the involved players, may become overly challenging. However, problems may be mitigated by a thoughtful intervention of standardization.

The paper reviews some of the most important efforts in research and industry to tackle E2E service quality and concludes with some recommendations for additional research and/or standardization effort required to be able to deploy mission critical or interactive real-time services with high demands on service quality, reliability and predictability on cloud platforms.

Keywords: Cloud Computing, Service Quality, End-to-End SLA.

1   Introduction

Over the last few years virtualization and Cloud Computing technology found their commercial success (e.g. Amazon EC2). This is surely tightly connected with the continuous and steep evolution that Information and Communication Technologies (ICT) have been recently undergoing. The wide availability of high-speed network connections is causing an inescapable shift towards distributed computing models where processing and storage of data can be performed mostly in cloud computing data centers.

Cloud Computing introduces a novel model of computing that brings several technological and business advantages: customers (a.k.a., *tenants*) can rent cloud services on a pay-per-use model, without the need for big investments for resources that have to be designed for peak workloads, whilst being at risk of remaining under-utilized for most of the time; providers may offer cloud services for rental, hosting them on big multi/many-core machines, where the big infrastructure investments may easily be amortized over hundreds or thousands of customers.

J. Altmann, K. Vanmechelen, and O.F. Rana (Eds.): GECON 2013, LNCS 8193, pp. 228–243, 2013.

This *multi-tenancy* nature of cloud infrastructures constitutes one of the major levers over which a high level of efficiency in the management of the hosted services may be achieved. Indeed, by leveraging to virtualization technologies, which allow for easy and seamless migration of virtual machines (VMs) among physical hosts, a provider may manage the physical infrastructure with a high efficiency. Physical resources may easily be shared among multiple tenants whenever appropriate.

Unfortunately, this enhanced level of resource sharing brings a number of disadvantages and challenges as well. Sharing the physical infrastructure leads to an increased level of temporal interference among the hosted services. As a consequence, one of the critical issues emerging in cloud infrastructures is the stability in the performance level of the hosted services.

Cloud providers are not the only ones to which the current observable unstable and unreliable performance of cloud services should be attributed. As it is well known, the Internet, over which most of the cloud offerings are accessible current, is entirely designed and deployed according to best-effort paradigms. Indeed, the Internet has always been multi-tenant by its nature.

However, the requirements of cloud customers are very likely to evolve quickly, as cloud technology is being more and more known and used worldwide. Many enterprise applications that might take tremendous advantages from the cloud model cannot be hosted on nowadays infrastructures due to their stringent performance requirements that cannot be met in nowadays cloud computing infrastructures, accessible and interconnected through the best effort Internet. Think of virtual desktop, Network Function Virtualization (NFV), professional on-line multimedia editing and collaborative tools, on-line gaming, just to mention a few.

Furthermore, virtualization is becoming increasingly interesting for telecom operators (a.k.a. *telcos*) who are increasingly willing to switch from hardware-based to software-based solutions.

Some of the world leading telecom operators have initiated [2] in early 2013 a new standards group for virtualization of network functions at ETSI [3]. Aim is to transform the way network operators architect networks by evolving standard IT virtualization technology to consolidate main network equipment types onto industry-standardized high-volume servers, switches and storage, which could be located in data centers, network nodes and in end-user premises [2]. This potentially offers some benefits, such as:

- Reduced CAPEX, lowering equipment cost
- Reduced OPEX
- Reduced time to market for new telecom services
- Increased scalability
- Reduced entry level/barrier for new players, and geographically targeted services
- Multi tenancy, multi user, multi services, telecom/network operator resource sharing/pooling

Virtualization and cloud technologies allow for an unprecedented degree of flexibility [2] in the management of the physical resources. However, they also introduce further variability and unpredictability in the responsiveness and performance of these virtualized network functions, which are often characterized by well-specified service levels (i.e., reliability and QoS constraints such as latency constraints) that have to be respected. Furthermore, end-to-end service quality is increasing in importance and is paramount for real-time and/or interactive services but especially for carrier grade telecommunication services such as for instance IMS (IP Multimedia Subsystem).[1]

An end-user requesting a service does not really care or need to know if the service requested and consumed is Cloud based or a traditionally hosted one. An end user mainly cares about the price for a service and the expected and received service quality – the *end-to-end service quality*.

This includes several issues, such as End-to-End service availability, End-to-End service performance (e.g. latency, jitter, throughput), End-to-End service reliability, End-to-End service accessibility and End-to-End service retainability. More details about the above issues can be found in [5].

In a Cloud deployment case, the end-to-end service scenario can get quickly very complex in terms of number of actors and providers involved in the end-to-end service delivery chain and hence all the boundaries between, i.e., the horizontal chain including User Equipment, Access Network, Core Network, Data Center and the top-down chain across the various cloud layers from Software-as-a-Service (SaaS) to Infrastructure-as-a-Service (IaaS). The scenario can easily get more complex in case of services spanning across multiple data centers or for instance 3rd party infrastructures involved in the DC (see Section 3 below).

Hence, in order to enable more telecom like applications and services to be run in a distributed cloud environment, networked systems need to become more intelligent and able to support end-to-end QoS by joint optimization across networking, computing and storage resources.

In order to provide the required end-to-end service quality for cloud based services, a Service Level Agreement (SLA) framework is required to express the required level of service quality and related Key Quality Indicators (KQIs), to measure, monitor, correct or police, repair and finally to guarantee the required level of service quality, when coupled with proper service engineering practices. A chain of multiple SLAs is required covering the end-to-end scenarios. This results in a complex system of multiple SLAs covering all the boundaries between actors and providers.

Additionally, those SLAs have different levels of technical content as an SLA between an end user and an application service provider might be quite different from an SLA between a Cloud Service Provider (CSP) and a Network Service Provider (NSP).

---

[1] More information is available at:
http://www.3gpp.org/Technologies/Keywords-Acronyms/article/ims

1.1   Proposition

This paper aims to highlight the importance of end-to-end service quality for cloud services especially for the case of telecom carrier grade services. We will mainly focus on the multi-tenancy aspects (as this enhanced level of resource sharing raises some issues in terms of stability and reliability of cloud services) as well as the area of Service Level Agreements for end-to-end scenarios.

Technology-wise, we have today some basic building blocks that may enable cloud infrastructures to exhibit stable and predictable performance to customers. Indeed, on the side of network provisioning, standards exist enabling the possibility to provide connectivity with end-to-end QoS guarantees, such as IntServ [12] and DiffServ [11].

Similarly, on the side of computing technologies, platforms for real-time and predictable computing are becoming increasingly accessible, not restricted to the traditional area of real-time and embedded systems, but recently spreading also extending into the area of predictable cloud computing [15,29].

However, one of the major obstacles that keeps hindering the potential for a worldwide deployment of these technologies and especially for telecom services, is the fact that, in many distributed and cloud computing scenarios, there is not merely a single business entity responsible for the service delivery. Instead, we may have multiple different, unrelated business entities with contrasting and competing requirements, interacting for the provisioning of end-to-end cloud services to customers and finally end users. For example, multiple cloud, storage and network service providers may be involved for the delivery of a distributed cloud service to a community of end users.

In this context, setting up proper SLAs among the involved players for delivering strong QoS guarantees to customers, may become overly challenging. However, the main problems arising in such interactions may be mitigated by proper SLA engineering techniques trying to fragment the overall problem into simpler ones to be tackled separately, when possible, and a thoughtful intervention of standardization.

The next section will present some of the related work existing in those areas followed by some scenarios to explain the potential complexity of actors involved at the present. Finally the paper identifies blank spots of required research and standardization work in this area.

2   Related Work

This section shortly reviews existing standards and research efforts addressing end-to-end Cloud/Network service delivery with QoS considerations. Due to space constraints, not each individual activity in this area can be mentioned.

2.1   Standards

ETSI. ETSI is currently involved in several activities related to the above mentioned issues. Of major importance towards the scope of end-to-end cloud service quality provisioning is the work [3] started by the ETSI NFV Reliability

& Availability sub group. A first report of that group is expected for late 2013. ETSI NFV detected the importance of end-to-end considerations and kicked off a Specification document in April 2013 on "NFV End to End Architecture Reference" (Work Item DGS/NFV-0010). A publication of a first version is planned for autumn 2013. However, the issue of service quality for virtualized network functions will be a key issue to work on inside the ETSI NFV activity and will be probably touched on by several working and expert groups of the ETSI NFV Group, such as, e.g., in the "Reliability and Availability WG". The work of this ETSI NFV consists of providing a pre-standardization study before considering later a broader standards proposal in a new or existing standardization group.

The second related ETSI activity is the Technical Committee (TC) CLOUD which aims to address issues associated with the convergence between IT (Information Technology) and Telecommunications. The focus is on scenarios where connectivity goes beyond the local network. TC CLOUD will also address interoperability aspects of end-to-end applications and develop formal test specifications to support them.[2] The recent related Technical Report from TC CLOUD is TR103125, V1.1.1, "Cloud, SLAs for Cloud Services" aiming to review previous work on SLAs including ETSI guides from TC USER and contributions from EuroCIO members and to derive potential requirements for cloud specific SLA standards. Connected to TC CLOUD is the third ETSI hosted and related activity, the Cloud Standards Coordination (CSC) task.[3] ETSI has been requested by the EC through the European Cloud Strategy [19] to coordinate with stakeholders in the cloud standards ecosystems and devise standard roadmaps in support of EU policy in critical areas, such as security, interoperability, data portability, reversibility and SLAs. Especially the subgroup dealing with Cloud SLAs might produce a highly interesting output document in regard to existing SLA standards when looking on use cases demanding end-to-end Cloud service quality. The final report towards the European Commission is expected for autumn 2013.

NIST. The Cloud Computing Group of the National Institute of Standards and Technology (NIST) has published and is currently working on a series of reports being of value to the topic of end-to-end cloud service quality.[4]

The NIST Cloud Computing Reference Architecture [20] contains a reference architecture widely used by industry, also introducing actors such as the "Cloud Broker", which might play a major role in the end-to-end cloud service delivery chain.

NIST Special Publication [21], in "Requirement 3: Technical Specifications for High-Quality Service-Level Agreements", highlights already the importance of how to define reliability and how to measure it. This is amplified by "Requirement 10: Defined & implemented Cloud Service Metrics" on the industry need for standardized Cloud Service Metrics.

---

[2] More information at:
http://portal.etsi.org/portal/server.pt/community/CLOUD/310
[3] More information at: http://csc.etsi.org/website/private_home.aspx
[4] More information can be found at: http://www.nist.gov/itl/cloud/index.cfm

NIST took this already to the next level and is especially addressing those two requirements in the NIST Cloud Computing Reference Architecture and Taxonomy Working Group (RATax WG) [22], in addition to other works on SLA taxonomy and Cloud Metrics [23].

Finally, in an updated Version 2 of Special Publication 500-291 "NIST Cloud Computing Standards Roadmap", which is currently undergoing internal review and approval process, NIST is also investigating on cloud Standards for Service Agreements. However, regarding end-to-end service quality, the document refers to considerations done recently by the TM Forum – more details on that in the next paragraph.

TMF. The Tele Management Forum (TM Forum) has started recently some effort on Multi Cloud Management which is potentially of high importance for the end-to-end cloud service quality topic.

TM Forum has created a set of business and developer tools to help service providers and all players in the multi-cloud value chain implement and manage services that span across multiple partners. Organized as "packs", these initial tools focus on managing SLAs between partners [24].

Document TR178 [30] is a good starting point into that topic as this technical report takes a wider view considering also related existing work at e.g. DMTF, OGF, NIST, ITU-T, OASIS and other TMF related activities.

The report recommends a set of business considerations and architecture design principles that are required to support end-to-end Cloud SLA Management with the aim to facilitate discussion regarding SLA consistency across Cloud Deployment Models and Services Models. TMF is currently planning the work on a version 2 of that document until late 2013 in order to add especially a section related to Cloud Metrics and Measurements. Furthermore, TM Forum started to work on several Multi-Cloud Service Management Reports (TR194-TR197) which are yet not finalized and published. Looking at the work started it appears that this work is essential to follow and potentially extend when reasoning about end-to-end cloud service quality matters. Some of the highlighted points will be also reflected in Section 4.

OGF. The Open Grid Forum (OGF) developed two Web Services (WS) Agreement Specifications. First, the GFD-R.192 WS Agreement Specification [45], a protocol for establishing agreement between two WS parties, such as between a service provider and consumer. And second, the GFD-R-P.193 WS-Agreement Negotiation specification [46], a protocol for multi-round negotiation of an agreement between two parties, such as between a service provider and consumer which works on top of WS-Agreement.

Furthermore, OGF started the Open Cloud Computing Interface (OCCI) working group,[5] aiming to realize a set of open specifications, protocols and APIs [39,40,43] for enhancing interoperability across various implementations related to the management of cloud infrastructures and services. Projects aiming to provide an implementation of the OCCI specifications include the

---

[5] More information is available at: http://www.opennebula.org/

well-known OpenStack[6] and OpenNebula.[7] The currently available specifications are GFD.183 OCCI Core [40], GFD.184 OCCI Infrastructure [39] and GFD.185 OCCI RESTful HTTP Rendering [43].

2.2   Research

IRMOS. The IRMOS European Project[8] has investigated how to enhance execution of real-time multimedia applications in distributed Service Oriented Infrastructures and virtualized Cloud infrastructures. One of the core components developed in IRMOS is the Intelligent Service-Oriented Networking Infrastructure (ISONI) [8,9]. It acts as a Cloud Computing IaaS provider for the IRMOS framework, managing (and virtualizing) a set of physical computing, networking and storage resources available within a provider domain. One of the key innovations introduced by ISONI is its capability to ensure guaranteed levels of resource allocation for individual hosted applications. In ISONI, each distributed application is specified by a Virtual Service Network (VSN), a model describing the resource requirements, as well as the overall end-to-end performance constraints. A VSN is a graph whose vertexes represent Application Service Components (ASCs), deployed as VMs, and whose edges represent communications among them. In order for the system represented by a VSN to comply with real-time constraints as a whole, QoS needs to be supported for all the involved resources, particularly for network links, CPUs and storage resources. To this purpose, VSN elements are associated with precise resource requirements, e.g., in terms of the required computing power for each node and the required networking performance (i.e., bandwidth, latency, jitter) for each link. These requirements are fulfilled thanks to the allocation and admission control logic pursued by ISONI for VM instantiation, and to the low-level mechanisms shortly described in what follows (a comprehensive ISONI overview is out of the scope of this paper and can be found in [4,8,9].

Isolation of Computing. In order to provide scheduling guarantees to individual VMs scheduled on the same system, processor and core, IRMOS incorporates a deadline-based real-time scheduler [15,18,31] for the Linux kernel. It provides temporal isolation among multiple possibly complex software components, such as entire VMs (with the KVM hypervisor, a VM runs as a Linux process). It uses a variation of the Constant Bandwidth Server (CBS) algorithm [10], based on Earliest Deadline First (EDF), for ensuring that each group of processes/threads is scheduled on the available CPUs for a specified time every VM-specific period.

Isolation of Networking. Isolation of the traffic of independent VMs within ISONI is achieved by a VSN individual virtual address space and by policing the network traffic of each deployed VSN. The two-layer address approach avoids unwanted cross-talk between services sharing physical network links. Mapping

---

[6] More information is available at: http://www.openstack.org/
[7] More information is available at: http://www.opennebula.org/
[8] More information is available at: http://www.irmosproject.eu

individual virtual links onto diverging network paths allows for a higher utilization of the network infrastructure by mixing only compatible traffic classes under similar predictability constraints and by allowing selection of more than just the shortest path. Traffic policing avoids the network traffic going through the same network elements causes any overload leading to an uncontrolled growth of loss rate, delay and jitter for the network connections of other VSNs. Therefore, bandwidth policing is an essential building block to ensure QoS for the individual virtual links. It is important to highlight that ISONI allows for the specification of the networking requirements in terms of common and technology-neutral traffic characterization parameters, such as the needed guaranteed average and peak bandwidth, latency and jitter. An ISONI transport network adaptation layer abstracts from technology-specific QoS mechanisms of the networks, like Differentiated Services [11], Integrated Services [12,13] and MPLS [14]. The specified VSN networking requirements are met by choosing the most appropriate transport network, among the available ones. Other interesting results from the research carried out in IRMOS include: algorithms for the optimum placement of distributed virtualized applications with probabilistic end-to-end latency requirements [16]; the use of neural networks for estimating the performance of Virtual Machines execution under different scheduling configurations [18]; techniques for reduced down-time in live-migration of VMs with time-sensitive workloads [37]; and others. The effectiveness of IRMOS/ISONI has been demonstrated for example through an e-Learning demonstrator [15].

SLA. Within IRMOS, an SLA management framework spanning across the three main cloud service models (SaaS, PaaS, IaaS) has been developed, through a combined approach of SLAs with real-time attributes (and QoS attributes in general) according to the needs of the service to be deployed and executed. A set of tools has been developed which support the tasks of the different actors (from application modeling down to resource virtualization) and an SLA life cycle between them. In IRMOS the SLA life cycle is structured in three phases:

- Publication phase
- Negotiation phase
- Execution phase

More details can be found in [25]. This paper also describes in detail the different types of dynamic SLAs among the different actors:

- Application SLA: agreement established between the Client as a business customer and the Application Provider; this SLA contains the high-level QoS parameters of the application required and defined by the Client.
- Technical SLA: agreement negotiated between the PaaS Provider and the IaaS Provider. This agreement contains low-level QoS parameters associated with the infrastructure.

Within the IRMOS project an extensive SLA state of the art analysis has been performed [26,27,28] also covering several other EC funded research projects such as RESERVOIR and SLA@SOI.

SLA@SOI. The SLA@SOI EU Project[9] developed an open-source framework addressing [41] negotiation, provisioning, monitoring and adaptation of SLAs through the entire cloud service life-cycle. The framework included [42] both functional and non-functional characteristics of services, such as QoS constraints, which can be formalized through an XML-based syntax.

OPTIMIS. The OPTIMIS EU Project [10] investigates on orchestration of cloud services [1] specifically addressing how to deploy intelligently legacy applications based on their preferences and constraints regarding trust, risk, eco-efficiency and cost factors. For example, in [17], a model for optimum allocation of cloud services is presented that considers a mix of trust, risk, eco-efficiency and cost factors in the overall optimization goal. OPTIMIS also investigates on how to properly leverage both private, hybrid, federated and multi cloud environments for services development and deployment.

ETICS. The ETICS (Economics and Technologies for Inter-Carrier Services) European Project investigated on the criticalities for the creation of a new ecosystem of innovative QoS-enabled interconnection models between Network Service Providers (NSPs) impacting all of the actors involved in the end-to-end service delivery value-chain. ETICS investigated on novel network control, management and service plane technologies for the automated end-to-end QoS-enabled service delivery across heterogeneous carrier networks.

The business models analysis [6] and the overall architecture [7] results from ETICS constitute fundamental building blocks allowing for the construction of management of network Inter-Carrier Service Level Agreements.

EC – Expert Group. In July 2013 an Expert Group on Cloud SLA's of the European Commission published a report on "Cloud Computing Service Level Agreements - Exploitation of Research Results" which provides a very detailed insight and analysis on research results achieved by European and National funded research projects [47].

3 Deployment Scenarios

Provisioning of cloud computing applications and services to end-users requires complex interactions among a number of players and business entities. There exist a nearly unlimited amount of scenarios with increasing number and type of actors, the figure below shows the potential complexity:

---

[9] More information is available at: http://sla-at-soi.eu/
[10] More information is available at: http://www.optimis-project.eu

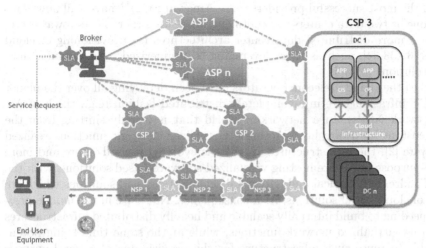

Fig. 1. end-to-end scenario(s)

The scenario includes for instance:

- One or more Cloud Service Providers (CSPs), including potentially Software-as-a-Service (SaaS), Platform-as-a-Service (PaaS) and Infrastructure-as-a-Service (IaaS) providers.
- One or more Network Service Providers (NSP), including heterogeneous networks such as the Access Network and Core Network NSPs.
- One or more Application Service Providers (ASPs)
- The Cloud Customer and End User, who may be the same or different entities, depending on the context.
- A multitude of heterogeneous user equipment, requiring potentially different access network technologies such as DSL, Wifi, LTE, ...
- And finally a Broker serving as contact point and contractual partner for the customer.

In early cloud deployments, NSPs played merely the role of providing connectivity among data centers and end-users through their communication networks, in a way that is service- and mostly also cloud-agnostic. As a consequence, delivering cloud based applications and services to end-users needs at least interactions among Access Network NSP(s), Core Network NSP(s) and Cloud Service Provider CSP(s). However, traditional data centers heavily centralized within a few geographical locations fall short when constraints on response-times become tight (e.g., real-time applications). Indeed, ensuring predictable and stable QoS levels in such conditions becomes overly challenging and requires carefully thought interactions among all these business entities.

Though, over the last years, such a picture has been undergoing quite a change. On one hand, CSPs have been expanding their presence on the territory by adding more and more data centers across the planet. Even though some of the most successful providers (e.g., Amazon EC2)[11] have still nowadays barely one or two data centers per continent, there are other efforts towards creating way more distributed data center architectures for provisioning of cloud services [32,33,34], such as those leveraging "containerized" and modular data center solutions [35,36].

On the other hand, Telecom operators have been deploying all over the planet their ICT infrastructure in a completely distributed fashion (e.g., think of Access Network NSPs). In a networking world that is heavily shifting from the use of custom hardware boxes towards virtualized network functions realized in software [2], the infrastructures of NSPs is evolving towards more and more general-purpose hardware hosting virtualized software-based solutions, with the need of addressing vertical and horizontal scalability of said solutions which are typical of cloud-based solutions. As a consequence, NSPs are in the unique position of needing to build internally scalable and heavily distributed infrastructures for hosting virtualized network functions, while at the same time being potentially able to reuse such infrastructure for the provisioning of general-purpose cloud services but with a novel, heavily distributed, close-to-the-edge and unprecedented low-latency infrastructure.

Generally speaking, distribution of cloud services so as to get closer to the edge and the end users is a must, while low latency becomes more and more important for users, whose requirements evolve at an amazing speed from needing a mostly storage-only cloud to needing full fledged remote desktop-like solutions.

Moving cloud services closer to the edge mitigates partially the problems for delivering cloud services with stable end-to-end QoS levels. Indeed, when interacting users are geographically close, the variability in the network response is highly reduced, mostly due to the reduction in the number of network segments and NSPs to traverse for closing a single round-trip interaction with the cloud. However, for users distributed across geographically distant locations, and for many cloud applications that already exist nowadays in which the interactions among users spread across an unimaginable number of data items spread all around the globe (e.g., think of collaborative tools such as videoconferencing, shared boards, interactive real-time editing of office documents or mastering of media contents), it is crucial that end-to-end QoS is still guaranteed through appropriate set-up of a properly interacting end-to-end cloud service supply/delivery chain, especially for those services that are to be delivered in a professional way. This requires proper interfaces and standards to allow, for example, the network management infrastructure (e.g., the OSS/BSS) to tie together with cloud management systems (e.g., Cloud Orchestrator), and possibly the existence of Cloud Brokering agents that, analogously to aggregator websites nowadays, are capable of interacting with all these systems to find suitable solutions for customers, matching their needs.

Consider again Figure 1 which clearly shows the potential complexity and especially the large amount of SLAs involved among all the actors. The customer wants to have a single point of contract, meaning one SLA about the service with

---

[11] More information is available at: http://aws.amazon.com/ec2

all characteristics and clearly defined quality metrics. In this set-up the Cloud Broker facilitates meeting of such customer requirement. The Broker then based on customer requirements as expressed in the SLA selects the right ASP as well as CSPs and NSPs in order to fulfill those requirements. This could be done all by the broker or in a more cascaded way. At the end, this whole process results in a large number of SLAs in order to clearly define the accountability between the actors when delivering the contractual defined and required QoS.

End-to-end QoS for cloud services can only be achieved through a careful negotiation of service levels among all the providers, both in the network and in the IT space. Furthermore it is required to have clearly defined quality metrics to monitor and report and finally to trigger countermeasures in case of SLA violation always with the overall target to keep the end-to-end service quality as required.

4 Conclusion and Outlook

End-to-end service quality for cloud services is heavily dependent on SLA handling in a multi-provider and multi-vendor setup, coupled with proper resource management strategies in a challenging environment with heterogeneous and potentially widely distributed resources. A major challenge for the management of end-to-end Cloud SLAs is the aggregation of individual SLAs across the vertical and horizontal end-to-end path with all their related metrics and KPIs (main metric of interest for the Service Provider)/KQIs (main metric of interest for the customer). TMF, as indicated above, started some work within the Multi-Cloud Service Management Activity which required further work especially regarding the integration/stacking of multiple SLAs. Furthermore additional research and/or standardization effort is required, e.g., to:

- Define clear, measurable metrics to be used to quantify service quality needs and expectations and to provide a common language between the multitude of vendors and providers. Work has been started on this at QuEST EB9 Group, TMF and NIST at least. SLA metrics require appropriate definition and categorization to align with expressed SLA objectives as well as to monitor for adherence to those objectives and report or trigger actions when those objectives are not met. There will be no real SLA management and hence no deployment for mission critical or interactive real-time services without crystal clear defined metrics and the definition of how to measure, report and manage them.
- Develop a more automated SLA management, as required to develop machine readable SLAs in order to achieve faster provider discovery, comparison and monitoring of service quality (see also related recommendations in [44], page 60, Section 6 Federation).
- Enhance the very complex end-to-end view across all the horizontal and vertical layers and actors, in order to ensure not just service quality but also issues like security and accountability for cloud based services (see also

related recommendations in [44], page 61, Section 7 Programmability & Usability and page 63, Section 9 Security).

- Design and engineer proper resource management and scheduling frameworks for cloud computing infrastructures, enabling the possibility to ensure proper levels of temporal isolation among VMs deployed by independent customers (see also related recommendations in [44], page 60, Section 5 Multiple Tenants).
- With the expected quick increase in number of available cloud data center locations across the planet, it will become more and more challenging to properly/optimally place but especially to dynamically relocate applications, VMs, data, across one or more cloud infrastructures, in order to achieve desired and desirable trade-offs among efficiency in management of the infrastructure and users' quality of experience and expectations; more research on scalable, adaptive resource management policies, coupled with agile software infrastructures, is needed for handling the cloud computing scenarios of tomorrow (see also related recommendations in [44], page 60, Section 6. Federation and page 61, Section 7 Programmability & Usability).
- Deal with energy efficiency, a critical issue that needs to be addressed at all levels of computing, from industrial deployments to research, and from hardware to software; designing SLAs containing QoS constraints, but at the same time capable of leaving a degree of flexibility to the CSP or other involved entities enabling more energy-efficient management of resources, need to be further investigated (see also related recommendations in [44], page 61, Section 7 Programmability & Usability).
- Tomorrow cloud applications will make more and more use of massive amounts of data, and normal users of cloud applications will expect/pretend that they can query amazingly huge data sets in one instant; resource management and scheduling for meeting QoS constraints and providing temporal isolation in presence of "big-data" types of workloads presents a set of novel challenges that have to be urgently addressed by research in the domain of cloud computing and virtualized infrastructures (see also related recommendations in [44], page 56, Section 1 Data Management).

As a final concluding remark, we highlighted in this paper some of the most important efforts in research and industry to tackle end-to-end service quality, but there is still significant work ahead in order to be able to deploy mission critical or interactive real-time services with high demands on service quality, reliability and predictability on cloud platforms.

Acknowledgments. The authors would like to thank Randee Adams and Eric Bauer for their valuable comments, suggestions and support.

References

1. Zsigri, C., Ferrer, A.J., Barreto, O., Sirvent, R., Guitart, J., Nair, S., Sheridan, C., Djemame, K., Elmroth, E., Tordsson, J.: Why Use OPTIMIS? Build and Run Services in the Most Suitable Cloud Venues. OPTIMIS Whitepaper (October 2012)

2. Chiosi, M., et al.: Network Functions Virtualisation – Introductory White Paper, SDN and OpenFlow World Congress, Darmstadt, Germany, October 22-24 (2012), http://portal.etsi.org/NFV/NFV_White_Paper.pdf
3. ETSI NFV Portal, http://portal.etsi.org/portal/server.pt/community/NFV/367
4. Voith, T., Stein, M., Oberle, K.: Quality of service provisioning for distributed data center inter-connectivity enabled by network virtualization. Elsevier Journal on Future Generation Computer Systems 28, 554–562 (2012)
5. Bauer, E., Adams, R.: Service Quality of Cloud Based Applications. Wiley-IEEE Press (December 2013) (tentative publication date), ISBN 9781118763292
6. Dramitinos, M., Kalogiros, C.: Final business models analysis (January 2013)
7. Zwickl, P., Weisgrab, H.: Final ETICS architecture and functional entities high level design (February 2013)
8. Voith, T., Kessler, M., Oberle, K., Lamp, D., Cuevas, A., Mandic, P., Reifert, A.: ISONI Whitepaper v2.0 (July 2009)
9. Oberle, K., Kessler, M., Stein, M., Voith, T., Lamp, D., Berger, S.: Network virtualization: The missing piece. In: Proceedings of the 13th International Conference on Intelligence in Next Generation Networks, pp. 1–6 (October 2009)
10. Abeni, L., Buttazzo, G.: Integrating Multimedia Applications in Hard Real-Time Systems. In: Proceedings of the 19th IEEE Real-Time Systems Symposium, Madrid, Spain (December 1998)
11. Blake, S., Black, D., Carlson, M., Davies, E., Wang, Z., Weiss, W.: RFC2475 – An Architecture for Differentiated Service. IETF (December 1998)
12. Wroclawski, J.: RFC 2210 – The Use of RSVP with IETF Integrated Services. IETF (September 1997)
13. Wroclawski, J.: RFC2211 – Specification of the Controlled Load Quality of Service. IETF (September 1997)
14. Rosen, E., Viswanathan, A., Callon, R.: RFC3031 – Multi-protocol Label Switching Architecture. IETF (January 2001)
15. Cucinotta, T., Checconi, F., Kousiouris, G., Kyriazis, D., Varvarigou, T., Mazzetti, A., Zlatev, Z., Papay, J., Boniface, M., Berger, S., Lamp, D., Voith, T., Stein, M.: Virtualised e-Learning with Real-Time Guarantees on the IRMOS Platform. In: Proceedings of the IEEE International Conference on Service-Oriented Computing and Applications (SOCA 2010), Perth, Australia (December 2010)
16. Konstanteli, K., Cucinotta, T., Varvarigou, T.: Optimum Allocation of Distributed Service Workflows with Probabilistic Real-Time Guarantees. Springer Service Oriented Computing and Applications 4(4) (December 2010)
17. Konstanteli, K., Cucinotta, T., Psychas, K., Varvarigou, T.: Admission control for elastic cloud services. In: Proceedings of the IEEE 5th International Conference on Cloud Computing (CLOUD 2012), pp. 41–48, Honolulu, Hawaii, USA (June 2012)
18. Kousiouris, G., Cucinotta, T., Varvarigou, T.: The Effects of Scheduling, Workload Type and Consolidation Scenarios on Virtual Machine Performance and their Prediction through Optimized Artificial Neural Networks. Elsevier Journal of Systems & Software (JSS)
19. European Commission: Unleashing the Potential of Cloud Computing in Europe. COM (2012) 529 final, Brussels (September 2012), http://ec.europa.eu/information_society/activities/cloudcomputing/docs/com/com_cloud.pdf
20. NIST Cloud Computing Reference Architecture. Special Publication 500-292 (September 2011), http://www.nist.gov/customcf/get_pdf.cfm?pub_id=909505

21. US Government Cloud Computing Technology Roadmap Volume I, Special Publication 500-293, vol. I (November 2011),
    http://www.nist.gov/itl/cloud/upload/SP_500_293_volumeI-2.pdf
22. NIST Reference Architecture and Taxonomy Working Group (RATax WG), Wiki,
    http://collaborate.nist.gov/twiki-cloud-computing/bin/view/
    CloudComputing/ReferenceArchitectureTaxonomy
23. Cloud Metrics Sub Group, Wiki, http://collaborate.nist.gov/
    twiki-cloud-computing/bin/view/CloudComputing/RATax_CloudMetrics
24. Multi Cloud Management,
    http://www.tmforum.org/MultiCloudManagement/13928/home.html
25. Gallizo, G., Kübert, R., Katsaros, G., Oberle, K., Satzke, K., Gogouvitis, G., Oliveros, E.: A Service Level Agreement Management Framework for Real-time Applications in Cloud Computing Environments. In: CloudComp 2010, Barcelona (2010)
26. Kübert, R., Gallizo, G., Polychniatis, T., Varvarigou, T., Oliveros, E., Phillips, S.C., Oberle, K.: Service Level Agreements for real-time Service Oriented Infrastructures. In: Achieving Real-Time in Distributed Computing: From Grids to Clouds. IGI Global (May 2011)
27. Katsaros, G., Cucinotta, T.: Programming Interfaces for Realtime and Cloud-based Computing. In: Achieving Real-Time in Distributed Computing: From Grids to Clouds. IGI Global (July 2011)
28. Oliveros, E., Cucinotta, T., Phillips, S.C., Yang, X., Voith, T., Middleton, S.: Monitoring and Metering in the Cloud. In: Achieving Real-Time in Distributed Computing: From Grids to Clouds. IGI Global (July 2011)
29. Xi, S., Wilson, J., Lu, C., Gill, C.D.: RT-Xen: Towards Real-time Hypervisor Scheduling in Xen. In: ACM International Conference on Embedded Software (EMSOFT) (October 2011)
30. TR178: Enabling End-to-End Cloud SLA Management. TM Forum
31. Checconi, F., Cucinotta, T., Faggioli, D., Lipari, G.: Hierarchical Multiprocessor CPU Reservations for the Linux Kernel. In: Proceedings of the 5th International Workshop on Operating Systems Platforms for Embedded Real-Time Applications (OSPERT 2009), Dublin, Ireland (June 2009)
32. Alicherry, M., Lakshman, T.V.: Network aware resource allocation in distributed clouds. In: Proceedings of INFOCOM 2012, Orlando, FL, pp. 963–971 (March 2012)
33. Valancius, V., Laoutaris, N., Massouli, L., Diot, C., Rodriguez, P.: Greening the Internet with Nano Data Centers. In: Proceedings of the 5th International Conference on Emerging Networking Experiments and Technologies (CoNEXT 2009), pp. 37–48. ACM, New York (2009)
34. Church, K., Greenberg, A., Hamilton, J.: On Delivering Embarrassingly Distributed Cloud Services. In: Hotnets, Calgary, CA (October 2008)
35. IBM Global Technology Services – Case Study. A containerized IT solution increases Port of Fos-sur-Mer efficiency (March 2012)
36. IBM Global Technology Services. Columbia County builds a scalable modular data center to improve availability, doubling IT capacity while leaving the same energy footprint (April 2010)
37. Checconi, F., Cucinotta, T., Stein, M.: Real-Time Issues in Live Migration of Virtual Machines. In: Proceedings of the 4th Workshop on Virtualization and High-Performance Cloud Computing (VHPC 2009), Delft, The Netherlands (August 2009)
38. Metsch, T.: Open Cloud Computing Interface - Use cases and requirements for a Cloud API. Open Grid Forum (2009)

39. Metsch, T., Edmonds, A.: GFD-P-R.184 Open Cloud Computing Interface - Infrastructure. Open Grid Forum (June 2011)
40. Nyren, R., Edmonds, A., Papasyrou, A., Metsch, T.: GFD-P-R.183 Open Cloud Computing Interface – Core. Open Grid Forum (June 2011)
41. Wieder, P., Butler, J.M., Theilmann, W., Yahyapour, R.: Service Level Agreements for Cloud Computing. Springer (2011)
42. Theilmann, W., Lambea, J., Brosch, F., Guinea, S., Chronz, P., Torelli, F., Kennedy, J., Nolan, M., Zacco, G., Spanoudakis, G., Stopar, M., Armellin, G.: SLA@SOI Final Report (September 2011)
43. Metsch, T., Edmonds, A.: GFD-P-R.185 Open Cloud Computing Interface – RESTful HTTP Rendering. Open Grid Forum (June 2011)
44. Schubert, L., Jeffery, K.: EC Cloud Expert Group Report. Advances in Clouds – Research in Future Cloud Computing, http://cordis.europa.eu/fp7/ict/ssai/docs/future-cc-2may-finalreport-experts.pdf
45. Andrieux, A., Czajkowski, K., Dan, A., Keahey, K., Ludwig, H., Nakata, T., Pruyne, J., Rofrano, J., Tuecke, S., Xu, M.: GFD-R.192 Web Services Agreement Specification (WS–Agreement). Open Grid Forum (October 2011)
46. Waeldrich, O., Battr, D., Brazier, F., Clark, K., Oey, M., Papaspyrou, A., Wieder, P., Ziegler, W.: GFD-R-P.193 WS-Agreement Negotiation. Open Grid Forum (October 2011)
47. Kyriazis, D.: European Commission Directorate General Communications Networks, Content and Technology Unit E2 - Software and Services, CLOUD. Cloud Computing Service Level Agreements: Exploitation of Research Results (June 2013), https://ec.europa.eu/digital-agenda/en/news/cloud-computing-service-level-agreements-exploitation-research-results

Estimating the Value Obtained
from Using a Software Service Platform

Netsanet Haile and Jörn Altmann

Technology Management, Economics, and Policy Program (TEMEP)
College of Engineering, Seoul National University
151-744 Seoul, South-Korea
netsanet@temep.snu.ac.kr, jorn.altmann@acm.org

Abstract. Service markets allow users to discover, purchase, and utilize services offered on a specific platform. As service platforms grow in number of users and variety of offerings, it raises the question of whether this phenomenon continues to benefit users. Based on a literature review, the paper identifies usability, service variety, and the number of personal connections accessible over the service platform as major determinants that contribute to the value to users. Based on survey data on the behavior of mobile service users, the relationship between user value and the determinants is analyzed and estimated. The results show positive correlations between all three determinants and the value. Using regressions, we estimate how much these determinates contribute to the user value. Mobile service users are satisfied with the usability of services of their chosen platforms, although the impact on the user value is the lowest. Users benefit the most from an increase in the number of their personal connections and the number of services they use.

Keywords: Network Effect Theory, UTAUT, Value Creation, Service Platforms, Survey, Multiple Regression.

1   Introduction

Service platforms can be considered one of today's highly valued technologies. In recent years, there has been a rapid growth in the number of services being developed and offered over various platforms. By January 2013, Apple's App Store contained 750,000 registered services. Google's Android operating system runs on many devices and competes with the iPhone. It comes with more than 700,000 services as of April 2013, that are offered through its software service market Play Store.

The introduction of mobile service platforms made the development and offering of services simple and helped their integration into users' daily lives [32]. From a business perspective, value creation is the main focus of service platform operators, both in the context of creating better value for customers purchasing their services as well as for their shareholders, who want to see their stake increase in value. Due to the novelty of technologies, delivery modes, and business models in service platforms, the definition of their value system is at its early stage. Therefore, the question

J. Altmann, K. Vanmechelen, and O.F. Rana (Eds.): GECON 2013, LNCS 8193, pp. 244–255, 2013.
© Springer International Publishing Switzerland 2013

whether the existing models from theories of network analysis and information systems explain the specific characteristics of the value creation process in service platform markets needs to be addressed.

Prior to the web services era, demand-side interdependencies in communication markets have been investigated in earlier literature [1]. Following these approaches, economic theories regarding information goods stated that usage of products in these markets is driven by the need for compatible (interoperable) products to exchange information and the need for complimentary products and services [2], [3]. The concepts of complementarities and network effects are adopted into theoretical models for platform leadership and value creation in e-businesses in recent studies [4], [5]. These studies introduced direct and indirect network effects which come from the installed base and the availability of complimentary services as value drivers for both providers and consumers. However, they provide a general overview of network effect markets, investigating reactions to an aggregated number of users without considering variations of user choices. In addition to this, a complete value function needs to account for the benefits from actual use of functions. For this purpose, we adopt the measures of usability introduced through the Technology Acceptance Model (TAM) and later extended into the Unified Theory of Acceptance and Use of Technology (UTAUT) [6] [7]. This paper applies measures (i.e., perceived usefulness and perceived ease of use) used in the UTAUT to capture the user value from the usability of a service platform. The paper addresses a research gap regarding the identification of determinants of a service platform user's value and the introduction of a measurement method. In detail, it responds to the question of what aspects of a service platform determine a user's value. It also addresses a question on how to estimate the value function of a service platform user.

Our main hypothesis is that the value creation process in mobile service markets is significantly influenced by personal experiences of the users' in relation to the usability of functions provided, size of personal networks built with other users, and the number of services a user chooses to utilize. In order to evaluate the relationships between service users' value and a set of variables measuring their usage experience, the study applied multiple regressions on survey data.

The contribution of our paper is that it builds an aggregated model based on a previously established research framework of IT usage and network effects [4], [5], [6], [7], [8], [9], [10], [11], [12]. Using this model, it presents an estimation of a value function of service platform users. The value function is computed empirically from the analysis of survey-based consumption data of service platform users. As the business model of service platforms is dominated by advertisement-based, charge-free offerings, the paper suggests a value measure that takes into account this fact. The results of the analysis are used to discuss the extent of impact on service users' value due to the ever increasing provision of new service offerings, improvements in usability, and the ability to connect to a larger number of other users via the service platform.

In the following section, we will give a short overview of service marketplaces, approaches using network effect theory, the Unified Theory of Acceptance and Use of Technology (UTAUT), and related literature on value creation. Section 3 presents the model proposed. After describing the data collection in section 4, section 5 presents the results and discussion of the estimated data. Section 6 concludes the paper.

2   Related Work

2.1   Software Service Markets

The term software services (services) is used to refer to software-as-a-service offerings that run on computing devices such as smartphones, tablet personal computer, and notepads. They are made available through service platforms or service marketplaces such as Apple App Store, Google Play Store, Windows Phone Store, BlackBerry App World, and Amazon App Store. The software services are downloaded from the platform to the users' devices, which run operating systems such as iOS, Android, Windows, and BlackBerry OS. The operating systems are free of charge or are obtained through a perpetual license. The software services are usually produced by third-party developers and are offered via the platform for a share of the sales price (e.g., for about 20-30%). Today, multiple OS-native and third-party software service providers operate in the service market. iOS and Android hold the largest shares in the market as they are adopted by more than 500 million users each [13]. In detail, App Store of Apple contained 775,000 services as of January 2013 [14], Google Play Store of Google has 700,000 services as of April 2013 [15], Window Phone Store of Microsoft 130,000 services as of February 2013 [16], and BlackBerry World of RIM offered 100,000 services as of March 2013 [17].

2.2   Unified Theory of Acceptance and Use of Technology

The Unified Theory of Acceptance and Use of Technology (UTAUT) focuses on identifying measures (factors, constructs) for a technology to be successfully adopted and used by the target market [7]. It is an integrated and updated presentation of the earlier Technology Acceptance Model (TAM) and the subsequent developments that have been made based on TAM [6].

2.3   Network Effects Theory

In empirical studies based on network effect theory, authors mainly put effort into proving the existence of network effects and estimating its value using regression analysis [18], [19], [20], [21]. Some of the studies use equilibrium analysis to explain problems such as market failure, competition, and path dependency of markets [2], [8], [9], [10], [11], [12], [22], [23]. Looking into these earlier studies of network effects, they provided a general theoretical framework showing responses of a potential market to an aggregated size of an installed base and complimentary products. Theories of network effects have also been adopted as value factors in web service markets in recent studies [4], [5].

2.4   Value Creation

Value creation describes the performance of businesses or the consumption decisions that increase the value of goods, services, or a business [24]. Creating value for a customer entails providing products and services that customers find consistently useful. In today's economy, such value creation is typically based on products and process innovation. Creating value for investors means delivering consistently high returns on their capital. This generally requires both strong revenue growth and attractive profit margins. These, in turn, can be achieved only if a company delivers sustained value for customers [24].

There have been a number of studies performed on the value creation process and value factors in platform-based markets in general [4], [25], [26]. A few studies also exist on IT service markets [5], [27], [28], [31]. These studies focus on value creation in e-business [4], adoption of mobile Internet [25], mobile service ecosystem [26], IT service platforms [5], [27], and on the evaluation of service platform business models [28], [31].

The theories of network effect and UTAUT are used in this paper as sources of determinants, explaining the value creation process. In constructing a service platform user's value model, the paper employs two value drivers (namely installed base and complementary services), which have been introduced by the theory of network effects. In addition to this, the paper also adopts perceived usefulness and perceived ease of use from the UTAUT measures of usability.

3   Model Specification

3.1   Determinants of Value of Service Platform Users

Identifying the major value determinants is important for modeling the value creation in service platforms. For this, we examined studies on the Technology Acceptance Model (TAM), its extended versions, the Unified Theory of Acceptance and Use of Technology (UTAUT), network effect theories for information goods markets, and the adoption of network effects concepts. We found that value creation in service platforms could be explained using three determinants: usability, service variety, and installed base.

Usability. Adopting the concepts of UTAUT [7], usability of a service can be described as the level of effort the user needs to access, understand, utilize the service platform and its offerings. It also entails the level, at which the service platform includes offerings that fulfill the user's functionality requirements. Usability of a service platform is enhanced by its functional and non-functional performance. Whether a user's experience meets the expectations determines the value of the user (Table 1). In this model, the value for perceived usability as a latent variable was obtained from the interaction of two proxy measures (Table 2). Those measures are the users' indication of their perceived level of usefulness (PER_USEFUL) and perceived level of ease of use (PER_EASE_USE) of their service platform [6], [7]. The reciprocal of the product (equation 1) is taken to represent the perceived usability of user i in the value model:

$$USAB_i = \frac{1}{PER\_USEFUL_i + PER\_EASE\_USE_i}$$ (1)

Table 1. Value determinants summary

Determinant	Definition	Source
Usability	Degree of performance of a system to accomplish the required functions as well as degree of difficulty to understand and use a system.	[6],[7]
Installed base	Quantity of existing users of a system.	[2],[4],[5],[9],[10], [11],[12]
Service variety	Quantities of services interoperable (compatible) with the system used.	[2],[3],[4],[5],[8],[29], [30],[9],[10],[11],[12]

Service Variety. Services, which run over the same service platform, are developed using a common standard. If a user adopts a service platform, the user is offered basic functionalities, enabling him to run further and complementing services. The existence of complementarities makes a product or service a more attractive offering to users [2], [4], [5], [9], [10], [11], [12], [29], [30]. The use of additional services could cost more for the user though. Therefore, the variety of services available determines the quantity of services and service categories a user has access to over this platform (Table 1). In this model, service variety accessed by the user is measured by the total number of services the user subscribed to or stored in their smart device (S_TOTAL) and the average number of services used per day (S_DAILY_USE)(Table 2). The number of services a user chooses to install and to use daily are assumed to indicate their valuation of the variety of services their service platform offers. We normalized the value using the maximum number of services expected to be installed and used daily. The resulting level of use of service variety is in the range [0,1]. Therefore, service variety for user i is represented in the model as shown in equation 2:

$$S_i = \frac{S\_TOTAL_i * S\_DAILY\_USE_i}{Max(S\_TOTAL_i * S\_DAILY\_USE_i)}$$ (2)

Installed Base. The installed base is the total number of a particular product or system in the entire market or product segment. However, when calculating the installed base of a market, it is important to exclude products that have been replaced by technology upgrades or are no longer in use. Therefore, the installed base corresponds to the size of the actual end-user base, indicating its popularity (Table 1). The installed base measure is particularly important if the adoption of a new product depends on a product (e.g., device, software) that is already installed in the market [11].

Table 2. Summary of variables and measures used in the value model

Variable	Measure	Description
Usability	Perceived Ease of use (PER_EASE_USE)	Level of ease, at which a user can discover, purchase, and utilize services on the service platform.
	Perceived usefulness (PER_USEFUL)	The ability of services offered on the platform in relation to the user's functional requirement.
Service variety	Number of services currently installed (S_TOTAL)	Total number of services the user currently has installed on his device.
	Number of services used per day (S_DAILY_USE)	The number of services the user uses frequently.
Installed base	Number of connections to other users (N_TOTAL)	Total number of contacts a user has stored in their communication and social media services.
	Number of active connections to other users (N_RECENT_INTER)	Number of other users the service user communicates with frequently.

In the context of service platform markets, one unit of an operating system activated corresponds to one user. The total number of devices with a certain operating system run by a single platform service user makes the installed base of the service platform. Current software service platforms are dominated by use scenarios which involve communication, collaboration, and exchange of information among users [5], [28], [30]. Thus, the number of other users that a user can connect with on a platform is an important determinant.

Similarly, the installed base is represented by the number of total connections stored by the user (Table 2). The number of connections (N_TOTAL), which the user chose to make over their social media, communication, and entertainment services, is taken as the indicator of their valuation of the installed base. In addition, the frequency of interactions (N_RECENT_INTER) with a part of those connections is also considered. The installed base value is also normalized to generate a value in the range [0,1]. Therefore, we define the installed base for user i as shown in equation 3:

$$N_i = \frac{\text{N\_TOTAL}_i * \text{N\_RECENT\_INTER}_i}{Max(\text{N\_TOTAL}_i * \text{N\_RECENT\_INTER}_i)} \tag{3}$$

3.2   Proposed Value Model

We construct a value model consisting of the determinants identified in the previous section. The model assumes that service platform users get value from their experience of usability of the service platform, the variety of services (functionalities) that they can utilize, and the number of communications (connections) that they can make with other users. When deciding on the adoption of a service platform, a user i is assumed to expect the value $V_i(USAB_i, S_i, N_i)$ of using the service platform to be greater or equal than the value of not using it. The value V_i is a function of $USAB_i$ (equation 1), S_i (equation 2), and N_i (equation 3).

To indirectly measure the value V, we introduce two more measures (Table 3), namely the time spent on using services (C_TIME) and the monetary cost of using services (C_USAGE). In detail, C_USAGE is the amount of money the user spent on purchasing services, fees paid for upgrading and access to content such as movies, music and games per day. C_TIME is the cost of time the user spends on using the service platform daily. The total cost, which is a function of C_TIME and C_USAGE, represents a lower bound to the value V that a user gets. A user would never use a service platform, if the value V were lower than the cost spent.

Table 3. Summary of the variable and measures used to estimate the user value in the model

Variable	Measure	Description
Total cost	Time spent on using services (C_TIME)	Amount of time a user spends on using services on average per day.
	Cost of using services (C_USAGE)	Amount of money a user spends on using services on average per month.

Based on these two measures of cost, the value of a user i can be estimated as shown in the following equation:

$$V_i(USAB_i, S_i, N_i) > TOTAL\_COST_i \ (C\_USAGE_i, C\_TIME_i) \qquad (4)$$

where V_i, $USAB_i$, S_i, and N_i are defined as described above. $TOTAL\_COST_i$ is a function of C_USAGE_i and C_TIME_i. It calculates the sum of $\ln(C\_USAGE_i)$ and $\ln(C\_TIME_i)$.

Service platforms are dominated by advertisement-based service offerings. In such an environment using willingness-to-pay for service usage as the only indicator of value would undermine the results. Therefore, we add the cost of time the user spends daily utilizing services as well. Based on the user's annual income, we estimate their approximate hourly income and use it as the cost of one hour of time spent.

Based on this value model, multiple separate relationships between the platform users' value (estimated through the total cost) and the explanatory variables can be measured. The value model (equation 5) is based on an additive logarithmic function.

$$TOTAL\_COST = \beta_0 + \beta_1 ln(USAB) + \beta_2 ln(S) + \beta_3 ln(N) \qquad (5)$$

The coefficients $\beta_0, \beta_1, \beta_2$, and β_3 indicate the intercept and the amount of change in the total cost (i.e., the proxy for the value of service users) as a result of the change in one unit of usability (USAB), service variety used (S), and number of connections (N), respectively. It describes their individual relationship with the resulting value (TOTAL_COST), assuming the other variables constant.

4   Method

4.1   Data Collection

A user survey has been conducted from May 1st to May 31st 2013 to collect the data for the analysis. The survey was distributed to global smartphone users and administered online, through social media and email. Anyone, who owned a smartphone, was eligible to respond to the survey. The survey questionnaire included 26 questions:

In total, 183 responses have been received. The characteristics of our respondents are: 78 students (43%), 51 (28%) employees of private companies, 43 (23%) government employees, and 11 (6%) self-employed. It is clearly a small sample to represent the whole population of mobile service users. However, it includes a good distribution of possible behaviors of new and experienced mobile service users: 140 (77%) of which have been smartphone users for more than a year. The respondents of the survey were users of different service platforms: 46 (25%) Apple iOS users, 98 (54%) Google Android users, 7 (4%) Microsoft Windows Mobile users, 27 (15%) RIM BlackBerry users, and 5 (3%) users of other platforms. Among the responses received, 177 valid records are used in the analysis. Observations with 0 service usage per day were omitted. Table 4 shows the measurement types of the main variables collected by using the questionnaire.

Table 4. Types of data collected for each variable considered in the study

Variables	Measures	Measurement types used
USAB	PER_EASE_USE	Likert scale (1-5)
	PER_USEFL	Likert scale (1-5)
S	S_TOTAL	20 Intervals, Range (1-200)
	S_DAILY_USE	8 Intervals, Range (0-21)
N	N_TOTAL	15 Intervals, Range (1-1500)
	N_RECENT_INTER	10 Intervals, Range (1-100)
V (Value)	C_TIME	17 Intervals, Range (0-8)
	C_USAGE	6 Intervals, Range (0-25)

5   Data Analysis Results

5.1   Time Spent on Using Services

The peak frequency on time spent on services is the range 0.5 hours to 1.0 hour. 35 subjects (20%) indicated this range. The second highest frequency with 32 subjects (18%) is the range 1 hour to 1.5 hours. The distribution of the frequency on time spent has a lognormal shape (Figure 1).

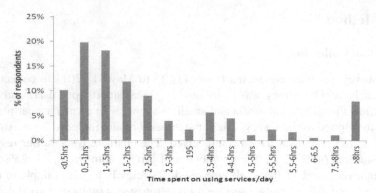

Fig. 1. Average time spent on using services per day

Only 71 of our respondents (31%) spent more than 2.5 hours a day on using any of the services on their smartphones.

5.2   Correlation

All explanatory variables (Usability (USAB), service variety (S), and installed base (N)), which have been identified in section 3, show positive correlations with each other as well as a significant correlation with the response variable (TOTAL_COST), representing the value to users (Table 5).

Table 5. Correlation between determinants and total cost

	USAB	S	N	TOTAL_COST
USAB	1			
S	0.66749	1		
N	0.49424	0.68236	1	
TOTAL_COST	0.47194	0.62693	0.60457	1

The strongest positive correlation (0.682) is shown between the number of services installed on users' smartphones (S) and the number of personal connections they have made over their communication and social media services (N). This correlation is in line with the fact that communication is the preferred functionality of services of many mobile platform users. The second highest positive correlation (0.667) is between usability of the platform (USAB) and service variety (S). In addition to this, TOTAL_COST (i.e., willingness-to-pay) and service variety show also a strong correlation (0.626). In general, these results confirm that users are willing to pay (through money and time spent) for communication with personal contacts and for service variety.

5.3   Estimation of Coefficients

Based on the data collected, we can estimate the coefficients of the model that is shown in equation 5 as follows:

$$TOTAL\_COST = 1.04 + 0.85 \ln(USAB) + 6.22 \ln(S) + 4.66 \ln(N) \quad (6)$$

As shown in Table 6, the explanatory power of the model is satisfactory with an adjusted R^2 of 0.44. The t-test detected statistically significant dependence of V on all 3 independent variables (USAB, S, and N). Both the F-test and P-value are sufficiently low to indicate good reliability of the model.

All of the estimated parameters have a positive sign. The estimated rate of change of V with respect to USAB, if S and N are fixed, is between -0.877 and 2.587, with respect to S, if USAB and N are fixed, is between 3.118 and 9.327, and with respect to N, if USAB and S are fixed, is between 2.484 and 6.837. The detail results of the regression are shown in Table 6 below. Service variety is estimated to be the strongest positive determinant of platform users' willingness to spend time and money on usage, if other factors are fixed.

Table 6. Model estimation results

Regression Statistics						
Multiple R	0.674					
R Square	0.455					
Adjusted R Square	0.445					
Standard Error	1.758					
Observations	177					

	Coefficient	Standard Error	t Stat	P-value	Lower 95%	Upper 95%
Intercept	1.045	0.164	6.367	0.00	0.721	1.369
USAB	0.855	0.877	0.974	0.33	-0.877	2.587
S	6.222	1.573	3.956	0.00	3.118	9.327
N	4.661	1.103	4.226	0.00	2.484	6.837

While having a positive impact, a change on the level of usability does not cause a significant increase in the willingness-to-pay for service usage, assuming other factors fixed. Personal connections and service variety have been identified as the two important determinants for service platform users. The rate of change of the total cost in response to one level increase in the number of personal connections to other users is significant (4.661), assuming other parameters fixed. The same goes for service variety. In this case, the rate of change is even 6.222.

6   Conclusion

Motivated by the globally increasing attractiveness of software service platform use and the paralleled increasing interest of developers to offer more services over these platforms, this paper aimed at proposing a model explaining the value of software service platform users. We explained the relevance of the theoretical framework in service platform markets and analyzed their implications. We chose three explanatory variables: usability, service variety, and installed base. Each of those variables can reasonably contribute to the service users' value. The dependent variable, user value, is proxied (substituted) through the cost of time that users spend on using the service platform and the spending on purchasing and using services. This is reasonable to assume as the user value needs to be higher than the cost that is incurred to a user. Otherwise, i.e., if the return in user value were lower, the user would not use the platform at all. Therefore, the estimate gives a lower bound on the value.

Based on a survey conducted among smartphone users, we estimated the coefficients of the value model. Most of its explanatory power of the model resides in the variable service variety and the variable installed base. It is remarkable that their explanatory power is stronger than the explanatory power of the variable usability.

Though efforts were made to include subjects revealing all possible behaviors in relation to the variables of interest, this study has limitations due to a small sample size. Further studies could be conducted involving a more representative sample size.

Acknowledgments. This work has been funded by the Korea Institute for Advancement of Technology (KIAT) within the ITEA 2 project 10014 EASICLOUDS.

References

1. Rohlfs, J.: A Theory of Interdependent Demand for a Communications Service. The Bell Journal of Economics and Management Science, 16–37 (1974)
2. Katz, M.L., Shapiro, C.: Network Externalities, Competition, and Compatibility. The American Economic Review 75(3), 424–440 (1985)
3. Economides, N.: The economics of networks. International Journal of Industrial Organization 14(6), 673–699 (1996)
4. Amit, R., Zott, C.: Value Creation in E-business. Strategic Management Journal 22, 493–520 (2001)
5. Lee, S., Kim, T., Noh, Y., Lee, B.: Success Factors of Platform Leadership in Web 2.0 Service Business. Service Business 4(2), 89–103 (2010)
6. Davis, F.D.: Perceived Usefulness, Perceived Ease of Use, and User Acceptance of Information Technology. MIS Quarterly 13(3), 319–340 (1989)
7. Venkatesh, V., Morris, M.G., Davis, G.B., Davis, F.D.: User Acceptance of Information Technology: Toward a Unified View. MIS Quarterly, 425–478 (2003)
8. Katz, M.L., Shapiro, C.: Technology Adoption in the Presence of Network Externalities. The Journal of Political Economy, 822–841 (1986)
9. Katz, M.L., Shapiro, C.: Systems Competition and Network Effects. The Journal of Economic Perspectives 8(2), 93–115 (1994)

10. Farrell, J., Saloner, G.: Standardization, compatibility, and innovation. The RAND Journal of Economics, 70–83 (1985)
11. Farrell, J., Saloner, G.: Installed Base and Compatibility: Innovation, Product preannouncements, and Predation. The American Economic Review, 940–955 (1986)
12. Arthur, W.B.: Competing Technologies, Increasing Returns, and Lock-in by Historical Events. The Economic Journal 99(394), 116–131 (1989)
13. Worldwide Smartphone OS share, http://www.icharts.net/chartchannel/worldwide-smartphone-os-share-2012-q1-2013-q1_m3zryyngc (accessed on June 2013)
14. Apple, http://www.apple.com/pr/library/2013/01/07App-Store-Tops-40-Billion-Downloads-with-Almost-Half-in-2012.html (accessed on June 2013)
15. Google Play, https://play.google.com/store/ (accessed on June 2013)
16. Windows Phone Store, http://www.windowsphone.com/en-us/store/overview (accessed on June 2013)
17. Blackberry World, http://appworld.blackberry.com/webstore/ (accessed on June 2013)
18. Hartman, R.S., Teece, D.J.: Product Emulation Strategies in The Presence of Reputation Effects and Network Externalities: Some Evidence From The Minicomputer Industry. Economics of Innovation and New Technology 1(1-2), 157–182 (1990)
19. Church, J., Gandal, N.: Network Effects, Software Provision, and Standardization. The Journal of Industrial Economics 85–103 (1992)
20. Gandal, N.: Hedonic Price Indexes for Spreadsheets and an Empirical Test for Network Externalities. The RAND Journal of Economics 25(1), 160–170 (1994)
21. Economides, N., Himmelberg, C.: Critical Mass and Network Evolution in Telecommunications. In: Toward a Competitive Telecommunications Industry: Selected Papers from the 1994 Telecommunications Policy Research Conference (1995)
22. Besen, S.M., Farrell, J.: Choosing How to Compete: Strategies and Tactics in Standardization. The Journal of Economic Perspectives 8(2), 117–131 (1994)
23. Liebowitz, S.J., Margolis, S.E.: Path Dependence, Lock-in, and History. Journal of Law, Economics, & Organization 11(1), 205–226 (1995)
24. Brandenburger, A.M., Stuart, H.: Value-Based Business Strategy. Journal of Economics and Management Strategy 5, 5–25 (1996)
25. Kim, H.W., Chan, H.C., Gupta, S.: Value-Based Adoption of Mobile Internet: An Empirical Investigation. Decision Support Systems 43, 111–126 (2007)
26. Basole, R.C., Karla, J.: Value Transformation in the Mobile Service Ecosystem: A Study of App Store Emergence and Growth. Service Science 4(1), 24–41 (2012)
27. Haile, N., Altmann, J.: Value Creation in IT Service Platforms through Two-Sided Network Effects. In: Vanmechelen, K., Altmann, J., Rana, O.F. (eds.) GECON 2012. LNCS, vol. 7714, pp. 139–153. Springer, Heidelberg (2012)
28. Smedlund, A.: Value Co-creation in Service Platform Business Models. Service Science 4(1), 79–88 (2012)
29. Zhu, F., Iansiti, M.: Entry into Platform-Based Markets. Strategic Management Journal 33(1), 88–106 (2012)
30. Gawer, A., Cusumano, M.A.: How Companies Become Platform Leaders. MIT Sloan Management Review 49(2), 28–35 (2008)
31. Gebregiorgis, S.A., Altmann, J.: IT Service Platforms: Their Value Creation Model and the Impact of Their Level of Openness on Their Adoption. TEMEP Discussion Paper 201295 (2012)
32. Kim, J., Ilon, L., Altmann, J.: Adapting Smartphones as Learning Technology in a Korean University. Transactions of the SDPS. Journal of Integrated Design and Process Science (2013)

An Experiment in SLA Decision-Making

Ulrik Franke[1], Markus Buschle[2], and Magnus Österlind[2]

[1] FOI – Swedish Defence Research Agency
16490 Stockholm, Sweden
ulrik.franke@foi.se
[2] Industrial Information and Control Systems
KTH – Royal Institute of Technology
Osquldas v. 12, 10044 Stockholm, Sweden
{markusb,magnuso}@ics.kth.se

Abstract. Decision-making with regard to availability service level agreements (SLAs) is investigated. An experimental economics approach was used to elicit the preferences for different SLA alternatives from the subjects ($N = 16$), all professionally working with IT management. A previously published scenario on downtime costs in the retail business was used in the experimental setup. Subjects made 18 pairwise choices under uncertainty. After the experiment, they were paid based on one of their choices, randomly selected. The subjects rarely behaved as expected utility maximizers in the experiment. This raises questions about company SLA management in real situations, and calls for further research.

Keywords: Service Level Agreements, Availability, SLA Management, Decision-making, Experiment.

1 Introduction

Today, IT is increasingly being provisioned as a service. Distributed systems technology provides the basis of the "cloud", where enterprises can buy advanced IT services "off the shelf", gaining flexibility and scalability. However, the economic implications are just as important to investigate as the technology [1].

A key non-functional property of IT services bought and sold is *availability*. Annual costs of unplanned downtime were in the billion dollar range already 15 years ago [2], and have hardly improved since. Stock prices fall when business operations are disrupted by IT incidents [3, 4], and reliability costs rank as an important IT frustration for executives [5]. However, to maintain high availability today, IT executives need proper service level agreements (SLAs). Such contracts link business operations to the IT services bought off the shelf.

How to write proper SLAs is interesting both to academia and practitioners. Management by contract [6] can be said to be at the heart of this research area, along with the primacy of the business perspective [7, 8] and the fact that negotiations have to take place between parties with asymmetric information [9]. Gartner [10] and ITIL [11] offer practical advice on availability SLA writing.

J. Altmann, K. Vanmechelen, and O.F. Rana (Eds.): GECON 2013, LNCS 8193, pp. 256–267, 2013.
© Springer International Publishing Switzerland 2013

The research question of this paper is: Do practitioners deviate from expected utility when procuring availability SLAs, and if so, how? Previous work identifies many potential deviations, e.g. bounded rationality [12, 13] and overconfidence [14]. This study extends previous theoretical work [15] with an empirical investigation. Our results show that practitioners do not necessarily behave as expected utility maximizers – indeed, they do so quite rarely in our experiment.

1.1 Outline

The remainder of the paper is structured as follows: Section 2 covers related work. Section 3 presents the availability investment model used in the experiment. Data collection methods are detailed in Section 4, followed by results in Section 5. Section 6 relates the outcome to previous findings and discusses the results. Finally, Section 7 offers some concluding remarks.

2   Related Work

Optimal SLA management is a growing field. [16] offers models for optimal service-window scheduling to minimize business impact, but does not address *unplanned* outages. [17] derives optimal SLA strategies, but does not focus on availability. [18] considers SLA specifications, but without quantitative risk analysis. [19] investigates the service procurer's optimization problem, but does not empirically study human decision-making. Neither does the game theoretic approach of [20]. Technically oriented work such as frameworks for bridging SLA templates [21] or intelligent SLA negotiation agents [22] are important for well-designed SLAs, but does not further our understanding of human decision-making.

Turning to decision-making research, [23] presents a game theoretic framework for SLA negotiation. A bargaining process is envisioned, where an equilibrium between client and service provider is found by counter-offers. This is different from our study, where the client is offered a *take-it-or-leave-it* contract.

[24] presents a study on decision-making for duplex gambles where 34 undergraduate statistics students played hypothetical gambles. The study shows that in the loosing form of gambles (like those in our study, where the decision maker cannot gain money from the gamble) a majority of respondents (78%) maximize the expected value of the gamble, being highly consistent. A similar study with 42 undergraduate psychology students is presented in [25], with results again showing that most respondents are maximizing the expected value.

3   The Decision-Making Problem

SLAs govern many non-functional requirements, but our focus is on *availability*. The *average availability* can be computed as the Mean Time To Failure (MTTF) divided with the total time of operation, i.e. the sum of MTTF and the Mean Time To Repair/Restore (MTTR) [26]:

$$A = \frac{\text{MTTF}}{\text{MTTF} + \text{MTTR}} \tag{1}$$

Availability is a good experimental topic for many reasons: Requirements are easy to understand, there is a tangible economic impact, and it is often at the heart of SLAs. In the experiment (cf. Section 4), participants were subjected to a decision-making problem re-used from [15], where more details can be found.

3.1   A Simple Investment Model

Availability investments have diminishing returns. Each additional hour of up-time comes at a higher cost. This is modeled by Eq. (2)

$$A = f(A_0, c) = 1 - (1 - A_0)e^{-\alpha c} \tag{2}$$

where $A \in [0, 1]$ is the availability resulting from an investment $c \geq 0$ made at an initial availability level $A_0 \in [0, 1]$, where $\alpha \in (0, 1)$ determines the shape of the function. Though simplified, it reflects some important real world characteristics.

An estimated average cost of 1 hour of downtime is the following [27]:

$$\frac{\text{Empl. costs/hour} \cdot \% \text{ Empl's affected by outage}}{+ \text{ Avg. Rev./hour} \cdot \% \text{ Rev. affected by outage}} \tag{3}$$
$$= \text{Estimated average cost of 1 hour of downtime}$$

If this cost is multiplied with the number of hours per operating year (e.g. 365 days · 24 hours for 24/7 systems) a maximum potential loss L is found. With availability A, the annual loss is $(1 - A)L$, e.g. $A = 95\%$ entails a loss of $0.05L$. In this simplified model, hourly cost is independent of outage duration.

By adding downtime costs and investment costs a net cost function is found:

$$\text{Net cost} = (1 - f(A_0, c))L + c \tag{4}$$

This net cost function has a level of investment c^* that minimizes the cost:

$$c^* = \frac{\ln(\alpha \cdot L \cdot (1 - A_0))}{\alpha} \tag{5}$$

3.2   The Variance of Outage Costs

A better model does away with averages and lets the outage cost depend on the time of occurrence, giving each hour a separate random cost variable L_i. The expected total cost becomes a sum over the set Out of hours when outages occur:

$$\text{Net cost} = (1 - f(A_0, c)) \sum_{i \in Out} E[L_i] + c \tag{6}$$

In the stochastic model, net cost variance becomes important. As shown in [15], the variance depends a lot on whether the outage hours are consecutive or non-consecutive, assuming that the covariance of consecutive hours is larger than that of non-consecutive. In practice, this is often the case: two consecutive outage hours in a retail business before Christmas probably have a greater covariance than one hour from before Christmas and one hour from a February Monday morning. Thus, the *number of outages* becomes important for the variance of downtime costs. In our model, this is modeled by a homogeneous Poisson process (HPP). The probability that a failure occurs n times in the time interval $[0, t]$ is

$$P(N(t) = n) = \frac{(\lambda t)^n}{n!} e^{-\lambda t} \text{ for } n \in \mathbb{N} \tag{7}$$

$N(t)$ belongs to the Poisson distribution: $N(t) \in Po(\lambda t)$. λt is the expected number of outages in a year: the product of λ, the intensity of the HPP [occurrences/time] and t, the length of the time interval.

3.3 An Actual Dataset of Revenue Data

The final component of the model is a dataset based on [28], a report from the Swedish Retail Institute, with statistics on the revenue distribution in the Swedish retail sector. Hourly and monthly data is given in Tables 1 and 2. Based on these statistics, a dataset of 13 hours times 365 days was generated and normalized, reflecting relative hourly revenues over the operating year.

Table 1. Hourly retail sector revenue distributions (normalized) for normal and pay weeks [28]

	Mo.	Tu.	We.	Th.	Fr.	Sa.	Su.	Sum
Normal week (Pay week)								
09.00-12.00	1 (2)	2 (2)	2 (2)	3 (3)	4 (4)	4 (3)	2 (2)	18 (18)
12.00-16.00	3 (3)	3 (3)	4 (3)	5 (5)	8 (8)	9 (9)	6 (6)	37 (37)
16.00-22.00	5 (5)	5 (5)	7 (6)	10 (11)	10 (11)	4 (5)	3 (4)	44 (47)
Total	10 (10)	10 (10)	12 (11)	18 (19)	22 (23)	17 (17)	11 (12)	99 (100)

Table 2. Monthly retail sector revenue distribution (normalized) over a year [28]

Jan.	Feb.	Mar.	Apr.	May.	Jun.	Jul.	Aug.	Sep.	Oct.	Nov.	Dec.
7	7	8	8	8	8	8	8	8	8	8	11

As seen in the tables, there is a lot of variance: A payment system outage during a single high revenue hour might cost as much as a dozen low revenue hour outages, if no transactions can be made with the payment system down. In the experiment, downtime costs are calculated by Eq. (6), substituting expectations with hourly costs from the normalized dataset described in Tables 1 and 2. To summarize, the subjects thus face two important features of availability SLA decision-making: diminishing marginal returns on investment, and variance of outage costs. While the data might not be representative of all industries (cf. [15] for a further discussion), its variance offers an interesting case. The problem is easy to understand, but the stochastic model makes it hard to solve.

4 Data Collection Method

To empirically investigate the preferences of IT professionals with regard to availability SLAs, an experimental economics approach was used with 16 research subjects. All of the subjects work in the intersection of business and IT, some with a focus on availability. The subjects participated in an evening course on Enterprise Architecture for practitioners in the field of enterprise IT. Based on their background, the subjects are more likely to be on the procuring than the providing side of an SLA, though this was not explicitly investigated.

First, the subjects were introduced to the problem presented in Section 3. Diminishing returns on investments were introduced to the subjects using textbook diagrams [29, 11] and a table [30]. The importance of variance was illustrated with the following thought-provoking wording on a PowerPoint slide: "99.9% availability 24-7 means almost 9 hours of annual downtime. Case 1: A single 9 hour outage. Case 2: 100 separate 5 minute outages. Which one do you prefer?" Then, Tables 1 and 2 – background facts in the experiment – were shown and remained on display throughout the session. It was explicitly pointed out that the decision-making problem is a simplified one, not aiming to capture the entire complexity of real systems and their availability, but rather to investigate the behavior of IT decision-makers under uncertainty.

The subjects were asked 18 questions, with no pre-test. Each question represented a binary choice between two SLA scenarios. Each scenario had an SLA price, a resulting minimum availability (percent) (by Eq. (2)) and a number of expected outages (by Eq. (7)). The subjects were asked to procure the payment service for a retail store with revenue streams/downtime costs according to Tables 1 and 2 and Eq. (6). The translated questionnaire can be found in Fig. 1.

Each subject received an initial endowment of 300 Swedish kronor (SEK) for each of the 18 questions. The subjects received the information that one percent unavailability would correspond to 47.45 hours of annual downtime with *average* cost of 100 SEK. As a motivation for making wise decisions, following the data collection an answer from each subject was selected at random, its outcome simulated according to Section 3 and the resulting amount was paid out. The subjects did not have calculators. All data was fully anonymized before analysis.

The 18 questions were grouped into 3 categories. In the first category the questions were phrased as follows:

1. Do you prefer to pay 6 SEK for 99% availability with 1 expected outage or 12 SEK for 99 % availability with 2 expected outages?
2. Do you prefer to pay 12 SEK for 99% availability with 2 expected outages or 18 SEK for 99 % availability with 3 expected outages?

i.e. both alternatives always offered 99% availability, but the first alternative was cheaper with fewer outages. This pattern was followed until:

6. Do you prefer to pay 60 SEK for 99% availability with 10 expected outages or 120 SEK for 99 % availability with 20 expected outages?

Consider the 18 questions below. Every question is a choice between two alternatives.
For every question your initial capital is 300 SEK that you should invest in order to get the most out of. One question will be selected randomly, simulated and paid out!
One percent unavailability corresponds to 47.45 hours downtime. 47.45 hours downtime cost 100 SEK *on average.*

1. Pay 6 SEK for 99% availability with 1 expected outage	Pay 12 SEK for 99% availability with 2 expected outages	7. Pay 0 SEK for 99% availability with 2 expected outages	Pay 15 SEK for 99.53% availability with 2 expected outages	13. Pay 0 SEK for 99% availability with 20 expected outages	Pay 15 SEK for 99.53% availability with 20 expected outages
2. Pay 12 SEK for 99% availability with 3 expected outages	Pay 18 SEK for 99% availability with 5 expected outages	8. Pay 15 SEK for 99.53% availability with 2 expected outages	Pay 30 SEK for 99.78% availability with 2 expected outages	14. Pay 15 SEK for 99.53% availability with 20 expected outages	Pay 30 SEK for 99.78% availability with 20 expected outages
3. Pay 18 SEK for 99% availability with 3 expected outages	Pay 30 SEK for 99% availability with 5 expected outages	9. Pay 30 SEK for 99.78% availability with 2 expected outages	Pay 45 SEK for 99.89% availability with 2 expected outages	15. Pay 30 SEK for 99.78% availability with 20 expected outages	Pay 45 SEK for 99.89% availability with 20 expected outages
4. Pay 30 SEK for 99% availability with 5 expected outages	Pay 48 SEK for 99% availability with 8 expected outages	10. Pay 45 SEK for 99.89% availability with 2 expected outages	Pay 60 SEK for 99.95% availability with 2 expected outages	16. Pay 45 SEK for 99.89% availability with 20 expected outages	Pay 60 SEK for 99.95% availability with 20 expected outages
5. Pay 48 SEK for 99% availability with 8 expected outages	Pay 60 SEK for 99% availability with 10 expected outages	11. Pay 60 SEK for 99.95% availability with 2 expected outages	Pay 75 SEK for 99.98% availability with 2 expected outages	17. Pay 60 SEK for 99.95% availability with 20 expected outages	Pay 75 SEK for 99.98% availability with 20 expected outages
6. Pay 60 SEK for 99% availability with 10 expected outages	Pay 120 SEK for 99% availability with 20 expected outages	12. Pay 75 SEK for 99.98% availability with 2 expected outages	Pay 90 SEK for 99.99% availability with 2 expected outages	18. Pay 75 SEK for 99.98% availability with 20 expected outages	Pay 90 SEK for 99.99% availability with 20 expected outages

Fig. 1. The questionnaire used (translation)

In the second category the questions were phrased as follows:

7. Do you prefer to pay 0 SEK for 99% availability with 2 expected outages or 15 SEK for 99.53 % availability with 2 expected outages?

In this case the number of outages was always 2, but the first alternative was cheaper with a lower availability. This pattern was again followed until:

12. Do you prefer to pay 75 SEK for 99.98% availability with 2 expected outages or 90 SEK for 99.99 % availability with 2 expected outages?

In the third and final category the questions were phrased as follows:

13. Do you prefer to pay 0 SEK for 99% availability with 20 expected outages or 15 SEK for 99.53 % availability with 20 expected outages?

The number of outages was 20, but the first alternative was cheaper with a lower availability. The availability numbers were the ones of the second category.

The subjects were allowed as much time as they needed in order to complete the questionnaire. The authors were available to answer questions related to the subjects' understanding of the questions.

5 Results

A visual guide to the different behaviors described below is offered in Fig. 2.

5.1   Category 1

Expected Behavior. The *expected* reward is the same in all alternatives: 1% expected unavailability means an expected loss of 100 SEK. Thus, a decision-maker that maximizes expected utility would always chose the cheapest alternative, i.e. never be willing to pay to spread unavailability over a greater number of outages. Such maximization of expected utility would be consistent with the findings of [24] and [25]. However, because of the large variance in the outage costs, a more risk-averse decision-maker would be willing to pay to reach a certain number of outages, determined by her level of risk aversion. Once that number is reached, she would not be willing to pay more for an even greater number of outages. Thus, there would be a unique turning-point, below which a risk-averse decision-maker would pay for more outages, and above which she would not pay for more outages. The expected utility maximizer and the risk-averse agent are the two types of decision-makers discussed in [15].

Observed behavior 7 participants (44%) maximized the utility by always choosing the cheapest alternative. 5 participants (31%) behaved as risk-averse decision-makers and exhibited turning-points. One participant had a turning-point at 3 outages, two at five outages, one at eight outages and one at ten outages. 4 participants (25%) exhibited *non-monotonic* preferences in the sense that they, at some point, were not willing to pay to go from n to $n + m$ outages, but were willing to pay to go from $n + m$ to $n + k$ outages, where $k > m$.

5.2   Categories 2 and 3

Expected Behavior. The *expected* reward changes with the alternatives: Each basis point (i.e. one hundredth of a percentage point) of expected unavailability has an expected cost of 1 SEK. Thus, a decision-maker that maximizes expected utility would always pay for increased availability at a rate of more than 1 basis point per SEK, and never pay for increased availability at a rate of less than 1 basis point per SEK. In the given case, the utility-maximizer would pay 30 SEK to reach 99.78%, but not 45 SEK to reach 99.89%. However, a moderately risk-averse decision-maker might forgo this principle in the category 2 questions (where two expected outages make for large variance), but not in the category 3 questions (where twenty expected outages make for small variance).

Observed Behavior. 1 participant (6%) behaved as a consistent utility maximizer, with a turning-point at 30 SEK in both cases. 1 participant (6%) behaved as a risk-averse utility maximizer, with a turning-point at 45 SEK in category 2 and 30 SEK in category 3. 3 participants (19%) behaved as flawed but consistent utility maximizers, with equal but non 30 SEK turning points in both cases. 4 participants (25%) exhibited extreme behavior (not illustrated in Fig. 2) in always choosing to pay for more availability (2 participants) or never choosing to pay for more availability (2 participants). 1 participant (6%) exhibited non-monotonic preferences in both categories 2 and 3. 1 participant (6%) behaved as a utility maximizer (30 SEK turning-point) in category 2, but was extreme in category 3 by always choosing to pay for more availability. 1 participant (6%) behaved as a flawed utility maximizer (15 SEK turning-point) in category 2, but exhibited non-monotonic preferences in category 3. 2 participants (11%) behaved as risk-averse utility maximizers in category 2 (turning-points at 45 SEK), but exhibited non-monotonic preferences in category 3. 2 participants (11%) behaved as risk-averse utility maximizers in category 2 (turning-points at 45 and 75 SEK), but were extreme in category 3 (one always choosing to pay for more availability, one never choosing to pay for more availability).

The results are summarized in Table 3. The payments, following random selection and simulations, ranged from a maximum of 261 SEK to a minimum of 123 SEK, with a median of 236 SEK and an mean of 216 SEK.

Table 3. A summary of the results. EUM = expected utility maximizer (i.e. no risk aversion of risk seeking), FUM = flawed utility maximizer (i.e. a non-optimal turning point), RUM = risk averse utility maximizer (i.e. paying more than a strict expected utility maximizer to decrease variance), Non-mon = non-monotonic preferences (i.e. multiple turning points), Extreme = always choosing to pay for more availability or never choosing to pay for more availability (not illustrated in Fig. 2).

Participant	Category 1	Category 2	Category 3
1	EUM	FUM	Non-mon
2	Non-mon	EUM	Extreme
3	Non-mon	Non-mon	Non-mon
4	EUM	Extreme	Extreme
5	Non-mon	Extreme	Extreme
6	RUM	Extreme	Extreme
7	EUM	Extreme	Extreme
8	EUM	FUM	FUM
9	Non-mon	FUM	FUM
10	EUM	FUM	FUM
11	RUM	RUM	EUM
12	EUM	EUM	EUM
13	RUM	RUM	Extreme
14	RUM	RUM	Extreme
15	EUM	RUM	Non-mon
16	RUM	RUM	Non-mon

6 Analysis

The experimental evidence is somewhat surprising, as few participants behave as (risk-averse) expected utility maximizers, whereas many exhibit non-monotonic or extreme preferences. Very few individuals were consistent with the ideal (risk-averse) utility maximizers hypothesized before the experiment; in essence only participants 11 and 12. The behavior of the respondents is different from those presented in [24, 25], especially the high amount of inconsistent respondents.

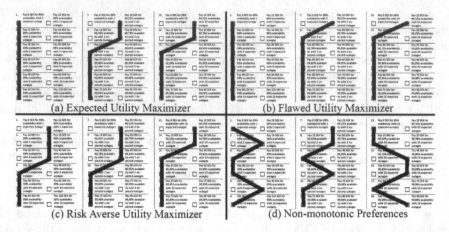

Fig. 2. Categories of behaviors found. This figure provides a visual guide to illustrate the different behaviors – the text of the questionnaire is more legible in Fig. 1.

As noted above, previous work has identified many deviations expected utility maximization. However, all the subjects were professionals, managing enterprise IT in their line of work. Therefore, their deviations from expected utility in decisions relating to SLAs are interesting. It might be the case that the incentives were simply too low to properly motivate the subjects (unfortunately, it is prohibitively costly to use realistically large incentives), especially as the subjects did not have calculators (though for all 18 questions, a mere three calculations suffice to find the appropriate turning-point in each category). Indeed, companies might always do their math properly in real situations with higher stakes. However, at least some practitioners self-report that their companies are immature in SLA writing [31], and thus might not be much better utility-maximizers than the individual decision-makers in the experiment. Furthermore, knowledge gaps can exist even between knowledgeable procurers and service providers, affecting SLA quality [32]. In light of the large deviations from expected utility, it would be interesting to redo the experiment on a larger student sample to see whether professional experience matters.

It is worth elaborating on two reasons why the expected utility is appropriate for the enterprise IT service SLA setting. First, expected (monetary) utility is appropriate because of the corporate context. Second, SLA decision-making does not aim to replicate decisions or decision-making principles of any actual individuals. It aims to do what is in the best interest of the enterprise. To this end, it is often a distributed process, in the sense that someone investigates business-side requirements, someone maps dependencies between IT services, someone does ROI calculations, and someone negotiates with service-providers, before someone (nominally) finally makes the decision and signs the contract.

This distributed nature of decision-making is both a strength and a weakness of the experimental setup. The strength is that all of the participants were relevant, in the sense that even though they professionally belong to different parts of the decision-making chain; they all have a role in it. The weakness is that decisions are rarely taken by a single individual. Still, a more complex (collaborative) experimental setup might have unnecessarily clouded the results.

The small number of participants ($N = 16$) clearly deserves a remark, as it limits the reliability. Follow-up experiments, with a larger number of participants, would obviously be desirable. However, it should be noted that this weakness of reliability is related to a strength of validity: all of the participants were actual IT management professionals, lending the result a greater credibility. Validity is further increased by the realistic data-set (re-used from [15]).

An improvement of the questionnaire would be to include baseline questions on binary choices between a sure thing (e.g. 100 SEK) and a lottery (e.g. lottery 1: 200 SEK with 40% probability, 0 SEK with 60% probability or lottery 2: 200 SEK with 60% probability, 0 SEK with 40% probability). This would clarify each subject's tendency to maximize expected utility or to avoid risk. A question related to professional experience would also have been interesting.

7   Conclusions

This paper presents an investigation of availability SLA decision-making with subjects from the IT management profession. The scenario required the subjects to make pairwise choices between alternatives, under uncertainty. Subjects were incentivized by a payment based on one of their choices, randomly selected.

The results indicate that decision-makers rarely maximize expected utility. Some previous work indicated that they would, whereas there are also many deviations identified in the literature. The implications for company SLA management in real situations require more research. The sample size ($N = 16$) is small and reliability thus moderate, whereas validity is high due to the background of the participants and the realistic data-set (re-used from [15]) used in the payment simulations.

In addition to re-doing our experiment with a larger number of participants, an interesting direction for future work is to investigate whether decision-support systems of various kinds could help improve SLA decision-making. Another interesting approach for future experiments would be to have research subjects act both as IT service providers and procurers, playing out a negotiation scenario. It would also be interesting to investigate the impact of varying years of experiences; how do experienced professionals compare with their less experienced colleagues, or with inexperienced students?

Acknowledgment. The authors thank Shahid Hussain, who acted as the discussant of this paper at a research seminar at KTH. Furthermore, the three anonymous reviewers offered a number of comments that have substantially improved the quality of the paper.

References

1. Marston, S., Li, Z., Bandyopadhyay, S., Zhang, J., Ghalsasi, A.: Cloud computing – the business perspective. Decision Support Systems 51(1), 176–189 (2011)
2. IBM Global Services: Improving systems availability. Technical report, IBM Global Services (1998)
3. Bharadwaj, A., Keil, M., Mähring, M.: Effects of information technology failures on the market value of firms. The Journal of Strategic Information Systems 18(2), 66–79 (2009)
4. Baek, S.I., Lee, S.J., Lim, G.G.: Exploring impacts of IT service failure on rm's market value. In: Fourth International Conference on Networked Computing and Advanced Information Management, NCM 2008, vol. 2, pp. 450–454 (September 2008)
5. Harris, K.: Gartner CEO and Senior Business Executive Survey, 2010: Perceptions of IT and Tactical Fixes. Technical report, Gartner, Inc. (March 2010)
6. Salle, M., Bartolini, C.: Management by contract. In: IEEE/IFIP Network Operations and Management Symposium, NOMS 2004, vol. 1, pp. 787–800. IEEE (2004)
7. Sauvé, J., Marques, F., Moura, A., Sampaio, M., Jornada, J., Radziuk, E.: SLA design from a business perspective. In: Schönwälder, J., Serrat, J. (eds.) DSOM 2005. LNCS, vol. 3775, pp. 72–83. Springer, Heidelberg (2005)
8. Buco, M.J., Chang, R.N., Luan, L.Z., Ward, C., Wolf, J.L., Yu, P.S.: Utility computing SLA management based upon business objectives. IBM Systems Journal 43(1), 159–178 (2004)
9. Hasija, S., Pinker, E.J., Shumsky, R.A.: Call center outsourcing contracts under information asymmetry. Management Science 54(4), 793–807 (2008)
10. Williams, D.: The Challenges and Approaches of Establishing IT Infrastructure Monitoring SLAs in IT Operations. Technical report, Gartner, Inc. (September 2010)
11. Taylor, S., Lloyd, V., Rudd, C.: Service Design (ITIL). The Stationery Office, TSO (2007)
12. Camerer, C.: Bounded rationality in individual decision making. Experimental Economics 1(2), 163–183 (1998)
13. Goo, J., Kishore, R., Rao, H.R., Nam, K.: The role of service level agreements in relational management of information technology outsourcing: An empirical study. MIS Quarterly 33(1), 119–145 (2009)
14. Vetter, J., Benlian, A., Hess, T.: Overconfidence in IT investment decisions: why knowledge can be a boon and bane at the same time. In: Proc. Thirty Second International Conference on Information Systems, ICIS (2011)
15. Franke, U.: Optimal IT Service Availability: Shorter Outages, or Fewer? IEEE Transactions on Network and Service Management 9(1), 22–33 (2012)
16. Setzer, T., Bhattacharya, K., Ludwig, H.: Change scheduling based on business impact analysis of change-related risk. IEEE Transactions on Network and Service Management 7(1), 58–71 (2010)
17. Courcoubetis, C., Siris, V.: Managing and pricing service level agreements for differentiated services. In: 1999 Seventh International Workshop on Quality of Service, IWQoS 1999, pp. 165–173 (1999)
18. Trienekens, J.J., Bouman, J.J., van der Zwan, M.: Specification of service level agreements: Problems, principles and practices. Software Quality Journal 12, 43–57 (2004)

19. Kieninger, A., Schmitz, B., Straeten, D., Satzger, G.: Incorporating business impact into service offers–a procedure to select cost-optimal service contracts. In: AMCIS, Proceedings, Paper 19 (2012)

20. Demirkan, H., Goul, M., Soper, D.S.: Service level agreement negotiation: A theory-based exploratory study as a starting point for identifying negotiation support system requirements. In: Hawaii International Conference on System Sciences, vol. 1, p. 37b (2005)

21. Brandic, I., Music, D., Leitner, P., Dustdar, S.: VieSLAF framework: Enabling adaptive and versatile SLA-management. In: Altmann, J., Buyya, R., Rana, O.F. (eds.) GECON 2009. LNCS, vol. 5745, pp. 60–73. Springer, Heidelberg (2009)

22. Silaghi, G.C., Şerban, L.D., Litan, C.M.: A framework for building intelligent SLA negotiation strategies under time constraints. In: Altmann, J., Rana, O.F. (eds.) GECON 2010. LNCS, vol. 6296, pp. 48–61. Springer, Heidelberg (2010)

23. Figueroa, C., Figueroa, N., Jofre, A., Sahai, A., Chen, Y., Iyer, S.: A game theoretic framework for SLA negotiation. Technical report, HP Laboratories (2008)

24. Davenport, W., Middleton, M.: Expectation theories of decision making for duplex gambles. Acta Psychologica 37(3), 155–172 (1973)

25. Lindman, H., Lyons, J.: Stimulus complexity and choice inconsistency among gambles. Organizational Behavior and Human Performance 21(2), 146–159 (1978)

26. Høyland, A., Rausand, M.: System reliability theory: models and statistical methods. Wiley, New York (1994)

27. Patterson, D.: A simple way to estimate the cost of downtime. In: Proc. 16th Systems Administration Conf.— LISA, pp. 185–188 (2002)

28. Bergström, F., Arnberg, J.: När handlar vi? – Om konsumtionsmönster i den traditionella detaljhandeln. Technical report, Handelns Utredningsinstitut (March 2005) (in Swedish)

29. Marcus, E., Stern, H.: Blueprints for high availability, 2nd edn. John Wiley & Sons, Inc., Indianapolis (2003)

30. Malik, B., Scott, D.: How to Calculate the Cost of Continuously Available IT Services. Technical report, Gartner, Inc. (November 2010)

31. Franke, U., Johnson, P., König, J.: An architecture framework for enterprise IT service availability analysis. In: Software & Systems Modeling, pp. 1–29 (2013)

32. Köppel, A., Böning, D., Abeck, S.: How to support the negotiation of service level agreements (SLAs) for your client/server application. In: Proc. SCI 1999 and ISAS (1999)

Information Security Investments: When Being Idle Equals Negligence

Maurizio Naldi[1], Marta Flamini[2], and Giuseppe D'Acquisto[1]

[1] Università di Roma Tor Vergata, Roma, Italy
naldi@disp.uniroma2.it, dacquisto@ing.uniroma2.it
[2] Università Telematica Internazionale UNINETTUNO
Roma, Italy
m.flamini@uninettunouniversity.net

Abstract. The Learned Hand's rule, comparing security investments against the expected loss from data breaches, can be used as a simple tool to determine the negligence of the company holding the data. On the other hand, companies may determine their investments in security by maximizing their own net profit. We consider the well known Gordon-Loeb models as well as the more recent Huang-Behara models for the relationship between investments and the probability of money loss due to malicious attacks to determine the outcome of the application of three forms of Hand's rule: status quo (loss under no investments), ex-post (loss after investment), transitional (loss reduction due to investment). The company is always held negligent if it does not invest in both the status quo and the transitional form. In the ex-post form, it is instead held negligent just if the potential loss is below a threshold, for which we provide the exact expression.

Keywords: Security, Privacy, Investments, Negligence, Hand's Rule.

1 Introduction

A company holding its customers' data is bound to protect them against data breaches. If its efforts (if any) are not enough, and data breaches do take place, it is reasonable to suspect that the company could have tried harder to protect those data and has therefore been negligent. It may be hard to prove a negligent behaviour, since that would imply a survey of the protection measures taken by the company, a survey of the attacks that may be reasonably expected, and an analysis of the actual attack responsible for the breach.

However, the application of a well-known principle, established seventy years ago by Judge Learned Hand, can be used to declare negligence. According to Hand's rule a company is held negligent if the cost of protection would have been lower than the expected loss (i.e., the product of the potential loss by its probability of occurrence). In [8] and [9], it has been proposed to apply Hand's rule to information security breaches.

But how do companies determine their security budget? If they suffer direct losses due to data breaches, it has been suggested that they should invest so as

J. Altmann, K. Vanmechelen, and O.F. Rana (Eds.): GECON 2013, LNCS 8193, pp. 268–279, 2013.
© Springer International Publishing Switzerland 2013

to maximize their expected net profit. This is the approach taken by Gordon and Loeb in [4] and, more recently, by Huang and Behara in [5]. Both go suggest models for the relationship between security investments and the probability of money loss due to attacks, and use those models to derive the optimal amount of security investments. In [3], [2], and [7], a sanctioning regime is analysed to spur companies (not suffering direct losses, but sharing the losses suffered by their customers) to invest in security, and a game between customers and companies is devised to arrive at the optimal amount of security investments.

Coupling a negligence detection tool as Hand's rule with the investment strategy dictated by such models allows us to analyse if such strategies, in addition to being optimal for the company, are also recommended (or actually urged) by Hand's rule, so that the company is held negligent if it has not invested as much as recommended by that strategy.

In this paper, we apply Hand's rule under profit maximizing investing strategies. We consider both the Gordon-Loeb and Huang-Behara models and examine the outcome of Hand's rule under the resulting strategies. Hereafter, we refer to the company responsible for protecting the data as the company for short, though its customers may be other companies as well as individuals. We consider three alternative interpretations of Hand's rule, differing for the definition of the loss term: status quo or ex-ante (full expected loss i no investment is made), ex-post (full expected loss if investment is made), and transitional (reduction of the expected loss due to the investment). In the status quo and transitional forms, we find that the company is always declared negligent if it does not invest in security. Instead, in the ex-post form, we prove that the company is declared negligent if the potential losses lie below a threshold (which we determine).

The paper is organized as follows. In Section 2, we describe the origin of Hand's rule and its transposition to security investments. In Sections 3 and 4, we apply Hand's rule to the strategies deriving respectively from Gordon-Loeb's model and Huang-Behara's model.

2   Hand's Rule for Negligence

Investments in information security help reduce the probability of data breaches and the subsequent losses. Poor investments (or the sheer lack of them) signal the unwillingness to counteract security attacks and mitigate customers' losses. According to the Learned Hand's rule for negligence, a comparison of the investments against the losses suffered by customers helps reveal the negligence of the company. In this section, we describe such rule and see how it can be applied in the context of information security.

In the *United States v. Carroll Towing Co.* decision in 1947, Judge Learned Hand proposed a test to determine whether a legal duty of care has been breached (i.e., if a negligent behaviour has been put in place). Though the case concerned an improperly secured barge, which had drifted away from a pier and caused damage to several other boats, the rule stated in that context is of general applicability. The rule states that if the cost B of taking precautions is lower than the expected loss that would have been avoided by taking those precautions, and due care has not been taken, then we have a case of negligence. The test can be expressed through the inequality

$$B < PL, \tag{1}$$

where L is the money loss, and P its probability (see Section II.G of [1]).

It has been suggested that Hand's rule can be applied to information security. In [8] it is argued that companies have a duty to provide reasonable information security practices under the common law of torts (notwithstanding contractual devices such as *hold harmless* clauses and indemnification agreements), and Hand's rule is the best analytical approach to establish such legal liability. Noticing again the failure of traditional tort negligence suits to hold breached retailers accountable for data breaches, Schneider proposed a set of remedies to deter negligent handling of customer data and Hand's rule as an approach to determine the level of care imposed on companies [9]. Assuming that both the probability of loss and the loss itself can be estimated with enough accuracy, the application of Hand's rule in the context of information security is quite straightforward. Here the party whose negligence has to be ascertained is the company holding the data and in charge of protecting them. The cost B of protection is represented here by the investment in security.

However, the original formulation of Hand's rule assumes that the expense removes the event leading to damage, so that the company faces a binary choice: either to spend and be sure that there is no damage or not to spend and accept the chance that the damaging event takes place. As noted by Markovits [6], Hand's rule can be generalized, allowing for the possibility that investments reduce the probability of loss occurrence but do not eliminate it. The definition of the right-hand side of the inequality (1) must be defined precisely, since it can lead to ambiguities. We consider here the following alternative definitions for the loss to use in the inequality (1):

- Status quo (ex-ante);
- Ex-post;
- Transitional.

In the status quo form, the investment is compared against the expected loss that would be faced if the service provider does not invest in security. The rationale for this form of Hand's inequality is that whatever the investment decided by the service provider, we compare it against what would happen if the service provider is inactive. In the ex-post form, the investment is compared against the expected loss resulting after the investment is made. Finally, what investments accomplish is to reduce the expected loss, so that it is likewise reasonable to compare the investment against that reduction of the expected loss. Since we now consider the effect due to the transition from a no-investment decision to the commitment to invest, we call this third form as transitional.

We recognize now that the expected loss is not an independent variable, since the probability of loss depends on the amount of investments in security. As companies invest more in security, the left-hand term of the inequality (1) increases, while the right-hand term (the expected loss) decreases: the test is more likely to be passed (the company is not held negligent) as investments grown (larger investments signal the willingness of the company to protect its customers' data). However, it leaves us with the problem of deciding the amount of investments for which the test has to be applied. In this paper, we assume that the company sets its level of security investments through some utility maximization procedure.

The regions of negligence resulting from the application of Hand's rule in its three forms are shown in Fig. 1. The broken curves represent the expected loss in the ex-ante and ex-post forms (right hand-side of the inequality). The solid line (bisectrix) represents the equality of expected loss and investments. The negligence region is the area where the solid line is below the broken curve. In the status quo form, the expected loss is determined in the absence of investments: it is a fixed value, irrespective of the actual investment. In the ex post form, the expected loss is a decreasing function of the investment. In the transitional form, we have instead to compare the distance between the two broken curves with the height of the solid line. The status quo is the least tolerant of the three (it gives the widest region of negligence).

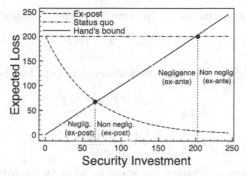

Fig. 1. Regions of negligence as determined by Hand's rule

3   Gordon-Loeb's Model for Breach Probability

After the description of Hand's rule in Section 2, we can now apply the rule by employing a model relating the probability that the loss due to a data breach takes place and the investment in security. We consider two couples of models, proposed respectively by Gordon and Loeb in [4], and Huang and Behara in [5]. In this section, we deal with the couple of models by Gordon and Loeb (hereafter referred to as the GL1 and GL2 models for short). We first describe the models and then find out whether the investments suggested by those models lead the company to being considered negligent if it does not comply.

Gordon and Loeb propose two broad classes of function to describe the relationship between the probability P of money loss and the investments I in security. Though in Gordon and Loeb's paper the loss is considered to be suffered by the company responsible for data protection, this assumption encompasses the case where the loss is suffered by the customer and the company is held liable for that loss. The functions proposed by Gordon and Loeb are respectively

$$P_{\text{GL1}} = \frac{V}{(\alpha I + 1)^{\beta}} \tag{2}$$

$$P_{\text{GL2}} = V^{\alpha I + 1},$$

where $\alpha > 0$ and $\beta \geq 1$ are two measures of the productivity of information security investments, and V is the probability of loss in the absence of investments. The probability of loss is decreasing in both α and β.

If the loss due to the data breach is L, and the probability of an attack is T, the expected loss is

$$X_* = LTP_*, \tag{3}$$

where the asterisk means that we can apply the formula to the GL1 as well as the GL2 model.

Gordon and Loeb adopt as a figure of merit the expected net benefit $ENBIS$, i.e., the reduction in the expected loss due to the investment minus the investment itself:

$$ENBIS = [V - P_*]TL - I. \tag{4}$$

The optimal amount $\hat{I}$ to invest in security is that maximizing $ENBIS$:

$$\hat{I} = \underset{I}{\text{argmax}} \quad ENBIS. \tag{5}$$

In [4], Gordon and Loeb obtain the following results for the two models:

$$\hat{I}_{\text{GL1}} = \frac{(\alpha\beta VTL)^{\frac{1}{\beta+1}} - 1}{\alpha},$$

$$\hat{I}_{\text{GL2}} = \frac{-\ln(-\alpha VTL \ln V)}{\alpha \ln V}. \tag{6}$$

We can now see how a company investing in security according to the outcome of Gordon-Loeb's model behaves with respect to Hand's rule. In this case, the negligence rule states that the company is held negligent if $\hat{I}_* < X_* = LTP_*$ and the company fails to invest the amount $\hat{I}_*$. Since we have $\hat{I} < VTL/e < VTL$ (Proposition 3 in [4]), the company is to be held negligent according to the status quo form if it does not comply with that investment.

For the ex-post form under the first model by Gordon-Loeb, we can instead prove the following theorem

Theorem 1. *Under the GL1 model in the ex-post form of Hand's rule, the company is held negligent iff the potential loss is* $L < \frac{1}{\alpha\beta VT} \left(\frac{\beta-1}{\beta}\right)^{-\frac{1}{\beta+1}}$

Proof. Under the GL1 model, where the probability of loss conditional on an attack is P_{GL1} in Equation (2), Hand's rule declares the company to be negligent if the following inequality holds

$$\hat{I}_{\text{GL1}} < \frac{VTL}{(\alpha\hat{I}_{\text{GL1}} + 1)^{\beta}}. \tag{7}$$

By replacing Equation (6) for $\hat{I}_{GL1}$, and after some manipulation, Hand's inequality (7) becomes

$$(\alpha\beta VTL)^{\frac{1}{\beta+1}} - 1 < \frac{\alpha VTL}{(\alpha\beta VTL)^{\frac{\beta}{\beta+1}}}. \tag{8}$$

If we pose $\lambda = \alpha\beta VTL$, the above inequality can be written as

$$\lambda^{\frac{1}{\beta+1}} - 1 < \frac{\lambda/\beta}{\lambda^{\frac{\beta}{\beta+1}}} \implies \lambda^{-\frac{1}{\beta+1}} > \frac{\beta-1}{\beta}, \tag{9}$$

whose solution is

$$\lambda < \left(\frac{\beta-1}{\beta}\right)^{-\frac{1}{\beta+1}}. \tag{10}$$

If we now replace λ by its full expression, we get

$$L < \frac{1}{\alpha\beta VT}\left(\frac{\beta-1}{\beta}\right)^{-\frac{1}{\beta+1}}. \tag{11}$$

Theorem 1 provides an upper bound for the expected loss to declare negligence. In Fig. 2, we show how that upper bound moves for two sample values of the αVT product: Hand's rule becomes more tolerant as β grows (the regions of non negligence - above the curves - get larger).

For the transitional form of Hand's rule, we can prove the following theorem

Theorem 2. *Under the GL1 model in the transitional form of Hand's rule, the company is always held negligent if it does not invest, excepting when the potential loss is $L = 1/(\alpha\beta VT)$*

Proof. Under the GL1 model, where the probability of loss is given by Equation (2), Hand's rule in the transitional form declares the company to be negligent if the investment is lower than the reduction of the loss due to the investment itself, i.e., if the following inequality holds

$$\hat{I}_{GL1} < VTL - \frac{VTL}{(\alpha\hat{I}_{GL1}+1)^{\beta}}. \tag{12}$$

By replacing Equation (6) for $\hat{I}_{GL1}$, the inequality becomes

$$(\alpha\beta VTL)^{\frac{1}{\beta+1}} - 1 < \alpha VTL\left[1 - \frac{1}{(\alpha\beta VTL)^{\frac{\beta}{\beta+1}}}\right]. \tag{13}$$

If we pose $\lambda = \alpha\beta VTL$, the above inequality can be written as

$$\lambda^{\frac{1}{\beta+1}} - 1 < \frac{\lambda}{\beta}\left(1 - \frac{1}{\lambda^{\frac{\beta}{\beta+1}}}\right) \implies (\beta+1)\lambda^{\frac{1}{\beta+1}} - \beta - \lambda < 0. \tag{14}$$

We now have to examine the behaviour of the function

$$h(\lambda) = (\beta + 1)\lambda^{\frac{1}{\beta+1}} - \beta - \lambda, \tag{15}$$

which makes up the left-hand term of the inequality (14). Its derivative is

$$\frac{\partial h}{\partial \lambda} = \frac{1}{\lambda^{\frac{\beta}{\beta+1}}} - 1 \begin{cases} > 0 \text{ if } \lambda < 1 \\ = 0 \text{ if } \lambda = 1 \\ < 0 \text{ if } \lambda > 1 \end{cases} \tag{16}$$

The left-hand term of (14) is first an increasing function of λ, reaches its maximum at $\lambda = 1$ and then decreases. Since its maximum is

$$h(1) = \beta + 1 - \beta - 1 = 0, \tag{17}$$

we have $h(\lambda) \leq 0$ (with a single zero in $\lambda = 1$), and the Hand's rule is always satisfied strictly, excepting the single point $\lambda = 1 \rightarrow L = 1/(\alpha\beta VT)$, where the investment exactly equals the reduction of the loss.

Though Theorem 2 identifies a case where the company is not held negligent if it does not invest, we have to consider that this case corresponds to a single value of the potential loss, whose chance of occurrence is extremely low, even in that case, the investment equals the expected loss. Though Hand's rule would not be satisfied in a tight sense, and the *favor rei* principle would lead the company to escape the negligence conviction, the chance of occurrence of that situation is so low that we can consider the company to be negligent for all practical cases.

For the second model by Gordon and Loeb, we can instead prove the following result

Theorem 3. *Under the GL2 model in the ex-post form of Hand's rule, the company is held negligent according to Hand's rule iff the potential loss is $L < \frac{e}{-\alpha VT \ln V}$*

Proof. Under the GL2 model, where the probability of loss conditional on an attack taking place is given by P_{GL1} in Equation (2), Hand's rule declares the company to be negligent if the following inequality holds

$$\hat{I}_{GL2} < V^{\alpha \hat{I}_{GL2}+1}TL. \tag{18}$$

By replacing Equation (6) for $\hat{I}_{GL2}$, and after some manipulation, Hand's rule (23) becomes

$$-\frac{\ln(-\alpha VTL \ln V)}{\alpha \ln V} < VTL \cdot V^{-\frac{\ln(-\alpha VTL \ln V)}{\alpha \ln V}}. \tag{19}$$

If we pose $\lambda = -\alpha VTL \ln V$, the above inequality can be written as

$$-\frac{\ln \lambda}{\alpha \ln V} < -\frac{\lambda}{\alpha \ln V} V^{-\ln \lambda / \ln V}, \tag{20}$$

which can be put in the form

$$\ln \lambda < \lambda V^{-\ln \lambda / \ln V} \longrightarrow \lambda < e. \tag{21}$$

If we replace λ by its full expression, we finally get

$$-\alpha V T L \ln V < e \longrightarrow L > \frac{e}{\alpha V T \ln V}. \tag{22}$$

Again, we can use the results of Theorem 3 to see how Hand's rule tightens when the model parameters change. In Fig. 3, we report the upper bound on the potential loss for two sample values of the αT product, as a function of the vulnerability V (the probability of loss in the absence of investments). We observe a characteristic very wide bathtub behaviour. Since a larger upper bound of the potential loss implies a tighter behaviour (negligence is declared for a wider set of cases), we see here that Hand's rule gets extremely tight both for the lowest and highest values of vulnerability.

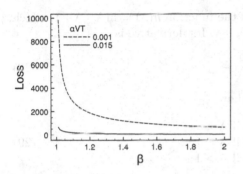
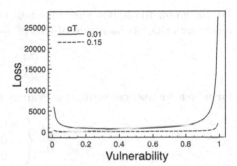

Fig. 2. Maximum potential loss for negligence under GL1 model (ex-post form)

Fig. 3. Maximum potential loss for negligence under GL2 model (ex-post form)

If we consider the loss reduction due to the investments rather than the actual loss (the transitional form), the liability of the company can instead be proven for any value of the potential loss, as stated in the following theorem

Theorem 4. *Under the GL2 model in the transitional form of Hand's rule, the company is held negligent according to Hand's rule if it does not invest, unless the potential loss is $L = 1/(\alpha V T \ln V)$*

Proof. Under the GL2 model in the transitional form, where the probability of loss conditional on an attack taking place is given by P_{GL1} in Equation (2), Hand's rule declares the company to be negligent if the loss reduction due to the investments is larger than the investments themselves, as embodied by the following inequality

$$\hat{I}_{GL2} < V T L - V^{\alpha \hat{I}_{GL2}+1} T L. \tag{23}$$

By replacing Equation (6) for $\hat{I}_{GL2}$, and after some manipulation, Hand's rule (23) becomes

$$-\frac{\ln(-\alpha VTL \ln V)}{\alpha \ln V} < VTL \left[1 - V^{-\frac{\ln(-\alpha VTL \ln V)}{\alpha \ln V}}\right]. \tag{24}$$

If we pose $\lambda = -\alpha VTL \ln V$, the above inequality can be written as

$$-\frac{\ln \lambda}{\alpha \ln V} < -\frac{\lambda}{\alpha \ln V}\left[1 - V^{-\ln \lambda/\ln V}\right]. \tag{25}$$

If we multiply both sides by the positive quantity $-1/(\alpha \ln V)$, the inequality becomes

$$\ln \lambda < \lambda \left[1 - V^{-\ln \lambda/\ln V}\right]. \tag{26}$$

By exploiting the identity $V = e^{\ln V}$ and moving all the terms to the left hand-side, the inequality becomes

$$\ln \lambda - \lambda + 1 < 0. \tag{27}$$

We have now to analyse the behaviour of the function $h(\lambda) = \ln \lambda - \lambda + 1$, which represents the left handside of this inequality. Its derivative is

$$\frac{\partial h}{\partial \lambda} = \frac{1}{\lambda} - 1, \tag{28}$$

for which we observe straightforwardly that

$$\frac{\partial h}{\partial \lambda} \begin{cases} > 0 \text{ if } \lambda < 1 \\ = 0 \text{ if } \lambda = 1 \\ < 0 \text{ if } \lambda > 1 \end{cases} \tag{29}$$

The function $h(\lambda)$ is first an increasing function of λ, reaches its maximum at $\lambda = 1$ and then decreases. Since its maximum is

$$h(1) = \ln(1) - 1 + 1 = 0, \tag{30}$$

we have $h(\lambda) \leq 0$ (with a single zero in $\lambda = 1$), and the Hand's rule is always satisfied strictly, excepting the single point $\lambda = 1 \to L = 1/(\alpha VT \ln V)$, where the investment exactly equals the reduction of the loss.

Again, since Theorem 4 states negligence excepting a single case, the same considerations made for Theorem 2 apply.

4   Huang-Behara's Model for Breach Probability

After investigating the models by Gordon and Loeb, we now turn to the models recently proposed by Huang and Behara. In this section, we show that their models can be seen as special cases of those proposed by Gordon and Loeb, so that we can exploit the results obtained in Section 3.

In [5], Huang and Behara propose again a couple of models for the probability that a loss occurs conditioned on an attack taking place. While Gordon and Loeb's models are stated with reference to their functional form, Huang and Behara distinguish between targeted and opportunistic attacks. Targeted attacks are directed at specific information systems; examples of targeted attacks are denial of service, website defacement, or a purposeful penetration into a banking system to transfer large amount of money by hackers. Instead, opportunistic attacks are created and released by attackers to look for and infect, opportunistically, any reachable and accessible information system via a network; examples of opportunistic attacks are viruses, worms, spyware, phishing, and spam e-mail.

For the two types of attacks, Huang and Behara propose the following expressions for the probability P of money loss conditioned on attack taking place, labelled respectively as P_{target} for targeted attacks and P_{opp} for opportunistic attacks:

$$P_{\text{target}} = \frac{V}{k_1 I + 1}$$
$$P_{\text{opp}} = V^{k_2 I + 1},$$

(31)

where $0 \leq k_1, k_2 \leq 1$.

By comparing Equation (31) with Equation (2), we find them strikingly similar. Actually, Huang-Behara's targeted model is equivalent to Gordon-Loeb's Type 1 model and Huang-Behara's opportunistic model is equivalent to Gordon-Loeb's Type 2 model (with $k_1 = \alpha$ and $k_2 = \alpha$) if the following positions hold:

$$\beta = 1,$$
$$0 \leq \alpha \leq 1.$$

(32)

The equivalence is completed by the fact that Huang and Behara derive the optimal amount of security investment through the same criterion as Gordon and Loeb, i.e., by maximizing $ENBIS$.

If we want to investigate how the company behaves with respect to Hand's rule, we can therefore exploit the results obtained for the models by Gordon and Loeb.

For targeted attacks, we can state the following results.

Corollary 1. *Under Huang-Behara's model for targeted attacks, the company is always held negligent in the status quo and ex-post form if it does not invest.*

Proof. We start with the proof for the ex-post form. With the positions (32), Hand's rule in the ex-post form given in Theorem 1 can be expressed as

$$k_1 V T L < \lim_{\beta \to 1} \frac{1}{\beta} \left(\frac{\beta - 1}{\beta} \right)^{-\frac{1}{\beta + 1}} = \infty.$$

(33)

Hence, the inequality is satisfied (and negligence is declared) for any finite value of the potential loss L. Since Hand's rule is always tighter for the status quo form (i.e., it declares negligence for a larger range of values for the potential loss), negligence is always declared a fortiori for the status quo form.

Corollary 2. *Under Huang-Behara's model for targeted attacks, the company is always held negligent in the transitional form of Hand's rule if it does not invest, unless the potential loss is $L = 1/(\alpha VT)$.*

Proof. In the transitional form, Theorem 2 holds irrespective of the value of β. Hence, it holds true when $\beta = 1$, so that the service provider is always held negligent (if it does not invest), excepting the single case where the potential loss is $L = 1/(\alpha VT)$, where the investment equals exactly the loss reduction.

Similarly for opportunistic attacks, we can exploit the equivalence with Gordon-Loeb's Type 2 model and prove the following results.

Corollary 3. *Under Huang-Behara's model for opportunistic attacks, the company is held negligent in the ex-post form of Hand's rule iff $L < -e/(k_2 VT \ln V)$.*

Proof. With the positions (32), Hand's rule in the ex-post form given in Theorem 3 can be expressed as

$$L < -e/(k_2 VT \ln V). \tag{34}$$

Corollary 4. *Under Huang-Behara's model for opportunistic attacks, the company is always held negligent in the transitional form of Hand's rule if it does not invest, unless the potential loss is $L = 1/(\alpha VT \ln V)$.*

Proof. Since Theorem 4 holds true irrespective of the value of α, it holds true when $0 < \alpha < 1$. Hence, the provider is always held negligent (if it does not invest), unless $L = 1/(\alpha VT \ln V)$.

For the status quo form, we know from Proposition 3 in [4] (recalled in Section 3) that the company is always held negligent under Gordon-Loeb's model, and therefore under Huang-Behara's model as well.

5   Conclusions

We have investigated how companies optimizing their investments in security could be held negligent according to Hand's rule, which compares the investment in security against the expected loss. We have considered a prominent couple of models proposed by Gordon and Loeb for the relationship between investments and the probability of loss in the case of an attack and a new couple of models proposed by Huang and Behara for the same purpose. The models by Huang and Behara (proposed for targeted and opportunistic attacks) appear to be just special cases of those proposed by Gordon and Loeb. We have observed that Hand's rule can be applied in several forms, depending on the way the expected loss is defined. We have considered three forms, which we have named the ex-ante (status quo), ex-post, and transitional form. If we compare the optimal investment against the expected loss in the absence of investment security (the status quo form), the company is always held negligent if it does not invest. Instead, if we consider the expected loss obtained as a result of the investment itself (the ex-post form), we have proved that the company would be held negligent if not investing when the potential loss (assumed to be known) is below a suitable threshold. In the transitional form, we have proved that the company is always held negligent if it does not invest, unless the loss has a precise single value (which we have determined). For all practical cases, the company would be declared negligent under Hand's rule for two of the three forms we have considered, and conditionally negligent (depending on the loss value) for the third one. Since the amount to invest has been evaluated as that maximizing the net benefit of the company, our findings represent as additional spur for the company to invest in security. Such a decision would spare the company a conviction in the case of a trial, should Hand's rule be applied in court as a negligence test.

References

1. Cooter, R., Ulen, T.: Law and economics. Addison-Wesley (2000)
2. D'Acquisto, G., Flamini, M., Naldi, M.: Damage Sharing May Not Be Enough: An Analysis of an Ex-ante Regulation Policy for Data Breaches. In: Fischer-Hübner, S., Katsikas, S., Quirchmayr, G. (eds.) TrustBus 2012. LNCS, vol. 7449, pp. 149–160. Springer, Heidelberg (2012)
3. D'Acquisto, G., Flamini, M., Naldi, M.: A game-theoretic formulation of security investment decisions under ex-ante regulation. In: Gritzalis, D., Furnell, S., Theoharidou, M. (eds.) SEC 2012. IFIP AICT, vol. 376, pp. 412–423. Springer, Heidelberg (2012)
4. Gordon, L.A., Loeb, M.P.: The economics of information security investment. ACM Trans. Inf. Syst. Secur. 5(4), 438–457 (2002)
5. Huang, C.D., Behara, R.S.: Economics of information security investment in the case of concurrent heterogeneous attacks with budget constraints. International Journal of Production Economics 141(1), 255–268 (2013)
6. Markovits, R.S.: Tort-Related Risk Costs and the Hand Formula for Negligence. The University of Texas School of Law, Working Paper (November 2004)
7. Naldi, M., Flamini, M., D'Acquisto, G.: A revenue-based sanctioning procedure for data breaches. In: The 7th International Conference on Network and System Security NSS, Madrid, June 3-4. LNCS. Springer (2013)
8. Rustad, M.L., Koenig, T.H.: Extending Learned Hands Negligence Formula To Information Security Breaches. I/S: A Journal on Law and Policy for the Information Society 3(2), 236–270 (2007)
9. Schneider, J.W.: Preventing Data Breaches: Alternative Approaches to Deter Negligent Handling of Consumer Data. Journal of Science & Technology Law 15(2), 279–332 (2009), Boston University School of Law

Author Index